Mechanism Design for Total Quality Management

Using the Bootstrap Algorithm for Changing the Control Game

Mechanism Design for Total Quality Management

Using the Bootstrap Algorithm for Changing the Control Game

Petter Ogland

Lulu Press
Raleigh, North Carolina

Lulu Press, Inc.
3101 Hillsborough Street
Raleigh, NC 27607

www.lulu.com

Published by Lulu Press 2014.
10 9 8 7 6 5 4 3 2 1

ISBN 978-1-321-45590-0

This is an edited version of the dissertation of the same name submitted to the Faculty of Mathematics and Natural Sciences at the University of Oslo. The original thesis was produced by Akademika Publishing in connection with the thesis defence in November 2013.

Dedicated to Dr. Lars Bratthall in appreciation of his suggestion that the PhD thesis should be published as a book.

Abstract

As society continues to develop in technological ways, side-effects of yesterday's solutions are becoming today's problems and systems tend to fail in increasingly spectacular ways. The more severe the consequences of organisational failure are, the greater is the need for approaches like total quality management (TQM) to control the organisation from a holistic perspective. On the other hand, to design and implement optimal control can be difficult, and about 80% of all TQM implementation projects tend to fail.

High failure rates in environments characterised by technological complexity and social distrust can be understood through game theory. Management and workforce are involved in a control game, and the TQM designer is playing a game with the organisation as a whole in trying to change the economic mechanisms that define the control game. The goal is to design mechanisms that make the control game align with TQM philosophy, but the easiest and most stable solution to this game often end up being both TQM designer and organisation developing policies and quality systems while forgetting to implement or only pretending to do so. By thinking more widely about the quality management system supporting the TQM policy as information infrastructure (II), however, and making use of the Monopoly game model for understanding the growth and development of II, the II design strategy known as the bootstrap algorithm (BA) becomes an interesting option to explore.

The hypothesis in this study is that the BA is an optimal strategy for gradually changing the game in a manner that will lead to sustainable TQM at the highest level of excellence. The claim is analysed by looking at twenty years of information systems action research that involves three Norwegian public sector organisations.

The outcome of research reports experiences in BA design using Total Systems Intervention (TSI) implementation methodology. Although the research focuses on challenges and weaknesses in the practical BA designs, resulting in problems and partial failures in TQM implementation, the outcome supports the BA hypothesis.

The analysis is based on considering three levels of gameplay. On the shop floor level, an audit game is played out between the TQM auditor and IT personnel. The "what gets measured gets done" motivational theory is a key to success for TQM implementation on this level, but depends on having established management commitment by winning the trust game on higher organisational levels. As the trust game is not a single-shot game, various techniques have to be used to gain trust in various situations for various elapses of time. Different game models are introduced and discussed for elaborating useful ways of thinking about different conflicts and challenges. The highest level of gameplay is the mechanism design game where the TQM designer fights the resistance of the organisation by trying to change the strategy sets and payoffs of the trust game and audit game in order to increase the basis of attraction for the game equilibrium that suggests walking the TQM talk and reducing the basis of attraction for TQM talk without walk.

The research makes contributions to II/BA and TSI theory through the Monopoly model of II dynamics, the reformulation of the BA as a genetic algorithm, and by suggesting game theory as an overall theoretical framework for TSI action research. The implications for practice are reduced failure rates for TQM implementation.

Preface

The reason for undertaking the study has been to improve the understanding of how to implement total quality management (TQM) in complex environments such as those represented by the Norwegian Tax Administration (NTAX). Although a bureaucracy like the tax administration is governed by rules and regulation and has a clear purpose of assessing and collecting tax in a correct and cost-efficient manner, a large bureaucracy making intense use of information technology can be a very complex system, and this is one of the reasons why traditional methods for implementing TQM in these type of organisations may not work.

However, based on my personal ideas and experiences in how to implement TQM in complex environments, first at the Climate Department of the Norwegian Meteorological Institute (DNMI) and later within the IT function of NTAX, IT Department Director Reidar Nybø at NTAX had me enrolled in a PhD programme for the purpose of seeing how NTAX could improve by collaborating with academic research networks. The idea was endorsed by the late NTAX Director-General Bjarne Hope and succeeding Director-General Svein Kristensen. During the years of PhD research my main contact at NTAX has been IT Strategy Director Karl Olav Wroldsen, who I had also worked closely with during the years of practical TQM implementation at NTAX. I want to thank all for giving me this opportunity, and in particular I want to thank Karl Olav for continual support and for taking care of practical issues at NTAX.

Although the main part of the study of the bootstrap algorithm (BA) as strategy for TQM mechanism design has been carried out as action research addressing specific processes at NTAX, my peer community during the period of research has primarily consisted of fellow information systems researchers at the Department of Informatics at the University of Oslo. First of all I want to thank my primary supervisor, Professor Jens Kaasbøll, for years of interesting discussions. Not only was I lucky in finding a supervisor who was perfect for the kind of research I was interested in doing, but also an outstanding human being who has been of tremendous importance to me during these years. I also want to thank my secondary supervisor during the early years of research, Doctor Lars Bratthall, and my secondary supervisor during the final years, Professor Ola Henfridsson. They have both been excellent.

Although it is impossible to mention all the people that have contributed to the continual doing and writing up of the research, I want to specifically thank Margunn Aanestad for discussions about the BA strategy and information infrastructure dynamics, Tone Bratteteig for getting me involved in debates about design theory, Jørn Braa for explaining how the BA has been used in practical action research, Eric Monteiro for inspiring lectures and discussions that lead to the development of the Monopoly model for TQM mechanism design, and Jo Herstad and Nigussie Tadesse Menghese for interesting discussions while sharing office.

I also want to thank Bendik Bygstad, Sundeep Sahay, Maja van der Velden, Sisse Finken, Christina Mörtberg, Nils Damm Christophersen, Petter Nielsen and Knut Staring for sharing valuable insights through discussions, and also thanks to Kristin Braa who together with the doctoral students made the weekly reading/writing group into an enjoyable and valuable source for discussion and learning.

Contents

List of illustrations

List of tables

List of abbreviations

AG	Office of the Auditor General of Norway (Riksrevisjonen)
AI	Artificial Intelligence
ANT	Actor-Network Theory
AR	Action research
AR	Register of stockowners (Aksjonærregister)
AWS	Automatic Weather Station
BA	Bootstrap Algorithm
BPR	Business process reengineering
BSC	Balanced Scorecard
CAF	Common Assessment Framework
CAR	Canonical Action Research
CAS	Complex Adaptive System
CDM	Custom Development Method
CobiT	Control Objectives for Information and Related Technology
CMM	Capability Maturity Model
CPM	Cyclical Process Model
CQI	Continuous quality improvement
CSF	Critical success factor
CSH	Critical System Heuristics
CSP	Critical systems practice
CST	Critical systems thinking
CWQC	Company-wide quality control
DNMI	Norwegian Meteorological Institute (Det norske meteorologiske institutt)
DSB	Data-assisted control of tax declarations (Datastøttet selvangivelsesbehandling)
DSR	Design science research
ECIS	European Conference on Information Systems
ECSN	European Climate Support Network
EDI	Electronic Data Interchange
EDT	Evolutionary drama theory
EFQM	European Foundation for Quality Management
EGT	Evolutionary game theory
ESS	Evolutionary stable strategy
FIN	Ministry of Finance (Finansdepartementet)
FOS	Notification of tax (Sentral forskuddsutskriving)
GA	Genetic Algorithm
HCI	Human-computer interaction
HISP	Health Information Systems Programme
IA	Internal Audit
IRIS	Information Systems Research Seminar in Scandinavia
II	Information infrastructure
IS	Information system
ISD	Information systems development
ISO	International standards organization
IT	Information technology
ITIL	Information Technology Infrastructure Library
JIT	Just in Time
LEP	Taxation of individuals (Likning etterskuddspliktige)
LFP	Taxation of companies (Likning forskuddspliktige)
NOA	Networks of Action
NP	Non-deterministic polynomial time
NTAX	Norwegian Tax Administration (Skatteetaten)
OR	Operations research (UK: "operational research")
PD	Participatory design
PDCA	Plan, do, check, act
PSA	Pre-filled tax declaration (preutfylt selvangivelse)
PSM	Problem structuring methods

PST	Postmodern systems thinking
QA	Quality assurance
QMS	Quality management system
RCA	Researcher-Client Agreement
RH	Research hypothesis
ROI	Return on investment
RQ	Research question
SE	Software Engineering
SEI	Software Engineering Institute
SITS	NTAX division for IT and services (Skatteetatens IT- og servicepartner)
SKD	Norwegian Directorate of Taxes (Skattedirektoratet)
SOSM	System of Systems Methodology
SPC	Statistical process control
SPI	Software process improvement
SQA	Software quality assurance
SSM	Soft Systems Methodology
TQC	Total Quality Control
TQM	Total Quality Management
TSI	Total Systems Intervention
UiO	University of Oslo
VSM	Viable Systems Methodology

1. INTRODUCTION

The purpose of this chapter is to motivate the study. The motivation starts by explaining why total quality management (TQM) is important but difficult to implement and how the bootstrap algorithm (BA) is an interesting approach for addressing the difficulties (section 1.1). This is followed by describing the knowledge gap related to the stability, impact and optimality in using the BA for implementing TQM (section 1.2). By focusing on how these gaps can be bridged, a precise statement of the aim of the study and research hypotheses follows (section 1.3). The chapter concludes by giving an overview of the components and structure of the thesis (section 1.4).

1.1 The Total Quality Management (TQM) challenge

This section starts by explaining why TQM is an important management philosophy and looks at some sociological explanations for why TQM is so difficult to implement (section 1.1.1). These sociological explanations will then be used for introducing two game theoretical models representing the challenges of TQM implementation; a quality control game that depends on having management commitment and a game of getting management commitment (section 1.1.2). In order to make sure that the process of game play optimises TQM implementation, a Monopoly game of mechanism design is introduced for redesigning the rules (mechanisms) of the quality control and management commitment games (section 1.1.3). The bootstrap algorithm (BA) for information infrastructure development is presented as a strategy for winning the Monopoly game of TQM mechanism design (section 1.1.4).

1.1.1 TQM is important but difficult to implement

The world is getting more complex all the time. We are becoming increasingly dependent on complex systems. When systems fail, they often fail in spectacular ways with increasingly severe consequences (Perrow, 1984). Examples include the 1979 Three Mile Island disaster, the 1986 Chernobyl disaster, and the 2011 Fukushima nuclear power plant breakdown. Beniger (1986) suggests that the history of information systems can be read as the ongoing development of increasingly sophisticated control systems in order to manage the increasingly complex service and production systems. Lash, Giddens and Beck (1994) identify the endless spiral of how complex solutions lead to complex failures with the process of modernisation. Beck (2000) believes we have reached a stage where people are beginning to become more concerned with the distribution of risk than the distribution of wealth.

Unless one believes that industries like nuclear power industry should be abandoned because the consequences of failure are too big, regardless of accident probabilities, the only way to deal with the problem is to spend resources on researching and developing elaborate quality management systems. Total Quality Management (TQM) is often used as a name for describing the general philosophy and methodology for improving organisational performance by focusing on quality control and process improvement. When the focus of the approach is software engineering, as is the case with this particular study, the general approach is often referred to as Software Process Improvement (SPI) (Humphrey, 1989).

Although TQM may provide a solution to the control problem, the general failure rate for TQM implementation is high, often suggested to be around 70-80% (Senge, 1999; Burnes, 2010). The reason for this high failure rate has been researched and discussed. Explanatory factors often mentioned are factors like lack of management commitment (Beckford, 2002), lack of customer focus (Oakland, 1999), inadequate understanding of statistics and probability theory (Deming, 1986), poor framing of the process improvement problems (Churchman, 1968) and challenges having to do with culture (Cole & Scott, 2000; Innomet, 2007). Most of these explanations take a management perspective on TQM implementation. Flood (1993), however, suggests that the fundamental problem has less to do with individual factors and more to do with systemic aspects of TQM implementation. As he sees it, TQM design and implementation aims to influence the control game describing the conflict between capital and labour in any organisation. TQM implementation can be used as a process of liberation, Flood argues, in the sense that it helps making processes and decisions visible and can make it easier for labour to stand up to capitalist oppression.

Gintis (2009) recommends using game theory as a unified language for behavioural sciences such as economics, biology, psychology, sociology and so on. Elster (1982) sees game theory as particularly useful in the context of the kind of critical theory that Flood advocates. Game theory draws inspiration from the analysis of games like Chess and Poker as models of situations involving more than one decision maker. Anything that can be described in terms of players, strategies and payoff can be said to be a game. While game theory takes the rules of the game as given, and makes predictions about the behaviour of strategic players, the theory of mechanism design is about the choice of rules ("mechanisms") to make the process of game play optimise some objective (Börgers, 2013, p. 2).

The model in figure 1 illustrates Flood's systemic perspective on TQM implementation as a game of mechanism design in the sense that the TQM designer can be seen as the principal trying to change the control game played by the agents inside the organisation. By continually redesigning the quality management system (QMS) used for describing the formal rules and payoff for parts of the control game, the TQM designer is trying to understand the behavioural psychology of the agents to create mechanisms that will make it rational for them to play the control game in a manner that complies with the requirements and expectations of TQM.

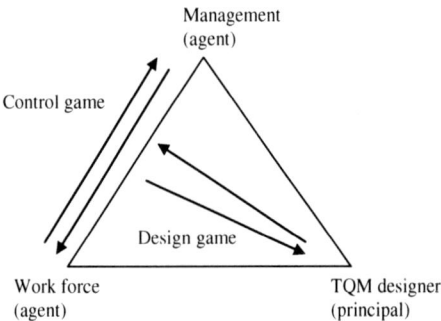

Figure 1: The mechanism design game of TQM implementation

In order to implement the mechanisms needed for changing the control game into a TQM game, Flood recommends the Total Systems Intervention (TSI) methodology. TSI is a methodology for managing system interventions for simple and complex problems through cyclic stages of problem formulation, problem solution and solution evaluation while maintaining an overall perspective grounded in the critical theory of Foucault, Habermas and others who tend to understand the social world in terms of oppression and liberation (Flood & Jackson, 1991).

From a practical point of view, the TQM mechanism design game is managed through the process of redesigning and implementing the QMS. While Flood (1993) does not specifically address the information systems literature dealing with the problems and methods in developing quality management systems and other information systems, particularly in Scandinavia there is a long tradition of information systems research based on a similar type of critical ideology (Bjerknes et al, 1987; Greenbaum & Kyng, 1991; Nygaard, 1996).

Although critical theory is useful for explaining TQM implementation failure by addressing the fact that the TQM designers are not doing information systems development in a social vacuum, thinkers like Brunsson and Jacobsson (2000) have pointed out that the class struggle perspective may also be somewhat ineffective or even misleading in the sense that this narrow perspective tries to understand the control game without understanding the game the organisation is playing with other organisations. While organisations may want TQM for the purpose of increasing productivity and improving quality, having a TQM-related certificate may also be a requirement for doing business, or being acknowledged as a TQM company may create certain competitive advantages. Brunsson and Jacobsson discuss the dynamics of what happens when an organisation wants to be seen as doing TQM while not having the will or the resources to actually do so. While the general nature of the mechanism design game in figure 1 remains the same, the kind of mechanisms the principal needs to design and implement may be different. One of the basic challenges for the TQM designer is to know whether and to which extent the organisation is committed to TQM.

1.1.2 Game models of TQM commitment and quality control

The Stag Hunt model is a game theoretical model used for analysing situations where there is a difference between risk and payoff (Binmore, 2007). The model is based on the idea that two hunters make an agreement on collaborating in hunting stag, but as each hunter is not certain that the other hunter will show up, he may end up with the impossible task of hunting stag by himself rather than doing the more simple but less profitable task of hunting hare alone. In table 1 the Stag Hunt model has been used for describing the game of trust between the organisation and the TQM designer as of whether they should commit to TQM (stag) or just pretend to be doing TQM (hare).

		Organisation	
		Commit to TQM (stag)	Pretend to do TQM (hare)
TQM designer	Commit to TQM (stag)	(3, 3) Best for both	(0, 2) Bad for TQM designer, good for organisation.
	Pretend to do TQM (hare)	(2, 0) Good for TQM designer, bad for organisation.	(1, 1) Acceptable for both

Table 1: Commitment to TQM understood as Stag Hunt

There are two pure Nash equilibria for the Stag Hunt game in the meaning that once a given equilibrium has been chosen by both players it is irrational for either player to change strategy. The equilibria in the Stag Hunt game in table 1 consist of either both players committing to TQM or both players pretending to do TQM.

The choice of both organisation and designer to commit to TQM is Pareto efficient in the meaning that it is not possible to achieve better payoff without at least one player getting a worse payoff. In other words, this equilibrium is payoff dominant. The challenge, however, is that the mutual pretending to do TQM is risk dominant. If the organisation is sceptical about the designer's ability to create a useful QMS, believing there is a risk that the designer

3

will pretend to do TQM, it is better for the organisation also to pretend. Symmetrically, if the designer believes there is a risk that the organisation is only talking about TQM without any intent on implementing it in a proper way, then confronting the organisation with error lists and improvement plans is more likely to produce harm than satisfaction, and it may be less risky to pretend to do TQM.

Once the game is stuck in the "pretend to do TQM" corner, it may become increasingly difficult to get out of the equilibrium. If stag hunt is played repeatedly, it can be seen that "pretend" is an evolutionary stable strategy (ESS) as lack of trust is being iteratively increased. On the other hand, "commit" is also an ESS as repeated mutual trust will also increase as a consequence of previous history of trust. A problem, however, is that the designer may sometimes fail due to incompetence or bad luck, and there may also be situations where organisation finds it necessary to talk about the importance of TQM without being able to back up the words with action, so it may not be possible to play the payoff dominant equilibrium every time.

Both for the organisation and the TQM designer it is clearly better to cooperate by committing to TQM. If they should be playing the inefficient Nash equilibrium in which neither is committed to TQM, they could shift to the efficient equilibrium where they both commit. However, the payoffs in the Stag Hunt game are structured in a manner that makes such as a shift hard to manage. The basin of attraction of the inefficient equilibrium is large and that of the efficient equilibrium is small. It is difficult for evolution to have the players go out of the basin of attraction of the risk dominant equilibrium and into the basin of the payoff dominant equilibrium (Binmore, 2007, pp. 68-69).

The Stag Hunt model provides a useful model for explaining the observations of Brunsson and Jacobsson (2000) in terms of why it is so difficult to implement TQM. In discussions relating to the importance of having management commitment to TQM implementation (Beckford, 2002), the model is particularly relevant. To illustrate this, table 2 is used for representing quality control as a game of Matching Pennies under the assumption that there is management commitment (Binmore, 2007, p. 4), i.e. the Pareto optimal solution to the Stag Hunt game is being played.

		Organisational unit being audited	
		Comply with standards (heads)	Ignore standards (tails)
TQM auditor	Audit (heads)	(-1, 1) Auditor looses (wasteful auditing), unit wins.	(1, -1) Auditor wins, unit looses (cannot continue irregular practice).
	Not audit (tails)	(1, -1) Auditor wins, unit looses (could have continued irregular practice).	(-1, 1) Auditor looses (he should have audited), unit wins.

Table 2: Quality audit understood as Matching Pennies

The Matching Pennies representation of the quality audit process, and more elaborate audit games based on the Matching Pennies scenario (Tapiero, 1996), is based on the idea that there are consequences for the unit being audited if the auditor finds and reports irregularities. If the Stag Hunt game is being played through the risk dominant equilibrium, this may not be the case. If there are no sanctions or incentives associated with the outcome of the audit game, the unit is most likely to continue business as usual and audits will just play along with the idea that everything is fine (Brunsson and Jacobsson, 2000).

Another way of referring to the conditions for making the Matching Pennies model valid is

4

the idea of "what gets measured gets done" (Peters & Waterman, 1982). When the TQM auditor is auditing and the organisational unit being audited ignore following standards, the Matching Pennies outcome is one utility point for the auditor managing to make a finding and minus one utility point for the unit being exposed. The payoff is based on the idea that auditor will be rewarded and the unit punished, but if nobody cares about the outcome the work done by the auditor is pointless and the unit can safely continue irregular practice without fear of being sanctioned. In other words, a principle like "what gets measured gets done" does not necessarily work when the inefficient equilibrium for the Stag Hunt game is being played.

Although the outcome of the Stag Hunt game is vital for the survival of the TQM programme and success of TQM implementation, the way to make sure that the Pareto optimal equilibrium in the Stag Hunt game continues to be played is by changing organisation culture (Hildebrandt et al, 1991). Cultural characteristics such fear, short-sighted focus on costs and profits and lack of system perspectives have to be replaced with values such as pride in work, joy in work, long-term goals, focus on continual improvement, and use of scientific reasoning (Deming, 1986).

1.1.3 The Monopoly model of information infrastructure dynamics

The popularity in use of cell phones and the internet from the 1990s and onwards has made a massive impact on society and culture in general (Goggin, 2006; DiMaggio et al, 2001). While sociologists study how society evolves as a consequence of technological evolution, information systems researchers make use of sociological knowledge for developing theories about how to develop information systems like the global system of cell phones, computers and the internet. In his reasoning about such large structures, Hanseth (2002) defines an information infrastructure as "a shared, evolving, open, standardized, and heterogeneous installed base", and uses the internet, electronic data interchange (EDI) networks and corporate infrastructures to exemplify what this means.

From the viewpoint of wanting to use the design and continual redesign of the organisational quality management system (QMS) as a way of gradually changing organisational culture towards values that fit with TQM practice, it could prove useful to think of the QMS as information structure as defined above. What this definition provides is a perspective of the QMS as something that is based on sustainable practice (installed base), which is heterogeneous in the sense of manifesting itself through different means and methods, standardised through technological standards and quality standards such as ISO 9001 or equivalents, evolving through breakthroughs and continual improvement and shared by the organisation as a whole. The infrastructure definition makes it natural to conceptualise the dynamics of the QMS as the growth and development of a network of local quality management systems. While local quality management systems are used for controlling quality and cultivating quality control practice for individuals and groups of people in an organisation, by viewing the network of all such systems as a whole the QMS becomes a technology for controlling the quality management practice and culture of the organisation as a whole.

In a lecture on information infrastructure theory, Monteiro (2006) suggested that a practical way of thinking about the difference between information system development and information infrastructure development was to compare with the designing of houses and cities. In the continuation of this he discussed the strategy used for developing a global health information infrastructure by showing a map of the world and jokingly describing the process as an attempt to "conquer the world". By seeing the growth and development of information infrastructure and control of cultural change as two sides of the same coin, certain aspects of the dynamics of information infrastructure can be modelled by the Monopoly board game. The Monopoly game can be seen to parallel the way information structures evolve by looking at real estate development for a city as a whole with the aim of conquering the world by bankrupting all the other players.

In figure 2 the Monopoly game as a representation of information infrastructure dynamics has been identified as the key to understanding TQM implementation by means of controlling the outcome of the Stag Hunt game of commitment to TQM which again will control the outcome of the Matching Pennies game of doing quality audits.

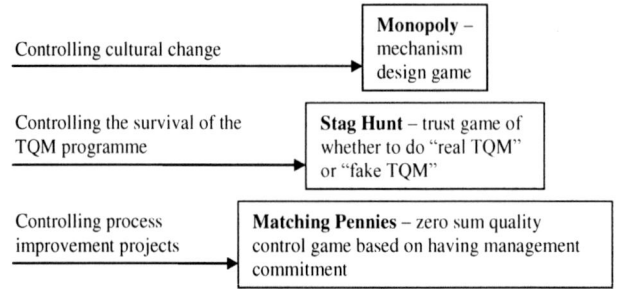

Figure 2: Three interdependent levels of control for managing TQM implementation

Unlike Matching Pennies and Stag Hunt, which are well-known models of strategic interplay from the game theory curriculum, Monopoly is more often viewed as a game of chance. Bewersdorff (2007), for instance, discusses Monopoly along with Snakes and Ladders as examples of games that can be understood by looking at the probabilities associated with going from one position on the board onto another. Unlike Snakes and Ladders, however, the Markov chain representing these transition probabilities does not represent a full understanding of the game but only the starting point for understanding how to trade properties and develop real estate monopolies, i.e. a game of strategy.

It is the interpretation of Monopoly as a game of strategy that makes it interesting as a model for understanding business and entrepreneurship (Axelrod, 2002, p. 11). As a game theoretical understanding of Monopoly requires mathematical models that are far more complex than what is needed for understanding the role of chance in the game, the existing body of knowledge on how to win Monopoly is largely a mixture of empirical expert knowledge supported by mathematical analysis through the use of computer simulations (Darzinskis, 1987; Frayn, 2005; Seidman, 2011; Koury, 2012).

Although the original version of Monopoly was created as a serious game for the purpose of analysing aspects of tax reforms (Kennedy & Waltzer, 2004), there have been doubts about whether the modern version of Monopoly can be used for modelling complex phenomena in a way that makes the model conclusions reflect non-trivial knowledge about the phenomenon (Abt, 1970). More recently, however, Monopoly has been used as a serious game in accountant education (Mastilak, 2012), sociological teaching about social class stratification and inequality (Crocco, 2011), how different outcomes of laws and policies may have on socio-economic systems (Wright-Maley, 2013). It has been used as an education tool for teaching mathematical reasoning, probabilities and statistics (Tostado, 2010), and it has been used as a basis for designing serious games for purposes like information systems development and software process improvement (Holeman, 1995). Orbanes (2002) argues that the strength of Monopoly as a serious game lies not in the specific commercial design but rather in the general design principles of the game and how such principles can be used for designing training games for educating workers or designing work in ways that will keep the workers motivated.

One way of making the Monopoly game into a model for understanding TQM mechanism design is by thinking about it as a two-player game where one player represents commitment to TQM and the other player represents forces that work against commitment to TQM. Monopoly properties can be thought of as QMS solutions, users of such solutions and quality management practice. Series of properties of the same colour can be thought of as business processes, property trading as getting access to data and management commitment to action, and property development as the education of users and redesign of solutions for improving practice. For the player committed to TQM the goal of the game is to redesign solutions and educate users and improve practice for the purpose of achieving TQM excellence while for the other player the goal is to control solutions, users and practices for the purpose of pretending to be doing TQM.

Although the official rules of Monopoly state that the object of the game is to become the wealthiest player through buying, renting and selling property, an alternative way of stating the objective is to say that it is to bankrupt all the opponents (Orbanes, 2007, p. 113). When translated to the language of TQM mechanism design this means that the purpose of those committed to TQM is to gain ideological hegemony by eliminating the "fake TQM" practice associated with those pretending to do TQM while the purpose of those pretending to do TQM is to eliminate the ideology that makes it impossible to maintain organisational status quo. Figure 3 shows the ideas being put into action.

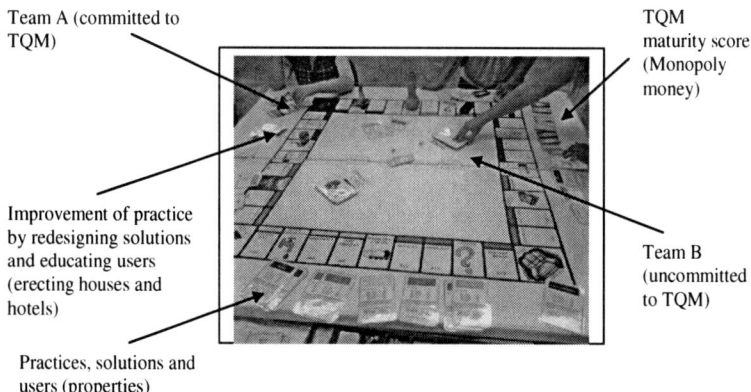

Team A (committed to TQM)

TQM maturity score (Monopoly money)

Improvement of practice by redesigning solutions and educating users (erecting houses and hotels)

Team B (uncommitted to TQM)

Practices, solutions and users (properties)

Figure 3: TQM mechanism design simulated by Monopoly game play

1.1.4 The Bootstrap Algorithm (BA)

When Monteiro (2006) talked about developing global health information infrastructure as conquering the world, the strategy he discussed was the strategy embedded in the 'networks of action' research method for developing information infrastructure through a process of managing a network of action research projects (Braa et al, 2004). This strategy had previously been defined outside the context of action research by Hanseth and Aanestad (2003) as the Bootstrap Algorithm (BA) reproduced in table 3.

Start with
   • simple, cheap, flexible solution
   • small network of users that may benefit significantly from improved communication with each other only
   • simple practices
   • non-critical practices
   • motivated users
   • knowledgeable users
1. Repeat as long as possible: Enrol more users
2. Find and implement more innovative use; go to 1
3. Use solution in more critical cases; go to 1
4. Use solution in more complex cases; go to 1
5. Improve the solution so new tasks can be supported; go to 1

Table 3: Bootstrap algorithm for information infrastructure design (Hanseth & Aanestad, 2003)

As seen from the table, the BA consists of an initialisation step and five steps managed through the use of a control loop. The purpose of the initialisation step is to identify a place within the organisation that can be used as a basis for growing and developing the information infrastructure. The control loop contains the logic needed for creating growth and development.

When using the Monopoly model for representing the information infrastructure, the BA becomes a Monopoly strategy. In the language of Monopoly the initial step of the BA consists of obtaining properties by rolling the dice and buying whatever is available. The control step then describes the mechanisms of how to trade properties to get monopolies and then develop them by erecting houses and hotels. This process continues "as long as possible", which means either until the BA has resulted in driving all other players out of the game or the player has been driven out of the game himself.

1.2 The knowledge gap in TQM-related BA research

For the practical purpose of TQM implementation the BA in table 3 describes the implementation approach in well-defined steps, there are examples of information infrastructure development failure when the BA has not been followed and success when the BA has been followed (Hanseth & Lyytinen, 2004), and there are accounts of how the BA has been used as part of an action research programme on the development of a global health information infrastructure (Braa et al, 2004; Braa & Sahay, 2012). So far, however, the important issue related to the stability and robustness of the BA has not been discussed in the literature (section 1.2.1). Another important issue not sufficiently discussed is the political positioning of the TQM designer within the management/workforce conflict and users/designers conflict needed for making the BA have an impact on TQM implementation success (section 1.2.2). A third important gap is the lack of reflection in BA literature on situations where the BA strategy may not be an optimal choice (section 1.2.3).

1.2.1 Stability, sensibility and robustness in BA-driven control

As pointed out by Flood (1993), TQM is based on systems theory. One way of trying to understand the BA in the context of systems theory is to think of the TQM mechanism design from the control perspective represented in figure 4.

While the visual representation of the TQM mechanism design in figure 1 focused on the

8

impact of a mechanism design like the BA on the control game represented by the QMS, the systems perspective in figure 4 provides a natural frame of reference for discussing the stability of the control system as a whole and the optimality of the BA for the purpose of controlling the QMS development. Stability is a fundamental concept in systems theory and the central idea is to make sure that whatever is being controlled by a control algorithm like the BA keeps within reasonable bounds and does not start oscillating out of control (DiStefano et al., 1990).

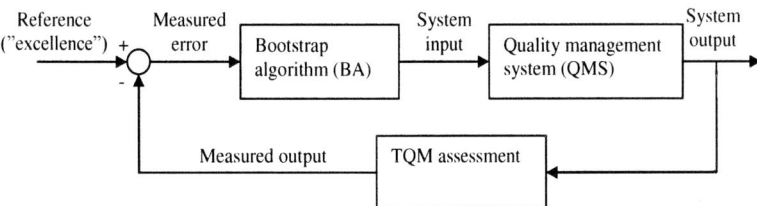

Figure 4: The TQM mechanism design seen from a systems perspective

As the QMS is an information infrastructure in the sense of being made up of a network of individual information systems, the BA control is an example of distributed control (Albertos and Mareels, 2010, pp. 59-65). With the controller represented in the shape of an algorithm, as is common in distributed control, the system can also be seen as an example of intelligent control (ibid, pp. 298-302). The purpose of the control is to make sure that the growth and development of the QMS continues in a stable manner.

Even though Hanseth and Lyytinen (2010) use the language of non-linear dynamics for describing the growth and development of information infrastructure, making it natural to think of the BA as a control algorithm for the QMS dynamics as illustrated in figure 4, their description is strictly verbal and not sufficient for a mathematical formulation of the control problem for analysis of stability and robustness by analytical means or simulation experiments. In order to develop precise models for describing the QMS dynamics, empirical studies with focus on time-series analysis and statistical process control (SPC) need to be carried out (del Castillo, 2002).

1.2.2 The impact of BA on TQM implementation success

The BA is an information infrastructure development strategy based on complex adaptive systems (CAS) ideas, which makes it a strategy for implementing TQM if we focus on the part of the information infrastructure that defines the organisational QMS. Since the 1990s there have been several attempts to view TQM implementation from the perspective of CAS by focusing on how to make the QMS adapt to technically and politically unpredictable situations through processes mimicking natural evolution (e.g. Kelly, 1994; Dooley et al., 1995; Goldberg, 2000; Palmberg, 2009).

While the logic of traditional TQM-related implementation methods is based on the assumption that a process cannot be improved before it is put in a state of statistical control (Taylor, 1911; Shewhart, 1931; Deming, 1986), the CAS strategies have been developed for the purpose of implementing TQM in complex environments where such basic assumptions are not met. This makes the CAS approach important and relevant, but as the writing about such strategies usually consists of using the CAS terminology as a hermeneutical tool for explaining process and outcome of implementation projects, rather than a systematic and critical empirical study of the method itself, there is a gap in normative theory as to whether such methods actually work.

In the view of the control diagram in figure 4, the question of whether the BA works or what kind of impact the BA has on TQM implementation is a question of how well the BA is performing as a control algorithm for regulating the growth and development of the QMS. Weinberg and Weinberg (1988) point out how system regulation problems can be understood as game problems in the sense that both the controller and the system are making moves and the purpose of a good control design is to make sure that the controller is playing a winning strategy. While such games are more often games against nature (i.e. decision under uncertainty or risk) than zero-sum games of strict competition where the regulated system is out to destroy the regulator (ibid, p. 243), it has been argued so far that TQM implementation is best understood as a zero-sum game. The use of the BA for playing the TQM mechanism design game has been conceptualised as a "conquer the world" battle for the purpose of establishing an organisational TQM doctrine and convert dissidents.

When looking more specifically at the BA in table 3 as a normative statement about how to win the Monopoly game of TQM mechanism design, the algorithm does not take into consideration the balance between technical and political complexity that define the Monopoly game. Looking at how to play the mechanism design game for changing the control game in figure 1 through the process in figure 4, the purpose of table 4 is to suggest scenarios where the BA is expected to have good impact and bad impact on TQM implementation success.

		Organisational control game	
		Dominated by technical complexity	Dominated by political complexity
TQM mechanism design	Aligning the BA with management interests	GOOD Traditional TQM engineering approach to process improvement where the TQM programme itself is viewed from a CAS perspective (Goldberg, 1989)	BAD The organisation is pretending to do TQM and the designer goes along with the pretence (Brunsson and Jacobsson, 2000)
	Aligning the BA with workforce interests	BAD The organisation wants to implement TQM by use of a framework like CMM but the designer is reading a hidden political message into the framework and tries to sabotage implementation (Ciborra, 1998)	GOOD Using TQM for improving social conditions as part of doing business process improvement and viewing the learning organisation as a whole from a CAS perspective (Flood, 1993; 1999)

Table 4: How a BA frame of action and the political context of organisation may impact on TQM implementation success

The upper left quadrant in table 4 represents the conventional way of implementing TQM that is being taught at schools of management. This way is consistent with the ISO 9000 guidelines of how to implement quality management methods, and is based on extensive engineering literature on operations research, systems development and statistical quality control (Masing, 1999; Juran & Godfrey, 2000; Dale, 2003). It has sometimes been pointed out that the Japanese style of implementing traditional TQM standards and methods through the process of continual improvement (kaizen) is a good example of how CAS works in a business context (Goldberg, 1989).

The upper right quadrant represents the case where the BA has no impact on TQM implementation because the TQM designer is not able to fight the "fake TQM" culture of the organisation and decides to join the culture rather than to fight it. This situation has previously been discussed as the risk dominant Nash equilibrium (inefficient equilibrium) to the stag hunt representation of the TQM mechanism design game.

The lower left quadrant represents a point of view that ISO 9000 and CMM standards, developed from military standards or American management practice based on "command and control" mentality, work contrary to what is actually needed for implementing TQM (Seddon, 1997; Ciborra, 1998; Rose, Aaen & Nielsen, 2008). Although this alignment approach may result in organisational improvement in a political sense, it is questionable whether such improvements will be measurable by the chosen ISO 9000 and CMM standards when the general message is "I want you to cheat" (Seddon, 1992).

The lower right quadrant represents the point of view expressed by Flood and Jackson (1991) that the methods of operations research, systems management and TQM are tools that can be used for breaking out of mental prisons created by organisational culture. If the TQM implementation process is stuck in the inefficient Nash equilibrium of both the organisation and the TQM designer pretending to do TQM rather than actually doing it, Flood (1993) prescribes a methodology for moving onto the efficient equilibrium. The role of CAS in TQM implementation is seen through the perspective of organisational learning (Flood, 1999).

When looking at the challenges in table 4 as a whole, the question of whether BA will impact on TQM implementation depends on how the BA manages to balance the focus on political and technical issues. If the TQM designer looks at the QMS development problem from an engineering perspective (upper left quadrant), there is a risk that the BA results in TQM failure by ending up in the upper right quadrant. If the TQM designer looks at the QMS development problem from a sociological perspective (lower right quadrant), there is a risk that the BA results in TQM failure by ending up in the lower left quadrant.

Hanseth and Monteiro (1997) argue the need for a balanced perspective on technological and sociological issues for the descriptive understanding of growth and development of information infrastructure, but when it comes to the important issue of how to apply the dual perspective in the normative theory beyond what can be seen in table 3, there is a gap in existing knowledge.

1.2.3 The BA and optimal mechanism design

When economists are using mechanism design for constructing auctions, an optimal mechanism design is an auction that makes the bidders play a game that produces optimal output for the seller (Nisan et al, 2007). When using the BA as a mechanism design for changing the control game, the optimality criterion relates to the question of how to implement the BA in a manner that makes the organisation rise to TQM maturity as quickly as possible and with as few costs as possible.

In order to investigate whether the BA can be used as an optimal TQM mechanism design it is necessary to clarify the difference between a BA design and a non-BA design. A challenge with how the BA is defined in table 3 is that it seems like the definition could be used as an abstract representation of any system development method. This impression is made even stronger by the way Hanseth and Lyytinen (2004) use the principles behind the BA for explaining why one information infrastructure project fails and another succeeds. The explanation accentuates complex political game play but ignores technical issues like choice of system development method and whether the method was followed in a competent manner.

However, as mentioned earlier, the difference between information systems design and information infrastructure design has been described as comparable to the difference between designing a house and designing a city. From a TQM perspective the difference between a BA strategy and a non-BA strategy could consequently be seen as the difference between focusing on the improvement of individual processes and focusing on the improvement of the organisation as a programme of improvement projects. In her study of CAS and TQM implementation, Palmberg (2009) describes these two perspectives on process improvement as characteristics of a CAS and a non-CAS perspective on TQM.

The purpose of table 5 is to suggest scenarios where the BA is expected to function as an optimal and non-optimal mechanism design strategy.

Organisational control game

		Complex QMS	Simple QMS
TQM mechanism design	BA strategy	OPTIMAL The BA has been designed for this environment (Hanseth & Lyytinen, 2004)	NON-OPTIMAL The CAS framework may cause the environment to look more complex than it is and prevent a discussion of how system development can be implemented in a more straight-forward manner (Checkland, 2005)
	Non-BA strategy	NON-OPTIMAL Traditional TQM implementation approach is likely to fail because the complex organisational system will behave in an unexpected manner (Senge, 1999)	OPTIMAL The traditional TQM implementation approach is expected to work when all critical success factors are being met (Beckford, 2002)

Table 5: Selecting strategy for TQM mechanism design to match the QMS of the organisation

The upper left quadrant represents the kind of cases used within BA literature for explaining the success of the BA approach, like how the development of the internet can be seen to have evolved by following the BA in a successful manner (Hanseth & Lyytinen, 2004).

The lower left quadrant represent the kind of cases used within BA literature for explaining how information infrastructure development projects failed because of violating the logic of the BA, as can be exemplified by some cases from the health sector (Hanseth & Lyytinen, 2004). When Senge (1999) points out that two out of three TQM implementation projects fail, his explanation is that the TQM designers and implementer do not understand the complexity of the quality management systems and organisational environments they operate in.

The upper right quadrant tries to capture the idea of applying methods for city development when the problem consists of building a single house. A criticism of the CAS perspective articulated by Checkland (2005) is that thinking about the world from a CAS perspective may prevent people from discussing what might be simple solutions to seemingly complex problems because they assume that the problems are inherently complex.

The lower right quadrant represents the situation where traditional TQM implementation literature describes how to deal with TQM design. Typical of such situations is that there is no significant technical or political complexity that might result in difficulties when trying to meet with key success factors for TQM implementation. Many of the well-known TQM success stories circulating in TQM literature, like TQM implementation at organisations like Xerox, Ford and Motorola seem to have been of this kind (Grant, Shani & Krishnan, 1994).

Researchers comparing the CAS and the non-CAS approach to TQM also exemplify how difference in organisational cultures is an important premise for whether to think about process improvement by focusing on the totality of business processes as a whole (CAS) or to think in terms of single processes (non-CAS) (e.g. Palmberg, 2009).

When looking at the challenges in table 5 as a whole, whether the TQM mechanism design will be optimal or not depends on how the BA matches the true complexity of the environment. If the TQM designer looks at every QMS development problem as an information infrastructure development problem (upper left quadrant), there is a risk that the mechanism design will be non-optimal by ending up in the upper right quadrant. If the TQM designer looks at every QMS development problem as an information system development problem (lower right quadrant), there is a risk that the mechanism design becomes non-optimal by ending up in the lower left quadrant.

The TQM implementation approach based on TSI includes a problem formulation step where the question of whether the QMS is simple or complex has to be seriously considered before the next step of choosing a suitable solution strategy (Flood, 1993). Although it appears that the combination of TSI and BA might solve the practical problem of optimal TQM mechanism design, this combination represents a new perspective that has never been studied before.

1.3 Aim of study and research hypotheses

The aim of the study is to contribute to the filling of the knowledge gaps about the practical use of BA as a TQM implementation method in complex environments where complexity refers both to technical complexity and social distrust. Another way to formulate this aim is to say that the research is concerned investigating the following hypothesis:

> **RH: The bootstrap algorithm (BA) is an optimal mechanism design for implementing TQM**

For the purpose of testing the RH, three supporting research hypotheses (RH1-3) have been constructed.

> **RH1: The BA can be implemented and managed in a state of statistical control**

> **RH2: The response to the BA treatment is performance improvements measurable by TQM assessments**

> **RH3: The BA is optimal for implementing TQM in complex environments**

While RH1 and RH2 are needed for testing whether the BA actually works, RH3 is needed for investigating whether the BA strategy is actually better than non-BA strategies when implementing TQM in complex environments.

Technical explanations in terms of how the hypotheses are to be made operational and how they are to be tested will be explained in chapter 2 and 3. The Climate Department of the Norwegian Meteorological Institute (DNMI) and the IT function of the Norwegian Tax Administration (NTAX) will be used as organizational context for testing and analysis of results. The Department of Informatics at the University of Oslo (UiO) will also play an indirect role in the study.

13

If the study should fail in the sense of one or more of the hypotheses being contradicted by observations in any of the organisations, this may contribute serious doubts about the BA as a general strategy for TQM mechanism design. On the other hand, if the study should succeed in supporting the hypotheses this can be interpreted to strengthen the hypotheses but will not be sufficient for validation. Regardless of outcome, the detailed description of how the BA hypothesis is being investigated over a long span of time in real environment should be an important contribution to BA and TQM research in itself.

1.4 Overview of papers and structure of thesis

The thesis consists of this summary document ("kappa") and six individually published papers as listed in table 6.

#		Theory	Method	Contribution
1	Øgland, P., 2009. The Game of Software Process Improvement: Some reflections on players, strategies and payoff. Krogstie, J. (Ed.): *Proceedings for Norsk konferanse for organisasjoners bruk av informasjonsteknologi, NOKOBIT 16*, Institutt for datateknikk og informasjonsvitenskap NTNU, 23-25 November 2009, Trondheim, Norway. ISBN 978-82-519-2493-1, pp. 209-222	Software Process Improvement (SPI), Evolutionary game theory	Case study	SPI evolves over a sequence of dramas
2	Øgland, P., 2009. The Pac-Man model of total quality management: Strategy lessons for change agents. *Systemist*, Vol 31, No 2&3, pp. 82-103.	TQM, EFQM, Game theory (in games)	Case study	The Pac-Man model produces optimal TQM strategies
3	Øgland, P., 2009. Measurements, Feedback and Empowerment. Critical systems theory as a foundation for Software Process Improvement. *The 17th European Conference on Information Systems (ECIS-17): "Information Systems in a globalising world; challenges, ethics and practice"*, 8.-10. June 2009, Verona.	Total Systems Intervention (TSI)	Design research	Critical systems thinking can improve SPI in politically turbulent organisations
4	Øgland, P., 2008. Software process improvement: What gets measured gets done. *31st Information Systems Research Seminar in Scandinavia (IRIS 31): "Challenging the Future: Context, Participation and Services"*, 9-12 August 2008, Åre, Sweden. (Awarded best paper)	Double-loop learning	Design research	The "What gets measured gets done" principle works at group level, not individually
5	Øgland, P., 2008. Designing quality management systems as complex adaptive systems. *Systemist*, Vol 30, No 3, pp. 468-491.	Complex adaptive systems	Case study	Explaining failure of quality systems initiatives
6	Øgland, P., 2007. Designing quality management systems with minimal management commitment. *Systemist*, Vol 29, No 3, pp. 101-112.	TQM, systems theory	Design research	Successful implementation of QMS can be done bottom-up
Kappa	Mechanism design for total quality management: Using the bootstrap algorithm for changing the control game	TQM, information infrastructure, game theory	Action research	The bootstrap algorithm is an effective strategy for TQM implementation

Table 6: Publications defining the thesis

The table includes an indication of theory, method and contribution for each of the publications. The different theories, methods and contributions linked with each of the six individually published papers represents small groups of pieces in a larger puzzle represented by the overall action research study using TQM, information infrastructure and game theory for showing how the bootstrap algorithm is an effective strategy for TQM implementation (kappa).

Figure 5 illustrates the structure of the thesis by representing the way the six chapters have been ordered in the style of a Vee diagram (Novak & Gowin, 1984). The diagram is a simplification of Gowin's original Vee diagram in the sense that the original six levels of abstraction have been replaced with three levels and some additional labelled arrows have been added along and between the conceptual and methodological legs of the Vee in order to better understand the logic of how the different chapters are connected.

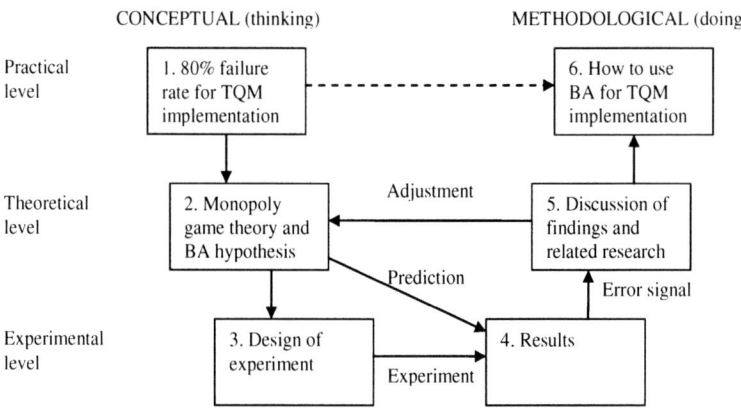

Figure 5: A Vee model of how the BA can be studied as part of an action research design

In this introductory chapter, chapter 1, the research has been motivated by the importance of doing total quality management (TQM) in an increasingly complex world while the failure rate for TQM implementation is about 80%. Axelrod's (2002) suggestion of using the Monopoly game for understanding business was then used to explain the failure rate, and the bootstrap algorithm (BA) was formulated as a hypothesis for how to win the Monopoly game of TQM mechanism design. The hypothesis was to be tested by use of an action research experiment.

In chapter 2 the Monopoly game theory of TQM implementation will be explained in more detail with a focus on the theory of games and mechanism design. The BA hypothesis from information infrastructure theory will also be explained by focusing on how to integrate it with the theory of systems and control design for the purpose of implementing TQM.

The purpose of chapter 3 is to explain how to test the BA hypothesis in the context of action research. The research design is described in the context of canonical action research (CAR) with emphasis on the five principles used for designing CAR.

The resulting action research narrative is presented in chapter 4. Each of the three cycles of research is described according to the cyclic process model (CPM) suggested by CAR, which means that the narrative will include organisational diagnosis, planning of action, implementation of action, evaluation of action and reflection on the results. The individually published papers will be mentioned briefly as references for understanding certain details of the action research narrative.

The purpose of chapter 5 is to analyse and discuss the findings by comparing and contrasting the outcome of the different action research cycles. The findings will also be compared to literature and related research. The individually published papers play a central role in this chapter as each of the papers accentuate important events or findings having to do with the research as a whole.

The conclusion in chapter 6 is written with the TQM designer in mind and tries to keep a practical focus by summarising and concluding about why and how the BA can be used for implementing TQM. The conclusion is written in style of lessons about the stability and robustness of the BA, how to make use of the BA for implementing TQM, and how to avoid pitfalls that prevent the BA from being implemented in an optimal manner.

2. LITERATURE REVIEW

The purpose of this chapter is to explain how and why the BA strategy might contribute in reducing the TQM implementation failure rates. The explanation starts by first framing implementation theory in a perspective that differentiates between descriptive kernel theory and normative design theory (section 2.1). The descriptive theory of TQM implementation is reviewed from a Monopoly perspective (section 2.2), and the normative theory of TQM implementation is reviewed from a BA perspective (section 2.3). A specific framework for how to design a BA for implementing TQM is produced (section 2.4), and implications from this framework on making the research hypotheses operational are clarified (section 2.5).

2.1 Information systems implementation research

This section starts by explaining how information systems implementation can be understood from the perspective of operations research (OR) and systems analysis (SA) (section 2.1.1). The practice of OR and SA can be understood partly as engineering science (systems theory) and partly as social science (game theory) (section 2.1.2). The empirical context of OR and SA consists partly of understanding a phenomenon (kernel theory) and partly of prescribing how to interact optimally with that phenomenon (design theory) (section 2.1.3).

2.1.1 Operations research (OR) and systems analysis (SA)

In literature reviews on information systems implementation research, the starting point of IS implementation research is sometimes referred to as studies dealing with operations research implementation (Lucas, 1981; Nygaard, 1996). Although the problem of IS implementation being a more general problem in the sense of the IS solution not necessarily having to be an optimum solution to some operations research problem, for the purpose of reasoning presented in this study it is nevertheless conceptually useful to start with the diagram in figure 6 showing how operations researchers (Phillips et al., 1976, p. 5) view the problem of operations research in the organisational context.

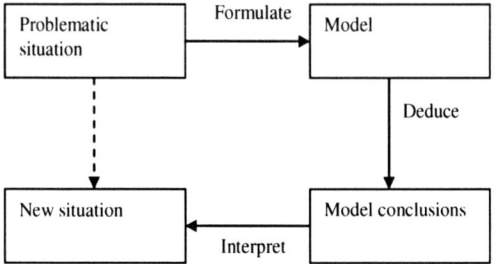

Figure 6: The operations research (OR) approach to change management

In the case of TQM implementation, when the TQM team is working on some specific problematic situation that needs to be improved, they may turn to the operations research literature and discover that the situation can be formulated through the use of some operations research model. If the model is not too complex, an optimal solution may be deduced. By interpreting the model conclusions in the real world by the process of implementing them, a new situation emerges that hopefully is an improvement over the old problematic situation.

In order to make sure that the new situation is an improvement it is necessary to have an information system for monitoring and giving feedback to the process of which the situation is a part. As statistical process control (SPC) and other statistical methods are typical tools used in quality management systems (Gitlow, 2001), the operations research approach in figure 6 can be reformulated as an information systems development (ISD) cycle where the terms analyse, design and implement replace the terms formulate, deduce and interpret in order to understand not only how the process is changed but also how the control system used for keeping the process stable is changed.

When looking at the problem of how to design a control system for the process defined by operations research, the TQM team may turn to the control theory literature. Beer (1959) suggested that the relationship between operations research and control theory should be described as operations research being the research carried out within the science of cybernetics. In his work on social science paradigms and organisational metaphors, Morgan (1997) has also suggested that cybernetics provide the most fitting metaphors for representing the TQM paradigm. Flood (1993) builds his theory of TQM on the basis that the kind of control theory suggested by Beer represents the typical worldview of the TQM practitioner, but argues that wider perspectives are needed for succeeding with TQM implementation.

Systems analysis (SA) has become a more common term for describing the logic of operations research when it moves beyond the confines of the assembly line and the automated factory to seek the solution of larger societal problems (Lilienfeld, 1978, p. 103; Nygaard, 1996, p. 97). The diagram in figure 7 shows how the logic of OR is embedded in SA when looking at the problem of how to implement TQM in complex environments.

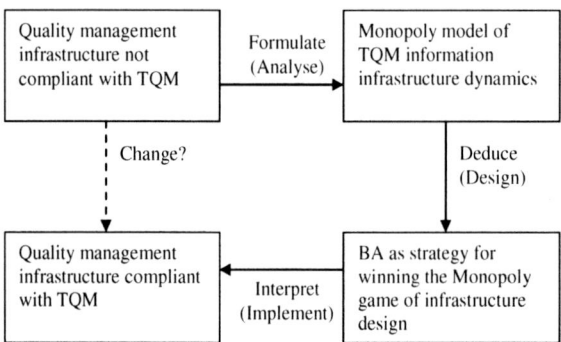

Figure 7: The systems analysis (SA) approach to change management

The most important difference between the OR approach in figure 6 and the SA approach in figure 7 is reflected in how OR was described as a research approach within a science of cybernetics. While the terms formulate/deduce/interpret describe the process of finding an optimal strategy for some OR problem, the terms analyse/design/implement have wider implications in the sense of also making sure that the strategy is running in a state of statistical control.

As mentioned when presenting the BA knowledge gap in section 1.2, thinking about the BA from a cybernetic perspective means that it is not only sufficient that the BA actually works as a strategy for winning the Monopoly game, but it must also be able to work if the initial conditions for game play are slightly changed. The BA strategy should also be able to withstand surprising moves from the anti-TQM Monopoly player and not corner itself into a position where the Monopoly game becomes a game of luck rather than a game of strategy.

When thinking about the SA model in figure 7 as an approach for developing the TQM mechanism design cybernetics in figure 4, the analysis consists of developing a model for representing the QMS dynamics between systems input and systems output, while the design consists of selecting TQM assessment method and a detailed control design fitting with the logic of the BA. In other words, the SA problem consists of widening the OR problem of finding the optimal strategy for playing Monopoly into a design problem for control and feedback systems (DiStefano et al, 1990). The change of perspective corresponds to a change from a game theory perspective to a systems theory perspective, as will be explained in the next section.

2.1.2 Systems theory and game theory

Krick (1969) describes the concept of a system as the fundamental concept in engineering. In science and engineering, the world is described to consist of systems being analysed and systems being created. In introductory literature on science and engineering, such as Krick's book, one can get the impression that scientists and engineers believe that the world consists (ontologically) of natural systems like the solar system and man-made systems like railway systems. In his study of how scientists in high energy physics are thinking and practicing the scientific method, Giere (1988) believes that the physicists think about their mathematical models and theories not only as models of reality but actual description of reality, and along with some other philosophers of science he believes that science progresses by getting closer to the truth about phenomena (Churchland & Hooker, 1985). Van Fraassen (1980), however, thinks differently. From his perspective the purpose of science is to create models of reality that are empirically fit. It is not a question of whether our model of the solar systems represents the truth about a phenomenon like a group of celestial objects but rather to which extent our model fits with our data when describing and making predictions about the phenomenon. The progress of science does not consist of getting closer to the truth about reality but in improving our models of reality.

Checkland (1981) argues along the same lines as van Fraassen when dealing with systems engineering. A prison, for instance, is a physical phenomenon, but there are many ways to understand it as a system. It can be thought of as a punishment system, a system for protecting society from criminals, a system for educating criminals and so on. In other words, the process of analysing the situation and formulating the problem, represented by the upper part of the diagram in figure 7, can lead to several alternative models. Which model is the correct one depends on the perspective of the viewer. In Scandinavian information systems research, the concept of 'power of definition' ("definisjonsmakt") has been used for describing how the formulation of the problem can be part of a political game (e.g. Bjerknes et al, 1987). Flood and Jackson (1991), and Flood (1993) in particular, have been arguing along similar lines when discussing how TQM problems are formulated.

It is not only during situation analysis and problem formulation that a game theoretic understanding can add insights to systems development process. The next step of deducing model conclusions or designing solutions can also be understood from a game perspective. Weinberg and Weinberg (1988) specifically suggest using game theory for understanding the design of control systems in feedback and systems control. In their example of constructing a thermostat the game becomes a game against nature rather than a political game, but by expanding the systemic scope for the unit of analysis it is easy to see how the regulation of temperature inside a factory could be used as a strategy in a power conflict between management and workforce (Hannemyr, 2009). In Scandinavian information systems research the identification of control games of this kind have played an important part for the identity of the research community (Nygaard, 1996). However, such control games do not always have to be defined by capital to exploit and oppress labour. In Chile there was a period of plans, experiments and prototypes of supporting the socialist government through use of cybernetic designs (Beer, 1974). Flood (1993) suggests that this particular "design for freedom" should be used as a general approach for designing TQM.

One difference between the deduce/define step in figure 7 as compared with the preceding formulate/design step and the proceeding interpret/implement step is that deduce/define goes from model to model conclusion without assuming any connection to the empirical situation on the left side of the figure. In the case of the OR model, when the problem is well-formulated, the deduction of model conclusions is a strictly logical process by mathematical reasoning through analytic or numerical means. The model conclusions follow logically from the model. In the case of SA, however, when there may be several possible solution designs to select from, different people will benefit differently on the solution (model conclusions) regardless of whether they all agree on the definition of the problem (model). Both the solution to the Iron and Metal study (Nygaard, 1996) and the "design for freedom" study (Beer, 1974) were based on political analysis of how to find an optimal solution within the solution space defined by the constraints of how the problem was defined.

The final step of interpreting the model conclusions through implementation in figure 7 can also be interpreted from the viewpoint of game theory. Churchman et al (1956) recognised the challenge of how operations research literature tended to focus on expanding the list of models of the engineering problem and proving theorems about how to draw conclusions from the models, but had less to say about the psychological, social or political problem of implementing the solutions. This resulted in studies trying to understand implementation failure and what could be done to prevent it (e.g. Huysmans, 1970; Lucas, 1981; Lucas et al, 1990). In the Scandinavian school of information systems research this scenario has sometimes been articulated as a conflict between designers and users (e.g. Greenbaum & Kyng, 1991). Ulrich (1983) has written about the conflict of designers and users from a general perspective, developing the method of Critical Systems Heuristics (CSH) for systematically analysing the political consequences of implementation. The method of CSH is important for Flood (1993) when he discusses how to evaluate how a TQM implementation project supports the view of the oppressed.

The OR and SA models in figure 6 and 7 illustrate the process of changing systems in the empirical world through the process of making a systems model, drawing conclusions from that model and making use of those conclusions in the empirical world. Although different writers mean slightly different things when referring to systems theory, from a mathematical perspective it usually refers to systems of differential equations, difference equations or similar structures (Luenberger, 1979; Berlinski, 1976). Although there may be no "systems" in the real world, as van Fraassen and Checkland see it, the first step in the OR and SA processes consists of deciding which parts of the phenomenon to be considered to define the system and how to formulate the system problem by use of a model. In the typical example where the empirical phenomenon is represented as a system of differential equations, a phase portrait representation of the model could be used for describing equilibrium points and attractors to characterise the stability and dynamics of the system. This kind of knowledge is essential if the problem is a control design problem. As with electrical or mechanical engineering, the idea is to design mechanisms like feedback loops to make sure that the system performance runs within the boundaries of wanted states. The final step in the OR and SA models is to implement the system to observe if it actually does as expected.

What was pointed out in this section was that each of the three transitions in the OR and SA models could be seen as political or game theoretical problems. Although the OR and SA models tell the designer to follow steps of analysis, design and implementation, the OR/SA method does not communicate that each of these steps can be viewed as decision trees representing choices to be made between alternative routes. More than that, the outcome of the decisions being made also depends on decisions being made by other decision makers. In other words, the SA process in figure 7 can be thought of as a game. The strategies for playing the SA game may be different from strategies used for playing Chess or Poker, but game theory is a language for reasoning about all kinds of games. Game theory is the mathematical theory of how rational decision makers should optimise the outcome of their decision in situations involving more than one decision maker (Binmore, 2007).

Among some scholars, e.g. Levine (2009), game theory is seen as one of four branches of economic theory where the other branches are decision theory, general equilibrium theory and mechanism design theory that all relate to game theory. Outside of economics, on the other hand, it is not uncommon to speak of game theory when referring to any of the theories above (e.g. Luce & Raiffa, 1957; Colman, 1995; Nisan et al, 2007), although others would argue that studying decision making in situations involving more than one decision maker (game theory) is a special case of decision theory (Peterson, 2009). However, decision theory can be considered part of game theory by describing decisions involving a single decision maker in situations of risk and uncertainty as games against nature (Colman, 1995). Mechanism design can also be seen as a part of game theory and is sometimes described as "reverse game theory" in the sense of designing game rules for meeting specific purposes rather than analysing what kind of strategic behaviour to expect when the rules are known (Binmore, 2007, p. 102).

In figure 7 the model in the SA process is a Monopoly game model. The SA problem consists of first describing the QMS infrastructure by use of a Monopoly model in terms of a system that explicitly states the rules of the game. The next step is to deduce model conclusions in terms of designing a control strategy for winning the Monopoly game. The final step consists of testing the model conclusions in the real world. If the approach was successful, the QMS infrastructure has been changed in a manner that makes it compliant with TQM. In other words, the rules determining behaviour in the organisation have been changed and the mechanism design game has been won.

However, winning the mechanism design game depends on being able to play the SA game well. There may be many alternative Monopoly representations of the QMS with different shareholder groups seeing the game differently as Checkland would point out. Once a particular Monopoly game has been chosen to represent the QMS, there may be many ways of deducing and designing winning strategies, depending on political perspectives and alliances, as the action research by Nygaard and associates exemplify. Finally, to successfully implement the solution depends on playing the human-computer interaction (HCI) game right in getting people to use the new QMS in compliance with TQM ideals.

2.1.3 Kernel theory and design theory

Systems theory and game theory serve two different purposes when studying a game like Monopoly. The systems theory of Markov chains can be used for finding facts about the system like the probabilities of landing on different colour groups and calculating how many rolls of the dice it takes on average for circling the board. Game theory, on the other hand, is focused on how to use the systems insights when considering what ought to be done for controlling the system in terms of preventing the opponents from winning.

There is nothing contradictory about systems theory and game theory from a theoretical perspective. Much of the classical literature on systems theory includes game theory as part of the systems approach (e.g. Churchman et al, 1956; von Bertalanffy, 1968; Lilienfeld, 1978). As both systems theory and game theory are mathematical theories, there are no theoretical dangers in mixing them as long as the resulting mixed theories make mathematical sense (Berlinski, 1976). When used empirically, however, they are used for reasoning about different types of situations. Systems theory is used for understanding a phenomenon, game theory is used for designing actions. Systems theory is concerned with "what is". Game theory is concerned with "what ought to be".

From the viewpoint of the philosophy of science the two statements are classified differently in the sense that the "what is" statement is referred to as descriptive or positivist theory while the "what ought to be" statement is referred to as normative theory (Peterson, 2009, pp. 3-4). Descriptive decision theory deals with how people are making decisions in real life, often conflicting with what the normative theories of how rational decision makers should be making decisions (Colman, 1995; Peterson, 2009), and could perhaps be seen as a kind of systems theory in the sense that descriptive game theory can be helpful for explaining the dynamics of the system as interaction is carried out through game play (Ariely, 2008).

Simon (1996) discusses the difference between the "what is" theory with the "what ought to be" theory as the difference between natural science and science of the artificial. Science of the artificial, or design science as he also calls it, is the science of making decisions. Engineers, managers, psychologists, economists and city planners make decisions, and even though the nature of their decisions is quite different, the maze is a useful model for describing the decision problem. He specifically mentions game theory and control theory as examples of formal design theories (ibid, p. 122).

Within information systems research the design science idea has been seen as an interesting way of theorising about the designing of artefacts such as constructs, models, methods and instantiations (March & Smith, 1995; Hevner et al, 2004). As the distinction in information systems research is not between design science and natural science, the nature of the "what is" theory used in natural science and social sciences is referred to as kernel theory (Walls et al, 1992). In this study this means that Monopoly systems theory (the probabilistic dynamics of the system) is used as kernel theory and Monopoly game theory (how to control the system in terms of preventing opponents from winning) is used as design theory.

Design theory is used for finding optimal strategies for systems development. Kernel theory is used for motivating and explaining the outcome of such designs. In trying to understand why there is an 80% TQM implementation failure, one approach is to back-track the cyclic structures in figure 6 and 7 by creating an error-cause tree as is done in figure 8.

What the search approach in the figure suggests is to start by looking at reasons for TQM implementation failure by evaluating the implementation strategy. If the implementation strategy was poor from a game theoretical perspective, the reason for failure may have more to do with cultural issues than the technical design of the quality management system (Brunsson and Jacobsson, 2000). On the other hand, if the implementation process worked fine but ended up adding more bureaucracy and no improvement in quality and productivity, the reason may be a quality engineering problem in terms of the TQM team having little understanding of statistical quality control and systems design (Deming, 1986; Seddon, 1997). However, if both the implementation strategy worked fine and there were no problems with quality management system design but there is still no measurable effect in terms of quality and productivity improvements, the reason may be that the TQM team had been improving processes that had little or no relevance on the parameters used for measuring organisational performance in terms of quality and productivity (Drucker, 1950; Deming, 1994). In other words, the explanation for failure was a poor analysis of the organisation as a system.

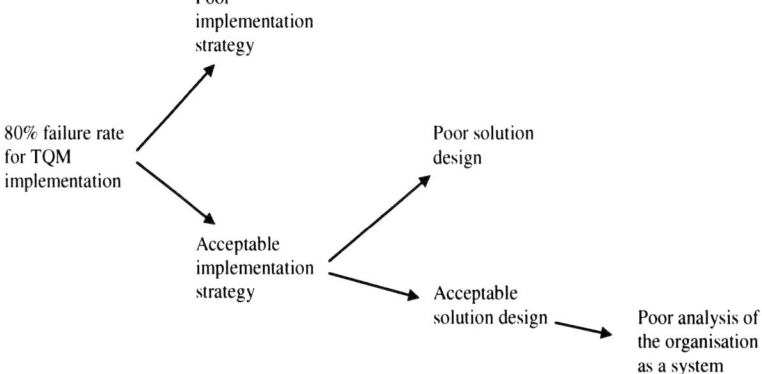

Figure 8: Error-cause tree for the ISD model inspired by the operations research approach

Although systems and control theory has been described as the natural language for discussing TQM (Juran, 1964; Deming, 1994; Flood, 1993), the logic of the diagram in figure 8 makes the games defined by relationships between systems and environments the central concern in empirical TQM implementation research. For instance, by regarding management as the system and the workers as the environment to be controlled, the relationship between system and environment can be seen as a control game representing social conflict (Braverman, 1974). In this context the mechanism design game is a game between the productivity experts (system) and the organisation as a whole (environment) where the experts try to change the control game between managers and workers in favour of management interests by changing the rules and payoff in the control game (Taylor, 1911). Alternatively, the mechanism design game could consist of humanistic researchers (system) and the organisation as a whole (environment) where the researchers try to change the control game in favour of worker interests (Lewin, 1946; McGregor, 1960).

2.2 Kernel theory: The Monopoly dynamics of TQM failure

The purpose of this section, as illustrated in figure 9, is to explain the Monopoly model as a model for understanding QMS information infrastructure dynamics from a kernel theory perspective.

The explanation will start by pointing out challenges in developing kernel theory for explaining failure in TQM mechanism design (section 2.2.1), and will then proceed by backtracking the error tree in figure 8 for reviewing literature on implementation error (section 2.2.2), design error (section 2.2.3) and analysis error (section 2.2.4) before explaining the information infrastructure concept (section 2.2.5) and showing how the Monopoly game can be used for representing information infrastructure dynamics (section 2.2.6).

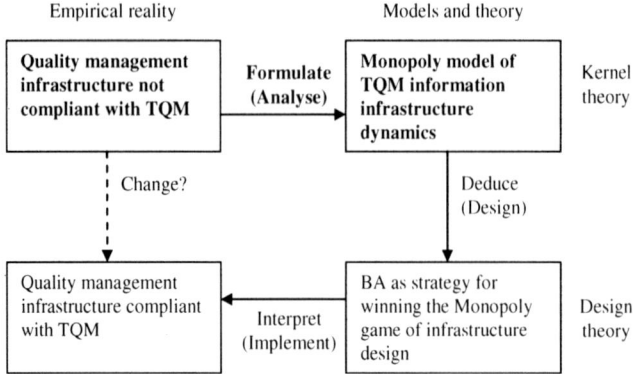

Figure 9: Kernel theory for changing culture by redesigning information infrastructure

2.2.1 Challenges for explaining failure in TQM mechanism design

Both the productivity expert and humanist research way of thinking about TQM implementation can be represented as design games in figure 1. As TQM is a management philosophy based on the idea that customer focus and continual process improvement will lead to business success, the relationship between management and workforce can be understood as a control game where management tries to make sure that the workforce practice is in compliance with work standards (Tapiero, 1996). The workers, on the other hand, may have individual or collective reasons for not wanting to be continually monitored and controlled (Braverman, 1974).

Technology plays an important part in the development of control systems. In the scientific management area, the dominant control technology consisted of controllers giving commands to the workforce according to written procedures and recording the results by use of stop watches and checklists (Taylor, 1911). As technology has developed, it has been possible to develop more subtle methods of controlling the workforce, and the use of computerised information systems has now become so dominant that the control systems are often more or less invisible (Beniger, 1986).

In figure 1 the way technology (represented by the TQM designer) changes the control game is referred to as a design game. The players in this game consist of the principal (consultants or action researchers in the role of TQM designer) analysing the control game played between the agents and trying to redesign the mechanisms of the game by redesigning the quality management system (QMS) in order to optimise the TQM implementation for the organisation as a whole.

There are many factors that motivate how to develop a QMS design strategy. A design theory for prescribing how to deal with situations depends on having a kernel theory for explaining how the various factors contribute in the dynamics of the system as a whole. One of the challenges in using systems theory for understanding complex systems of this kind is that there are important events happening on different scales. In meteorology there are scale models representing different scales of time and space that have to be integrated for predicting how local weather will unfold (Tarbuck & Lutgens, 1994). In general, however, how to integrate different scale models into a coherent multi-scale model representation of a phenomenon is not easy. As Lemke (2000) points out, not only are there challenges in multi-scale modelling, but the customary way of thinking about the social world in dual terms of material and a mental components makes it difficult to develop coherent models of ecosystems with cultures (semiotic practice) such as the human social systems.

2.2.2 Analysis: What can't be measured can't be managed

The use of measurements and statistical analysis is fundamental to quality control and TQM (Shewhart, 1938; Deming, 1986). In a paper dealing with challenges in information systems action research Baskerville (2007) refers to a hospital study where the administrative staff wanted physicians to cut costs by improving decisions. Inspired by the theory of "what can't be measured can't be managed" an information system was developed for the purpose of both aiding the physicians in their decision processes and to make it possible for the organisation to learn from wrong decisions and thus systematically work towards hospital excellence. The IS implementation turned out to be a failure, however, as the physicians refused to expose their decisions to non-peer groups such as the administrative staff. The story illustrates a challenge with both the control game and the design game in figure 1 when the organisation can be characterised as a professional bureaucracy in the sense where the mangers (administrative staff) represent the replaceable resources while the workers (physicians) are the irreplaceable experts with the dominant organisational power. In the context of figure 8, the intervention failed due to "poor analysis of the organisation as a system". What turned out to be a successful strategy for the technology side of the design game for this particular case was to redefine the control game as a peer-control game and develop a quality management system that allowed the physicians to control themselves and have control over their own process improvements without intervention from administrative staff.

2.2.3 Design: The case against ISO 9000

In order to use measures and statistical analysis it is necessary to have quality standards to measure against (Taylor, 1911; Shewhart, 1938). As TQM practice gradually developed as an approach for controlling all aspects of the organisation, quality standards continue to be introduced and developed in new areas, including quality standards such as ISO 9001 for the design of quality management systems (Hoyle, 2006) and the Capability Maturity Model (CMM) for the software industry (Zahran, 1998).

Peter Axel Nielsen and other Scandinavian IS researchers have written about the business models hidden inside the CMM standards (e.g. Rose, Aaen & Nielsen, 2008). They argue that these models are based on American management principles that do not work equally well in other cultures. Ciborra (1998) also warns against the CMM standards and total quality control culture in general. Seddon (1997) makes a similar argument against ISO 9000. He argues that the ISO 9000 series developed from military standards and that the quality practice these standards support is a practice associated with a "command and control" culture which is very different from the sort of quality practice associated with TQM and successful quality management.

In the context of the model in figure 1, what this kind of research suggests is that technology tends to create equilibria in the control game that are not necessarily the kind of win-win equilibria recommended by Deming (1994) and other TQM scholars. In the context of figure 8, the failure occurred due to "poor solution design".

2.2.4 Implementation: Organisational hypocrisy

Whether it is true or not that ISO 9000 and other quality standards are based upon ideologies that contradict ideals and principles of TQM, empirical research can at least show examples of the standards being implemented in the spirit of such ideologies (Seddon, 1997). Focusing on the ideals and realities of TQM implementation, Brunsson and Jacobsson (2000) describe further challenges to the design game in figure 1 by saying that the control game is not defined exclusively by players inside the organisation. Quality standards like the ISO 9000 standards are part of a global network of management consultants, auditors, standardisation committees and related communities or what can be described as a standardisation industry. Although it is in the interest of this industry that the ISO 9000 standards deliver what they promise, the industry also has to deal with organisations that have been told to comply with such a standard without necessarily having the time, resources or right motivation for doing this.

As a consequence of this, what emerges is a culture of "organisational hypocrisy" in the sense that TQM theory becomes detached from TQM practice. Organisations want to be acknowledged as excellent by getting certified against regional and international quality standards and spend time and resources in maintaining an image of being compliant with TQM while not necessarily being compliant. Because networks like the ISO 9000, CMM or audit industries in general depend on having users and customers, promises are made and rules are bent to give the impression that TQM is being implemented while in reality it is difficult to say what is happening (Brunsson 1989; Brunsson and Jacobsson, 2000; Power, 1997).

In the context in figure 1, this means that the design game in the model is part of a larger and more complex game. The failure in figure 8 occurred due to "poor implementation strategy". Not only do the TQM implementers have to make sure that the mechanisms defining the control game results in a win-win situation that allows two parts to cooperate but they also have to make sure that this equilibrium is not a "hypocrisy" equilibrium where everybody ends up believing they are continually improving organisational performance through TQM while what they are actually doing is sweeping problems under the carpet until the belief is broken as some disaster sooner or later happens.

2.2.5 The information infrastructure paradigm

The information infrastructure paradigm (Ciborra, 2000; Hanseth & Ciborra, 2007) is a way of thinking about information systems development (ISD) from a network perspective similar to how Brunsson and Jacobsson (2000) wrote about the ISO 9000 industry as a global network creating globalised TQM hypocrisy. While the hypocrisy theory is useful for understanding the dynamics of standardisation from the agent perspective in the design game in figure 1, the information infrastructure paradigm may be more useful for understanding the game from the principal side.

Hanseth (2002) defines an information infrastructure as "a shared, evolving, open, standardized, and heterogeneous installed base" using the internet, electronic data interchange (EDI) networks and corporate infrastructures to exemplify what this means. The concept of a standard is interesting in the context of TQM design. A typical information infrastructure narrative often deals with issues like how different players try to impose different standards for integrating systems, like a conflict over what data exchange format should be used for dealing with some specific context (Braa et al, 2007). In order to document and understand how such games are played out in real life, Hanseth and Monteiro (1998) have suggested using the anthropological research approach known as actor-network theory (ANT).

ANT was originally used for writing case studies about scientists making use of network politics in their daily scientific work and thus getting a better understanding of social aspects of the scientific method (Latour, 1987). In order to deal with such problems, ANT deals with multi-scale modelling and how to coherently integrate material and mental components of social systems (Lemke, 2000). The generality of the approach has made it useful for focusing on the role of networks when trying to understand all sorts of social phenomena (Latour, 2005). While the system unit in an information system perspective makes it natural to analyse process, monitoring and feedback for individual systems and how these systems relate to each other through game theory, making the network the unit in information infrastructure makes topological analysis a natural approach with evolutionary game theory (EGT) as a possible approach for analysing how the different networks interact.

The potential usefulness of the information infrastructure paradigm for planning TQM implementation can be explained by using the networks in figure 10 for illustrating a story told by Legge (2002) about TQM implementation from an ANT perspective. The first challenge for the TQM consultant is to convince top management about TQM in order to establish a centralised TQM topology that covers at least a vital part of the organisation. At this stage the topology will break into individual pieces when the central station is removed, so the next step is to identify and cultivate champions for the TQM idea inside the organisation in order to make the topology decentralised. As TQM theory and practice continues to be cultivated through the organisation, the final goal is to end up with the distributed network where TQM has been implemented in the sense of the network becoming more or less indestructible as every station has been enrolled.

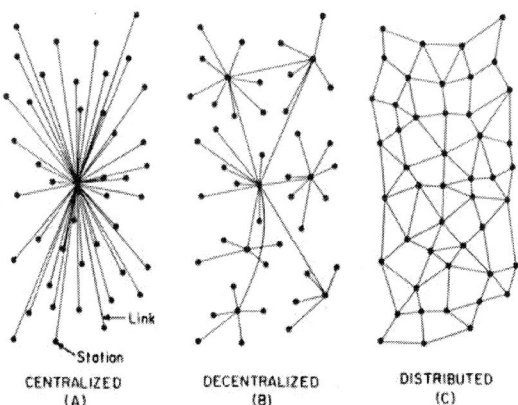

Figure 10: Three different actor-network topologies (Hansson, 2009)

In the context of organisational hypocrisy, the principal using the information infrastructure design strategy (BA) in the design game (figure 1) should be interpreted as a principal trying to redesign the control game played by the agents by gradually trying to replace the regulations and incentives used in the hypocritical game with new regulations and incentives gradually introduced by having the new TQM network replace the old network.

2.2.6 The Monopoly board game

Explaining the way the information infrastructure design strategy was used in the context of a global health information systems programme (HISP), Monteiro (2006) suggested, somewhat jokingly, that the strategy could be described as a "world domination game" as more and more countries were enrolled in the HISP network as the information infrastructure was developed. Although this comment may not have been intended to be taken literally, there is a similarity between the logic of information infrastructure design and the logic of "world domination" parlour games such as Risk and Monopoly.

The benefit of using a game like Monopoly or Risk as a general model of the TQM implementation process is that such games can be understood as mathematical models allowing the researcher to formulate the TQM implementation problem in a manner which makes it possible to deduce model conclusions to be implemented (figure 6). As the Monopoly board game is the more well-known of the two, both in terms of the public knowledge about parlour games and the extent these games have been used by scholars (Axelrod, 2002; 2009; Bewersdorff, 2007), this framework will be used for analysing the TQM implementation problem in general terms. Some of the characteristics of the Monopoly game are listed and compared with characteristics of how information infrastructures grow and develop in table 7.

	Information infrastructure	**Monopoly board game**
Goal and constraints	Conquer the world	Make all competitors loose
	A large network of information systems is developing in a manner that is difficult to predict	Game dynamics have strong element of chance
Opening	Technical standards are vitally important as they limit and direct further development	Properties are vitally important for getting an income. Ownership to properties also limits and directs further development of the game
Middlegame	Having monopoly on series of standards makes it possible to control technological evolution	Having monopoly on a series of properties is necessary for property development
	Gateways	Negotiating and trading properties is necessary for getting ahead in the game
	The information infrastructure dynamics is non-linear but there are attractors	Movement around the game board is ruled by dice but properties are not visited with equal frequency. The jail functions as an attractor.
Endgame	Increasing returns	Monopoly follows the "rich getting richer" dynamics. At one stage the wealth of one player may start to increase at the cost of all the others.
	Lock-in	Once monopolies start to develop the game will reach a phase where nothing can be done but wait for the game to end

Table 7: Using the Monopoly board game to model information infrastructure dynamics

To elaborate on the comparison of concepts in table 7, the content of the first table column suggests a way of grouping ideas.

Goal and constraints

When discussing the purpose of Monopoly, Axelrod (2002, p. 118) makes a point out of the game being a zero-sum game. To win at Monopoly is equivalent to making everybody else loose, but this can also be interpreted as being able to survive as long as possible. When thinking of information infrastructure development and TQM implementation, it may be more practical to think in terms of how to survive when a significant challenge of the game is that it is difficult to predict what will happen next.

For the purpose of finding appropriate solution concepts of dynamic games, Jim Dolan has suggested that "success for player p" should be defined as the state (date-event pair) where player *p* has at least one move left (Gross, 2005). This solution concept is useful for analysing Monopoly and information infrastructure development because it is difficult to know when the game will end. The longest game play of Monopoly on record lasted 70 days (Orbanes, 2007, p. 185), and there is a theoretical possibility that a game of Monopoly can go on forever (Friedman et al., 2009). For this reason the early rounds (local tournaments) in world championships in Monopoly consist of each player playing three 90-minute games and making the player with the most wealth at the end of each game the winner (Orbanes, 2007, p. 143). For information infrastructure development and TQM implementation that may take many years or even decades to complete, Dolan's solution concept makes it possible to talk about success without knowing the final outcome of game play.

Opening

When using Monopoly to model information infrastructure dynamics, properties play a similar fundamental role in Monopoly as standards do in information infrastructures. When integrating information systems it is necessary that they are able to communicate with each other through common standards. In the case of TQM implementation quality standards and frameworks like EFQM, CMM and ISO 9001 are important because they make it possible for the organisation to communicate with auditor networks and participate in practitioner networks for discussing different ways of implementing the standards and ways of sharing best practice.

Middlegame

According to Axelrod (2002, p. 178), at the moment a player builds the first monopoly in the game, the opening game ends, and the middlegame begins. The building of monopoly marks the transition from equal opportunity for all into decreasing opportunities for some. The building of the first monopoly brings an end to an economy based on plenty and introduces one increasingly based on scarcity.

There is a similar dynamics in information infrastructure once standards are being adopted and used for developing the infrastructure. Solutions based on obsolete technological standards erode while solutions based on fashionable standards grow. In the case of TQM implementation there have been fads and fashions by methods, standards, management consultants talking about concepts like quality circles, benchmarking, continual quality improvement (CQI), just-in-time (JIT), business process reengineering (BPR), Six Sigma, and Lean Production as if they represented different approaches although they often tend to be new packaging of the same old TQM ideas (Cole, 1999). While such fashions may seem ridiculous from an engineering perspective, they can be important for getting management interest and commitment. Just as the Monopoly game, in infrastructure development it is necessary to get control over "properties of the same colour" to be able to start cultivation and development, like it is important for TQM implementation to be able to work on business processes. Only with an understanding of the process as a whole is it possible to carry out 80/20 analysis and find out which few important tasks to improve in order to create significant impact on business performance.

In computer and telecommunications theory a gateway is a term used to denote an object linking two different networks or different communication protocols or standards. It is often used to denote a converter or translator between different formats. By using the story of how the internet was established in Scandinavia, Hanseth (2001) illustrates the important role of gateways for developing information infrastructure. In the Monopoly game a series of properties may be distributed between two or more players, and each of these players can be seen as gateways between such colour series. How to negotiate and trade properties is an important aspect of Monopoly game play, and computer simulation studies are used to improve the understanding of how such negotiations and trades should be done (Yasumura et al., 2001; Loffredo, 2008).

The dynamics of how information infrastructures grow and develop is generally unpredictable but have been described through the use of non-linear dynamics and attractors (Hanseth & Lyytinen, 2010). The dynamics of Monopoly is usually described through the use of Markov chain theory (Ash & Bishop, 1972; Stewart, 1996a; 1996b). The board game consists of 40 positions (states). The transition probability from one state to another can be calculated by considering the outcome of the rolling of the dice and the drawing of chance and community chest cards. Something that can be seen from this kind of analysis is the role of the Jail position on the Monopoly board as an attractor. The rules of Monopoly requires a player to go to Jail whenever landing on the "go to Jail" position, drawing a "go to Jail" card, or rolling doubles for the third time on the same turn (Orbanes, 2007, p. 41). The consequence of this is that certain properties, like those of the orange series, are more likely to land on that others, and the frequency pattern for players landing on properties has to be taken into consideration when deciding which properties to buy, trade and develop.

Based on the Markov chain theory, Luenberger (1979) shows how the traditional 1935 definition of the Monopoly game is just one configuration of an infinite number of Monopoly game designs that can be created by changing the number of positions on the board and the data on property deeds and chance cards. Thinking about Monopoly games as a class of games makes it possible to design specific Monopoly games for specific tasks such as studying and teaching how to implement the Capability Maturity Model (CMM) for controlling software development (Yilmaz & O'Conner, 2012).

Endgame

How information infrastructures become standardised is sometimes described by referring to the ideas of economist W. Brian Arthur of how increasing returns tend to magnify historical events (path-dependency property) and to trap the dynamics into dominated standards (lock-in property) (Auriol & Benaim, 2001). Similar mechanisms can be observed in the endgame of Monopoly as the distribution of wealth becomes increasingly skewed and one player starts to dominate the game and wins by driving everybody else out (Seidman, 2011).

2.3 Design theory: Monopoly strategy for TQM implementation

The purpose of this section, as illustrated in figure 11, is to show how the BA can be seen as a strategy for winning the Monopoly game of TQM information infrastructure design by the process of reviewing Monopoly literature and literature dealing with CAS and TQM implementation.

The review will start by addressing the objective to be optimised by TQM mechanism design and how the Monopoly game should be analysed for finding good mechanism design tactics (section 2.3.1), and will then proceed by commenting on Monopoly tactics such as using CAS for thinking about how to buy properties (section 2.3.2), using TSI for thinking about how to trade properties (section 2.3.3) and using the principle of "what gets measured gets done" for thinking about how to develop properties (section 2.3.4) before summarising the tactics as part of a BA strategy of how to play Monopoly (section 2.3.5).

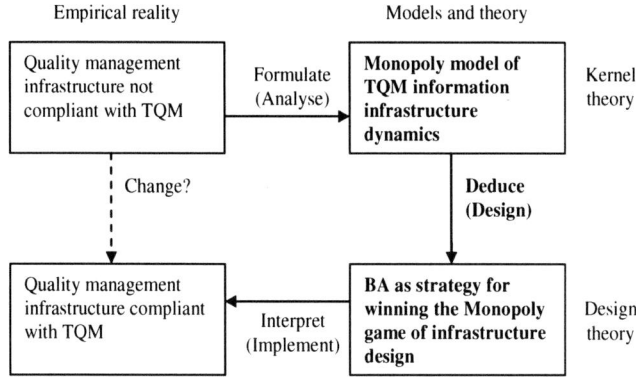

Empirical reality   Models and theory

Figure 11: Design theory for changing culture by redesigning information infrastructure

2.3.1 Objectives and tactics in TQM mechanism design games

Mechanism design is the study of how a principal can design or redesign games that are played by agents for the purpose of making game play optimise some objective. The mechanisms are typically regulations and incentives for changing the equilibria for strategic game play. Examples of the use of mechanism design in economics and political science are the designs of elections, auctions and markets (Nisan et al., 2007).

In the context of the TQM implementation problem, the general assumption is that the way this game is usually played results in 80% implementation failure. The quest for TQM mechanism design is to look at how the Monopoly model captures critical aspects of the TQM implementation game and then try to change the equilibria of the organisational TQM games by playing the Monopoly representation of the mechanism design game in a successful manner.

The objective to be optimised in TQM mechanism design

The pyramid model in figure 12 depicts quality management through a perspective of three levels. At the bottom level there are business processes. At the next level is the information infrastructure (quality management system) used for controlling the business processes. At the top level is the objective function used for evaluating whether the information infrastructure helps the business processes perform at an optimal level in terms of high productivity, low cost and zero defects. On the left side of the pyramid there are standards that are relevant for designing and evaluating the information system in the general mass production context. On the right side there are standards for dealing with software engineering.

The system of business processes may typically consist of processes for customer management, dealing with suppliers, development, production and calibration of control instruments (Hoyle, 2006). The purpose of the information system is to read sensor data from the product realisation process, and then send control signals produced by the control algorithm in order to make sure the system of business processes performs at an optimal level.

In the context of quality management, the objective function used for evaluating whether the information systems is keeping the process in optimal control is often referred to as the maturity of the quality management system (Crosby, 1979). Different assessment standards use different criteria and scales for measuring maturity levels, but they can usually be scaled to produce scores between 0 and 1.

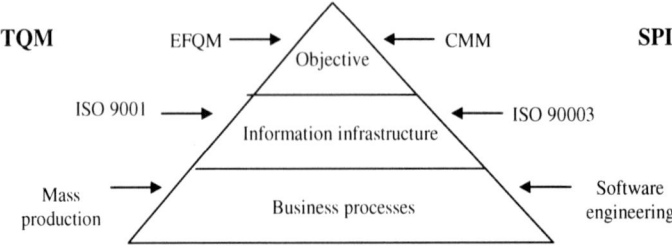

Figure 12: Pyramid model for optimising the business processes through quality management

From the viewpoint of the TQM mechanism design game, it is necessary but not sufficient to have a global standard such as the EFQM or CMM frameworks for measuring implementation progress. There is also a need for measurable optimisation criteria such as the cost and duration of the implementation process. If the dynamics of the system of business processes are sufficiently well understood, having a control goal and optimising criteria should be sufficient for evaluating possible strategic solutions to the TQM mechanism design game from a systems perspective in the sense of thinking about the solutions as control designs and evaluating such designs from the perspective of stability and robustness (Albertos & Marcels, 2010).

The political nature of TQM mechanism design games

The TQM mechanism design game consists of the designer influencing the strategy sets and payoffs of the control game by modifying the information infrastructure (quality management system, QMS) at the mid level in figure 12, assuming that the standards at the top level are given, for the purpose of changing the practice at the bottom level. The strategy set is related to the standards and procedures used by the QMS while the payoff is related to how organisational practice is measured or audited against the standards and how the results are fed back into the organisation.

Taylor (1911) exemplifies the idea in his case study of how to carry pig iron by a method of having labour constantly monitored by stopwatch and given feedback on when to work and when to rest while using salary incentives for preventing the process to break down. In his case the physical labour is described at the bottom level of figure 12, the controls at the mid level, and the object function at the top level in terms of a balanced scorecard based on the four ideas of "science, not rule of thumb – harmony, not discord – cooperation, not individualism – maximum output, in place of restricted output" (ibid, p. 123).

The Monopoly game of mechanism design Taylor was playing consisted of trying to convince management of the benefits of running organisations based on cultivating practice based on science, harmony, corporation and efficiency. What he was fighting against was what he saw as the existing culture of "rule of the thumb", discord, individualism and "soldiering" (inefficiency). The early stages of his Monopoly play started by "buying properties" in terms of getting involved with any organisation that would be interested in his ideas, such as the Bettlehem Steel Company in Pennsylvania, and then starting to "trade properties to get monopolies" in terms of getting control over certain tasks and practices such as carrying pig iron or shovelling. This would then allow him to "develop properties" in terms carrying out design research on how to optimise the chosen task and develop control systems for making sure that optimal work was carried out in a sustainable manner.

Carrying out these kind of interventions were not without problems. Taylor reflected that "if he had lived where the [workmen] lived, they would have brought such social pressure to bear upon him that it would have been impossible to have stood out against them. He would have been called [...] foul names every time he appeared on the street, his wife would have been abused, and his children would have been stoned. Once or twice he was begged by some of his friends among the workmen not to walk home, about two and a half miles along a lonely path by the side of the railway. He was told that if he continued to do this it would be at the risk of his life. In all such cases, however, [...] he told them to say to the other men in the shop that he proposed to walk home every night right up that railway track; that he never had carried and never would carry any weapon of any kind, and that they could shoot and be d***" (ibid, pp. 40-41).

Despite conflicts escalating to the level of Taylor having to explain himself to the supreme court about the social implications for the quality of life for the workers in organisations when methods of scientific management were introduced (Taylor, 1947), scientific management spread all over the world. Whether Taylor won or lost the Monopoly game of mechanism design depends on one's perspective. One perspective would be to say that scientific management was a dehumanising practice of treating workers as machines whose main legacy is today's industrial automation by robots and computers (Clegg et al, 2005). Another perspective is to say that Taylor was the Isaac Newton of laying the foundation for the science of work upon which little of similar scope has been added since (Drucker, 1974). This second perspective can be supported by pointing out how action research was based on the method of scientific management (Lewin, 1920; Gold, 1999, p. 295), how operations research, management science and systems analysis is an extension of scientific management (Churchman, 1968, pp. 17-18), and how scientific management became what is currently described as total quality management (TQM) as it met with Japanese culture (Ishikawa, 1985; Shingo, 1987, pp. xv-xvi).

A main challenge for playing the game of TQM mechanism design, as can be seen by looking at the experience from the mechanism design of scientific management, is that the scientific study of process improvement has political implications and should be expected to be met with resistance. The negative interpretation of scientific management as a way for management to control the workforce through a process of deskilling (Braverman, 1974) is a challenge for making either of the two mistakes in table 4 from the introductory chapter. The first mistake is for the TQM designer to focus on the science of scientific management or TQM without realising the political context where the approach is being put into use. The other mistake is to see frameworks like scientific management and TQM as being political by themselves without looking at the social context.

Use of analysis and simulation for understanding the implementation game

In order to play the Monopoly game of TQM implementation in a way that promotes science, harmony, cooperation and efficiency, components that characterise a TQM culture, the TQM designer must not only understand the Monopoly dynamics of the QMS information infrastructure, he must also develop skills and theoretical understanding of how to play the Monopoly game of TQM mechanism design. Darzinskis (2007) illustrates this point in his comments on Bewersdorff mathematical explanation of how Monopoly works.

Bewersdorff (2007) presents an explanation of Markov chains and how they can be applied to games like Monopoly and Snakes & Ladders. The result of the calculation for Monopoly is two charts detailing the best investments in Monopoly. One chart ranks the monopolies according to how much rent income they will generate for the owner. The second chart ranks monopolies according to their return on investment (ROI), expected rent divided by cost. Thus one sees, for example, that the highest rent comes from the green colour group, and the best monopoly measured by ROI is the orange colour group. Bewersdorff suggests these charts may be useful for deciding what properties to buy and where to buy houses.

The problem, as Darzinskis (2007) sees it, is that the results of the Markov chain calculation are not really useful for decisions Monopoly players have to make. Players must buy nearly every ordinary property they land on in order to advance their chances of getting a monopoly and to block opponents from getting monopolies, so properties' ROIs and rents are mostly irrelevant to the property buying decisions. After players trade properties, almost every player has one monopoly, not two or three or four, so the problem of deciding where to build the next house is not an issue. The player must put the house on his lone monopoly. Only after reaching the later stages of the game, usually after one of the players has been eliminated, do players have a choice about which monopoly to build out. Even in this regard, the chart is not useful, Darzinskis argue, as there is too much data to memorize and Monopoly culture discourages players from consulting charts in the middle of a game.

The important decisions Monopoly players make involve trading, Darzinskis says, deciding which monopoly to take and which monopoly to allow an opponent to take. The data from a Markov chain calculation do not help much. What Monopoly players need to help them make this decision is the outcome of thousands of Monte Carlo computer simulations of Monopoly game play. He concludes by suggesting Monopoly players to have a look at his own specific findings based on Monte Carlo experiments of Monopoly game play (Darzinskis, 1987).

Bewersdorff focuses on the Monopoly rules and makes use of mathematical representations (Markov chains as kernel theory) for understanding the dynamics of Monopoly game play. Based on these insights he suggests implications for strategy design. Darzinskis, on the other hand, tries to find efficient designs for a winning strategy by running thousands of simulations. One might say that Bewersdorff understands the dynamics of Monopoly without knowing how to play it while Darzinskis knows how to win Monopoly without understanding the game. From an academic perspective, however, the Monopoly game would be best understood by mixing the insights and methods used by Bewersdorff and Darzinskis in a manner that could be used for testing the design ideas arising from Bewersdorff's approach using Darzinskins simulation methods, and explaining the outcomes of Darzinskis experiments by referring to Bewersdorff's kernel model.

When using the Monopoly game for explaining information infrastructure dynamics in section 2.2.6, this was done from the Bewersdorff perspective. By representing information infrastructure dynamics as a Monopoly game, the game can be analysed in a similar way as done by Bewersdorff, and the analysis will provide suggestions on strategy design. In the telling of the early days of TQM from the perspective of scientific management, the focus was on Frederick Taylor as a TQM designer, and his story became similar to the Monte Carlo experiments Darzinskis talk about.

The challenge in developing a Monopoly strategy for TQM mechanism design consists of two parts. The first part is to review results from digital simulations like those of Darzinskis and analogue simulations like the story of scientific management to suggest possible strategies.

34

The second part consists of explaining these strategies in the context of the kernel theory related to the Monopoly representation of information infrastructure in section 2.2.

The role of tactics in the Monopoly strategy of TQM mechanism design

In the language of game theory a strategy is something that is defined at the start of game play and continues to the game ends. The concept of a game tree is useful in the context of design theory. In game theory a game tree is a directed graph whose nodes are game positions in a game and edges are moves. The complete game tree for a game is the game tree starting at the initial position and containing all possible moves from each position. The number of leaf nodes in the complete game tree is the number of possible different ways the game can be played. In this context the strategies of the game correspond to a path from the initial node to a leaf node.

In a game like Monopoly, some of the moves are consequences of chance and some are consequences of decision making. No literature reviewed in this study mentions any calculations or estimates of the size of the complete game tree for Monopoly, but it seems likely to be expected to be of astronomical size and far beyond what can be analysed by brute force computer methods. What can be done, however, is to make use of computer analysis of partial game trees.

The concept of a tactic will be used to refer to a sequence of moves that limits the opponent's options and may result in tangible gain, following the language conventions of Chess literature (Seirawan, 2005). As a consequence of this definition, a strategy can be seen to be made up of a sequence of tactics, and specific tactics for Monopoly such as buying properties, trading properties and developing properties will be discussed. Furthermore, by conceptualising the strategy as an algorithm, the tactics can be thought of as subroutines to be used when dealing with specific time-event situations.

2.3.2 Property buying tactics: Complex adaptive systems (CAS)

In his comments on the rent and ROI tables calculated by Bewersdorff, Darzinskis (2007) said that these tables had little relevance during game opening as players should buy nearly every ordinary property they land on in order to advance their chances. In his book he discusses property buying tactics in more detail (Darzinskis, 1987). Although he maintains that buying every property one lands as a rule of the thumb for beginners (ibid, p. 74), his general comment is that most players buy more properties than they should, especially after the first 30 minutes of play (ibid, p. 80). Buying property shrinks cash reserves that could otherwise be invested in high-profit houses, so it makes sense to buy property only when there is good reason to do so, and there are three such reasons. Firstly, buy to assemble a monopoly or to prevent an opponent from assembling a monopoly. Secondly, buy to gain veto power over trades between opposing partner. Thirdly, buy to gain cash profit from investments.

To support his various claims, Darzinskis refer to probabilities derived from Monte Carlo experiments. He says, for instance, that a set of 1000 experimental games showed that players owning monopolies are 33 percent more likely to bankrupt their opponents when they do not buy the third property of a broken colour group. In other words, when landing on an unsold red property and the two other red properties are owned by separate players, Darzinskis advice is not to buy. Koury (2012), on the other hand, has been more phenomenological in his approach towards understanding Monopoly in the sense of trying to describe the world of Monopoly tournament gaming based on 35 years of observation, participation, discussion and reflection, and has been sceptical about whether Monopoly computer simulations based on artificial intelligence (AI) are capable of producing sufficiently good results (ibid, p. 30). He illustrates this point by writing about experiences and observations from the world of Monopoly tournament play, including a story where a professional tournament player lost the game to a 12 year old girl by giving the child a second orange property in exchange for a third light blue property completing his first colour group. What the professional had not anticipated was the "irrationality" of a third player who traded the final orange group for getting a complete set of utilities which subsequently resulted in the 12 year old winning the game and the professional spending the rest of the tournament shaking his head repeating to himself "There was no reason for him to do that, there was no reason for him to do that" (ibid, pp. 31-32).

While Darzinskis computer simulations were based on the usual game theory assumption that people know the rules of the game and are acting strategically, Ariely (2008) argues that "people are predictably irrational" in the sense that they are often acting strategically according to a different set of rules, like when an adult is playing Monopoly in a way (deliberately or not) that will improve the chances of a child to win. Koury's story illustrates psychological and sociological aspects of Monopoly play. It is not sufficient to understand the game in isolation. It is also necessary to practice Monopoly by playing a wide range of personalities in order to develop an understanding for the psychology of game play (Koury, 2012, p. 31).

Axelrod (2002, pp. 173-177) discusses three points in relation to using insights from the game opening of Monopoly for business and entrepreneurship. The first point corresponds to Bewersdorff approach of developing and analysing a Markov chain model of the Monopoly game to understand the proper odds of the game. In Monopoly some of this is known in advance due to the multinomial probability distribution for the roll of the dice, such as how it takes about five turns to get around the board, each player will probably roll doubles once each time around the board, and each player will probably land on four of the 28 property spaces each time around the board. To complete the Markov chain model, however, the sixteen chance and sixteen community chest cards have to be taken into consideration. As these cards are never shuffled in the course of the game, remembering the cards gives a competitive advantage. What the Monopoly model teaches in this case, Axelrod argues, is to understand the difference between generic probabilities related to the type of business one is dealing with (probability of the dice) and the specific probabilities that applies for the particular case in question (the gradual understanding of the sequence of chance and community cards as the game unfolds).

Axelrod's second point deals with understanding the psychology of the players. As the original Monopoly design included different tokens such as a car, a hat, a shoe etc to represent each of the players, the token a given player chooses might reveal something about his psychology and range of preferred strategies. Koury (2012) supports this idea with various stories involving how certain tournament players are attached to certain tokens. Orbanes (2013) refers to research based on polling players on the Facebook Monopoly fan page, members of a Monopoly association, students and teachers who use Monopoly in the classroom and gamers in general, and lists social and psychological treats associated with each token. Axelrod (2002, pp. 122-129) suggests this aspect of Monopoly can be carried over to the real world in terms of making use of how people present themselves for understanding their psychology and being conscious about how one presents oneself.

Axelrod's third point is the importance of being clear about the purpose of the game. Koury

(2012, pp. 100-101) explains how he was able to set the world recorded for fastest game of official tournament play of Monopoly by playing against people who had internalised the game in an unbalanced manner by paying too much attention to emotional aspects of the game and too little attention to logical aspects. They did not fully understand aspects of Monopoly that makes it into a game of strategy. In the official rules for Monopoly the object of the game is described as "to become the richest player by buying, renting and trading properties" (Orbanes, 2013, p. 244). Axelrod compares this with what he calls the "real objective" of Monopoly, namely to bankrupt all opponents. The lesson here is to understand the difference between descriptions derived from non-structuralist ethnographical research and the kind of precise mathematical models needed by engineers, economists and other planners in need for making social change.

Complex adaptive systems (CAS) and the opening gameplay of Monopoly

Kurt Lewin's systems approach to change management has been described to consist of three steps; a situation is unfrozen, it is changed, and is then refrozen (Goldstein, 1994). The same logic of unfreeze-change-refreeze is applied in the classical plan-do-check-act (PDCA) approach to process improvement and TQM implementation by use of statistical process control (SPC) in first making sure that the process to be changed is in a state of statistical control, then redesigning it, and finally stabilising the solution to make sure it is once again in a state of statistical control (Shewhart, 1938; Deming, 1986; Juran, 1989).

As discussed earlier, however, TQM implementation is not always carried out in predictable environments. Dooley et al (1995) argue that the paradigm of complex adaptive systems (CAS) is a better foundation for TQM implementation than traditional systems theory in such circumstances. Although they referred to literature showing how the CAS approach had been used for solving practical engineering problems (e.g. Kelly, 1994), their main point was how the CAS literature provided useful metaphors for thinking about organisational development.

As pointed out by Simon (1996), when CAS became an important perspective in systems theory it made an impact on how to frame decision problems in a manner where they could be solved through approaches like genetic algorithms (GA). The GA is a search algorithm simulating the process of natural selection by trying to evolve a population of potential solutions to a problem by trial and error rather than trying to explicitly design a solution (Holland, 1995). For instance, use of evolutionary programming for analysing the Monopoly board game has made it possible to understand more about Monopoly strategies than has been previously known by conventional analytical mathematical approach (Frayn, 2005; Kotrik, 2012).

CAS is a useful framework for understanding the opening game play of the Monopoly representation of TQM mechanism design because it provides a good match with Axelrod's three points. Considering his first point, the reason why TQM programme management based on GA makes more sense than the traditional TQM implementation approach is because it is designed to operate in an unpredictable environment, which makes it possible to make the generic aspects of the Markov chain representation of the Monopoly board as part of the GA framework. Learning will then take place as the process improvement projects within the TQM programme succeed and fail while a better understanding of the organisational environment is recorded as "the sequence of chance and community chest cards" is being revealed. The GA approach also fits with Axelrod's second point as the success and failure of individual process improvement projects will provide learning about the psychology of the opponents to the TQM philosophy. Finally, corresponding to Axelrod's third point, as the

GA is a mathematical algorithm it is necessary with an explicit representation of the conflicts in the organisation not only in the diplomatic language of "getting rich by buying, renting and trading properties" but by addressing the "real objective" of the game by explaining the criterion for defining game over.

2.3.3 Property trading tactics: Total Systems Intervention (TSI)

Axelrod (2002) talks about the three phases of Monopoly as opening, middle game and end game. Although the opening and end game are not totally dependent on luck, the most obviously strategic aspects of Monopoly come into play during the middle game. Seidman (2011) breaks the middle game down into two phases; trading properties and developing properties.

When Darzinskis commented on the rent and ROI tables by Bewersdorff by saying that they were of limited use for making decisions about which properties to buy and which to develop, he did not mention the possible usefulness of the tables in the context of trading. Koury, however, illustrates the importance of understanding the difference between the retail value and market value of a property. His explanation for how he set a world record by winning a Monopoly game in 15 minutes and 38 seconds was based on three incidents (Koury, pp. 100-101). The game started by a player landing on Oriental Avenue (light blue), but didn't want it and put it up for auction. Koury bought the property at the price of $110 because nobody wanted to pay more than retail value. The next player rolled a 3 and an 8 and landed on Vermont Avenue (light blue) and bought it. However, as she had not been willing to pay more than retail price at auction, Koury asked her if she would sell it to him for a $20 profit. She accepted. Next Koury rolled a 4 and a 5 which gave him Connecticut Avenue (light blue). Within 45 seconds of game play he had three hotels up, and in less than 15 minutes he had bankrupted all the others and won the game.

For Axelrod (2002, pp. 95-102) there are no significant differences between trading properties in Monopoly and trading in other contexts. The most important aspect of trading in Monopoly is that it changes from a game where "you roll dice, and you move around the board, and you buy properties from the bank, and you pay and collect rent, and ..." to a situation that consists not of playing a game but playing people (ibid, p. 96).

Total Systems Intervention (TSI) was developed in the late 1980s as a method for mixing different types of system methods in sequences for the purpose of solving real world problems while maintaining an overall critical social perspective (Flood & Jackson, 1991). The approach could in principle be used for solving any sort of problem dealing with organisational change, for instance the implementation of information systems (Dahlbom & Mathiassen, 1993, p. 287), although the example used for illustrating the approach was TQM implementation. In the early 1990s, a series of TSI studies were conducted in relation to TQM implementation and a specific method for implementing TQM through the use of TSI was developed (Flood, 1993).

The three boxes on the circumference of the circle in figure 13 represent the three key processes in TSI. The creativity process consists of addressing the interaction issues to be solved ("mess") at the centre of the figure by using metaphors or other methods in order to frame it as a problem. The choice process consists of choosing relevant methods needed for whether the problem needs to be elaborated and reformulated, whether it is sufficiently well-formulated to be solved or whether the solution needs to be evaluated. The implementation process consists of implementing the chosen method and evaluating the results.

The TQM implementation process consists of following the TSI cycle in clockwise manner after having entered the cycle through the creativity step or any other step. The TSI cycle can also be run anti-clockwise whenever there is need to reflect upon the outcome of a process. Due to the way TSI addresses the whole problem lifecycle process from the vague understanding of the problematic situation as a mess until it has been properly understood, solved and evaluated, different types of data need to be collected depending on the methods used at the creativity, choice and implementation stages of the cycle.

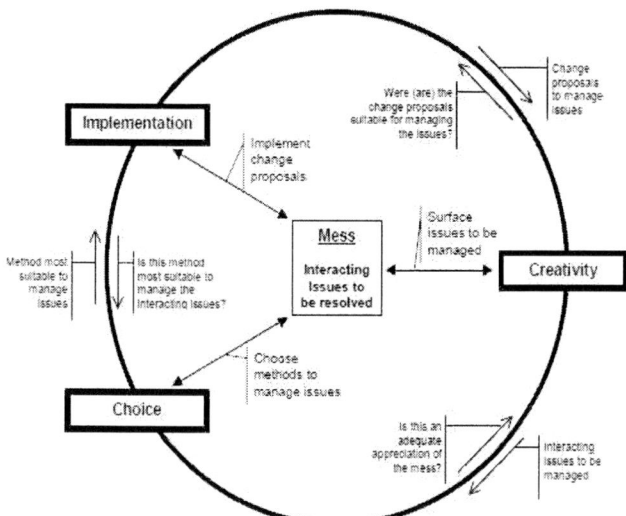

Figure 13: Total systems intervention process (Mehregan et al, 1998, p. 167)

As TSI has been designed to match with all types of system methods, both problem structuring methods (PSM), solution methods from operations research (OR) and related fields, and solution evaluation methods like Critical System Heuristics (CSH), nine such system methods were used for illustrating the logic of TSI when it was first introduced (Flood & Jackson, 1991, pp. 35-41). Later, other example methods have been added to illustrate how TSI can be used for managing a wide spectre of situations (e.g. Jackson, 2003).

The mess at the centre of the TSI flowchart in figure 13 can represent any type of situational context from task management via business processes management to system management of organisational units such as departments or the organisation as a whole. When implementing TQM there are models and methods designed for dealing with each of these layers of perspective, and there are empirical examples of how TSI has been used for researching how to develop quality strategies at the systems level (Flood, 1991; Green, 1992; 1993), how to use the viable systems method (VSM) for designing quality management systems at the process level (Flood & Isaac, 1993; Flood, 1993), and how to apply methods like fishbone charts in an optimal manner at the task level (Flood, 1993).

The System of Systems Methodology (SOSM) represented by the diagram in figure 14 was the starting point for developing TSI. The purpose of this diagram was to assist the choice process in TSI by providing an overview of suitable methods for dealing with groups of problems. As TSI continued to develop, Flood replaced the SOSM with more general choice methods while Jackson continued to elaborate on the philosophical and practical aspects of SOSM to be used in TSI and other frameworks.

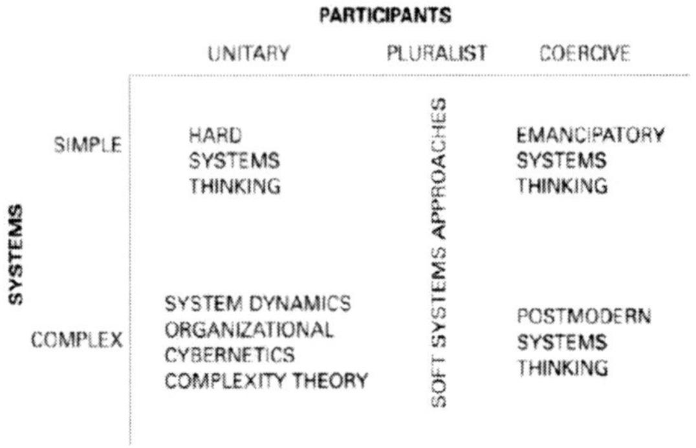

PARTICIPANTS

	UNITARY	PLURALIST	COERCIVE
SIMPLE	HARD SYSTEMS THINKING	SOFT SYSTEMS APPROACHES	EMANCIPATORY SYSTEMS THINKING
COMPLEX	SYSTEM DYNAMICS ORGANIZATIONAL CYBERNETICS COMPLEXITY THEORY		POSTMODERN SYSTEMS THINKING

SYSTEMS

Figure 14: System of systems methodology (Jackson, 2003)

The categories in SOSM are based on the idea that every mess can be understood as having to do with system complexity and relationship between participants. Systems are either simple or complex. As Flood and Jackson are somewhat mathematically imprecise in what they mean by simple and complex systems, this study will assume that the classification can be though of as similar to the classification of systems of differential equations as well-posed and ill-posed problems (Tikhonov and Arsenin, 1977). Relationships between participants can be irrelevant (unitary) when the focus is on solving a well-formulated problem, it can be exploring (plural) when some sort of debate or discussion is needed for formulating the problem in a mutually meaningful way, or it can be filled with tension (coercive) when solutions are being evaluated and participants wonder how the solution influence power and structure.

When dealing with TQM implementation from an information infrastructure perspective, the initial system analysis may typically consist of viewing the existing situation as complex-coercive. What the SOSM suggests in such cases is to investigate the postmodern systems thinking literature. As the information infrastructure paradigm makes use of ANT as one of its philosophical foundations, the information infrastructure paradigm can be seen as part of postmodern systems thinking.

In the same way as Axelrod described the trading aspect of Monopoly as playing people rather than playing a game, the TSI perspective on TQM implementation goes beyond the typical systems engineering context of TQM by seeing traditional OR as just one out of six problem contexts the TQM designer has to deal with ("hard systems thinking"). Although the unitary engineering aspect of TQM is of fundamental importance, the TSI framework helps seeing how engineering skills are important game skills that have to be supported with the trading skills needed for dealing with pluralist and coercive problem contexts.

The TSI is not a specific trading tactic, but it represents a way of thinking about each and every process improvement project from a trading perspective. While ANT was suggested as a kernel theory for explaining how the world is a network of negotiations, TSI is a design theory explaining how negotiations should be carried out for the purpose of solidifying and expanding the net. TSI can be integrated by CAS, as the SOSM differentiates between simple and complex systems, and CAS can be integrated by TSI by formulating the TSI as a GA, but

TSI and CAS are not the same (Jackson, 2003; Flood, 1999).

It should also be emphasised that the TSI models in figure 13 and 14 are design models for aiding the decision process. TSI is based on critical systems thinking ("emancipatory systems thinking") which means that decisions shaped by TSI are to be understood as decisions in environments involving more than one decision maker (Flood & Jackson, 1991). TSI can also be seen as an attempt to synthesise different paradigms as the SOSM represents a systematic approach for leading the TSI user in and out of different types of systems thinking (Jackson, 2000; 2003). As this could be interpreted as the TSI user having to change paradigmatic beliefs in terms of ontology, epistemology and axiology in order to make the chosen methodology work, TSI has been subject to criticism, reflection and reformulation (e.g. Tsoukas, 1993; Flood, 2004).

Given the perspectives on the philosophy of science discussed in section 2.1, however, the difference between natural science and social science does not have anything to do with ontology, epistemology or axiology but rather the question of whether the unit of analysis is seen as a system ("natural science") or a game ("social science"). From a design theory perspective, the purpose of TSI is simply to aid the problem solver through an optimal sequence of steps that makes sure that appropriate systems methods are used at the appropriate stage of problem solving. As long as this perspective is kept in mind while interpreting the different types of systems thinking represented in the SOSM, the purpose of the TSI becomes to find an optimal route through a complex maze (central design problem) that includes the opening and closing of black boxes for finding routes through other types of complex mazes at a deeper level (specific methodologies categorised by SOSM) before returning to the maze at the surface level.

This way of accepting the original TSI format by adopting an overall integrative philosophical perspective rather than making it work as a central hub in a system for communicating different methods based on different scientific paradigms could be seen as support of what Dahlbom and Mathiassen (1992) see as a need for a systems development philosophy. On the other hand, when Dahlbom and Mathiassen (1993) articulate their philosophy of systems development it is a non-integrative philosophy that centres around the idea of conflict between incommensurable paradigms of knowledge, such as the mechanistic versus the romantic, Habermas' three types of knowledge and the four sociological paradigms of Burrell and Morgan. Although there are similarities in the writings of Flood and Jackson with the writings of Dahlbom and Mathiassen, not at least in the central role of critical theory as a basis for a systems philosophy, there are epistemological differences. While Flood and Jackson make use of systems thinking as a unifying perspective, Dahlbom and Mathiassen are more concerned with the dialectics of conflicting philosophical perspectives as a way to aid the reflective practitioner. However, for the purpose of this study it is the way that the TSI and SOSM can be interpreted through van Fraassen's integrative philosophy of science that makes it useful (Øgland, 2009c).

When comparing the context of buying and trading properties in the Monopoly game of TQM mechanism design, a difference between TSI and CAS is that CAS is a way for discussing the TQM programme as cultivation of individual process improvement projects while TSI is the TQM implementation method used for each project. In the language of Monopoly this means that TSI is the approach used for managing individual monopolies, going through stages of buying, trading and developing properties for each colour group, while CAS is a framework for managing the portfolio of such real estate projects.

2.3.4 Property development tactics: What gets measured gets done

Brady (1978) suggests developing one Monopoly colour group at a time up to its optimal level. What is the optimal level may vary from group to group, but as a rule of the thumb one should aim for three houses on each property (Brandreth, 1985; Koury, 2012). Darzinskis (1987, p. 100) used Monte Carlo experiments for finding out whether it was beneficial to delay buying houses until there were enough liquid assets to put at least three houses on each monopolised lot. The outcome of his experiments, however, suggested that it would be better to start building houses immediately.

Axelrod (2002, p. 189) suggests these kind of Monopoly tactics are universally applicable for all kinds of business. Whether the businessperson holds several ventures or is the runner of a small shop, the 80/20 tactic of focusing on the most important issues first and getting them under control should be carried out despite temptations to move in too many directions at the same time.

Wuffle (1978) does not object to the 80/20 tactic but sees it as a fundamental problem with the Monopoly game that it models with world of real-estate management from a perspective that ignores the role of labour and unions in property development. Wuffle interprets this politically by seeing Monopoly as an ideological tool teaching and cultivating capitalist values in preparing children for society, making them develop a false consciousness that will allow them to accept the oppression of the ruling class rather than fighting the oppression. In the context of this study, however, the lack of detail in the way the Monopoly game models the conditions for property development means that the Monopoly model has to be extended in order to deal with the challenge of how to motivate construction workers into building houses and hotels on the given colour series.

The motivational theory of "what gets measured gets done" (Peters & Waterman, 1982) is based on the idea that clear goals and feedback improve efficiency and learning. The statement can be formulated in different ways, and in organisational context it is often interpreted similar to "workers tend to do what they believe managers focus on as important" (Schein, 1985).

Although measurements and statistical analysis is the basis for TQM, there are different opinions on how such results should be used for motivating people to improve. For instance, Crosby (1979) was of the opinion that organisations should give out awards to teams and individuals as part of a strategy for enrolling the organisation in the TQM ideology. Deming (1994), on the other hand, was worried that external goals would result in people being motivated by rewards rather than by the pleasure of doing a good job and was negative to rewards and prizes. Nevertheless, it should be possible to use the principle of "what gets measured gets done" in both cases as long as suitable methods for monitoring, measurements and feedback can be found.

Although the "what gets measured gets done" idea can be seen as a useful way of interpreting the idea of property development in Monopoly when using the Monopoly model to represent the real world, there is no such mechanism in the game. As long as a player have the necessary monopolies and cash resources, and the bank has not run out of houses, property development can be carried out without having to think about construction workers, labour unions, regulations and so on. The motivational "what gets measured gets done" game is an extension to the Monopoly game in order to make it deal with the real problems of TQM implementation.

A game extension does not necessarily change the nature of a game. Salen and Zimmerman (2004) identify cybernetic ideas like "what gets measured gets done" as a fundamental principle for successful game design, arguing along with Csikszentmihályi (1990) that clear goals and feedback are important for creating "flow" and making games sustainably enjoyable. In this sense, the extension of the game should not change the overall feel of the game. It makes the process of erecting small green houses and little red hotels slightly more complicated, but it is a conservative extension of the game in the sense that nothing else is altered.

2.3.5 The BA as a Monopoly game strategy

Using the metaphor of how a computer goes through a recursive bootstrap process for making itself ready to be used when started, Hanseth and Aanestad (2003) suggests that the development of information infrastructures can be understood as similar process. More recently Hanseth and Lyytinen (2010) have reformulated the BA to consist of three design principles and twelve underlying design rules. Table 8 shows how the three bootstrap design principles align with stages of the bootstrap algorithm. The twelve design rules correspond with the statements in the algorithm, although they are different in number and are formulated in a slightly different manner.

Bootstrap Design Principles	Bootstrap Algorithm

A. Design initially for direct usefulness
B. Build upon existing installed bases
	Start with
	   • simple, cheap, flexible solution
	   • small network of users that may benefit significantly from improved communication with each other only
	   • simple practices
	   • non-critical practices
	   • motivated users
	   • knowledgeable users

C. Expand installed base by persuasive tactics to gain momentum	1. Repeat as long as possible: Enrol more users 2. Find and implement more innovative use; go to 1 3. Use solution in more critical cases; go to 1 4. Use solution in more complex cases; go to 1 5. Improve the solution so new tasks can be supported; go to 1

Table 8: The bootstrap design principles and the bootstrap algorithm

The BA is made up of two parts. The first part consists of identifying the installed base that should be used for cultivation and expansion. In the context of the actor-network diagrams in figure 10, the centralised topology can be a way of visualising the initial step of the BA. The second part of the BA is a control loop that tries to expand and strengthen the actor-network. This can be visualised by the transition from diagram A to diagram B in figure 10 by linking the initial network with other networks in order to obtain a decentralised topology. The stop criteria for the algorithm is that it continues as long as possible, meaning that it either ends when the topology has become completely distributed as shown as diagram C (win) or it breaks down for some reason (loose).

The design principles in table 8 are useful for showing how the BA serves two objectives. They are used for strengthening the existing installed bases and they are used for expanding the installed bases.

As an example of how the BA works in practical situation, the action research network

43

associated with health information system programme HISP (Braa et al, 2004) has a centralised topology with Oslo as the centre, but the idea is to make it decentralised and distributed. When it is distributed, nobody is in control but all are coordinating themselves against each other. Latour (1988) has shown how the network of researchers within the scientific community can be understood along the ways of being run by a BA. Mechanisms like quality control by use of peer-review make it possible to avoid central control while still making sure that the scientific network remains standardised and consistent (Luhmann, 1990). The collective development of an internet encyclopaedia like Wikipedia is another example of a distributed knowledge network monitored and controlled by simple standards and peer-review mechanisms (Tapscott & Williams, 2006).

As the Monopoly game is used as a model for understanding the TQM implementation game, the OR logic of figure 6 makes it necessary to see the BA as a strategy for playing the Monopoly game. By using figure 15 as illustration, the BA starts at the GO position and iterating the control loop can be thought of as completing cycles around the board.

Figure 15: TQM implementation represented by a Monopoly board game

The initial BA step corresponds to the opening of the game where properties are being bought more or less at random, corresponding to the idea of identifying installed bases of quality management practice consisting of technological solutions (standards) and users.

As the BA enters the control loop the middlegame starts in the sense that each of the statements within the control loop can be interpreted has having to do with negotiating and trading properties or developing properties. The properties (tasks to be improved) are linked together in colour series, and it is not possible to cultivate and improve a process unless all the tasks are being monitored and controlled. Furthermore, not all the processes are of equal value for the purpose of implementing TQM. The dark purple series just after GO are cheap to buy and produces little income. The dark blue series just before GO are expensive to buy and produces much income. However, the dynamics of the game is dominated by forces of chance so it does not help to own expensive properties if nobody lands on them. Due to the fact that the Jail position functions as an attractor in the sense that players are often sent to jail means that the orange and red series are the ones most frequently landed on. When implementing TQM it is consequently important for the TQM designer to understand which parts of the information infrastructure that correspond to the different colour groups and use this knowledge when cultivating and developing quality management practice by improving solutions and educating users.

After iterating the BA control loop for a certain period, some quality management practices are cultivated and matured while others become increasingly difficult to do something about. The endgame is characterised by the fact that there are fewer decisions to be made as the effects of path-dependency and lock-in makes the TQM implementation go on auto-pilot either towards TQM success or TQM failure.

Viewing the BA through the Monopoly game is helpful for understanding the relationship between the BA and CAS. When thinking about the Monopoly game as a model about making strategic decisions in an unpredictable environment, it becomes obvious that it may be better to focus on a population of installed bases rather than one single installed based in the initial step of the BA as it takes time to realise whether chance or trading will make it possible to get the monopoly necessary for cultivation and development. The model is also useful for pointing out that not all standards and processes are equally important. While such perspectives are represented in the GA by the way it focuses on populations and makes use of a fitness function for evaluating this population, thus a natural part of CAS, it is not explicitly stated in the BA design principles and algorithmic statements.

The Monopoly game is also useful for understanding the relationship between the BA and TSI as the difference between programme management and project management within the field of information systems (Boddy et al, 2005). While the control perspective in the BA focuses on the growth and development of the population or network of process improvement projects, the control perspective in the TSI is on the individual process. However, as TSI goes further than traditional process improvement in the sense of putting more emphasis on problem structuring and solution evaluation in addition to the usual problem solving focus, the property development in Monopoly makes a useful match in the sense that there is problem structuring in trying to get a colour monopoly, there is problem solution in the actual development by erecting houses and hotels, and there is an evaluation in the sense of how the solution interacts with further gameplay including the possibility of future needs for selling and mortgaging. The BA, on the other hand, represents the logic of how to handle multiple property development around the game board and thinking strategically about development in relation to what the other players are doing.

2.4 The BA as a mechanism design for the TQM game

So far this chapter has been selectively reviewing literature on Monopoly and information systems implementation while focusing on the kernel theory and design theory of the TQM implementation game. The purpose of this section is to specify the pseudo-code of the BA in table 3 by thinking about BA as ISD prototype development and ISD programme management.

2.4.1 Thinking about the BA as ISD prototype development

One way of interpreting the BA is to think of it as an approach for managing the decision process in the prototype information systems development cycle (Kendall & Kendall, 1988), now often referred to as agile software development (Cockburn, 2002) or lean software development (Poppendieck & Poppendieck, 2003). While popular agile methods such as SCRUM often focus on having short decision and feedback loops with the customer in order to make sure that project priorities are aligned with customer priorities, the BA extends this principle by not only looking at customer satisfaction but also analysing customers or users from the perspective of motivation, knowledge and how the solution under development fits with existing practice.

When interpreting the BA from this perspective, the TSI comes in as a handy tool for selecting system methods for structuring the system development problem together with the user or from analysing the users (simple-plural, complex-plural), solving the problem in terms of developing a prototype (simple-unitary, complex-unitary) and evaluating how the solution affects the network (simple-coercive, complex-coercive).

The initial step of the BA in table 3 may be thought of as running an initial TSI cycle in figure 13 by first evaluating the situation either from a simple-coercive or a complex-coercive perspective, depending on whether one chooses to start by assessing the totality of the situation or whether there is an obvious way of identifying a part of the situation that fits with the initial criteria of the BA.

Having gotten an initial impression of the organisational context, the BA is ready to enter the control loop where each BA loop consists of one or more loops around the TSI wheel to complete an ISD prototype cycle of analysis, design, implementation and evaluation. The prototype development then continues by developing and expanding the solution by enrolling more users, finding more innovative use and minimising risks by addressing problems in order to deal with complexity and criticality while maintaining a focus on improving the existing solution so new tasks can be supported.

This method of using the BA logic for running the TSI process is more opportunistic than the way the TSI was originally designed for implementing TQM by a waterfall approach that started out with top management seminars and then gradually worked itself down the organisation in order to address quality problems and opportunities for improvement (Flood, 1993, chapter 9). The BA logic does not exclude this traditional top-down approach to TQM implementation, but the way the BA acts on local situations to achieve global results is more like a bottom-up approach.

2.4.2 Thinking about the BA as ISD programme management

In project management literature the management of more than one project is often referred to as programme management (Boddy et al, 2005). As the purpose of the BA is to design information infrastructure, a natural interpretation of this may be that the BA represents an approach for managing several system development life cycles at the same time, meaning programme management rather than project management.

The 'networks of action' approach (Braa et al., 2004) can be thought of as an illustration of how the BA is being used for managing health information systems development in different countries. The health information systems programme (HISP) is a process aimed at administrating health information systems development projects in many different locations. From the viewpoint of the actor-network diagrams in figure 10, the HISP can be thought of a decentralised network with Oslo and Johannesburg as the two most important stations. While all remaining stations and links in the network are important, they are not crucial. If political or technical problems should make it impossible to continue HISP development in one particular station, that station and its links are removed from the network, but the network may still continue to develop and expand.

One of the main theoretical references in the BA design theory is a book on genetic algorithms and complex adaptive systems written by the inventor of the genetic algorithm (Holland, 1995). There are no explicit references to the GA in the BA literature, but there are references in the GA literature on how to address the type of problems that the BA is trying to solve (Goldberg, 2000).

If the BA could be formulated in the language of a GA, then it would be easier to formulate and evaluate the stability and impact of BA on TQM in situations such as those illustrated by the HISP example. There are different ways of formulating the GA. The pseudo-code version in table 9 has a level of abstractness that seems suitable for using it as a way of communicating the BA strategy in a more operationally precise manner.

1. Choose initial population of individuals
2. Evaluate the fitness of each individual in that population
3. Repeat on this generation until termination (time limit, sufficient fitness achieved, etc.):
3.1. Select the best-ranking individuals for reproduction
3.2. Breed new individuals through crossover and/or mutation (genetic operations) and give birth to offspring
3.3. Evaluate the individual fitnesses of the offspring
3.4. Replace the worst ranked part of population with offspring

Table 9: Genetic algorithm (Øgland, 2009b)

The overall structure of the GA in table 9 and the BA in table 3 are similar in the sense of consisting of some initial steps and then a control loop. While the BA talks about a network of users and solutions, the GA talks about a population of individuals. The GA population can be defined to consist of the solutions and users in the BA and visualised as stations in the actor network diagrams in figure 10. The fitness in step 2 of the GA can be understood as how fit the solutions are in terms of user satisfaction or extent of use.

The control loop, starting with the evaluation in step 3 of the GA, breaks down either when the actor network has become fully distributed as illustrated by the rightmost topology in figure 10, making it impossible to increase the information infrastructure, such as reaching the highest possible TQM maturity score, or when the actor network is destroyed, as would happen if the central node in the leftmost actor network topology in figure 10 were to be removed.

The five step cultivation process making up the inner loop of the BA is represented by the steps 3.1 to 3.4 in the GA. The first control step in the BA of enrolling more users is formulated in a reverse manner by step 3.1 in the GA by focusing on the solutions and users within the existing focus that we believe can be important for further cultivation. Step 3.2 then corresponds with control step 2 in the BA in terms of finding more innovative use. The BA steps 3-5 also relate to this particular step as we want the new individuals (innovative use) to explore more critical cases, more complex cases and make sure that the existing solution is able to support new tasks.

Step 3.3 of the GA consists of evaluating the fitness of the innovative use, and in step 3.4 what seemed like innovative use, modified solutions and new users that did not turn out to be as helpful for the purpose of strengthening and expanding the network as expected are kept out of focus as the next control cycle is ready to begin.

The 'networks of action' story (Braa et al., 2004) may be useful for giving a more concrete example of how the BA translates into a GA. The two first steps of the GA consisted of software developers and hospital personnel in South Africa and information systems research scientists at the University of Oslo. The HISP solution used in South Africa was fit for the users, and there was interest in exporting it and modifying it to work in other countries. A population of individuals consisting of solutions and hospital personnel in different countries emerged. The research team focused on individual cases by enrolling students from different countries into a PhD research programme in Oslo (step 3.1). The PhD students and the action researchers worked on making the HIPS solutions fit to the local context, dealing with technical and political issues (step 3.2). Assessment of the progress of research and development was conducted (step 3.3). Occasionally political conflicts, research funding, technical problems or other issues resulted in some HISP development sites being removed from focus while new sites or new opportunities were enrolled into the area of focus (step 3.4).

As indicated in the book by Braa and Sahay (2011), the way HISP has survived for almost 20 years suggests that it is possible to implement the BA in a statistically stable manner (RH1). Although not always equally successful at every site, the general impact of the BA approach for developing health information systems has been good (RH2). Whether the BA can be seen to represent an optimal strategy, however, is difficult to say (RH3).

When it comes to the issue of using the GA representation of the BA for implementing TQM, the use of TSI can be done in exactly the same way as described in the context of agile development of individual systems. The steps 1 and 2 of the GA consist of viewing the mess as simple-coercive or complex-coercive in order to evaluate technical complexity and social distrustfulness for a population of problems to be solved by TQM methodology. The GA then starts the control loop and allows it to be continued either until a sustainable maximum TQM maturity level has been reached for the whole organisation or the TQM programme collapses. The 3.1 step in the control loop consists of using problem formulation methods (simple-plural and complex-plural) for identifying innovative use and new opportunities. The 3.2 step makes use of hard systems thinking (simple-unitary or complex-unitary) for breeding new individuals. Step 3.3 makes TSI evaluate the solutions (simple-coercive or complex-coercive). Step 3.4 changes the focus of the TQM programme by eliminating some improvement projects less likely to succeed with new projects that are hoped to have a greater impact for increasing the TQM maturity score.

2.5 Operational research hypotheses

The bootstrap algorithm (BA) is an information systems development (ISD) strategy that consists of gradually changing the current game played by the agents (organisational members) until the equilibria fits with the goals of the principal (designer). The main research hypothesis in the first chapter stated that the BA is an optimal mechanism design for implementing TQM. After having specified the type of BA to be used for changing the TQM game as a programme management method for information systems prototype development, following the operations research approach in figure 6 in the way illustrated in figure 16, it is now possible to make the BA research hypotheses operational by addressing the design theories associated with Monopoly, TQM, TSI and GA.

As illustrated in figure 16, the operational hypotheses will relate explicitly to the Monopoly game model and Monopoly game theory for understanding and predicting information infrastructure dynamics (kernel theory) and prescribing actions in the real world (design theory). As the testing of the hypotheses are carried out at the implementation step represented by the bottom left arrow in the diagram, the BA has to be understood both as the theoretical construct on the bottom right side of the diagram and as the bootstrapping practice on the bottom left side as the BA is being interpreted and used in the real world.

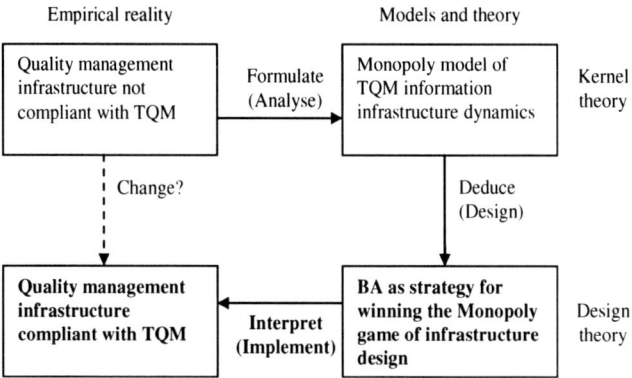

Figure 16: The operations research approach to change management as used in this study

2.5.1 The stability hypothesis (RH1)

A fundamental premise for the main hypothesis is that the TQM implementation programme does not break down before TQM has been implemented. As TQM is supposed to be implemented in an environment characterised by technical complexity and social distrust, there is a danger that the TQM implementation team gives up after being frustrated by the complexity or that they get thrown out for making political mistakes. The BA, however, is designed to deal with such environments through the means of continual improvement (IS prototype development, section 2.4.1) and risk management (IS programme management, section 2.4.2).

By following the BA trajectory, each improvement project is supposed to develop opportunistically by aligning with powerful actors and continually reconfiguring the semantic aspects of the network. The TSI approach provides a link between the verbal descriptions in the BA and the different systems methodologies needed for various stages of the TQM implementation process. If an individual improvement project should fail, for reasons technical, political or a mixture between the two, the BA should be resilient to such individual failures by thinking about it as programme management rather than project management. An individual failure may be regrettable, but not fatal as long as the network and larger population of improvement projects survive. The logic of the GA explains how the BA focus can be continually updated as the network changes.

By focusing on the GA representation of the BA, a natural parameter to observe for monitoring BA stability is the number of individuals in the population defined by the GA. By using statistical process control (SPC) it is possible to plot the number of individuals for each GA loop and then use the SPC outcome for taking corrective action if there are signs of the process being out of control.

The research questions used in *paper 4* and *paper 5* relate to the expected stable performance of the BA as the algorithm is being put to practical use.

Research question 1.1 (RQ1.1)

As known from feedback and control system theory, cascade and feedback design plays an important role for making unstable systems stable and keeping stable systems stable

(DiStefano et al, 1990). For the purpose of implementing TQM the "what gets measured gets done" principle has been used for creating stability through double-loop learning of both making sure that standards are being followed and critically challenged. In *paper 4* the "what gets measured gets done" principle is explored by reviewing literature on why one should expect it to work and then try to explain situations where it appeared to fail.

- RQ1.1: How can one use the "what gets measured gets done" principle for explaining success and failure of quality management initiatives?

Research question 1.2 (RQ1.2)

By making use of the design theory of complex adaptive systems (CAS) for developing the BA the solution is trading off efficiency for resilience and complexity (Kelly, 1994). However, as pointed out Perrow (1984), when complex systems fail, they often do so in unpredictable and disastrous ways. In *paper 5* the use of CAS for designing quality management systems (QMS) is explored from the perspective of trying to explain why and how CAS-based QMS initiatives can fail.

- RQ1.2: How can one explain the success and failure of quality management initiatives on a systemic level?

2.5.2 The impact hypothesis (RH2)

Brunsson and Jacobsson (2000) doubt it is possible to change the hypocritical TQM game because the hypocrisy is founded on a global industrial network related to quality standards and audit practice. The BA, however, suggests a way of changing the game by identifying groups of users (workers and managers) making use of the QMS the way it was designed and then cultivate a network of proper TQM practice by improving the QMS and enrolling more users.

To expand an actor-network by enrolling more users means that negotiations are carried out that result in new members becoming part of the network. One of the reasons why Brunsson and Jacobsson (2000) believe that the hypocritical or fake TQM is more likely to survive than the proper or real TQM is because it is much easier to commit to an idea by words than by practice. In the introductory chapter the problem was be illustrated by what is known as the stag hunt model in game theory. In this model both "real TQM" (impact) and "fake TQM" (no impact) were identified as Nash equilibria for stag hunt, but the way the size of the basin of attraction for the equilibria are different explained why "fake TQM" was a more likely outcome.

The reason to believe that the BA would have an impact on TQM implementation in the stag hunt context is because of its political nature. While TQM itself has been analysed from different political perspectives, some suggesting that it is a means for capital to control labour (Boje & Winsor, 1993) while other conceptualise it as a tool for liberating the oppressed (Flood, 1993), the politics of BA is the politics of technology as a third player in this control game. When using the Monopoly model for representing the TQM mechanism design game, the TQM designer (principal) is trying to change the regulations and incentives of the existing quality control game (played by agents) in order to replace existing organisational ideology with the TQM ideology.

The two-player version of the zero-sum Monopoly board game is used as a model on how to gain cultural monopoly through a process of cultivating "real TQM" while forcing out the "fake TQM" mentality. As the BA makes technology into a political actor in itself, the approach should be able to succeed in continually changing tactics to remain within the two impact quadrants in table 4. In other words, by using the BA to focus on TQM as a technological problem it should reduce the risk of being trapped in "fake TQM" by being politically naïve and it should also reduce the risk of sabotaging installed bases of TQM by being a political fanatic.

What this means in practical implications for the earlier formulation of RH2 is that the way the impact of the BA treatment is to be evaluated by "performance improvements measurable by TQM assessments" has to be done from the perspective of technology and not perspectives that favour either management or workers in the control game. Although the purpose of the Monopoly game is to change the cultural mentality in order to make TQM practice achievable, whether the mentality of the individual agents has changed or not is irrelevant as long as the revised control game makes it rational for the agents to do "real TQM".

The research questions used in both *paper 1* and *paper 3* are concerned with the impact of the BA by trying to understand quality management infrastructure dynamics in two slightly different ways.

Research question 2.1 (RQ2.1)

Whether a game is expected to being played once or repeatedly has consequences for what kind of strategies are expected to be played (Binmore, 2007). In *paper 1* the theory of evolutionary game theory (EGT) is used for exploring how some types of conflicts or interactions could be seen as repeated game play in software process improvement (SPI) and how the total game of implementing SPI or TQM can be understood both as Monopoly being played once and being played repeatedly in a potentially never-ending game tournament.

- RQ2.1: How can one use EGT for understanding TQM information infrastructure dynamics?

Research question 2.2 (RQ2.2)

Integrating BA with the TSI approach for implementing TQM means that there are certain ideological assumptions associated with the TSI approach carried over to the way the BA is being used (Flood, 1993). In *paper 3* the purpose is to explore how the ideology of critical systems thinking (CST) can be integrated with ANT and other ideas that are important for understanding how the BA is expected to have an impact on information infrastructure dynamics.

- RQ2.2: How can one use CST for understanding TQM information infrastructure dynamics?

2.5.3 The optimality hypothesis (RH3)

Even though the research should support the idea that the BA is a stable algorithm resulting in TQM implementation success, this does not eliminate the possibility that the TQM could have been implemented in more cost-efficient ways using alternative algorithms or methods. In table 5 there were four scenarios created by the use of the BA strategy and non-BA strategies in simple and complex environments. Only in complex environments is the BA expected to be optimal, while non-BA strategies are needed for dealing with simple environments in optimal ways. Using the BA in simple environments or non-BA strategies in complex environments is expected to be non-optimal.

After having explained how the Monopoly model can be used for thinking about the relationship between the BA and TSI, it should be easier to see how to work in parallel on applying the BA on the complex issue of managing the population of improvement projects while the TSI is used as a project management framework for managing the individual process improvement projects. As BA programme management process is a single process, the implementation and improvement of this process is done through TSI, but as the management of this particular process has to be done in parallel with the other process improvement projects, it is managed as part of the BA programme management system. In other words, the BA depends on TSI and TSI depends on the BA.

The practical implications for the earlier formulation of RH3, in terms of how the BA is implemented through the use of TSI, is that it is to be expected that the BA is optimal in the sense of simultaneously representing the two optimal quadrants in table 5 while avoiding the two non-optimal quadrants.

As pointed out by Simon (1996), what is an optimal solution depends on how the problem is framed. By only operating in classes of BA and non-BA strategies in simple and complex environments, there are limits to what can be learned about optimal design of the BA in practical situations. On the other hand, if one were to formulate more complex objective functions one could face the problem that most practical problems beyond a certain level of complexity are difficult to frame. Often a satisfactory solution is the best that can be practically achieved.

In order to provide deeper understanding of whether the BA is an optimal mechanism design in the sense of changing the control game to meet with the BA objectives of TQM in a cost-efficient manner, focus will also be kept on this hypothesis. In spite of the fact that a hypothesis of this kind will almost certainly be impossible to justify, the hypothesis is nevertheless important for the purpose of asking questions that can improve current understanding when explaining whatever might be the outcome of a particular BA study. As learning usually comes from reflecting upon failure (Lyytinen & Robey, 1999), the benefit of having an optimality hypothesis is that almost any outcome is bound to result in learning.

The research questions in *paper 2* and *paper 6* are focused on how to optimise the BA strategy for the purpose of implementing TQM.

Research question 3.1 (RQ3.1)

Although the TQM Monopoly game deals with the conflict between the TQM designer and the organisation as a whole, the subgame of Monopoly having to do with trading (getting management commitment) is a rough representation of the negotiations and tradings that go on in a real world TQM implementation (Legge, 2002). The purpose of *paper 2* is to explore how TQM designers may optimise their interaction with managers by considering the Pac-Man video game as a possible representation of the trading subgame.

- RQ3.1: How should one design the details of the BA to optimise the interaction between TQM designer and management?

Research question 3.2 (RQ3.2)

Another subgame of Monopoly that is a rough representation of real life is the way Monopoly ignores workers, unions, construction sites etc when it comes to property development

(Wuffle, 1978). The purpose of *paper 6* is to explore how TQM designers may optimise their interaction with workforce when it is uncertain to which extent management is committed to TQM.

- RQ3.2: How should one design the details of the BA to optimise the interaction between TQM designer and workforce?

3. METHODOLOGY

The purpose of this chapter is to give an explanation of the research methodology in terms of why certain data have been collected, what data have been collected, from where data have been collected, when they were collected, how they were collected, and how they have been analysed. The explanations starts by commenting on the chosen methodology of canonical action research (CAR) (section 3.1), and then makes use of the five CAR principles for discussing how data collection and data analysis is constrained by researcher-client relationships (section 3.2), a cyclic process model (section 3.3), choice of theory (section 3.4), trying to create change (section 3.5), and the aim of developing knowledge through reflection (section 3.6). The chapter concludes with a summary (section 3.7).

3.1 Using canonical action research (CAR) as research design

The purpose of this section is to explain why canonical action research (CAR) has been chosen and how CAR has been used. The explanations starts by commenting on how the use of CAR as a research methodology grew out of reflective practice (section.3.1.1), and then comments more specifically about the three philosophical issues of CAR and scientific method (section 3.1.2), CAR and design science research (section 3.1.3), and CAR and 'networks of action' (section 3.1.4).

3.1.1 From reflective practice to canonical action research

If the purpose of research is to carry out an empirical investigation of a strategy in a real environment rather than a laboratory, the research method is often referred to as action research (Collins & Hussey, 2002; Reason & Bradbury, 2006). Although there are several ways of doing action research described within the information systems literature (e.g. Kock, 2007), the research method used in this study started out as reflective practice and has gradually matured in rigour by interacting with the community of people doing and debating action research and related research strategies such as design science research. Even though the perspective and framing of methodology has changed over the time spent studying how to manage TQM implementation in complex environments, the research practice itself has in principle been very much the same since the informal start in 1992.

When trying to describe the research methodology covering the whole period of research, there are several relevant options for positioning the approach within the methodology literature. Some of these different types of framings have been used in the individually published papers. One natural frame could be to focus on the PDCA research method embedded in TQM, and then describe how this research method relates to statistical hypothesis testing (Shewhart, 1938; Deming, 1986), and how this approach has been used for doing quality improvement research within the healthcare community (Grol et al, 2004). Although this would have matched well with the methodological thinking behind the study from the beginning to the present, statistical process control (SPC) has played an important but not vital part in the research. The focus has been more on the phenomenological understanding of the consequences of the BA on TQM implementation than on testing specific aspects of the BA.

An action research approach that could have been used for compensating the phenomenological focus would be to align with Flood (1993; 2004) by following his example in the way he and his collaborators studied TSI as a TQM implementation method. This has also been an important influence on the study as TSI plays an important part in how the BA has been implemented. Although this way of doing action research, based on how Checkland and Holwell (1998) describe the nature of social science and action research, has been an important influence on action research within the Scandinavian part of the information systems research community (Nielsen, 2007), the way this approach distances itself from traditional scientific conventions about theory and hypothesis testing made it an unnatural choice.

Another important influence was the 'networks of action' research approach used for studying the growth and development of the global health information infrastructure (Braa et al, 2004). This approach exemplified a way to study information systems programme management by the way of managing a network of action research projects, a perspective that contrasted it with the way PDCA- or TSI-driven individual action research projects typically would be designed. A challenge with this approach, however, was that it was described more like an action research management method than an action research method.

Although elements from all of these three different ways of thinking about and doing action research were part of the action research practice, canonical action research (CAR) (Davison et al., 2004) has been chosen as a reference for describing the research design used in this study. CAR is based on five principles, all of which have been important for designing how to investigate the BA hypothesis. As CAR is used as a post-rationalisation, the action research was not explicitly designed to meet any of these principles or underlying criteria when it was constructed, but the principles and criteria nevertheless provide a practical way of describing what was done.

3.1.2 Canonical action research and scientific method

One way of thinking about action research is to say that it is a research model used for developing and testing a theoretical framework (F) by applying an action research method (M) aimed at creating social change in an area of concern (A). This perspective is represented in figure 17, and the model illustrates how the research may produce theoretical knowledge (F), practical knowledge about how to design and implement the research method (M) and improved contextual understanding (e.g. verbal descriptions) of the area of concern (A).

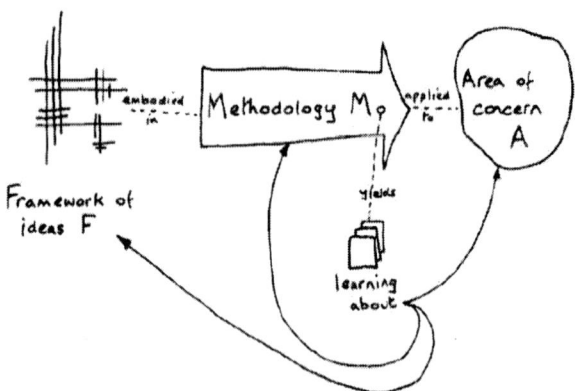

Figure 17: A general model of scientific research (Checkland & Holwell, 1998)

When investigating the use of BA for implementing TQM, the area of concern (A) is TQM implementation in situations characterised by technical complexity and social distrust, the methodology (M) is the action research method, and the framework (F) refers to the kernel and design theories discussed in chapter 2. The BA hypothesis as represented by the written algorithm in table 3 is part of F. The practical interpretation of the BA as an activity that requires certain skills and resources is part of M. The use of BA as a development process integrated with the research process is part of A.

The way the unit of analysis can be seen as part of all components F, M and A of figure 17 has created some debate among information systems researchers. For instance, MacKay and Marshall (2007) criticise the model in figure 17 for not distinguishing between the methodology M of action research and the methodology M' under investigation, such as the BA. From their point of view, in the outcome of research there is a difference between what is learned about action research (M) and the use of the BA (M'). From the viewpoint of this study, however, this kind of comment seems to ignore the fact that the BA is present in all three components of the model. It is represented as a theoretical construct (F), as part of the research strategy (M) and as a practice and empirical construct (A). On the methodological level the action research method or the BA are never investigated individually but only as an integrated whole, and the learning about M is learning about the BA research process. The rejection or failure to reject the BA hypothesis is carried out as a consequence of the interplay between the theoretical BA (F) and its physical interpretation (A).

3.1.3 Canonical action research and design research

Another debate in the information system community concerns whether it is possible to integrate the design science approach used by engineers for things like developing quality management systems through the PDCA research approach with the sociological action research approach (Iivari & Venable, 2009). One position in this debate is that the type of action research represented in figure 17 deals with the construction of sociological knowledge that is typically represented through stories, something that is significantly different from the mathematical theories and physical constructions developed through design science research. Although they do not believe that action research and design science research are incommensurable, they believe that it takes considerable effort for producing methods that makes it possible to integrate these two types of research. This view is also reflected in the fact that action design research methods have been developed for filling this gap (e.g. Sein, Henfridsson et al, 2011).

This study, however, has followed the alternative position in the debate that states that there is no significant difference between action research and design science research (Järvinen, 2007). The way this is done is by focusing on the F component in figure 17 as to represent where the study aims to make a contribution. This does not mean that the rich narratives about TQM implementation in the A component are irrelevant, but producing such stories and narratives is not an aim in itself. The purpose of the narratives should be to challenge and enrich the theoretical understanding of the BA and the Monopoly model of TQM implementation in the F component of the figure (Øgland, 2009c).

3.1.4 Canonical action research and networks of action

During the first years of this study, the outcome of the TQM implementation research consisted, among other things, of research reports describing new methods for doing quality control of geophysical data. Although these reports included literature reviews and methodology chapters, what was written in those reports had little to do with the BA hypothesis of TQM implementation. The difference between the networks of action (NOA) approach and the conventional action research approach is that they operate on two different levels. The NOA approach is a methodology for managing action research programmes by developing an action research infrastructure through the use of the BA. The development of specific quality control methods can be seen as individual design science or action research projects managed by the NOA. It is at the level of the NOA where the BA plays a part in the study. On the level of the individual action and design science research projects, the TSI approach has been used without any reference to the BA.

However, as the action research programme is a process, it may be possible to think of different strategies for improving such processes, which means that the NOA can be made subject to action research itself, and may consequently be studied through the lens of TSI and CAR.

3.2 The CAR principle of Researcher-Client Agreement (RCA)

When action research is carried out in the style of an external researcher entering the organisation and testing out some strategy through a process of interventions, there is a risk that the client organisation may question the process, the results or both. In order to prevent awkward situations where the researcher is denied access to data, prevented room of action or denied publishing the results, the first principle of CAR is to make sure that there is a mutual researcher-client agreement (RCA) (Davison et al, 2004, pp. 69-71).

When action research is carried out by an inside researcher in his own organisation, as is the way this study has been designed, the situation is slightly different but not necessarily less politically challenging. As pointed out by Coghlan and Brannick (2001, p. 63), "while doing any research in an organisation is political, doing research in and on your own organisation is particularly so. (...) Political forces can undermine research endeavours and block planned change. Gaining access, using data, disseminating and publishing reports are intensely political acts."

Even when the researcher is using his own process as the unit of analysis, as is done in this study with the researcher executing the BA as a TQM mechanism design strategy, the situation can be political (McNiff & Whitehead, 2006). Whitehead (1993), in particular, illustrates the case of how the assumingly straightforward case of doing reflective research on one's own work process in one's own organisation can be an intensely political and uphill battle.

3.2.1 The Norwegian Meteorological Institute (DNMI)

Between the years 1992 and 1998, the researcher worked for the Climate Department of the Norwegian Meteorological Institute (Det Norske Meteorologiske Institutt, DNMI). The RCA consisted of having a formal title as 'research scientist' and working within a team of climatological research scientists and executives on developing, maintaining and improving an information system KLIBAS for collecting geophysical data, doing quality control and presenting data for the public and research community through the use of statistical applications and data exchange formats.

The organisational culture at the Climate Department of DNMI was informal. There was no written RCA beyond the job title and the unwritten expectations that the growth and development of KLIBAS should also be combined with publications of scientific work. As the Climate Department was primarily doing applied climate research, the usual research outlet was the Klima journal edited and published by the department, but papers were also submitted to conferences and there were different Nordic and international research projects going on. There was also a close contact with the Department of Geosciences at the University of Oslo and Instrumenttjenesten AS (ITAS) associated with the Norwegian University of Life Sciences.

Although there were no restrictions on what kind of outlets the researchers at the Climate Department should use for publishing their research, framing the KLIBAS research as design research concerned with methods of quality control and process improvement was better fit with the unspoken peer expectations than doing action research with a strong sociological bend.

3.2.2 The Norwegian Tax Administration (NTAX)

When working on the challenge of implementing TQM within the IT function of the Norwegian Tax Administration (NTAX) between 1999 and 2005, a RCA was written in 2000 as the researcher was given the formal job title 'assistant director' of the IT department and a formal job description presenting general tasks and responsibilities for leading the quality management group with the aim of implementing TQM for the IT function. It was not stated that TQM should be carried out through the use of action research, although how TQM makes use of the 'scientific method' embedded in the PDCA-cycle and pragmatic hypothesis testing through the use of statistical process control (SPC) was occasionally brought up in discussions.

Although there was no natural outlet for publishing action research reports on TQM implementation, the software lifecycle methods used by the IT function produced a steady stream of technical documents as information systems were developed, and continued to live through annual cycles of maintenance and improvement. Integrating the quality management reports with the life cycle documents was filling a gap in the sense that it helped implement a part of the quality management system (QMS) that had been specified on a high level but not yet been put into practical use. As quality control and process improvement are involved with understanding problems and testing solutions, the standard format for writing scientific reports was a natural way of writing quality management reports.

Unlike the case of DNMI, there was at NTAX no peer community of researchers, but to a certain degree it seemed possible to align interests with the internal audit and the national TQM practice community by attending the annual meetings of Excellence Norway, the annual meetings of the ISO 9000 quality management community, and by being member of Statkonsult's steering group for network of quality management in the Norwegian public sector and attending such practitioner meetings. Although this was not the same as the being part of the research community and international research networks at DNMI, the way research is an integrated part of how TQM works made it possible to conceptualise and carry out TQM as action research.

In principle it should be possible to turn TQM practice into action research in any environment by aligning research focus with the quality control and process improvement focus in TQM and then practice into research by being explicitly reflective (Schön, 1983; McNiff & Whitehead, 2006).

3.2.3 The University of Oslo (UiO)

In 2005 the researcher changed formal job title at NTAX from 'assistant director' to 'research scientist'. The job title change was assisted with a RCA in the shape of a job description explaining tasks and responsibilities in terms of doing applied research on quality management within the organisation. It was also explicitly stated that the researcher should collaborate with leading quality control experts and international research communities, and that the quality of the research should be controlled by making sure that the first step of the process was to make the research part of a PhD process.

The RCA was further developed in 2006 as a contract between NTAX and the University of Oslo for getting the researcher enrolled in the PhD programme managed by the information systems group at the Department of Informatics at UiO.

3.3 The CAR principle of the Cyclical Process Model (CPM)

One challenge in doing research in real-world environments rather than a controlled laboratory setting is that the environment may be difficult to understand and it may change over time. Unlike the operations research model in figure 6, where there is a linear development from formulation of problem, deduction of solution and interpretation of the solution in the real world, what may seem as a reasonable formulation of the problem at an early stage of the action research process may later have to be adjusted if it turns out that the deduced solutions do not have the anticipated effect. Perhaps the initial understanding was inadequate, or perhaps changes in the environment caused problems in the process of collecting and analysing data, or perhaps the problem evolved and changed nature along with the research and what was a solution to the old situation is not a solution to the new situation.

Problems of these kinds are well known in TQM literature and are generally solved by conceptualising process improvement as a cyclic process, sometimes referred to as the plan-do-check-act (PDCA) cycle (Shewhart, 1938; Ishikawa, 1985; Deming, 1986). If one is suspicious of the outcome of a PDCA experiment, it can be cycled through once more, perhaps by changing some parameters, or it can be tested in a different environment. As pointed out by Davison et al (2004), action research often makes use of a similar cyclical process model (CPM) for compensating the lack to total controllability in a real-world environment. The CAR process model (figure 18) is reformulation of an action research model from organisational science (Susman & Evered, 1978) by making the entrance and exit points visually explicit, re-labelling each of the five stages, and presenting the centre of the model as the RCA rather than the development of the client-system infrastructure.

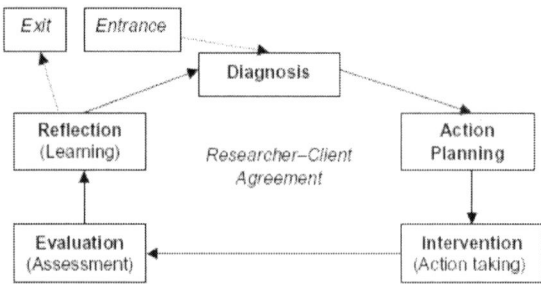

Figure 18: CAR process model (Davison et al, 2004)

Although the PDCA and the CAR process model express the same idea, there is a slight difference in the sense that the purpose of the CAR process is to produce knowledge about change management for publication in academic outlets while the focus on the PDCA is process improvement and in-house learning. This slight difference in perspective can be seen from the viewpoint of the CAR model by the way the diagnosis has been extracted from action planning and the reflection from evaluation in the action research model while the PDCA deal with these issues as the three stages of planning (understanding problem and formulating hypothesis), doing (carry out the experiment), and checking (testing the hypothesis and drawing conclusions) (Shewhart, 1938). The PDCA model, on the other hand, puts more emphasis on how to respond to the production of knowledge ("act") by making the organisational decision maker rather than the journal editor the customer of the process (Deming, 1986).

As the two models essentially describe the same process, only with a slight difference in customer focus, there is no conceptual impediments for turning an already existing PDCA-driven TQM implementation project into an action research project (Grol et al, 2004). In fact, as a TQM implementation programme typically consists of managing several PDCA process improvement projects at the same time, each such PDCA process could be used for designing action research processes. This is also the approach used in each of the individually published papers listed in table 6. Exactly how this has been formulated varies somewhat from paper to paper, attempting to engage in information systems research debates about research methodology.

For the purpose of using the CAR process model for investigating the BA hypothesis (RH), it is the PDCA used for designing and improving the TQM programme management as a whole that has to be addressed. As this study deals with three consecutive attempts to implement TQM in different organisations and situations, the overall PDCA or CAR process model makes three iterations. The first cycle deals with the testing of the RH at the Climate Department of DNMI. The second cycle deals with the testing of the RH at the IT function of NTAX. The third cycle is a renewed attempt at testing the RH at NTAX through collaboration with UiO.

CAR/CPM	Qualitative data	Quantitative data
Step 1: Diagnosis	TSI/SOSM: soft systems thinking Observations, interviews, and document reviews for making a diagnosis (building a game model)	
Step 2-4: Finding and testing a treatment		TSI/SOSM: Hard systems thinking, system dynamics, organisational cybernetics, complexity theory Find a treatment (strategy) by analysing the game model. Consider the strategy as an empirical hypothesis, collect quantitative data by putting it to use and apply statistical methods for evaluating the results.
Step 5: Reflection	TSI/SOSM: Emancipatory systems thinking, postmodern systems thinking Validation of diagnosis (game model) by reflecting upon why the treatment did or did not work optimally.	

Table 10: Using TSI for data collection and data analysis during different steps of the CPM

Each cycle of the CAR process model consists of five steps. The first step of the cycle is making a diagnosis. As the BA is a solution to the problem of implementing TQM infrastructure in complex environments, the diagnosis consists of describing the nature of the complex environment through the use of the Monopoly model. The next three steps consist of

61

formulating the BA hypothesis in relation to the empirical context, doing the experiment and evaluating the outcome of the hypothesis test. The fifth step consists of reflecting upon what the outcome of the BA test contributes to the Monopoly theory of TQM implementation. As the different stages of the CPM address different kinds of subproblems, TSI has been used for guiding the process of data collection and data analysis as illustrated in table 10.

As was discussed in section 2.3.3, the TSI/SOSM approach has been designed for the purpose of coordinating different systems methods needed at different stages when solving problems. Despite how such systems methods have been researched and developed within different scholarly traditions, traditions positioning themselves against other traditions exemplified by epistemological categories such as mechanistic/romantic, Habermas' three types of knowledge, four paradigms of social science (Dahlbom & Mathiassen, 1993), the methods could be seamlessly integrated by viewing them from the perspective of constructive empiricism (van Fraassen, 1980).

3.3.1 Step 1: Diagnosis

Collecting and analysing data during the first step of the CAR model is done for the purpose of understanding the organisation in the sense of making a diagnosis. When integrating the CPM with a TQM implementation methodology like TSI this means that the three TSI steps of creativity, choice and implementation have to deal with the question of understanding the "mess" (figure 13). From the viewpoint of the SOSM in figure 14, both complex-pluralist and simple-pluralist situations require problem structuring methods in the shape of "soft systems approaches". There are many such methods to choose from (e.g. Rosenhead & Mingers, 2001), and common to most of them is that they can be seen as workshop methods for discussing, framing the problem and committing to action.

A challenge for using methods like soft systems methodology (SSM) for diagnosing the problem in a situation dominated by technical complexity and social distrust, as is the situation in this study, is that SSM assumes an environment where it is possible to express and share ideas without fearing to upset those in power. Alternative soft methods like drama theory (Bennett et al, 2001) are more focused on understanding conflict, but they also require safe environments where conflicts can be explored, simulated and discussed.

Although ideas from SSM and drama theory, such as using diagrams and focusing on conflict when collecting and analysing data, have been important for each of the three rounds on diagnosis done in this study, none of the formal problem structuring methods has been used in a formal manner. As the diagnosis was typically carried out when entering a new organisation, the data collection consisted of document reviews, observations, interviews, discussions and informal talks. Data was then analysed by trying to see whether it was possible to build a rough Monopoly board model to capture the dynamics of the quality management infrastructure.

As Checkland (1981) argues that SSM can be understood within a phenomenological tradition, it might be possible to say that the way CAR is used in this study could also be understood from a phenomenological perspective. At least CAR based on constructive empiricism and phenomenology share the idea that the purpose of diagnosis is not to develop a "truthful" description of some external reality, as there may be as many equally truthful ways of describing a phenomenon as there are people engaging in it, but rather to find a useful model for the purpose of grasping a shared understanding of the situation and committing to action. On the other hand, the challenge of the diagnosis was not only to turn the mess into a problem, it was also necessary to explain why change was not happening. This is the reason Flood (1993) recommends the Viable Systems Methodology (VSM) as a diagnosis tool. Unlike SSM, which tries to develop a systemic understanding of the situation by network models in the shape of "rich pictures", VSM is more explicitly concerned with the control structure of the QMS by looking at a particular type of control diagram.

The way VSM makes use of a mathematical structure, such as the VSM control diagram as a tool for understanding the organisation, makes Jackson (2000) describe VSM as a structuralist approach. Although philosophers and social scientists may argue about the philosophical differences between different methodologies, like the differences between phenomenology and structuralism (e.g. Dahlbom & Mathiassen, 1993, pp. 232-233), for the purpose of this study it has been more important to find out how to integrate the different methodologies rather than to stress the differences in the scholarly traditions they came from. The philosophy of constructive empiricism (van Fraassen, 1980) seems very useful for this purpose.

As the simple idea guiding van Fraassen's philosophy is that science is concerned with building empirically adequate models of reality, rather than searching for truth, SSM and VSM are different only in the way that SSM is primarily concerned with building models based on how people make sense of the world in different ways while VSM tends to view the world by comparing empirical data with feedback and control templates. The output of the diagnosis step is not to find the truth about some part of the empirical world but to develop a useful model of that world. Where van Fraassen talks about Bohr's model of the atom (ibid, p. 44) or the Copernican model of the solar system (ibid, p. 45), this study is concerned with the Monopoly model of TQM implementation.

3.3.2 Step 2: Action planning

After the use of TSI during diagnosis resulted in an initial Monopoly representation of the QMS, the next step was to plan for action. With the Monopoly board representing the outcome of applying soft systems approaches in the SOSM (figure 14), the relationship between the participants is no longer pluralist but unitary. The TSI wheel (figure 13) can then use 'creativity' by figuring out whether the systems are simple or complex and then apply 'choice' for finding appropriate action planning methods from the realms of hard systems thinking, system dynamics, organisational cybernetics or complexity theory.

Action planning is essentially a mathematical exercise in the sense that the aim of the process is to analyse the Monopoly game model created in the first CPM step and deduce a winning strategy in the shape of a BA to be implemented as an intervention in the third CPM step. The type of mathematical analysis needed depends on the complexity of the Monopoly model created during diagnosis. If the problem has an analytical solution, this will be the most desired outcome. However, as discussed in section 2.3, the complexity of the Monopoly game makes it more realistic to hope for numerical solutions by digital or analogue simulations. If even this should be too much to ask, British mathematician Keith Devlin suggests using "soft mathematics" in the sense of applying the mathematical concepts as tools for verbal reasoning (Devlin, 1997; 2007).

Data collection and analysis depends on what kind of mathematical approach is being used. If the model can be solved analytically, there is no data collection and analysis beyond reviewing the relevant mathematical literature and verifying that model conclusions are correctly deduced from the model. In the case of analysing the model by use of computer simulation, the model have to be represented as a computer model, data will be produced and analysed by use of statistical methods as part of how the simulations are carried out. In the case of analogue simulation, experiments have to be designed and steps similar to those in digital simulation can be carried out, although the experiment may also produce qualitative data that could be used in the analysis.

In the case of using "soft mathematics", which has been a dominant approach in this study, there are no restrictions on data collection and analysis. Literature review, discussing with scholars and practitioners, looking for analogies, performing experiments, or collecting whatever type of data through any type of analysis method could in principle be applied if it serves the purpose of "deducing" model conclusions from the model.

Once the model conclusions have been found, the second step of action planning is to make the conclusion operational to make sure it can be practically implemented. For the purpose of designing action it is necessary to collect ideas that might lead to an operational design. Although the basic design has been explained in section 2.4 of the literature review, further detail for making practical designs has been developed by reading trade magazines and academic literature, visiting other organisation, searching the internet, participation in practitioner groups and discussion forums (the online Deming Network DEN, the American Quality Society AQS), taking part in practitioner conferences (the Norwegian ISO 9000 annual conference, the annual Excellence Norway conference), and reading trade magazines.

Although this kind of data collection should be carried out through out the action cycle, at the beginning of each action research cycle the researcher collected data from inside and outside the organisation to get some ideas on how to prepare the BA action. Data from within the organisation was the same data used for diagnosing, but the data analysis now consisted of making flowcharts and pseudo-code algorithms for the purpose of figuring out how to implement the BA in a practical manner.

Data collected from the outside included visits to the Swedish Meteorological and Hydrological Institute, Det Norske Veritas, Tandberg Data and The Norwegian Police Administration, attending quality practitioner conferences and reading trade magazines like Quality Magazine and Quality Progress.

Unlike the diagnosis that was carried out by focusing on aspects of constructive empiricism that fitted with phenomenology and structuralism, the first part of action planning follows a very different type of intuition. At this stage the scientist is working as a mathematician. The purpose is to deduce model conclusions, and if the mathematical model is sufficiently complex it may be necessary to collect and analyse data, but this should be thought of as a heuristic. The problem of deducing model conclusions is a mathematical problem that has nothing to do with the phenomenon that the model is supposed to represent. The deductive relationship between the model and model conclusions is important for the study as a whole as it should be used for showing how empirical inadequacy of the model conclusions should imply inadequacies in how the model was formulated in the first place.

The second part of action planning is of a different philosophical nature. Once the precise model conclusions have been established, the next few steps of CAR consists of trying to test the actions in what might be described as a positivist way of thinking (Kock et al, 1997; DeLuca, 2005; DeLuca & Kock, 2007). Although it is common among IS researchers and social scientists to see phenomenology and positivism as fundamentally different research methods based on incommensurable research paradigms (e.g. Dahlbom & Mathiassen, 1993; Collis & Hussey, 2003), constructive empiricism allows these ways of thinking to be integrated in CAR as they deal with the two fundamentally different issues of building a model of a phenomenon to be understood and testing the validity of such a model.

3.3.3 Step 3: Intervention

From the perspective of the TSI, both intervention (CPM step 3) and evaluation (CPM step 4) are included in the 'implementation' step of the TSI cycle starting with action planning. As the intervention can be thought of as a project, the type of data and data analysis methods used for project management are needed at this step (Boddy et al, 2005). Resource management is particularly important for deciding which actions to take. At DNMI and NTAX a person clocks in and clocks out at work. At the later stages of action research it has gradually become a habit of using a stopwatch. The practice has consisted of capturing the costs of different types of actions by using checklists for measuring the impact of an action and using a stopwatch for measuring how many man-hours are invested in doing the action.

3.3.4 Step 4: Evaluation

To evaluate the impact of BA on TQM implementation, some kind of TQM assessment model is needed. If the organisation has adopted a formal TQM approach which includes a TQM assessment framework like EFQM, CAF, ISO 9004, ISO 15504 or CMM, then such a framework can be both practically and theoretically useful for measuring impact.

In the first action research cycle, however, there were no such frameworks, so the impact of BA on TQM had to be measured by use of proxy data. In the second cycle all the assessment standards were used at various times, although the EFQM model was the one used most consistently over time. In the third cycle proxy data were used in combination with the ISO 9004:2000 assessment model.

In order to register growth and improvement through the TQM assessment models, monitoring and measurements, feedback control and improvement has to be carried out all over the organisation. Different types of data may be relevant for different parts of the organisation. Numerical data about time, cost and quality were recorded at the task level. Statistics from the task level were included in the monitoring and control at the process level. At the system level, quality audits were carried out through the use of observations, document studies and interviews.

3.3.5 Step 5: Reflection

Planning action, taking action and evaluating action could be seen as technical problem solving in the TSI context and thus represented one or more cycles through the TSI wheel characterised by unitary relationships between the participants. The process of reflecting, however, represents a change of perspective and can be seen as a cycle through the TSI steps of creativity, choice and implementation from the perspective of thinking about relationships between participants as coercive.

Unlike the method used during CPM steps 2-4 of collecting numerical data and applying statistical methods for data analysis, the data collection and analysis during the final reflection is more similar to what was done during diagnosis in the sense that it does not only look at the BA Monopoly strategy in isolation but whether the Monopoly diagnosis captured the essence of the problematic situation ("mess").

Flood (1993) recommends using the methodology of Critical Systems Heuristics (CSH) for evaluating TQM implementation. However, as Flood and Jackson (1991) identify CSH as a method suited for analysing simple-coercive situations, other methods are needed for the postmodern systems thinking (PST) in complex-coercive situations. Due to the focus on information infrastructures in this study, actor-network theory (ANT) was the most obvious methodological choice.

However, as the researcher himself is an important actor in the actor-network, it is difficult to write convincing success stories of the type illustrated by Latour when he goes about explaining the social construction of scientific facts (e.g. Latour & Woolgar, 1979; Latour, 1987; Latour, 2005). As the BA is supposed to function as a guide on how to act politically when implementing TQM, what should be the focus for reflection are the challenges and failures met when applying the BA.

Specifying learning in terms of explaining what went wrong is to a large extent based on personal reflections. Sometimes these reflections are checked or triangulated against reflections made by other stakeholders or by discussing with fellow scientists or people who have not necessarily been involved in the situations. In the end, however, the data collected at this stage represent the researcher's own interpretations and reflections.

Although ANT is based upon the idea that scientific facts are socially constructed (Latour & Woolgar, 1979; Hacking, 1999), making it potentially fit with the constructive empiricist philosophy, the ANT method has been used in a pragmatic rather than scholarly manner when narrating how the action research has unfolded in some of the individually published paper and the overall story in chapter 4. What this means is that the idea of understanding socio-technical systems as political networks (EGT models) without engaging in debates between ANT scholars and others concerning how the philosophy of science underpinning ANT may be similar or different from constructive empiricism (e.g. Cordella & Shaikh, 2003). Rather than posing such questions, the use of ANT has been done in the same way as all other methods selected from the SOSM (figure 14), simply by assuming that the methods make sense from the viewpoint of constructive empiricism, and then apply the methodology pragmatically for making the CAR approach work.

3.4 The CAR principle of theory

Theory plays an important part in TQM. The reason for this, according to Deming (1994), is that there is no learning without theory. If one is not explicit about why a certain process is expected to perform in a state of statistical control, it is difficult to improve knowledge by acknowledging error and adjusting the explanatory model. The original formulation of the BA in table 3 is somewhat problematic in this respect. The nature of the pseudo-code makes it unclear how to interpret both the statements and the internal relationships between the statements in the algorithm.

According to Davison et al (2004, p. 74) "CAR theory commonly takes the following form: In situation S that has salient features F, G and H, the outcomes X, Y and Z are expected from actions A, B and C. Changes to theory typically take place in the reflection stage of the CAR process and lead the project into an additional process cycle". As pointed out in chapter 2, the theory as a whole used in this study can be split between kernel theory and design theory. Statements in design theory can be formulated in a way that matches what is said about CAR theory above, but may need kernel theory for explaining why one should expect outcomes X, Y and Z from actions A, B and C in a situation S that has salient features F, G and H.

The kernel theory used for understanding bootstrapping is the theory of non-linear dynamical systems with focus on the growth and development of the internet as the prime empirical example (Hanseth & Lyytinen, 2010). Although this provides important conceptual and practical insight on the problem the BA is designed to solve, the BA still remains vague because there is no explicit mathematical model based on dynamical systems theory used for describing the empirical case of the growth and development of the internet. The kernel theory is not sufficiently precise to allow the researcher to predict consequences of how the BA will perform and allow him to revise the model as the experiments fail. In chapter 2, however, the Monopoly game was suggested as a model for making the BA testable hypothesis in the context of a Monopoly theory of how information infrastructures grow and develop.

Using the Monopoly model to represent the dynamics of how information infrastructure grows and develops makes the kernel theory more precise in the sense that the problem is formulated as a mathematically precise dynamic game, and it puts constraints on the interpretation of the BA as the BA is supposed to be deduced from the Monopoly model as a winning strategy. In regard of the constraints CAR puts on theory use, the main research hypothesis (RH) needs to be formulated along the line of "In situation S that has salient features of being technically and/or politically complex, the outcome of TQM implementation success is expected from following the BA strategy."

As pointed out by Davison et al (2004, pp. 74-75), the way CAR deals with theory puts constraints on how problems are formulated, how interventions are designed and how they are evaluated. As the issue of problem formulation and design of interventions has been discussed in chapter 2 and summarised above, stressing the role of the Monopoly model for meeting these requirements, the main implication for evaluation is that the treatment statement "in situation S with salient feature F, G and H, the outcome X, Y and Z is expected from action A, B and C" implies having predictor and response variables corresponding to actions A, B, C and outcomes X, Y and Z.

3.4.1 Dependent variables

In order to understand how the BA impacts on TQM implementation success, instruments and data for measuring TQM implementation success are needed. If the organisation has chosen a standardised TQM framework such as ISO 9000, EFQM or CMM such frameworks often include instructions on how to measure TQM maturity. For instance, both ISO 9004:2000 and CMM make use of a maturity scale from one to five, while EFQM uses a percentage scale.

The main research instrument, for evaluating TQM maturity and how the information infrastructure was evolving within the study, was based on using the EFQM excellence model. At the most abstract level, the EFQM model can be visualised as the nine box "cause and effect" diagram in figure 19, where the five enablers of leadership, policy & strategy, people, partnerships and resources and processes are assumed to impact on results in terms of people results, customer results, society results and key performance results. Each box has a percentage weight indicating its importance for the purpose of achieving organizational excellence. When using the model for conducting TQM audits, the weights represents the maximum score achievable for each box, meaning that the total score of a TQM assessment by use of the EFQM model is measured in terms of fractions between 0.0 and 100.0 percent.

There are different ways of using the EFQM model for doing organisational assessments, from simple checklists to complex audit procedures by use of external EFQM experts. The validity and reliability of the EFQM assessment method as a research tool depends on what kind of methods are being used to support the assessment.

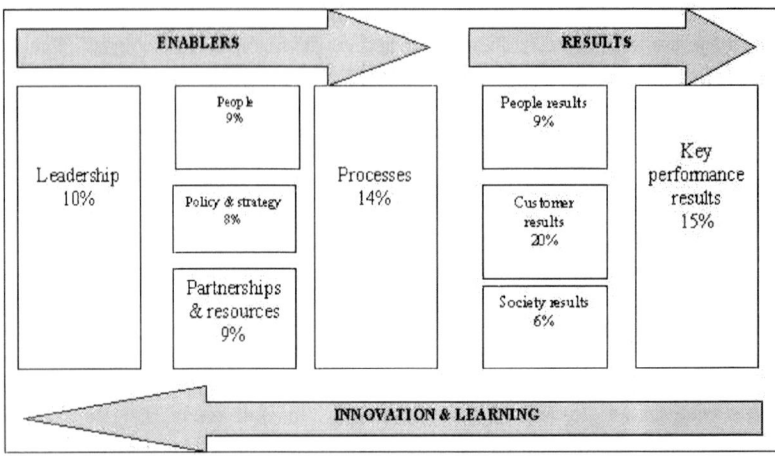

Figure 19: EFQM excellence model (Oakland, 1999)

During the period of research when the focus was on the IT function of NTAX as a whole, the first EFQM assessment was conducted in August 2001 and the final EFQM results were published in the monthly quality improvement status report of October 2004. Before deciding on the EFQM model, other assessment models were used. For the purpose of having a unified framework for communicating and monitoring TQM progress, assessments prior to August 2001 were converted into the EFQM format. The first uses of the EFQM model made as exact measurements as possible of the experimental subjects that had been enrolled into the TQM network by use of the BA. In order to provide scores for the parts of the EFQM model where there were insufficient data, subjective estimates were applied in order to be able to use the results of the assessments as part of the annual quality planning. The BA was used to extend the installed base of quality management practice into a larger TQM network. As a consequence of this, the reliability and validity of the assessment results increased as of covering a larger part of the organisation and having deeper, richer and more reliable data.

To make the EFQM model into an operational research instrument, different tools, methods and standards were used. As far as possible, the ISO 19011 standard was used for conducting quality audits. The CobiT audit standard was repeatedly used for defining objects to audit, along with frameworks like CMM, ISO 15504 and ISO 9001:2000. Whenever it was possible to measure quality characteristics and conduct SPC analysis, this was done. Checklists were developed and used for checking whether NTAX documentation standards and programming standards were being followed. Interviews were used for trying to understand why behaviour did not correspond with standards and procedures. Observations and general conversations with representatives of management, workforce and other control units such as the Internal Audit and the National Audit also provided important information.

The way EFQM data was collected through a bottom-up process of sampling from controls and audits can be illustrated by the NTAX software lifecycle model in figure 20. On the top of the figure there are quality control processes related to system acceptance as a new information systems went through initial stages of analysis, design, implementation, use, evaluation and then into a potentially everlasting maintenance and improvement cycle of repeating the four or five steps of the model depending on whether the system requirements had changed or not. The quality control processes were defined as quality control procedure V10 and acceptance procedure N7. Both of these procedures and all other standards and procedures used in the NTAX part of the study were developed by the organisation before the researcher arrived or were developed at the time of the study with minimal interaction with the researcher.

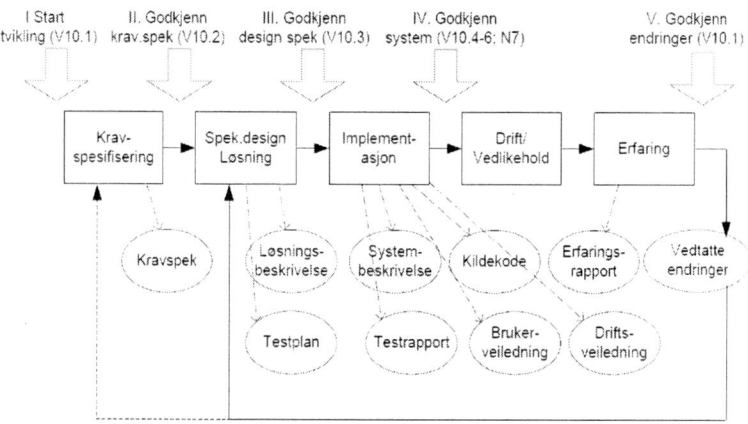

Figure 20: The NTAX software lifecycle model

The only design carried out by the researcher was the development of research instruments in terms of checklists and audit formats in order to check that the organisation was behaving in compliance with its own prescriptions. At the most basic level this consisted of yes/no checklists comparing the documents encircled in figure 20 with the NTAX standards describing the expected format and content for such documents. When making use of the checklists as parts of audits, the audits were sometimes written to match with the CobiT audit standards or other international or de facto quality management standards.

Although controls and audits were carried out repeatedly, often following the annual maintenance cycle described in figure 20, it was not possible to repeat all audits used for updating the EFQM on an annual basis. As the EFQM assessment for one year would not necessarily be completely independent of the assessment done for previous year, one of the basic criteria for monitoring the TQM level through use of SPC was not met. However, as many controls and audits were done repeatedly, the EFQM score chart was updated on a monthly basis, resulting in fluctuations up and down the maturity scale, and it seemed reasonable to use SPC for monitoring the level of change from one year to another.

The EFQM assessment model was only used during the first period at NTAX when the BA was implemented from the viewpoint of the quality department. At the next stage of research, when the BA was implemented from the IT staff position trying to grow and develop TQM by making interventions from the outside, the EFQM assessment model would not be of any use until the BA was able to make the installed base of quality control related to COBOL programming practice extend into managing a larger improvement programme. Instead of using EFQM data, the changes in quality indexes specifically designed and used in the

COBOL quality control practice were used as dependent variables.

At DNMI there were some discussions of using ISO 9001 and CMM for monitoring the TQM level associated with KLIBAS-related work practice, but there was limited management interest in such TQM standards at the time. When trying to understand the impact of the BA on TQM in retrospect, proxy data based on annual finance and productivity measurements for the Climate Department at DNMI were used as dependent variables.

3.4.2 Independent variables

Independent variables (predictor variables) relate to the actions A, B and C in the CAR theory statement. In the first supplementary research hypothesis (RH1) the issue of implementing the actions A, B and C in a manner that caused the BA to run in a state of statistical stability was used to indicate how to focus the design of independent variables. If the BA should break down, it cannot have any impact on TQM implementation success, so a variable measuring the stability of the BA is important.

In the part of the study where the EFQM assessment model was used as a dependent variable, there were attempts to also use the EFQM model for evaluating the BA implementation in terms of doing EFQM assessments of the quality function within the IT department of NTAX. Similar to how the EFQM was used for assessing the whole organisation, also in the case of the assessments of the quality function the process started out with alternative models like ISO 9004:2000 and the Common Assessment Framework (CAF) (EIPA, 2012) that were reformatted to fit with the EFQM model for the purpose of eliminating problems that could be helpful for the purpose of improving the performance of the BA.

In the part of the study at NTAX dealing with the COBOL process, research was carried out from an individual position within IT staff rather than on behalf of the quality department. Although it may be possible to use the EFQM format for personal self-assessment, as would be done if one were running a single-person company, the focus of NTAX had moved from EFQM to ISO 9000, so the ISO 9004:2000 standard was used for measuring BA stability.

In the DNMI part of the study, the organisation had not committed itself to any particular formal TQM framework at the time, so there was no obvious way to measure BA stability. In retrospect, the way Climate Department productivity indicators have used for measuring TQM level has been matched by using productivity indicators for systems development in terms of focusing on the development in production rates of technical KLIBAS reports.

3.4.3 Extraneous variables

In order to characterise the "in situation S with salient features F, G and H" part of the research hypothesis, the organisational settings consisting of DNMI, NTAX and NTAX in collaboration with UiO could be seen as extraneous variables in the sense that organisational culture and the way the TQM action research experiment was designed in the different settings could be seen to have an impact on the output. Unlike the independent variable relating to the way the BA was specifically implemented and controlled, features like organisational culture and experimental setting was beyond what the researcher was able to control.

3.5 The CAR principle of change through action

According to Davison et al (2004, p. 75), "the essence of CAR is to take actions in order to change the current situation and its unsatisfactory conditions. [...] A lack of change in the unsatisfactory conditions suggests that there was no meaningful problem, that the intervention failed to address the existing problem(s), or that the existing situation could not be altered because of political or practical obstacles that were neglected when the RCA was established."

3.5.1 Data collection

The data collection process in all three research environments were similar in the sense that data was collected through a process of observations, document studies, informal interviews, discussions and collection of numerical data to measure the state of the situation before and after the implementation of the planned intervention.

At DNMI the primary focus was on running time and error statistics for computer programs being part of the continually developing KLIBAS system. This narrow focus had to do with the DNMI culture being easy-going which caused few problems when asking about access to data, how to produce and distribute error reports, making observations and conducting informal interviews. The complexity of the situation had to do with the enormous amounts of meteorological data that was produced all the time, how to develop efficient methods of quality control, automatic if possible, and how to serve the KLIBAS customers by providing different types of climate statistics and data exchange formats.

Data collection at NTAX represented other types of challenges. The culture was different. It was intensely political with hidden agendas, people were suspicious, and there was a general resistance to change. Getting access to data often required several rounds of negotiations, and interviewing people was often difficult and had to be planned in advance and had be carried out in formal or semi-formal ways by use of audit interview guides and formal checklists. On the other hand, the software development methodology at NTAX was much more elaborate than at DNMI as it involved about 60 programmers rather than just a handful and was carried out along with the lifecycle model in figure 20.

In using the lifecycle model for designing research, data collection typically consisted of two steps. As soon as the software engineers had finished a particular step of the process, such as having written the test plan as part of system specification step, the researcher got hold of the report and checked the format and content against the NTAX standards. A checklist was completed and returned to programmers along with a preliminary audit report that also included results from last years check and supplementary observations and with a request for an interview with the programmers in order to find out whether they had been following the correct procedures and whether the preliminary audit report was adequate.

After a string of such audits along each of the business processes, the audits were appended to a general report assessing the status of the whole system development process prior to the stage of acceptance defined by procedure N7 in figure 20. The report was then handed over to management as part of the background material for deciding whether production was ready to start. The handover of the quality control report represented the implementation of the final step in NTAX audit procedure V10. The outcome of this procedure was a decision of whether the solution was accepted or not accepted as compliant with the NTAX quality management standards. If it was not accepted, then there were two outcomes. Either it resulted in a recommendation to management that production could not start or that it could start provided that the software engineer community committed themselves to improving quality control practice. If management took notice of the recommendation, the management signatures and comments were used as data for documenting management commitment.

When starting the collaboration with UiO in 2006 for the purpose of studying the use of BA for implementing TQM at NTAX from a different perspective, the data collection was narrowed down to collecting error statistics from the quality management practice for COBOL programming. This process had earlier been studied both as an individual task and as part of the software development process. From the viewpoint of the software development process, compliance with the programming standards were part of the implementation step in figure 20, but from 2006 onwards the focus on COBOL programming was only seen from the isolated task management perspective.

For practical reasons, as most of the time was being spent at UiO, most of the interaction between the researcher and the software programmers were done through email. There were also some informal conversations and interviews carried out in the corridors at times when the researcher visited NTAX to write on the action research report, but no systematically planned interviews with semi-formal interview guidelines as had been done in other cases. There were also discussions and interviews with managers concerning the COBOL standards, but these were also carried out whenever an opportunity came along rather than something being specifically planned ahead of time. Data was also collected by having email discussions with the quality department.

Data from the interviews and discussions were used in the action research reports as anonymous quotes. When communicating through email the number of emails and the time it took to get a response from the programming community was recorded and used as data for understanding how willing the programmers where to comply with the standards.

3.5.2 Exploratory data analysis

Depending on whether data analysis was part of building the model (diagnosis) or testing the model (planning, doing and evaluating action), different modes of thinking and different types of data analysis were used. This distinction is sometimes referred to as exploratory and confirmatory data analysis (Collis & Hussey, 2003, p. 197).

During the diagnosis stage of the action research cycle, data collection consisted of recording symptoms and data analysis consisted of making the diagnosis. At DNMI the main tool for inductive data analysis was systems thinking. The research diaries from this period consisted of system diagrams along with verbal commentary. The way of reasoning with system diagrams was not supported by any particular method beyond the kind of practical systems thinking used in object oriented programming (Wang, 1996) and quality control (Mitra, 1993). The fact that the KLIBAS project was making use of an Oracle database system meant that there were diagrams developed in the style of relational database diagrams. There were some attempts to use formal system design methods (Page-Jones, 1988), but the systems thinking remained fairly non-formal. Although the BA was designed according to CAS principles, the CAS literature in use (e.g. Kelly, 1994) was strictly verbal without any diagrams.

The part of the study taking dealing the IT function of NTAX as a whole started out using the same type of systems thinking that had been applied at DNMI but gradually grew more sophisticated by using methods similar to dynamical systems diagrams (Senge, 1990) and control diagrams (Beer, 1972). Towards the end of this period the TSI way of mixing different systems thinking methodologies was applied (Flood, 1993). Whenever audits or discussions were carried out, the researcher always brought along pen and paper and drew systems diagrams to help facilitate the discussion.

The part of the study focusing on the COBOL programming practice in isolation tried to expand on experiments done by using game models to describe social relationships in the previous part of the study and gradually the game perspective became the central model perspective of the study. Different books and articles on game theory, drama theory and game design were consulted (e.g. Miller, 2003; Dresher, 1981; Rosenhead & Mingers, 2001; Salen & Zimmerman, 2004), but no particular guide or formal approach was used for analysing data for the purpose of developing game models.

During the whole period of research descriptive statistics in the shape of tables and graphs were used for developing system models and game models. One of the most used statistical data analysis method was the Pareto analysis for presenting frequency tables or frequency histograms by ordering the categories by counts (Deming, 1986). The method was typically used for understanding the distribution of errors inside a system and aiding the researcher to focus on the most error prone processes.

3.5.3 Confirmatory data analysis

For the purpose of testing models or aspects of models, the focus was generally on three types of methods used for (a) finding out whether a process is stable, (b) finding out whether a process has changed after being submitted to an intervention, and (c) finding out whether one process has impact on another process through the use of regression and correlation analysis.

For the purpose of investigating process stability, statistical process control (SPC) was used (Shewhart, 1933). The method was usually applied in its most simple form by assuming the time series associated with the process being investigated were normally distributed and consecutive measurements being statistically independent. Even though there are SPC techniques for dealing with more complex situations (e.g. Wheeler, 1993), the simplified approach was generally sufficient for understanding whether a process was in a state of statistical control or not. There were some experiments with applying a method of SPC for short runs (Clark, 1999, pp. 86-90) at the beginning of the NTAX period, but as the adjustments to the control limits due to better but more complex methods in the cases they were applied had little effect on the way the charts were used, the original SPC design was used while keeping in mind that a more sophisticated statistical analysis should be applied when needed.

Shewhart (1938) compares the use of statistical quality control in industry with the use of statistical methods in scientific research. The planning, production and evaluation of industrial products in a mass production context can be compared with developing a hypothesis, doing an experiment and evaluating the results. When comparing the two processes, Shewhart (ibid, p. 150) says that "the problem of judging whether a state of statistical control exists is essentially one of testing the hypothesis that assignable causes have been eliminated".

If one considers the H0 hypothesis that there are still assignable causes one would expect to find error signals in the SPC. However, if one has observed a process over a long time and not discovered any error signals, then it should be possible to reject H0 on a pragmatic basis.

As pointed out by Deming (1986), the type of pragmatic hypothesis testing implicitly done when making use of SPC is not the same as the Neymann-Pearson statistical hypothesis testing method as it does not involve any concept of significance levels. For the purpose of discussing consequences of intervening in processes, however, the Neymann-Pearson categorisation of type I and type II errors is still useful (table 11).

		Fact	
		H0 is true Assignable causes exist.	H1 is true Assignable causes have been eliminated.
Action	Fail to reject H0	Ok	Type II error
	H0 rejected	Type I error	Ok

Table 11: Type I and type II error when testing the SPC hypothesis

Significance testing has only been sparingly used in the study. Occasionally a Student's t-test has been used for comparing the outcome of a process before and after an intervention. However, in order to make the test work it is necessary to have the process in a state of statistical control before the intervention is done, to identify the distribution of the original stationary process, and then bring the process into a state of statistical control after the intervention in order to compare the sample average from the two populations. In practice, however, it may be difficult to collect sufficient data both before and after the intervention in order to make the test meaningful. Deming (1986) argues that such kind of significance tests are of minimal use in a TQM context as the outcome of a successful intervention will be so obvious that the change of process parameters can be easily seen by visual inspection when the SPC has to be updated for further control.

The third type of statistical analysis used as part of deductive data analysis is regression and correlation analysis (Bhattacharyya & Johnson, 1977). This type of analysis has been used for predicting "year of zero defects" or when certain levels of TQM maturity is expected to be reached by looking at annual error volumes and maturity measurements. Although linear regression has been dominant when making these such predictions, exponential and logistic regression curves have also been used when the underlying system dynamics suggest this to be more relevant. The issue of significance of correlation coefficient has played a minor part in daily TQM practice as the challenge has not been to prove that there is continual improvement (e.g. negative auto-correlation in a time series of error signals) but rather to predict the time when maturity levels have been achieved. Whenever dealing with matters of significance concerning Pearson's correlation coefficient the methods and procedures described by Rowntree (1981, chapter 8) have been used.

	Hypothesis	Method for testing the hypothesis
RH1	The BA can be implemented and managed in a state of statistical control	Statistical process control (SPC)
RH2	The response to the BA treatment is performance improvement measurable by TQM assessments	Correlation analysis, $\alpha=0.05$
RH3	The BA is optimal for implementing TQM in complex environments	Search for counter-evidence

Table 12: Dominant method used for testing each of the three supporting BA hypotheses

How the confirmative data analysis techniques relate to the BA hypotheses is presented in table 12. Although it might in principle be possible to collect data before the BA intervention and then compare with data after the intervention, the BA is not a temporary intervention but rather a way of managing the TQM programme that has to be continued potentially forever. Rather than focusing on whether the BA had an impact on TQM implementation success, the data analysis technique used for testing RH2 focuses on the strength of the impact.

74

As mentioned earlier, the optimality hypothesis RH3 is difficult to test through the use of statistical means without having rivalling treatments (methods) to compare against. The hypothesis is nevertheless important for the purpose of making sure that the BA is implemented in an efficient manner, so the focus of the RH3 test will be to search for empirical counter-evidence to the BA being optimal.

3.6 The CAR principle of learning through reflection

According to Davison et al (2004, p. 76), "both researchers and clients must reflect on the outcomes of each intervention and determine whether the project should be continued". Without both the client and researcher reflecting upon the ongoing outcome of the research, it may be difficult to find out whether the research has reached a stage where it should exit the CPM or continue another cycle. In order to solve this situation, CAR suggests systematic use of reports and meetings for making sure that there is an ongoing reflection through all stages of action research.

3.6.1 TQM implementation progress reports

The research processes at DNMI were extensively documented. Table 13 lists administrative reports in the KLIBAS note series used for reporting progress on TQM implementation to the various shareholders.

	1995	1996	1997	1998	1999
January	-	KLIBAS 03/96	KLIBAS 04/97	KLIBAS 04/98	KLIBAS 03/99
February	-	KLIBAS 05/96	KLIBAS 06/97	KLIBAS 06/98	KLIBAS 05/99
March	KLIBAS 02/95	KLIBAS 08/96	KLIBAS 08/97	KLIBAS 08/98	KLIBAS 07/99
April	KLIBAS 05/95	KLIBAS 10/96	KLIBAS 10/97	KLIBAS 10/98	KLIBAS 09/99
May	KLIBAS 07/95	KLIBAS 12/96	KLIBAS 12/97	KLIBAS 12/98	KLIBAS 11/99
June	KLIBAS 09/95	KLIBAS 13/96	KLIBAS 14/97	KLIBAS 14/98	KLIBAS 13/99
July	-	KLIBAS 16/96	KLIBAS 16/97	KLIBAS 16/98	KLIBAS 15/99
August	KLIBAS 11/95	KLIBAS 19/96	KLIBAS 18/97	KLIBAS 20/98	KLIBAS 17/99
September	-	KLIBAS 21/96	KLIBAS 20/97	KLIBAS 22/98	-
October	KLIBAS 14/95	KLIBAS 23/96	KLIBAS 22/97	KLIBAS 24/98	-
November	KLIBAS 17/95	KLIBAS 25/96	KLIBAS 24/97	KLIBAS 26/98	-
December	KLIBAS 02/96	KLIBAS 02/97	KLIBAS 02/98	KLIBAS 01/99	-
Annual status	KLIBAS report 01/96	KLIBAS report 03/97	KLIBAS report 07/98	KLIMA report 09/99	KLIMA report 05/00

Table 13: DNMI progress reports

The first few progress reports in March, April and May 1995 reported only on the AUTO part of KLIBAS and then AUTO and SYNOP, but from June 1995 onwards progress for the system as a whole was reported. The reports were written in Norwegian. From October 1997 onwards the reports were written in English as the researcher became enrolled in the Nordic FREYR climatological quality control project. From May 1999 onwards the reports were restructured to fit the format of the NORDKLIM climatatological quality control project.

The annual reports were different from the monthly progress reports. The first reports from 1995, 1996 and 1997 gave a short overview of major improvements and minutes from all KLIBAS meetings. The 1998 report was an overview of all the KLIBAS documentation developed between 1991 and 1999. The 1999 report is the proceedings for the EUMETNET meeting which includes the paper that described the outcome of the BA research with suggestions for further research.

The progress reports written for the first five years of the NTAX study were modelled on the DNMI progress reports. As there was no formal TQM model in use, the structure of the IT strategy plan was used as a format for structuring the progress report until July 2001 when the format was redesigned to match the EFQM structure. All the plans and progress reports are listed in table 14. From the tenth progress report and onwards the documents were formally archived as official NTAX documents for internal use.

	2000	2001	2002	2003	2004
Plan	-	SKD	SKD nr 64/01	SKD 2003-003	SKD 2004-026
January	-	SKD	SKD nr 60/01	SKD 2002-075	SKD 2003-095
February	-	SKD	SKD 2002-001	SKD 2003-001	SKD 2004-002
March	-	SKD nr 08/01	SKD 2002-016	SKD 2003-005	SKD 2004-010
April	-	SKD nr 10/01	SKD 2002-023	SKD 2003-013	SKD 2004-016
May	-	SKD nr 13/01	SKD 2002-028	SKD 2003-025	SKD 2004-023
June	SKD	SKD nr 18/01	SKD 2002-033	SKD 2003-037	SKD 2004-028
July	SKD	SKD nr 23/01	SKD 2002-038	SKD 2003-045	SKD 2004-034
August	-	SKD nr 29/01	SKD 2002-049	SKD 2003-049	SKD 2004-048
September	SKD	SKD nr 32/01	SKD 2002-051	SKD 2003-055	SKD 2004-055
October	SKD	SKD nr 38/01	SKD 2002-057	SKD 2003-072	SKD 2004-063
November	SKD	SKD nr 45/01	SKD 2002-061	SKD 2003-082	-
December	SKD	SKD nr 51/01	SKD 2002-067	SKD 2003-088	-
Annual status	-	SKD 2002-003	SKD 2002-080	-	-

Table 14: NTAX progress reports

From January 2005 the monthly progress reports were first written as notes from the researcher to the director of the IT department and later to the director of IT strategy in the staff of the NTAX director general. These reports focused mainly on reporting progress according to the plan and contract established between UiO and NTAX. Challenges in getting access to data and interacting with the IT department was occasionally brought up and solved, but more detailed discussions related to progress of research was conducted through meetings. After being enrolled in the PhD programme at UiO the meetings were held about once or twice a year.

3.6.2 Individual process improvement reports

The NTAX action research reports were written for the client with the purpose of creating action and are listed in table 15. The format of the reports followed a conventional research report structure with introduction, literature review, methodology, results, discussion and conclusion in order to produce theoretical learning about the particular theme being investigated.

Research was conducted at three levels. The first seven process improvement studies in table 15 are described as task improvement as they dealt with specific aspects of the NTAX lifecycle model in figure 20. Each report analysed and compared practice from different business processes, like the ability to comply with the COBOL programming standards in business processes like PSA, FOS, LFT and LEP. All the eleven business processes in the middle section of the table, the second level of research, followed the life cycle model. The action research report was focused on making a total analysis and evaluation based on the controls and quality audits at stages 1-6 of procedure V10. It was written as input for the system acceptance procedure N7.

The third level of research was on the quality management system itself as the sum of all quality management practice found on the task and process levels. One type of action research processes was used for investigating how the currently documented system and current practice complied with TQM standards like ISO 9001, CAF, CMM and ISO 15504. Another type of research focused on investigating how the current set of standards used in the QMS was being updated according to the procedures defined by NTAX. A third focus was on monitoring and measuring the quality department in order to improve its internal efficiency and impact on the organisation as a whole.

	Research	2001	2002	2003	2004	2005
Task improvement	COBOL programming	SKD nr 61/01	SKD 2002-018	-	SKD 2004-001	SKD 2005-003
	CobiT M4 (internal audit)	-	SKD 2002-037	-	SKD 2004-009	-
	CobiT PO10 (project management)	-	SKD 2002-054	-	-	-
	CobiT PO9 (risk management)	-	-	SKD 2003-012	-	-
	CobiT A4 (documentation)	-	-	-	SKD 2004-113	-
	CobiT M2 (internal control)	-	-	-	-	SKD 2005-009
	CobiT (all 34 audit processes)	-	-	SKD 2003-087	SKD 2004-084	-
Business process improvement	PSA	-	SKD 2002-026	SKD 2003-014	SKD 2004-015	SKD 2005-011
	WebPSA	-	SKD 2002-027	SKD 2003-016	-	-
	DSB	-	SKD 2002-042	-	-	-
	FOS	-	SKD 2002-070	SKD 2003-091	SKD 2004-105	-
	LFP (vår)	-	-	SKD 2003-038	SKD 2004-031	-
	LFP (høst)	-	-	SKD 2003-073	SKD 2004-073	-
	FTS	-	-	SKD 2003-085	-	-
	LEP (skatteberegning)	-	-	-	SKD 2004-075	-
	ALTINN	-	-	-	SKD 2004-109	-
	LEP (forhåndsskatt)	-	-	-	SKD 2004-112	-
	AR	-	-	-	-	SKD 2005-011
System improvement	ISO 9001	SKD	-	-	SKD 2004-061	-
	Common Assessment Framework (CAF)	-	SKD 2002-006	-	-	-
	CMM & ISO 15504	-	SKD 2002-032	-	-	-
	NTAX standards	-	-	SKD 2003-048	-	-
	Self-assessment of quality department	-	-	SKD 2003-054	SKD 2004-106	-

Table 15: NTAX process improvement reports

The formulation and evaluation of the BA hypothesis relates specifically to this third level research that is more concerned with the TQM programme than the individual process and task improvement action research studies on the two first levels. Nevertheless, the development of the task and process improvement projects on the first and second levels of research are vital for understanding the TQM programme management at the third level.

After the study changed direction from looking at TQM implementation from the viewpoint of the quality department to a more formally defined action research viewpoint from the perspective of the IT staff of the NTAX director-general, only the COBOL action research process from the top of table 14 was kept alive. Table 16 contains a complete list of COBOL action research reports covering both periods.

Title	Identification	Size
Tilsyn med kvalitetssikring og intern kontroll ved standardisering av COBOL-programvare for likningsår 2009	SKD 31.01.11	250 pages
Standardisering av COBOL-programvare for ligningsår 2008	SKD 21.09.10	230 pages
Standardisering av COBOL-programvare for ligningsår 2007	SKD 22.02.10	110 pages
Opprydding og standardisering av COBOL-programvare	SKD 27.01.08	101 pages
Opprydding og standardisering av COBOL-programvare	SKD 18.05.07	86 pages
Opprydding og standardisering av COBOL-programvare	SKD 24.01.06	96 pages
Opprydding og standardisering av COBOL-programvare	SKD 2005-012	75 pages
Opprydding og standardisering av COBOL-programvare	SKD 2004-001	78 pages
Opprydding og standardisering av COBOL-programvare	SKD 2002-018	32 pages
Opprydding og standardisering av COBOL-programvare	SKD nr 61/01	20 pages

Table 16: NTAX process improvement reports written as part of the COBOL study

As can be seen from table 15, the six most recent COBOL action research reports were written for the client and the organisation but were not archived in the same formal manner as the earlier reports as they were now output of a research process rather than part of quality management system processes such as V10 and N7 shown in figure 20. It can also be seen from the table that the action research reports grew in size and complexity.

It would also be possible to present an overview of the 295 action research reports from the DNMI part of the study in a similar manner to what was done with the NTAX reports in table 16. However, as the BA hypothesis deals with the issue of managing the TQM programme more than the specific nature and outcome of the individual process improvements within such a programme, for the purpose of understanding the part of the study dealing with DNMI it is sufficient to understand that such a table can be constructed.

3.6.3 Research diaries

Following the advice of McNiff and Whitehead (2006), research diaries have been continually updates as the action research has been evolving. An overview of diaries is given in table 17.

Although the research diary has been useful for returning to previous reflections on why certain interventions had failed and what might been considered as interesting ideas for further development at a certain stage, the most important aspect of the diary keeping has been as a method for doing what Schön (1983) calls "reflection-in-action", using the diary for encouraging a process of thinking while writing and making diagrams.

The diary has also been used for "reflection-on-action", especially in the period before the formal start of the PhD project in 2006, in terms of spending some hours during the last week of the year for reflecting upon how the TQM implementation process had worked during the year as a whole and thinking about new ideas for the upcoming year.

Diary	Format	Size
January 2013 to present	Big (A4)	80 x 2 = 160 pages
September 2012 to January 2013	Big (A4)	80 x 2 = 160 pages
June 2012 to September 2012	Big (A4)	80 x 2 = 160 pages
June 2011 to June 2012	Small (A5)	96 x 2 = 192 pages
January 2011 to June 2011	Big (A4)	96 x 2 = 192 pages
September 2010 to January 2011	Big (A4)	96 x 2 = 192 pages
February 2010 to September 2010	Big (A4)	96 x 2 = 192 pages
February 2008 to February 2010	Big (A4)	74 x 2 = 148 pages
June 2005 to October 2010 (NTAX diary)	Small (A5)	96 x 2 = 192 pages
January 2003 to January 2008	Big (A4)	144 x 2 = 288 pages
August 1998 to January 2003	Big (A4)	96 x 2 = 192 pages
November 1995 to April 1998	Small (A5)	96 x 2= 192 pages

Table 17: Research diaries

3.7 Summary

The purpose of the methodology chapter was to explain how the research started out as reflective practice in 1992 and how it has gradually matured in rigour in terms of trying to meet the ideas and principles of canonical action research (CAR). Data have been collected and analysed in different ways, as illustrated in the comments on each of the five principles of CAR. Although the collection and analysis of data involves both qualitative and quantitative data, data about technical systems and human affairs, it was argued that CAR provided an integrative research methodology for collecting and analysing data that was consistent with the ontology, epistemology and axiology of the constructive empiricist philosophy of science.

The constructive empiricist philosophy of science has been developed as a constructive alternative to scientific realism. Constructive empiricism advocates the view that "scientific activity is one of construction rather than discovery; construction of models that must be adequate to the phenomena, and not discovery of truth concerning the unobservable" (van Fraassen, 1980, p. 5). In other words, the philosophy has a constructive epistemology in the sense that knowledge about the world is constructed by the process of making models of phenomena, and it has an anti-realist ontology in the sense that it is concerned with the usefulness and not the truth of the models vis-à-vis the real world. For example, to ask whether quarks or angels exist for real is a philosophical question but it is not a scientific question in the context of constructive empiricism (ibid, p. 11; van Fraassen, 2002).

When thinking about science as construction of models to represent the phenomena, it is useful to distinguish between theoretical models and data models embedded in the theoretical models (van Fraassen, 2008). For example, in a theoretical model using differential equations to represent the movements of a pendulum, coefficients and initial conditions used in the model are based on data models (probability models) of the length and mass and initial height and speed of the pendulum (e.g. Giere, 1988, pp. 70-71). In figure 21 the perspective on science as use of embedded data models in theoretical models for representing phenomena is illustrated by the way the research has been designed for this CAR study through the use of various data models embedded in a theoretical game model.

Applying CAR in the context of constructive empiricism means to investigate and improve the usefulness of the theoretical model in figure 21 for understanding the process of TQM implementation in organisations like NTAX. The figure can be used for summarising how CAR has been used as a research design.

The first step in the CAR cyclic model consists of diagnosing the organisation in order to understand what is preventing the organisation from changing and reaching a level of TQM excellence. Starting with a game theoretical framework to formulate the problem, such as the Monopoly framework represented by the mouse and cat game in the diagram, the researcher investigates the phenomenon by collecting data, producing data models and coming up with a revised and improved Monopoly model. The diagnosis consisted of making a full clock-wise cycle through the diagram by starting on top with Monopoly theory and ending on top with a Monopoly model of the organisation.

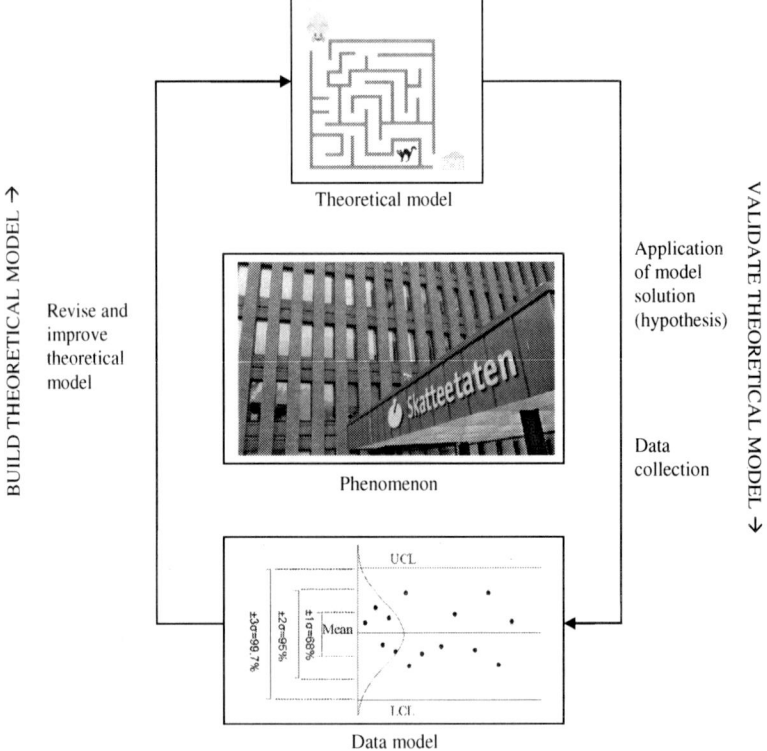

Figure 21: Research wheel (based on: Rudestam & Newton, 1992, p. 5)

The next four steps in the CAR cycle is the treatment that consists of turning a model *of* something into a model *for* something. The action planning consists of analysing the Monopoly model of NTAX for the purpose of finding an optimal action plan (game strategy). Because of the nature of the Monopoly model this game strategy can be thought of as a bootstrap algorithm (BA). The BA is then carried out as an intervention in the organisation while collecting data. After the completion of the intervention, the outcome of the BA is evaluated in terms of creating data models of performance parameters. Reflecting upon the outcome of the experiment, the theoretical model is once again revised and improved. In other words, the treatment also consisted of a making a full clock-wise cycle through the diagram by starting with the Monopoly model resulting from the diagnosis and validating this by investigating whether the model conclusions would have the expected impact when being tried out in practice.

As can be observed from this summary, and is being illustrated in table 18, there are three modes of thinking involved in how CAR is used. The CAR diagnosis relies heavily on qualitative data and may explain why action research is sometimes categorised as phenomenological research (e.g. Avison et al, 1999; Collis & Hussey, 2003). There are, however, constraints associated with the diagnosis in terms of how the output of the diagnosis is going to be used for deducing a treatment and consequently has to be formulated in the shape of a game model. These constraints are found in the CAR methodology when considering the semantic representation of the kind of theory CAR defines suitable for doing action research.

PDCA	CAR (figure 18)	Research wheel (figure 21)	TSI (figure 13 & table 10)	OR/SA (figure 6)
Plan (P)	Diagnosis	1. Application of model solution (assuming the researcher has a default theoretical model as he enters the situation) 2. Data collection 3. Revise and improve theoretical model	a. Creativity (plural) b. Choice (SOSM) c. Implementation SOSM: Soft systems thinking	Formulate (analyse)
	Action planning	Find treatment: Deduce solution from theoretical model	a. Creativity (unitary) b. Choice (SOSM) c. Implementation	Deduce (design)
Do (D)	Intervention (Action taking)	Test treatment: 1. Application of model solution 2. Data collection 3. Revise and improve theoretical model	SOSM: Hard systems thinking, system dynamics, organisational cybernetics or complexity theory	Interpret (implement)
Check (C)	Evaluation (Assessment)			
	Reflection (Learning)		a. Creativity (coercive) b. Choice (SOSM) c. Implementation SOSM: Emacipatory systems thinking or postmodern systems thinking	
Act (A)	Exit or enter new cycle	-	-	-

Table 18: How the steps in PDCA and CAR relate to steps in other cyclic models

The second mode of thinking is the CAR action planning where a mathematical analysis of game problem is used for deducing a game strategy. Although this mode of thinking is vital for the process of action research for finding the optimal treatment for a given problem, little is said about this in CAR literature. A possible reason for this may be because this represents a step that can be described as mathematics rather than social science, just like physics or natural science becomes mathematics in similar situations, but even though complex mathematical problem may have to be solved by mathematicians or in collaboration with mathematicians there is also literature explaining less complicated game theory results for the social scientist who wants to use the theory without getting too deeply involved in the mathematical details (e.g. Luce & Raiffa, 1957; Colman, 1995).

The third mode of thinking relates to the action planning, intervention, evaluation and reflection after the game strategy has been deduced. At this stage the CAR consists of testing a given strategy which means that it has to focus on numerical data and statistical analysis. Some IS scholars see this part of the CAR design as particularly important for optimising the quality of research and have been arguing the need for using a positivist mindset when doing CAR (e.g. Kock et al., 1997; DeLuca, 2005; DeLuca & Kock, 2007).

As has been summarised in this section, the CAR methodology has been implemented according to the philosophy of constructive empiricism which means that CAR is interpreted as no different from the scientific method used by natural scientists. The three modes of thinking in CAR corresponds to the three modes of thinking among physicists in trying to formulate some natural phenomenon as a mathematical problem (e.g. differential equations to represent the behaviour of a pendulum), solving the mathematical problem possibly with the assistance of mathematicians, and validating the understanding by empirical investigations of the mathematical solution.

4. RESULTS

The purpose of this chapter is to present the research results by describing the process and outcome of three cycles of action research. The first cycle deals with practical BA design for implementing TQM in a technically complex environment (section 4.1). The next cycle focuses on the challenges of BA design when the situation is also politically complex (section 4.2). The final cycle focuses on how the "what gets measured gets done" principle was used as part of the BA design (section 4.3).

4.1 First action research cycle – June 1992 to October 1999

The first cycle describes the development of a TQM programme management method that in hindsight can be described as an implementation of the BA in the complex environment of the Climate Department of the Norwegian Meteorological Institute (DNMI). The main insights from this cycle in terms of practical implementation of the BA are discussed in *paper 5*. In *paper 1* there is also a brief mention of how the experiences during the first cycle influenced BA expectations in later cycles. The walk-through of the CPM provides context for understanding the papers from the viewpoint of the Monopoly-based interpretation of information infrastructure dynamics.

4.1.1 Diagnosis

The understanding of the challenges at DNMI from the perspective of TQM was something that gradually evolved as it became apparent that the isolated software engineering (SE) perspective was not sufficient for understanding the important role of the environment where the SE practice was being carried out.

The KLIBAS project (1989-95) at DNMI was established for the purpose of replacing an old climate database system with a new system. The new system was going to be developed around an Oracle database on a UNIX platform, replacing old FORTRAN software with new software written in C, C++ and Visual Basic. As the previous solution had consisted of fragmented routines and work practice that made it difficult to produce weather statistics by combining weather data from different routines, an overall aim of the project was to make the new KLIBAS database system capable of integrating data across systems and platforms.

In June 1992, the new UNIX machines were running, but there were still difficulties and disagreements on how the relational database should be designed. The political game of the KLIBAS project group was based around making the research scientists and executives collaborate. The research scientists were split in two age groups. The younger scientists had a theoretical background in geophysics which included courses in computer science, and they were generally interested in the latest trends and developments in information systems development (ISD). The older scientists were more or less self-taught in FORTRAN programming and were less interested in trends and fashions in ISD.

As the executives lacked the formal education of the research scientists, they acted as if they were afraid of being exposed of not doing things right, generally being unwilling to share printouts of computer programs or to share knowledge in general. The younger scientists, on the other hand, had theoretical understanding of ISD but lacked experience and needed the practical know-how of the executives. The tension between these two groups resulted in hidden agendas and occasional verbal confrontations, but the middle position of the older scientists prevented conflicts from becoming too intense.

In addition to the political conflicts, the organizational culture was characterised by research scientists working in isolation with climate research on specific types of geophysical data, sometimes having one or more executives to assist in doing some of the more trivial parts of the work, like getting data into the database, doing simple forms of quality control, and responding to public requests by delivering computer-generated printouts of weather statistics.

From a TQM perspective, there were few problems related to customer satisfaction, process quality and product quality. There was a steady demand for the kind of services the Climate Department could offer. With the researchers being involved in the whole process of setting up and controlling weather stations, deciding what data to collect, how to perform quality control and how to use the data for statistical presentations and climate research, there was little need for formalised TQM models and methods.

On the other hand, this management approach of putting the experts in charge was not equally successful when running an ISD project. There was no research scientist whose research depended on turning the isolated work practices into one fully integrated system, although all the isolated communities saw large advantages of getting access to more data. The whole of DNMI expected the new KLIBAS database system to be important for all kinds of use, and by the time of 1992-93 other departments were starting to question the progress of the project. There were also worries inside the Climate Department because maintenance contracts for the old computer system were not being renewed while the KLIBAS project group did not seem to be able to agree on how to conceptualise the new system nor being able to deliver prototype examples that would match the quality of the old software solutions. In other words, the most relevant TQM-related problem for the Climate Department at DNMI was the KLIBAS project itself.

In trying to understand the dynamics of the KLIBAS information infrastructure, the Monopoly model in table 19 shows the eight most important business processes, related to specific types of geophysical data mentioned in *paper 5*, and how each of these processes can be broken down in tasks of data collection, quality assurance (QA) and applications for delivering data and statistics.

JAIL (or "just visiting")		Data	QA	Apps.	Data	QA	Apps.	Free Parking	
		Precipitation stations			**Automatic weather stations (AWS)**				
Apps	Aanderaa stations							**SYNOP** stations	Data
QA									QA
Data			DNMI Monopoly						Apps.
Apps.	Radio-sonde data							**METAR** stations	Data
QA									QA
Data									Apps.
Collect $200 in salary as you pass GO		**Climate stations**			**HIRLAM data**			Go to Jail	
		Apps.	QA	Data	Apps.	QA	Data		

Table 19: A Monopoly representation of the KLIBAS information infrastructure

There are four players to consider in this game of Monopoly. In addition to the players defined by the tensions between the young and old researchers and the executives, the action researcher became a fourth player in the sense that his background in computer science (numerical analysis) rather than geophysics made him view the KLIBAS project as algorithms, methods and systems. The technocratic perspective, represented by the computer scientist's way of understanding organisations as systems, can be used for representing the zero-sum ideological conflict that is assumed when using the Monopoly model.

While researchers and executives had special responsibility related to one or two coloured series on the Monopoly table, the aim of action research was to integrate the fragmented KLIBAS infrastructure by making use of data from different colour series when developing the QA properties. In order to do so, however, it was necessary to have access to data and know how data was going to be used, so property development was in principle not possible without first establishing a local monopoly.

In order to complete the diagnosis, the way the processes have been placed on the Monopoly model are done in the style of starting with the cheap properties that are not too expensive in terms of developing houses and hotels but give relatively modest returns. For instance, the radiosonde data routine, representing the procedure of collecting data from weather balloons, doing quality control and making data exchange formats and statistical presentations, was only useful for particular types of research and was managed left-handedly by an old researcher through the assistance of an executive who took care of all the practical issues.

The Aanderaa automatic weather stations were slightly more important as the data was being used more actively in research, but there were inconveniences in the physical operation of the stations and they were gradually replaced by other types of automatic weather stations (AWS) represented by the orange series. Although it was relatively cheap to develop properties within the Aanderaa series, such development would be unlikely to have much impact on the total game of information infrastructure development. However, by following the Monopoly board clockwise each new colour series represent stations and routines that were increasingly complex and important for DNMI as a whole.

The first of the four corners of the game, labelled "collect $200 in salary as you pass GO" represent the annual progress assessment of how the infrastructure development is progressing from the viewpoint of the individual player. The states marked "Jail" and "Go to Jail" represent the consequences of system development failure. They function as an attractor in the information infrastructure development in the sense that they model a development dynamics that explains why the high profit green and dark blue series are equally unattractive as the cheap purple and light blue series because it is less likely for a player to land on them.

The free parking state indicates the situation of doing things that have no impact on game play. No penalties are paid, but neither is there any capital gain. Free parking represents a short time for reflection-on-action to compensate the continual reflection-in-action as the information infrastructure development game is being played.

4.1.2 Action planning

When implementing TQM by use of BA, the initial step of the BA consists of identifying a small network of quality control practitioners who might benefit from improved communication with each other only. In the KLIBAS case, it seemed like a good idea to start with precipitation observations collected on a weekly basis from a population of about 700 stations spread all over the country. Late 1993, a method for getting data into the new database system was established, and software for producing data lists and simple statistics were made. Developing software for doing quality control followed early 1994, making the quality control practice of the precipitation group into a vital part of the actor-network.

By the end of 1994, the actor-network also included quality control practice related to the more complex Climate and SYNOP stations plus two types of automated weather stations. Still the actor-network was fairly fragmented in the sense that quality control practice within the precipitation station group did not make use of precipitation observations collected from the other types of stations and vice verse. A simple solution to this problem was to duplicate precipitation data from the other types of stations into the precipitation station database. This solution caused redundancy and a risk that producing the same type of statistics by drawing precipitation data from the precipitation data tables and the automatic weather stations tables would result in different outcome due to different types of quality control practice. Nevertheless, the BA recommends starting with simple practice before moving on to more complex cases.

The case of making the KLIBAS project itself a node in the TQM actor-network was facilitated by the fact that the younger scientists and the project manager in particular wanted to follow the trends of popular ISD by applying project quality assurance. A report describing the quality management principles for use in ISD projects was written (Kjensli & Moe, 1992), but after a failed attempt to assign an executive outside of the KLIBAS project group as quality auditor, the report was shelved. Although this did not affect the material side of the actor-network, it had consequences for the semiotic aspects of the network as it helped creating awareness of quality management. At this time TQM was a management fashion, and DNMI decided to implement ISO 9000 quality management in parts of the organization, although not within the Climate Department.

In May 1995 the KLIBAS project was formally completed (Moe, 1995), although only parts of the historical data had been loaded onto the new database systems, and only a fraction of the software had been developed. From the perspective of the head of the Climate Department, the project managers and other members of the KLIBAS team who wanted to spend more time of climate research and less on database development, it was useful to say that the ISD project had completed with the delivery of a successful initial version of the KLIBAS database system, handing over the responsibility for maintenance and further improvement to line management.

The formal termination of the KLIBAS project had consequences for the semiotic part of the actor-network, but as the material part of the network was hardly working at all, what had to be done in practice was that the material KLIBAS system had to be developed almost from scratch. The author of this thesis being one of the people responsible for ISD, the task seemed close to impossible both in scope and complexity, but reading a book on complex adaptive systems (Kelly, 1994) resulted in the idea that information systems development could be thought of in terms of biological growth and cultivation. As a consequence of this idea, the development quickly entered into the mode of the control loop of the BA where the KLIBAS prototype was expanded and improved in directions of more critical cases and more complex cases using events for triggering action rather than previously established plans.

The KLIBAS control algorithm was distributed between four modules named CHECK_MAIL (Øgland, 1999d), MAILSTAT (Øgland, 1999c), KAPO (Øgland, 1999f) and DRIFT (Øgland, 1998; 1999a; 1999h). The evolution of the algorithm was described in the C programming language in the technical reports. The diagram in figure 22 illustrates the logic of how it worked.

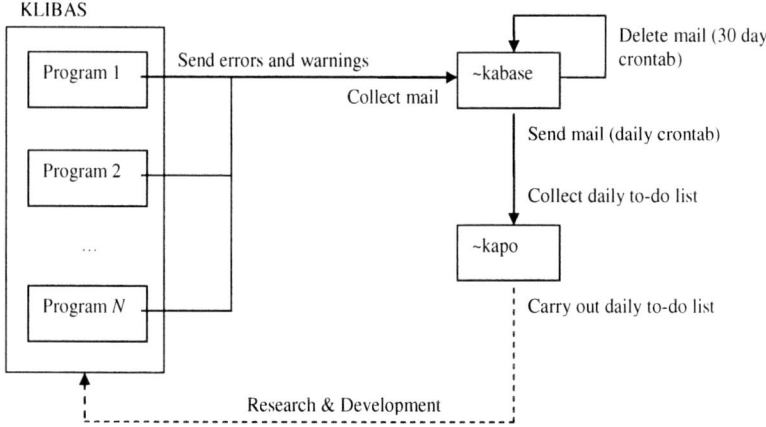

Figure 22: TQM programme management: The KLIBAS control algorithm

The KLIBAS database system consisted of a network of computer programs, some interacting with people and some not. All of the programs were designed in a manner that caused error and warning signals to be sent to the email account of the system user ~kabase. The program CHECK_MAIL used statistical process control for monitoring the volume of mails and deleted mails older than a certain age in the account to make sure it would not run out of memory. The program MAILSTAT performed a Pareto analysis of the errors and warnings collected in the mailbox by presenting a to-do list where the priority of each program was associated with the number of errors and warnings. The to-do list was sent to the user ~kapo every night, so that daily planning of tasks would be the first mail ~kapo read when logging on to the computer to read mail. The program KAPO was used for structuring the problem solving process, and the program DRIFT was used in the aid of writing monthly status reports.

The KLIBAS control algorithm can be seen as an implementation of the BA in the sense that it aims at cultivating and growing the network of computer programs by a process that is driven by the use of the programs. This means that the BA statements in table 3 involving subjective judgement are largely substituted by statistical reasoning and judgements created by the artificial intelligence embedded in the system by the way the daily to-do lists were designed. In the end, however, it was up to research and development whether to follow the suggestions provided by the system.

4.1.3 Intervention

The motto behind the BA approach was "productivity before quality" in the sense of first trying to achieve a stable production and then focus on product and process improvement rather than spending too much time planning before getting on with developing the system, as had been the case with the KLIBAS project.

Aligning BA strategy with TQM actor-network

Due to the poor quality of the KLIBAS solution when the project was officially ended, opportunities for improvement were many, and it was not obvious where to start. Following the ideas of complex adaptive systems, the idea became to focus on a population of simple improvement opportunities and then try to make KLIBAS operational in a bottom-up fashion. From the almost infinitely large population of improvement opportunities, a moderate sample was selected by looking at the structure and dynamics of the TQM actor-network within DNMI. Exploiting positive feedback in the sense of finding improvement opportunities that would align with the "rich getting richer" dynamics of Monopoly was particularly relevant.

One important opportunity for improvement was to make sure that the database was updated with fresh data (SYNOP) as they arrived electronically at DNMI for being used as input for the weather forecast models. The new KLIBAS technology allowed this to be done in ways not previously possible (Øgland, 1994a). Having the database updated to the latest hour resulted in a new situation for the Climate Department, and new "climate products" were developed in terms of having statistical overviews and analyses describing the previous week and month available to the public or specific subscribers more or less instantly after the final observations had arrived. This new situation also required new methods for doing quality control. While the standard way of controlling data had depended on waiting for observation logbooks to arrive several weeks later, the new control methodology had to depend more on automatic checks and update by use of interpolation and extrapolation (Øgland, 1997a; 1997b).

The SYNOP strategy was aligned with the actor-network in the sense that the head of the Climate Department was the person who had taken the initiative for the new monthly climate product. As this new product quickly became popular, it not only was seen to serve a public need, but it also worked as evidence for the success of the KLIBAS project. In this way the SYNOP strategy was politically important and a political success, but it did not align equally well with the rest of the TQM actor-network as it did not support existing quality control practices based on checking logbooks and weather maps. On the contrary, the new approach was later made part of a strategy of work automation (Øgland, 2000).

Working with online data suggested there might be possibilities for expanding the TQM actor-network beyond the Climate Department and into the Forecast Department (Øgland, 1999e). After researching this opportunity, however, it turned out that the observational quality needed for making use of the HIRLAM data in forecast models was not compatible with the precision needed for making use of the data within the Climate Department, so that put a momentarily stop for further expansion in that direction.

Another important opportunity for improvement arose when a research scientist studying wind observations asked whether it would be possible to get access to the wind observations from the METAR airport observations that arrived DNMI in parallel with the SYNOP observations. The METAR strategy was interesting from a BA perspective in the sense that it provided a gateway into establishing a new routine by working directly with the climate research scientist who would be responsible for this routine. Through several years of software development and process improvement, the METAR routine was gradually established (Øgland, 1995c; 1999i).

Efforts were also made in the direction of collaborating with the more established work practices related to precipitation stations, climate stations, Aanderaa automatic weather stations, agricultural automatic weather stations and semi-automatic precipitation stations. In *paper 5*, there is a simplified model of the TQM actor-network used for explaining how ideas from the first AR cycle at DNMI was later used as a basis for the BA design in the second AR cycle at NTAX.

To summarise the presentation above, the overall BA strategy was to cultivate the initial KLIBAS solution by analysing the needs and opportunities of the actor-network in terms of collaborating and improving existing practice, developing new practice, identify powerful nodes and gateways in the network that would make it larger, stronger and more stable. Trading and developing properties like SYNOP and METAR were particularly important as they seemed to represent "rising star" positive feedback qualities which could prove useful for getting control over the actor-network as a whole.

The CAS philosophy driving the BA made the overall strategy opportunistic, chaotic and driven by a myopic concern for fixing details in software and making sure system documentation was up to date. In total, the first cycle of the action research resulted in 436 reports of administrative, technical or scientific nature. Many of the reports were distributed beyond DNMI, and 101 research reports were made generally available through the Norwegian BIBSYS system.

Quality control of automatic weather stations

In 1996 and 1997 much effort was spent on establishing a work practice for handling of data from the Aanderaa automatic weather stations on KLIBAS in a similar way to how it had worked on the old platform. Data from the old system was stored on tape and loaded into the new database structure, new software was written, a quality handbook was made and some new features were added to make it easier to monitor how the routine was working (Nordlie & Øgland, 1995; Øgland, 1999b). Although the transition turned out successful, it was more work than had been originally estimated, especially the cost of loading data from tape into the database system, and considering the not too critical importance of the Aanderaa data in relation to other types of data and work practices at the Climate Department, perhaps too much effort had been put into completing this particular task when there were other more important tasks waiting.

In contrast to this, the work with the agricultural automatic weather stations (AWS) followed a different approach. In the same way as the Aanderaa stations, the routine was owned by a research scientist and managed by an executive, but in this case it was rather poorly managed despite the fact that the observations themselves were of greater strategic importance for DNMI and the Climate Department as a whole. After establishing a routine for automatically downloading data into the Oracle databases in 1994 and analysing the existing specifications and practice for quality control, a system of automatic quality control was implemented and then used as input for monthly quality control reports that was used for establishing a monthly quality control meeting between the Climate Department and the Instruments Department who were responsible for the AWS working properly (Øgland, 1995a).

Unlike previous BA interventions that were primarily done in terms of software development, in this case it was the meeting between the two departments that was the essential part in growing and improving the TQM actor-network at DNMI. As mentioned in a reflective study on how organizational culture impacts on the outcome of quality audits, this particular instance of subcontract quality audit within DNMI was successful because of mutual trust, common goals and having a discussion structured around facts made visible by quality control statistics in graphs and tables (Øgland, 2009a).

Quality control of automatic weather stations as a basis for TQM

In parallel with making changes in the material actor-network related to the data quality of automatic weather stations by writing and publishing a monthly quality control report, it seemed useful to try a similar approach for strengthening the part of the TQM actor-network related to the development and maintenance of the KLIBAS software. What resulted was a monthly progress report on automatic weather stations, presenting quality control statistics related to the growth and performance of the software used for running this system rather than the quality of the weather stations themselves (Øgland, 1995b).

A challenge with this approach was that there was no real audience for this kind of publication after the KLIBAS project had terminated. On the other hand, from the perspective of the BA practitioner this kind of document was useful for reflecting upon how to set up priorities for further process improvement. In order to make the document more useful, it was gradually expanded until it became a general status report for the whole KLIBAS system and could then function as a kind of hub or central node for the material TQM actor-network (Øgland, 1995d). Furthermore, by using methods like statistical process control (SPC) for monitoring the stability of processes and Pareto analysis for sorting problems by the frequency of how often breakdowns occur, much of the decision making process could be automated. In fact, the monthly status report was an efficient way of cultivating the CAS principles into a precise genetic algorithm (Øgland, 2009b).

The KLIBAS management approach also matured in terms of becoming a more rigorous form of action research. While the early KLIMA research reports had focused on development and analysis of new methods of statistical quality control (Øgland, 1993a; 1993b; 1994b; 1997c; 1997d), some of the final KLIMA research reports tried to align research focus with problems that were manually or automatically recorded (Øgland et al, 1999). As a consequence of documenting the ISD process in this way, the BA process was given a TSI-like process structure as illustrated in figure 23.

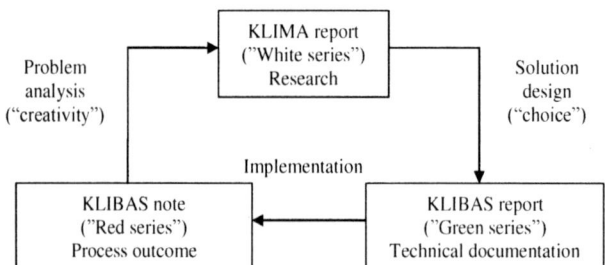

Figure 23: Documentation of the BA/TSI process at DNMI

The logic of the structure in the figure is similar to the three phases of creativity, choice and implementation in TSI. In the DNMI/KLIBAS case the creativity process consisted of identifying a problem from the KLIBAS status report or another data report and then formulate and analyse the problem by writing a research paper to be published as one of many such papers in a research report.

Among the various metaphors and models used by TSI in the process of formulating the problem, most problems within the KLIBAS process were either of the simple-unitary type in terms of data flow and data quality problems in search of optimal solutions in terms of algorithm and computer programs, or they were of the complex-unitary type in terms of describing work practices in need of optimal solutions in terms of procedures, quality handbooks and computer software for supporting existing practice. The problems were formulated as KLIMA research reports either dealing with algorithms (e.g. Øgland, 1997a) or work practice (e.g. Øgland, 1999j). Although problems of hermeneutical or political nature were always present and had to be handled in one way or another, they were never written down in terms of KLIMA research reports.

The choice process consisted of using the formulation of the problem for redesigning software or work practice. The internal KLIBAS report series was established as a part of the KLIBAS project in 1994 and were given a green layout which gave them a distinctly different look from the KLIMA reports. Depending on whether the problem would be simple-unitary or complex-unitary, different methods had to be used depending on whether the problem required changes in individual computer programs, changes in how various computer programs or computer systems were to interact, of whether the solution to the problem was a quality handbook or some procedures to be used by the executives. Unlike the clearly defined methods and groups of methods in TSI, there were no specific standards or methods for developing software and work practice at KLIBAS beyond each individual problem solver doing his best and trying to learn from what fellow problem solvers were doing.

Although the KLIBAS documentation includes results of test, it was only when the solution had been running in a production environment for a long time that problems or opportunities for improvements started to accumulate. In 1995 a new series of red KLIBAS documents were developed for the purpose of describing the performance of programs and work practices. As mentioned above, the birth of the document series started with the monthly quality control of observations from automatic weather stations and then expanded in volume by a parallel series of monthly status reports for the whole of KLIBAS. A complete list of all red KLIBAS reports was presented through table 13 in chapter 3.

Expanding the actor-network beyond the boundaries of DNMI

Having participated in commissioned climate research (Øgland & Førland, 1993), having written research reports on new methods of quality control of geophysical data (Øgland, 1993a; 1993b), and presented research on improved methods of statistical quality control at the Nordic Meteorological Conference (Øgland, 1994b), the author of this theses was asked to represent DNMI at the Nordic NORDKLIM Quality Control Project. The project helped expand the TQM actor-network beyond boundaries of DNMI and make it part of a Nordic "network of actions". This was practically useful and fitted with the overall BA strategy in terms of defining a readership for reports that had to be written as part of the BA/TSI process anyway, like the monthly status report (Øgland, 1999k).

In 1999 the actor-network was about to expand further into being part of a European Network as the researcher was asked to present a paper about quality management of data and dataflow at a EUMETNET conference in Oslo. The internal TQM network was linked with other Nordic networks through a NORDKLIM project (1996-2000) aimed at sharing insights and building a common platform for quality control. As part of the ECSN within the European Meteorological Network (EUMETNET), the ideas about implementing TQM as part of the climate database development process were presented (Øgland, 2000).

4.1.4 Evaluation

The stability hypothesis (RH1)
After spending a couple of years of running the BA in the initial mode in trying to understand the nature of TQM as practiced within the Climate Department of DNMI, the BA process moved into a state of statistical control in the sense of managing interventions over a network of six work practices each year for a period of six years. The experiment was terminated in a controlled manner, and the time series show no reason not to accept the hypothesis of the BA was implemented in a state of statistical control (RH1). The BA was in a state of statistical control in managing to keep focus on between three and ten work practices each year.

The impact hypothesis (RH2)
As there were no EFQM assessments or any other TQM assessment carried out at DNMI during the period of the experiment, alternative performance indicators need to be used for showing implication of the BA for TQM. One possibility could be to have a look at the change in production volumes of KLIMA research reports produced by the Climate Department of DNMI. Although the KLIBAS system was used for producing regular types of weather statistics for making comments to the press and responding to requests from the general public, the KLIMA reports often depended on extensive use of KLIBAS data. One way of testing the hypothesis of the BA having an impact on organizational performance (RH2) could be to see whether there was a positive correlation between the volume of technical KLIBAS reports describing system changes and the volume of KLIMA research reports being written. In figure 24 the annual volumes of KLIBAS technical reports have been used as predictor variable and the annual volumes of KLIMA research reports as response variables.

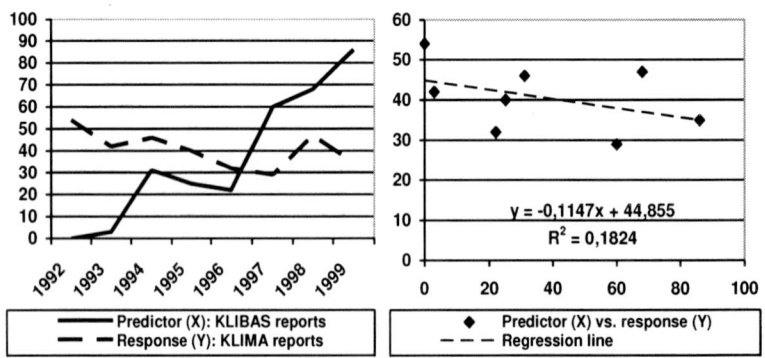

Figure 24: Output comparison between ISD documentation and commissioned research at DNMI

The diagram on the left side in figure shows a steady increase in the annual volume of technical reports increased as the BA/TSI matured, but unfortunately there seems to be no corresponding increase in the annual production of KLIMA reports. The diagram on the right side indicates a sample correlation of $R = -0.4271$ between technical productivity and research productivity. Given the sample size of $n = 8$, the correlation is not big enough to reject the null hypothesis of population correlation $r = 0$ at a 5% level of significance.

An alternative test consisting of correlating the annual volume of KLIBAS technical reports with the income of commissioned research (million NOK) is presented in figure 25. Financial numbers have been collected from the DNMI yearbook of 2000.

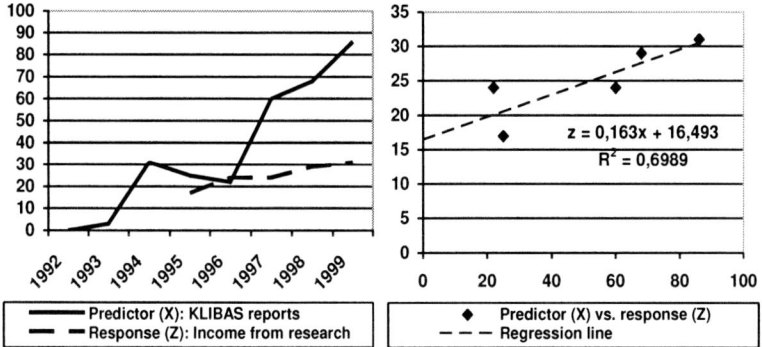

Figure 25: Comparison between ISD documentation and income from commissioned research

The diagram on the left side in the figure shows a steady increase in both annual volume of technical reports and income from commissioned research associated with the publication of KLIMA research reports. The diagram on the right side indicates a strong sample correlation of $R = 0.836$ between technical productivity and income from commissioned research. Unfortunately, the small sample size of $n = 5$ prevents the null hypothesis of population correlation $r = 0$ from being rejected at a 5% level of significance.

As the parameters chosen for testing the impact of BA on TQM are crude in the sense that there may be reasons for increase in commissioned research beyond the improvement of the KLIBAS database making such research more easy to facilitate, the outcome of the RH2 test does, nevertheless, not contradict the assumption that the BA had a significant impact on TQM implementation.

The optimality hypothesis (RH3)

There was no attempt to test RH3 in terms of considering whether the BA in figure 22 was an optimal control algorithm.

4.1.5 Reflection

The way the RH2 hypothesis was tested by a crude choice of parameters in the first cycle of action research was indicative of some of the challenges within that cycle. Although the use of frameworks like ISO 9000 and CMM were explicitly addressed as important and relevant for improving TQM practice and assessing TQM levels (Øgland, 1998), the task of managing the existing network of KLIBAS systems and research programmes proved too demanding to allow the necessary resources for figuring out how alignment with TQM standards could be efficiently accomplished.

This was unfortunate as DNMI was discussing the use of ISO 9000 for managing quality for the whole or parts of the organisation, and aligning KLIBAS with ISO 9000 might thus have made it possible to use the ISO 9001 compliance checklist as an objective function for measuring the impact of the BA for implementing TQM at the Climate Department. Although the BA had worked well as a bottom-up approach for developing TQM, it was missing the important means of addressing the strategic issues that would be necessary for getting more management commitment to TQM.

93

Another important challenge during the first cycle was the difference between the type of "science of the artificial" approach, in the sense of using artificial intelligence and cognitive theory for investigating questions on how to do quality control of KLIBAS processes and products (Øgland, 1999g), and the geophysical theory for investigating problems related to weather and climate the rest of the research community were using. Although the two research domains are related in the sense that an understanding of the dynamics of the geophysical systems is necessary for understanding how to design quality control methods for such systems, the problem of developing and implementing such quality control methods was considered an engineering problem from the perspective of the climate researchers, not a research problem. There was no community of practice of design science research at the Climate Department of DNMI although there were communities of practice of software engineering and climate research.

Not being part of a community of practice for the relevant type of research also resulted in difficulties in getting the right kind of feedback on how to improve and mature the research practice. In retrospect the research on quality control methods could be seen as successful in the sense that the research has been quoted and stimulated further research (e.g. Vejen et al, 2002; Araya & Alfaro, 2008; Araya, 2010; Kvalobs, 2011), but when submitting sample publications and a complete publication list for scientific assessment at the University of Oslo in 1997, the general response was that the research approach would benefit if it could be cultivated as part of a relevant PhD programme.

From the perspective of the Monopoly board in table 19, there was significant progress in the sense that an ideological position based the belief in artificial intelligence was able to buy properties, trade and develop at the expense of those believing in geological data processing by use of human intelligence. Nevertheless, while the machines were ready to take over human labour, there were few people ready to take over the responsibility for controlling and developing the machines. In other words, even though the action researcher was building houses and hotels on different colour series, the Monopoly game never entered the end game stage where the whole of the Climate department would succumb to the belief in systems, artificial intelligence and automation of all activities.

Nevertheless, the generally successful running of the BA narrated in section 4.1.3 can be explained by looking at Monopoly in table 19. The Radiosonde stations were avoided, as table 19 would predict, and when the BA entered the Aanderaa stations and started building houses and hotels this should have also have been avoided if the BA practitioner had reflected more deeply on the Monopoly representation of the actor-network at the time. However, having experience with property development at the light blue Aanderaa series was useful when the opportunity for buying and trading into the lucrative orange and red series of AWS and SYNOP arrived.

The experience with the expensive green and dark blue series of HIRLAM data and Climate stations were somewhat similar to that of the cheap purple and light blue series, as the Monopoly model predicted. The narrative tells a story of how getting involved in HIRLAM data would be strategically useful for expanding the TQM actor-network beyond the bounds of the Climate Department, but due to the way the HIRLAM was placed just behind "Go to Jail" in table 19 indicated that this would be a high hanging fruit that would strategically unwise. The same was the case with the Climate Stations, the core process of the Climate Department, because the Climate routine was too complex, involved too many people and did not interact with the smaller routines.

From the viewpoint of a Monopoly player basing his ideology on artificial intelligence and cognitive psychology, the brown, orange, red and yellow series of precipitation stations (especially the automated ones) and data from AWS, SYNOP and METAR that were arriving electronically with hardly any quality assurance and no applications beyond the ability to extract data from the Oracle databases in their raw format, were the most attractive properties to get control over. The "science of the artificial" ideological version of TQM was instantly fertile in this environment where it was possible to interact with the Instruments Department that had a similar technical rather than geophysical understanding of data processing.

Running round and round the Monopoly board, landing on Free Parking to write research reports, landing on GO to write status reports, and otherwise serving others when landing on properties not owned or getting help from others when they landed on properties own by the researcher would explain the success of the BA despite the lack of sufficiently long series of relevant data for making the statistical argument that was aimed at in section 4.1.4.

4.2 Second cycle – November 1999 to January 2005

The second cycle describes further testing the BA hypothesis within the IT function of the Norwegian Tax Administration. Main insights from this cycle are more fully described in *paper 1*, *paper 2*, *paper 3* and *paper 5*. The focus in *paper 4* and *paper 6* is on events and insights from the second cycle that also carry over into the third cycle. The walk-through of the CPM provides context for understanding the papers from the viewpoint of the Monopoly-based interpretation of information infrastructure dynamics.

4.2.1 Diagnosis

In *paper 1* the most characteristic symptoms of the IT function of NTAX are presented. The Hamlet narrative used in that paper provides a diagnosis that also includes the action researcher and the relationship between the organisation and the action researcher as a viewpoint for understanding the TQM mechanism design game. Part of the message in that paper is the need for the action researcher to make game models for understanding the politics of the environment and being able to learn from failed interventions. The paper draws attention to drama theory as a problem structuring method that can be used for analysing a situation with the aim of developing more mathematically precise models. The idea of how drama theory can be used is illustrated through the Hamlet narrative which is efficient for focusing on issues like politics, corruption and survival, aspects that are addressed in games studied within the branch of game theory known as evolutionary game theory.

The Monopoly game can be studied from the viewpoint of evolutionary game theory. Just like Hamlet, the Monopoly narrative is a zero-sum conflict filled with questionable motives, politics through trading, and the quest for ultimate survival with all but one player going bankrupt in the end. The Monopoly board for the TQM information infrastructure dynamics of the IT function at NTAX is represented in table 20 by including the business processes listed in chapter 3.6.2 as colour series and the five steps in the NTAX software life cycle development model (figure 20) as the five properties within each colour series.

Similar to how the diagnosis was conducted through use of the Monopoly model in the DNMI case, the colour series have also in the NTAX case been arranged around the board in manner of increasing importance and complexity.

95

The cheapest properties are within the purple FTS ("felles testsystemer") series just after passing GO. In regular Monopoly the throwing of the dice makes it unlikely to land on properties in this series. At NTAX the FTS was an administrative system developed for the purpose of coordinating the test activities for all the other systems (business processes) represented around the table. Having control over the FTS would be a way of getting access to important aspects of all the other colour series and could have been an important TQM strategy, but the system was underdeveloped, implemented in a different manner than specified and run by people who had no authority over the IT function as a whole. Although it would perhaps not have been all that difficult to take over these properties by use of quality audits, the expected payoff would be small compared with other colour series.

JAIL (or "just visiting")	LEP						FOS					Free Parking
DSB												PSA
				NTAX Monopoly								
FTS												LFP
Collect $200 in salary as you pass GO	ALTINN					AR						Go to Jail

Table 20: A Monopoly representation of the NTAX information infrastructure

The light blue DSB ("datastøttet selvangivelsesbehandling") was more important from a strategic perspective. The purpose of the process was to maintain the software used at the local tax offices to assist the control of annual self-declaration taxes. The quality standards and routines used all over the table had been developed by the group maintaining this business process, so auditing here would result in low hanging fruit in the sense that few formal errors were expected to be found, but as the DSB system itself did not interact with the taxpayers themselves, the system would have less impact for installing TQM in the organisation as a whole than those of other colour series.

Turning clockwise around the Monopoly board, the business processes have been arranged in a manner of increasing importance and complexity. The green and dark blue series represent systems in the process of being developed, AR ("aksjonærregister") being the national stockholder register and ALTINN being a shared internet portal for different governmental institutions, going through the initial cycle in the NTAX software lifecycle model in figure 20. From a quality management perspective the sooner errors are detected and corrected, the less costly the error detection and correction will be at later stages. However, from a TQM implementation perspective development projects are notoriously difficult. Development is often done in a climate where quality has to compete with other project management factors such as cost and time, and there is limited use for TQM methods like SPC which come into play when processes start repeating themselves. Getting involved in QA for project management would be resource demanding in terms of making it difficult to also have enough resources for trading and developing other colour series, and although it would be of extreme importance for NTAX to control project development, the process would be more likely to focus on fire fighting than research and learning.

The business processes represented by the brown, orange, red and yellow series, however, were all mature processes that were assumed to be following quality management practice according to NTAX rules and regulations. All of these business processes were important for NTAX. They all interacted with the tax payer and they were complex systems that depended on competent use of software engineering and management involvement. Both the department of finance (FIN) and the national auditor general (AG) were important shareholders.

In terms of understanding the different cultural or ideological positions that define the players in the Monopoly game, *paper 3* explains how the NTAX culture could be understood both from the viewpoint of Brunsson's (1989) network-sociological perspective of TQM-related "organisational hypocrisy" and Flood's (1993) class-oriented sociological perspective of TQM as strategy for liberation from oppression. As pointed out in the paper, the two sociological perspectives can be united through the systems perspective known as critical systems theory (CST).

Although hypocrisy and political liberation are important concepts for understanding the logic of the Monopoly representation of the information infrastructure dynamics, the diagnosis used in *paper 3* was coloured by the fact that the paper was written as a reflection on the TQM implementation process in progress rather than an initial impression of what was going on at NTAX during the planning phase. When entering the IT function of NTAX in 1999, "hypocrisy" did not seem like an obvious term to use for characterizing how the strategic and operational levels of the organization were clearly disconnected, as using such a word would be a malevolent characterization. The general impression, at this early stage, was that there were two cultures at play. One group of people enjoyed writing strategies, mission statements and going to meetings and conferences with people of similar kind. Another group of people found enjoyment in practical work, such as computer programming or project management, and fraternized with people who shared such interests. As long as no serious problems occurred and everybody was happy, this decoupling did not seem to bother people in any serious way. In retrospect, however, the way the term "organisational hypocrisy" is used in a non-malevolent sense by Brunsson (1989) would be a good way of describing the symptoms that were obvious at the very beginning and became even more obvious over time when getting to know the NTAX culture.

With a more clinical understanding of the NTAX culture, as represented by *paper 3*, the Monopoly model could be used for representing the TQM information infrastructure dynamics at NTAX as a zero-sum two-player game between "fake TQM" and "real TQM". The action researcher, of course, would be playing on the "real TQM" team with the aim of implementing TQM by bankrupting the "fake TQM" player.

As the action researcher had just entered NTAX and was consequently becoming more and more a part of the NTAX culture himself, it has in retrospect been useful to see that Gartner Group found similar symptoms and made a similar diagnosis in their investigating the IT function.

"There is today poor compliance between the strategic, tactical and operational levels of the organization. [NTAX] carries out strategy processes, but the strategies are not deployed into concrete tactical and operational decisions. This means that the organization is managed according to other factors like habits, personal preferences and technical details." (Gartner, 2010, p. 5)

"The annual budget process constitutes the essential part of the prioritization process. From the budget a certain amount is allocated to projects, and each service is allocated a certain budget amount to be used for development. Budgets are based on last year's budget and not on the strategy. Many public organizations formulate strategies that have limited impact on tactical and operational decisions. The observation, as we observe it at NTAX, is consequently not atypical of public organizations." (Gartner, 2010, p. 5-6)

The business logic of the annual budgets described here can be interpreted as a control game where it is not necessarily an advantage for NTAX to improve processes in terms of cost efficiency as this can lead to budget cuts. On the contrary, it may be more beneficiary for the organisation to maintain a high level of complexity that can be managed in a flexible manner in order to make sure that budget allocations stay stable, and it is a business logic that applies to all sections, groups and departments within the organisation. The situation illustrates how complex systems, political tensions and organisational hypocrisy can be linked together.

4.2.2 Action planning

The general idea was to implement the BA in a similar way as it had been done at DNMI by using a system similar to what was presented in figure 22. Unlike the DNMI case, however, the action researcher did not have direct access to the programming facilities, so rather than developing a system of computerised data collection and analysis based on an automated exchange of emails, what had been achieved automatically now had to be carried out manually through audits and inspections (***paper 5***).

However, some aspects of the DNMI practice were easy to duplicate, such as the establishment of a monthly quality report. At DNMI much of the content of such reports were automatically generated as software had been developed specifically for the purpose of data collection, analysis and presentation through graphs and tables. At NTAX this had to be done by hand, which made the monthly report more costly to update and maintain. Ideas like defining audit objects based on Pareto analysis could still be done, but now the process of collecting, analysing and presenting data had to be done through frameworks like the Balanced Scorecard, CAF or EFQM. Table 21 is a summarised version of what was presented in some of the first SKD assessment reports, and by comparing the numerical assessment scores of each of the nine categories with the maximum score shown in figure 19, it was possible to produce a Pareto analysis based on the individual scoring.

Unlike the case at DNMI, however, where this kind of Pareto analysis was a vital key for making the decision process more or less completely automated, the EFQM categories were only used as a reference when making decisions at NTAX. First of all it required too much work to make proper assessments, so each category was based on sample audits and subjective estimations. Secondly it seemed like a poor idea to spend one year on, say, "processes" and the next on "people results". All these categories had to be addressed indirectly all the time. As a consequence of this, the implementation of the BA became much more subjective in terms of ongoing decision making than what had been the case at DNMI.

The approach had to rely more on experience and intuition, using the Monopoly board game as an overall map of what kind of projects that might be good to get involved in and which ones to avoid.

EFQM assessment category	Assessment results
1. Leadership	Autocratic leadership at the top, which may not be unusual in a bureaucratic organisation.
2. Strategy	First IT strategy was published in 1988. Second strategy was published in 1998 with explicit mention of TQM as a quality management strategy for the IT function. More detailed aspects of quality management were regulated through the document describing IT security systems, policies and standards (SPS) from 1996.
3. People	A HR unit within the IT department was established around 1997-98.
4. Partnerships and resources	Some functions were outsourced. Financial resources from the ministry of finance (FIN) seldom represented a major problem as managing the tax processes are of national importance.
5. Processes	A quality management system (QMS) inspired by the ISO 9001 standards had just been established. The QMS was to a large degree based on a more systematic way of working that had been introduced with the FLID information systems development project (1992-97).
6. Customer results	There were few measurements or investigations concerning how the IT function was viewed by the rest of the organisation. In cases where the whole business process was digitalised, such as producing tax forms, the external customer (tax payers) seemed to be satisfied with how the tax system was being modernised.
7. People results	No significant problems with turnover or sickness.
8. Society results	No significant problems related to environmental and ethical standards.
9. Key results	At Christmas time a representative of FIN visited NTAX to give a public talk about the budget. No indication of FIN not being satisfied.

Table 21: Assessing the organisation through the use of the EFQM categories

Although not being fully aware of the CST literature at the time of setting up the initial action plan, a book on quality management for information systems development with perspectives similar to that of CST (Bang et al., 1991) was an important source of inspiration during the period 1999-2000. Although the focus of the book was practical rather than political, it addressed issues of power, structure and how to make use of action research. As such it was helpful for framing the problematic situation as having to do with technical complexity and organizational politics, and although it would take a few years before the language of CST was used as part of the study, the problem context was identified as highly complex and highly political. In January 2004, as the ideas of CST-driven TQM was introduced to the study by reading Flood (1993), it was noticed that the problem context that had identified within the IT function of NTAX could be labelled "complex-coercive" within the SOSM in figure 14 and individual process improvement projects could be thought of as running cycles through the TSI model in figure 13 with each iteration hopefully reframing the problem and changing solution strategies based on the logic of the SOSM.

Before the discovery of TSI, however, the understanding of technical and political complexity was based upon TQM theory from the perspective of complex adaptive systems (CAS) (e.g. Kelly, 1994; Dooley et al., 1995; Dooley, 1997) and the prior experience in applying the CAS approach at DNMI from 1992 to 1999 (Øgland, 2000; Vejen et al, 2002). The treatment used for handling the complex-coercive situation at NTAX, before applying TSI for reflecting upon how problem definitions change, consisted of using a Genetic Algorithm (GA) as a basic procedure for implementing TQM (Holland, 1995; Øgland, 2009b). As mentioned in section 2.4.2, the GA is a search heuristic that mimics the process of natural evolution. It consists of managing a population of search strategies that are repeatedly tested against the problem. Components from the most successful strategies are used as building blocks for a new generation of strategies while the less successful are forgotten. The way this was applied to TQM was by running several improvement projects at the same time, expecting many of them to fail, but reusing components of the more successful projects as a continually larger part of the IT function was gradually managed to get under control.

The treatment was in other words a very simple approach. Rather than playing along with the organisational hypocrisy of inventing policies, strategies and standards, the idea was to use every opportunity as it unfolded for auditing and checking whether some small part of the large and complex quality management system was working according to what was written in the NTAX standards and regulations. Further details about similarities and differences between the action planning at DNMI and NTAX, how the designed was based on CAS ideas and what can be learned from how these designs succeeded and failed are discussed in *paper 5*.

4.2.3 Intervention

The Norwegian Tax Authorities (NTAX) is considered one of the most modern parts of the Norwegian administration. It consists of the Directorate of Taxes and local tax offices employing a total of about 6000 people. At the time when the major part of the research was conducted, the IT department consisted of about 600 people (500 in Oslo and 100 in Grimstad) and was part of the Directorate of Taxes. At the Directorate of Taxes the term 'IT function' has been used to refer to all aspects of NTAX that can be seen as a part of how the computerized information systems are being developed, used, maintained and improved. Consequently, this is a somewhat loose term that tended to be interpreted differently depending on situation and context. In this study, however, it refers to the IT department and the "system owners" outside the IT department responsible for documenting and managing the software development processes unless otherwise specified. The quality management system (QMS) was designed to help the IS owners control and improve IS processes, and the task of the action researcher as head of the quality management group (situated within the IT department) was to make sure that the QMS was implemented according to internally defined and accepted NTAX strategies, policies and standards.

In the IT strategy of 1998 it was stated that the IT function should be managed according to the principles of TQM. As a consequence of this, many software process improvement (SPI) initiatives were conducted, including Capability Maturity Model (CMM) assessments, ISO 15504/SPICE assessments, use of ITIL standards, use of CobiT audit standards, developments of strategies, policies and standards for quality management, and attempts to redesign the existing QMS to fit with the requirements of ISO 9001:2000. The quality organization consisted of the quality management group (housing between three to five people) and external experts and consultants doing independent audits and assessments. The internal audit (IA) group and the national auditor general (AG) also played important roles in making sure that quality assurance and internal control functioned according to what was acceptable by the ministry of finance (FIN). The quality function used the EFQM model as an overall assessment tool between 1999 and 2005 with monthly updates based on the results of individual audits and controls.

The consequences of looking at the BA intervention from this broad perspective is analysed in more detail in *paper 1*. An issue that is problemised in that paper is the role of the type of standards mentioned above. From a TQM implementation perspective standards like CMM function like a translation of managerial power and commitment into documents and procedures that may be used for creating regulations and incentives for motivating software engineers and other IT personnel to behave in ways that fit with the TQM ideology.

Game opening

As expected from the Monopoly model, game opening started with random events in the sense of the action researcher trying to buy properties whenever the dice made him land on something that provided an opportunity for initiating a quality control and process improvement project. After a sequence of unlucky throws, the researcher landed on the implementation property within the red PSA ("preutfylt selvangivelse") series. Lack of compliance with COBOL programming standards had caused a severe problem as one of the key programmers died, leaving a legacy of spaghetti software behind him than another programmer desperately had to sort out in order to make the partially completed self-declaration tax forms be sent to the tax payers on time with correct information. The situation was close to disaster and the whole organisation took notice. As explained in deeper detail elsewhere (Øgland, 2006b), the combination of events, existing quality standards and routines and the personality and characteristics of the people involved made it natural to see the COBOL programming practice as the installed base for quality management that should be cultivated and expanded through the use of the BA. In *paper 4* and *paper 6* there are further comments about the COBOL process, but this story will be explained in more detail in the context of narrating the third action research cycle in section 4.3.

Although the COBOL programming is an important task in COBOL-oriented systems developing, as failure in the COBOL programming can have severe consequence for the system as a whole, implementation is only one of the properties in a NTAX Monopoly colour series. The next random event that helped pushing the game forward was the conclusion of the NTAX WebPsa project. In 2002 NTAX launched a solution where tax payers could log onto the internet to read their annual tax self-declaration, correct errors, fill in missing data, and return it to the local tax office at the click of a button. The WebPsa solution was part of this system, and due to the importance of preventing failure, at the request of the project manager the action researcher was asked to verify as much as possible so that the solution would get the necessary green light signature from NTAX management to be ready for production on time. In *paper 2* the green light signature is characterised as similar to the "power pellets" in the Pac-Man video game in the sense that it can for a short period change the nature of the TQM implementation game from the quality auditor being a general nuisance to suddenly becoming an important political factor.

The involvement with the WebPSA project resulted in two reports, one report summarising audits for launching the WebPSA solution and one report for supporting the greenlightning of the annual production start of the general PSA where the WebPSA was only a part (SKD 2002-26 and SKD 2002-27 in table 15). In the development of both reports, audits were conducted as far as possible to meet with the quality control structures and procedures shown in figure 20. Next year the procedure was repeated. Reports were written for PSA and WebPsa, and by taking advantage of what had been done the previous year, the reports grew in thickness and quality. In the case of WebPSA, only two reports were written as the project was completed and maintenance became part of the PSA process, but the PSA process continued to be monitored and as part of the annual greenlightning process throughout the action cycle.

Middlegame

In Monopoly the middlegame starts the moment one of the players manages to create the first monopoly (Axelrod, 2002, p. 178). Although it is unclear how many if any monopolies the "fake TQM" player had managed to create over time, getting involved with the PSA routine created a first monopoly for the action researcher. Further random events made him try to create a light blue monopoly with the DSB process, by being asked by the head of the IT department to evaluate the process for the purpose of finding out whether it was properly documented. As explained in *paper 1*, there were reasons for NTAX wanting to have a look at this process that the action researcher did not fully understand at the time, and without a proper greenlightning procedure it turned out difficult to maintain and develop the DSB monopoly. Contact was maintained with the DSB group, but the costs of involving with the group were larger than the benefits.

The orange FOS ("sentral forskuddsutskriving") series on the Monopoly board was a highly attractive series. The FOS process was responsible for predicting next years tax percentage for individual tax payers so that the government can draw the right amount of advance tax with each pay check and then later handle the surplus or deficit when the correct taxes are calculated by the PSA routine. Already having bought the implementation property through the involvement in the COBOL programming process, it would be interesting whether it would be possible to trade the other properties in order to develop a full monopoly. As with most attempts to get involved in activities at NTAX, several rounds of negotiations had to be carried out, but eventually properties were traded and the action researcher could start property development by carrying out audits and controls that would result in increased compliance with existing quality management routines and development of new standards and procedures. The story of the FOS is highlighted in *paper 3* as it illustrates some of the fundamental challenges regarding how people inside the system perceive their own quality management system. As told in the paper, the FOS case illustrates the "organisational hypocrisy" where not only the individuals inside the system believe they comply with TQM when they are not, but when this belief also seems to be shared with management, internal audit, national audit and so on. A whole network of make-believe TQM becomes visible, and the network does not like being confronted with the facts of non-compliance.

Having found the "power pellet" in the greenlight signatures for the large annual production systems, further attempts at building monopolies by acquiring different colour series around the Monopoly board were done, as shown in the list of business process improvement reports in table 15. Some attempts at acquiring monopolies were successful, such as LFP and LEP, while others, like ALTINN and AR were not.

Endgame

Implementing TQM by the method of genetic algorithms worked quite well from 1999 to 2005. Each year resulted in a larger output of quality control reports, involvement in projects, enlargement of the quality management group, more visible control and improvement along all directions with the IT function. The "rich getting richer" positive feedback dynamics of Monopoly game play were paying off. By the end of this period, however, the action researcher made some political mistakes, and the QMS collapsed. Despite the fact that the researcher had been deliberately following a method designed for dealing with complex-coercive environments, the way of implementing this method ultimately lead to failure. In *paper 6* the endgame is explained in more detail by focusing on what kind of mistakes were done and what happened. In *paper 1* the endgame is compared with the fifth act of Hamlet, suggesting that the outcome could have been predicted from the events mentioned in the first act and the nature of drama. Unlike a conventional game of Monopoly when players start on equal terms with $1,500 each, the first act of the drama was more like the Italian rules of

Monopoly were money and properties are unevenly distributed before the game play is ready to commence (Albertarelli, 2000).

4.2.4 Evaluation

In comparison with the DNMI cycle, it was easier to evaluate the effect of the BA at NTAX because there was a more obvious focus on obtaining a reliable assessment framework that could be used for measuring continual improvement of the organisation as a whole. As pointed out in *paper 1*, however, this search for a framework was not without problems, even though it was gradually realised that the EFQM assessment model would be a highly useful model as it was also being used by tax administrations in Denmark, Sweden and the UK.

Unfortunately, the EFQM model was not a simple model to use. As it is supposed to provide an assessment of the organisation as a whole, it requires the collection and analysis of all types of data, and it generally required far more resources than were possible to put into it at NTAX. Resources for EFQM assessment had to be constrained by the amount of resources spent focusing on analysing a few select processes such as PSA, FOS, LFP and LEP at a deep level while also "building houses and hotels" through the process of doing CobiT audits and other task oriented control and improvement (seven first rows in table 15). Nevertheless, all data collected over a year were used for recalculating the EFQM score for the IT function of NTAX, and the EFQM score was also adjusted on a monthly basis as soon as results from ongoing audits and controls could be used. Results were published in the monthly status reports. The resulting time series is shown in the graph of the left side of figure 26. The SPC chart on the right side shows the EFQM increments in terms of how much the annual EFQM average changed from one year to another.

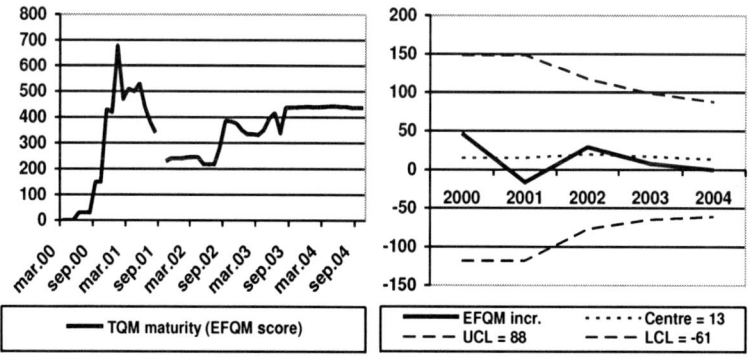

Figure 26: Time series of EFQM scores and annual average of EFQM increments

The reason for the gap in the time series between July 2001 and October 2001 on the left side in figure 26 is because the initial idea was to use the Balanced Scorecard (BSC) as a TQM maturity indicator, but these early measurements were later translated into EFQM scores as the EFQM assessment model became the standard reference from October 2001 and onwards.

The diagram on the right side of figure 26 shows the initial steps in establishing a SPC diagram for testing whether the TQM improvement rate is in a state of statistical control. The SPC was carried out on an annual basis using subgroups of twelve months. Process centre and control limits have been updated through the use of accumulated data, and as the diagram seems to indicate that they are stabilising, this might indicate that they could be frozen to be used as control values for further use of the SPC chart assuming that an average EFQM increase of 13 score units with upper and lower control limits as indicated in the diagram would predict the behaviour of the process for the next 5-10 years or so.

The stability hypothesis (RH1)

EFQM measurements were also used for controlling and improving the way the BA was implemented. This was done by the process of annual EFQM assessments of the quality function. In figure 27 the BA maturity (EFQM score) is plotted against the organisational TQM maturity (EFQM score from figure 26), using annual averages of the organizational EFQM scores for the purpose of comparison. In the presentation of EFQM increments in the annual BA assessment, on the right hand side of figure 27, control limits are updated by use of accumulated data until the EFQM increments appear to become sufficiently stable.

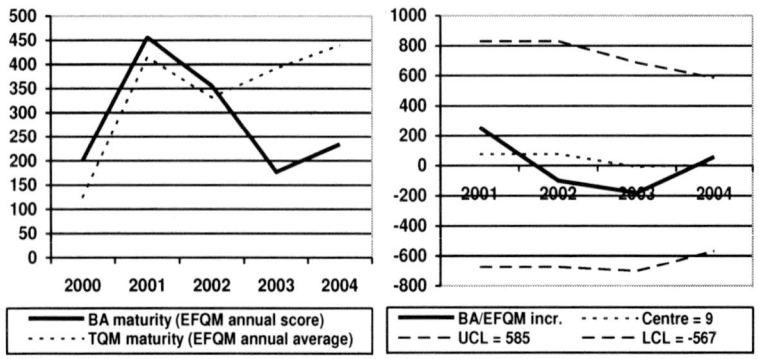

Figure 27: EFQM assessments of BA and EFQM increments for BA

As mentioned when discussing the stability hypothesis (RH1) in the DNMI case, a way of looking at the BA stability without taking the EFQM framework into consideration would be to see how many improvement projects the TQM programme is able to manage on an annual basis. As will be discussed further in chapter 5, at NTAX the TQM programme quickly reached a level of stability were it was able to manage between 5 and 19 improvement projects each year. However, the SPC in figure 27 can also be interpreted as a comment on BA stability in the sense that the maturity of the BA is expected to increase in a predictable manner from year to year without too much variation. With only four measurements it is not a very reliable indicator, but at least it gives no reason to believe the process being out of control

The impact hypothesis (RH2)

The assumption in the second supplementary research hypothesis (RH2) was that improved control on how the BA was implemented would impact the outcome of the BA. In figure 28 EFQM assessments were used both as predictor variables (BA maturity) and response variables (organisational TQM maturity).

From the diagram on the right side, it can be seen that the sample correlation coefficient R is 0.8040. However, due to the small sample size it is not possible to reject the null hypothesis of $r = 0$ and $R \neq 0$ at a 5% level of significance.

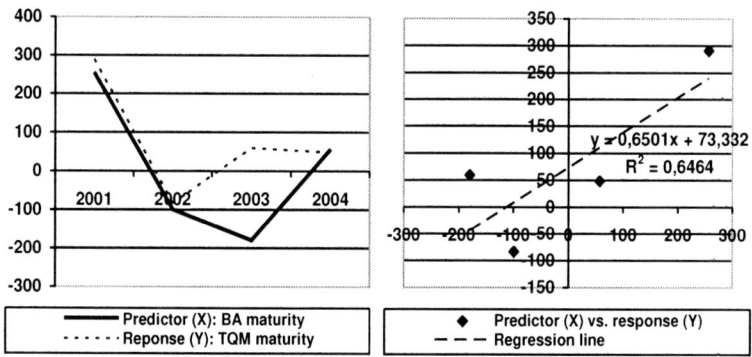

Figure 28: Visual comparison and correlation plot for BA maturity and TQM maturity

Regardless of what might have been the outcome of the statistical analysis, the poor quality of both the predictor data and response data would cause concerns as to whether the results could be trusted. The relevance of the plots in the figures 26, 27 and 28 is that the data reflect the way the action research was planned, and had it not collapsed by the end of this cycle, it seems reasonable to believe that the quality of predictor data, response data and the correlation results would improve with further iterations.

The optimality hypothesis (RH3)

In order to evaluate optimality hypothesis (RH3), it is necessary to estimate the expected time it would take to implement TQM by use of BA. Assuming that the time series of EFQM scores will follow the pattern of a S-shaped logistic curve

$$x(t) = 1000/(1 + be^{-at})$$

with slow growth in the beginning, then a middle period of great improvements, and a final period where the process slows down as it reaches ultimate maturity, the organisational TQM maturity measurements have been transformed by a reverse logistic equation

$$y(t) = \ln(1000/x(t) - 1)$$

on the right side of figure 29. Using a linear regression line to find the optimal fit with the transformed data then produces the logistic curve presented on the right side of the figure.

The logistic regression curve on the right side of the figure was created by reversing the transformation of data on the left side of the figure. The regression line can then be algebraically represented as

$$x(t) = 1000/(1 + 5.67e^{-0.3328t}).$$

The logistic curve is plotted from 1990, ten years before the TQM implementation started in 2000 until the regression curve predicts the top level of excellence has been achieved in 2025 as the predicted EFQM exceeds the value of 999. In other words, if the implementation process had not broken down, the model predicts that the consequence of applying BA the TQM implementation process would have taken 25 years.

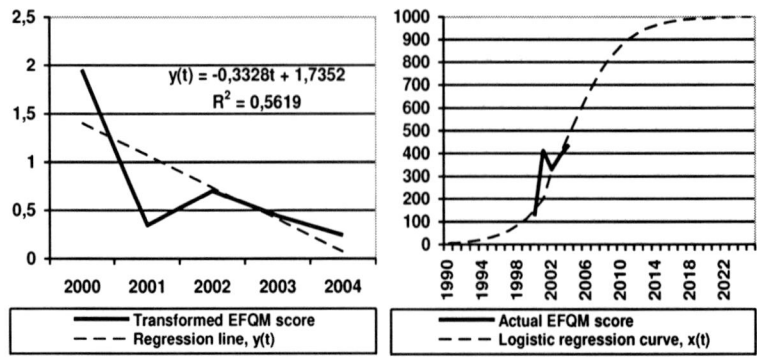

Figure 29: Logistic regression for estimating period of time for NTAX to reach TQM excellence

4.2.5 Reflection

Despite the fact that the BA process went out of control in the sense of being terminated by the process owners, during the period of its run there were no clear indications of it being out of statistical control. It was statistically predictable in the sense of being able to manage an average of 12 improvement projects each year, and the maturity of the way the BA was implemented in the Quality Department was continually improving at a rate of nine EFQM units per year. Although the measurements are not capable of producing results of high statistical reliability and validity, they are supported by the way the process had been designed to be stable by use of the GA framework (section 2.4.2) and how the action researcher felt confident in the process being stable. The BA process used a couple of years in going through the initial steps of the BA to identify a workable installed base and develop an initial control algorithm, but then the output level rose quickly to a sustainable capability level. There seems to be no reason to doubt the stability hypothesis (RH1).

The impact hypothesis (RH2) is more problematic. There are EFQM measurements supporting the idea that there was a positive correlation between the growth in BA maturity and growth in organisational TQM maturity, but the data quality is poor and the statistical analysis is not significant at the 5% level. Nevertheless, there is nothing in the data that suggests that the BA had no impact or a negative impact on TQM maturity. On the contrary, the action research treatment, as narrated in section 4.2.4, went along according to the predictions inherent in the Monopoly model used for diagnosing the TQM information infrastructure dynamics. The properties and colour series identified as high value and low value during the diagnosis generally turned out to be of similar high and low value when dealing with them during treatment. As the TQM implementation ended in failure, the Monopoly model was clearly not a perfect model for understanding the TQM information infrastructure at NTAX, but at the level the Monopoly model has been used so far there is nothing in the results that contradict the Monopoly theory. Monopoly is a game of chance and skill, winning consistently also requires a certain element of luck. However, as will be pointed out in the general analysis and discussion (chapter 5), the more detailed analysis of the game provided by the individually published papers relate much of the failure to aspects of "property development", having more to do with the consequences of how interaction with various groups were carried out than specifically which groups they were and which processes and tasks they were related to.

The failure could to a large extent be explained by inadequate theory-in-use for understanding the way certain political games were a part of organisational culture. At DNMI it was feasible to construct a BA based on the engineering logic of complex adaptive systems (CAS), handling complexity caused by social distrust in the same manner as technological complexity, but when trying to implement the BA in a large bureaucracy it was not sufficient to handle issues in an improvisational manner by spreading risk and doing everything in small steps. It was also necessary to understand the nature of decision making in an environment of several decision makers and conflicting goals.

The idea of using game theory for understanding the complex behaviour of hired quality auditors vis-à-vis the quality department was introduced in one of the NTAX reports (Øgland, 2004), but the theory was never used as a social theory for understanding and predicting behaviour in NTAX as a whole. Acknowledging the need for a better understanding of the political aspects of the organisation, how to use the critical theory in the style of Habermans and Foucault was investigated in 2004 by studying Flood (1993) on how to implement TQM through the use of TSI, and reading some texts by Derrida and Foucault, but there was never sufficient capacity available for a critically digesting and figuring out how TSI could be integrated with how the BA was being executed. In the language of Schön (1983), political challenges where handled intuitively as reflection-in-action rather than scientifically by a process of reflection-on-action.

Concerning the optimality hypothesis (RH3), the way the BA was implemented at NTAX was obviously far from optimal as the TQM implementation process failed. Nevertheless, the approach was more sophisticated than it had been during the DNMI period, despite the differences in outcome. The way the BA implementation improved at NTAX in comparison to DNMI consisted of at least two important issues. Firstly, using the EFQM assessment model for measuring the maturity of both the BA implementation and the organisational TQM level made it possible to develop testable design hypotheses for the purpose of improving the BA implementation. Of course there was an ongoing learning by trial and error also at DNMI, perhaps even more so than at NTAX because a technical environment gave a much more obvious response when something was not working, but because of the "niceness" and lack of explicit political conflicts at DNMI made it less obvious to frame control designs through the language of game theory. The use of game theory is the second important learning that differentiates the NTAX implementation of the BA from the DNMI implementation.

When it comes to the predictions in section 4.2.4 about how long period of time one should expect for reaching the TQM level of excellence when applying the BA approach, the result is pure speculation. The data quality is poor and the method of prediction is highly unreliable as small changes in the initial conditions should result in large changes in the outcome. Nevertheless, for the practitioner it is essential to make theoretical predictions, in the style of what the logistic regression does, because the difference between theoretical predictions and practical results gives an opportunity to challenge the theory and learn from failure (Deming, 1986). Even though the TQM implementation process at NTAX reached a premature end, the predictions based on the results from the logistic curve are of importance for action research as a benchmark or reference for the evaluation of similar types of TQM implementation studies.

4.3 Third cycle – February 2005 to June 2011

The third cycle describes further testing of the BA hypothesis within the IT function of the Norwegian Tax Administration in the context of collaborating with the University of Oslo to see whether working with internationally leading BA experts will increase the impact on TQM implementation results. Main insights from this cycle are more fully described *paper 4* and *paper 6.* The walk-through of the CPM provides context for understanding the papers from the viewpoint of the Monopoly-based interpretation of information infrastructure dynamics.

4.3.1 Diagnosis

The practical problem motivating the third cycle of action research was how to continue the use of BA for implementing TQM from the perspective of being an outside researcher rather than an inside quality manager. The diagnosis of the challenge of how to implement TQM was essentially the same as in the second cycle in terms of how the Monopoly board was constructed

As the information infrastructure develops, the Monopoly board may have to be adjusted in order to make sure that the Jail attractor fits sufficiently well with the attractor dynamics of the empirical reality. Going from the position of collecting and analysing data as a quality manager to the position of collecting and analysing data as a research scientist could for instance make it more difficult to access data and create change, which would mean that some business processes would be considered more complex and would be in need of being moved clockwise while other systems that were less influenced by the manager/researcher issue would move the other way. However, as the research would be a continuation of working with the people and processes that had been dealt with during the previous cycle, there seemed to be no reason to expect changes in organisational behaviour of the sort that would result in a reconstruction of the Monopoly model.

The basic conflict defining the Monopoly game was still the same. Winning at Monopoly from the viewpoint of the action researcher meant to bankrupt the "fake TQM" players. The "fake TQM" of NTAX was still characterised by parts of the organisation wanting to maintain a façade of doing TQM while in reality there was often little or no connection between what was written down in policies, strategies and standards and what was carried out in real life.

4.3.2 Action planning

Although the outcome of the previous cycle did not change the understanding of the TQM information infrastructure dynamics as represented by the Monopoly game board, there were important lessons to be learnt in terms of how to use the BA for playing the Monopoly game. An important BA tactic for developing Monopoly properties was based on the motivational theory of "what gets measured gets done" (Øgland, 2001). In 2006, while discussing action planning with Aanestad, co-creator of the original BA in table 3, this theory of "what gets measured gets done" was discussed, questioned and ended up being thought of more like a hypothesis than a fact in the context of BA.

As pointed out in section 2.3.4, when trying to explain the logic of the "what gets measured gets done" principle, it is not the measurements themselves that create action but it is the belief among those being measured that there are sanctions and incentives associated with the measurements. In *paper 6* the action plan based on the idea of trying to make the people on the floor believe that measurements matter when the people on the management level do not care is presented and discussed. Of course, this strategy had been used since the very start of the second cycle, but it had not been explicitly formulated in this way before. The idea of "what gets measured gets done" had been assumed as self-evident, at least when the measures are easy to understand and used in efficient feedback loop. In fact, a test had been carried out using a stopwatch for measuring the time of arrival to NTAX meetings for the Project Group of the IT Department (of which the Quality Department was a subgroup). Although there was no intent on using the measurement to anything as feedback to the meeting, it had a striking effect on reducing the average delay of arrival for the group as a whole.

Another important design issue was the integration of TSI with BA described in section 2.3.3. As explained earlier in the chapter, designing problem solving in cycles similar in form and content of TSI were present already with the first cycle (figure 23) and even more so during the whole second cycle when things became more political, but an explicit use of TSI did not occur before January 2004 when starting to read and study CST and TSI theory. In order to improve the BA design it seemed vital to make more explicit use of TSI by systematically addressing SOSM framework.

Bringing the third cycle of action research up to the level of trying to interact with a scholarly community of action researchers and other academics interested in information infrastructure, systems theory and quality management meant that it was no longer possible to play the opening of the Monopoly game in the usual way of buying every property one could land on. What was needed, though, was a handful of strategically chosen properties that could be used for studying the "what gets measured gets done" hypothesis while preparing the next step of acquiring monopolies and erecting houses and hotels for the purpose of reaching and going beyond the level of TQM implementation achieved during the previous cycle.

As the COBOL standardisation process had proved instrumental in the previous BA experiment, it seemed like a good idea to focus on this while forgetting the other processes for a while. As mentioned in *paper 6*, the COBOL process represented a prototype design based on the idea of creating "meaningless" control loops of monitoring and feedback without taking management commitment into consideration. What matters in getting these feedback systems to work is whether the people being monitored believe there is management commitment. Whether there is real management commitment or the workers are only bluffed to believe so does not matter (Harding, 2003). The control loops are meaningless in the same way as properties with houses and hotels are meaningless as long as nobody lands on them. Getting COBOL properties in colour series that get a lot of management attention is consequently a possible strategy for making sure that the "meaningless" monitoring and feedback routines become meaningful as part of greenlight signatures related to important production processes.

The main design idea for the BA is to start by focusing on the COBOL process as the installed base in the initial step, and then gradually advance the actor-network in the five control steps by getting control of business and production processes that make it possible to create monopolies and start property development. With a better utilisation of the "what gets measured gets done" idea it might be possible to win the Monopoly game more easily than was the case with the BA implementation used in the second action research cycle.

As a replacement for the EFQM assessments that stopped by the conclusion of the second cycle, ISO 9004 assessments were used as an alterative representation of the Monopoly money as Det Norske Veritas (DNV) got hired to prepare the IT function to comply with the ISO 9001 standard just after the second cycle completed (*paper 1*). Using ISO 9004 for measuring BA maturity by self-assessment could be of strategic importance in relation to how DNV addressed requirement 8.2.2 "internal audit". By using the 8.2.2 requirements as a basis for the BA it might be possible to position the action research in a way that it would be possible to enrol in the ISO 9001 actor-network and then implement TQM by taking control of this network.

4.3.3 Intervention

The initial instructions of the BA had now been completed. The "simple, cheap, flexible solution" consisted of the quality management used by the COBOL programmers for making sure that COBOL software was gradually conforming to requirements. The users consisted of COBOL programmers, the whole pyramid of managers between the programmers and the head of NTAX, and the network of IS researchers interested in knowledge about TQM, SPI and ISD to be obtained from the COBOL study. The internal audit was also included as an extended part of the network in order to continue the approach based on the "what gets measured gets done" motivational psychology that was part of the SPI design for the COBOL process.

The "small network of users that might benefit significantly from improved communication with each other" consisted partly of the programmers themselves who would benefit from adopting a common standard in order to avoid repetition of hopeless situations from the past where it had been almost impossible for one programmer to understand the software developed by another. The academic SPI network was also considered a small network that might benefit significantly from improved communication if it was possible to frame the COBOL research in a manner which made the findings relevant and interesting for the rest of the network.

The quality control practice itself was extremely simple. Within the COBOL programming environment at NTAX quality control software had been developed for the different users to run checklists for measuring the status of their pool of COBOL programs against the NTAX standards. In the IT strategies of 1998 it was stated that COBOL software should be standardised, but as there were no specific deadlines, all that had to be done was to make small improvements each year which would then make it possible to predict when the software would conform to the standards. The data collection for the action research consisted of monitoring progress and giving feedback to individual programmers or groups of programmers.

Although the COBOL software was critical for the organization as a whole, with the possibility of errors in the COBOL having national consequences, the process of designing the action research around this particular process seemed non-critical in the sense that it had been a relatively unproblematic process during the second cycle of action research. It seemed unlikely that interventions in a process that consisted of making sure programmers were following standards they had democratically developed themselves should cause sufficient political tension for bringing the action research to a halt.

In the case of meeting the BA initial instruction of having motivated users, it was clear that some of the COBOL programmers were motivated in trying to comply with standards while others were not. One of the reasons for choosing the COBOL process had to do with easy access to data because the individual who had been in charge of the project that delivered the COBOL standard and the quality control software remained highly motivated in making the group as a whole confirm to the standard (Øgland, 2006b). However, as experience during the second cycle had shown that not all programmers were equally motivated to follow the standards, the initial TQM actor-network in the COBOL study consisted of those 80% of the population who were motivated.

The case of starting with knowledgeable users was somewhat similar. The standard had been developed as part of a participatory design process, it had been presented and discussed in an open meeting with the NTAX director-general and IT director present, and programmers had been trained in use of the quality control software. Some individual programmers disagreed with the principles of the standards, some were indifferent, and there were new programmers beginning in the organization without being told about the standards and quality control software. However, a rough estimate would be that about 90% of the programmers at the beginning of the third action research cycle had sufficient knowledge about COBOL programming, the COBOL standards and the quality control software to be able to control and improve their own software.

Round 1 – April 2005 to January 2006
The COBOL process survived four iterations of the BA test conducted through the second AR cycle. Each instance of iterating the process was identified by the publication of an evaluation report. In the final evaluation report, published in January 2005, the COBOL problem was analysed through the lens of system dynamics by the way of describing a set of differential equations for modelling the behaviour of stocks and flows of software errors associated with each of the nine systems and how these parameters were linked together in a dynamic system. The research questions were motivated by control theory in the sense of trying to understand the system in terms of how it could be characterised as observable, controllable and stable.

The first iteration of the control loop for the third cycle was done in parallel with the initial instructions of the BA. Before being enrolled in the information systems actor-network at UiO there was an attempt to become enrolled in an actor-network of academic and industrial research related to statistical quality control. From this perspective, the system dynamics models and control theory models that had evolved from the second cycle of action research seemed like an appropriate way of framing the problem to make it interesting. After discussing with academic communities in Trondheim, Bergen and Oslo, a professor of applied statistics at the Department of Mathematics at the University of Oslo indicated that he might be interested in providing PhD supervision.

As a consequence of this, first iteration of the COBOL process within the third action research cycle started on the 20th of April 2005 with the publication of a note to the COBOL community at NTAX motivating the research, explaining the approach and the need for cooperation. The primary idea was to contribute to the understanding and development of the interconnections between statistical process control and dynamical process control (del Castillo, 2002). However, nothing further evolved from this as the professor left for a sabbatical, and there was also a question of whether this kind of strictly theoretical approach would benefit the more pragmatic needs of NTAX, even though the similarly theoretical study of the dip test had proved pragmatically efficient for the action research carried out in the first action research cycle.

As explained in section 4.3.1, the fact that DNV was being engaged for doing a formal ISO 9001:2000 assessment of the IT function, with the purpose of developing a certifiable quality management system, was another factor to take into consideration when deciding how to formulate the COBOL problem. As the ISO 9000 standards and the EFQM model had been used for evaluating both the quality department (stability of BA) and the organization (impact of BA), with results shown in section 4.2.4, the organizational focus on ISO 9001:2000 seemed like good motivation for integrating ISO 9000 as part of the design theory for the COBOL research.

From the viewpoint of TSI, the first iteration of the third cycle was primarily concerned with problem structuration in terms of trying to frame the COBOL standardisation problem in different ways that would match both industrial and academic interests. A turning point happened when getting enrolled into the Information Systems PhD programme at the Informatics Department at the University of Oslo. As a consequence of this, the COBOL evaluation per January 2006, previously consisting of trends and overviews of COBOL error statistics mixed with control theory and behavioural psychology, was rewritten to include sections on actor-network theory (ANT) and complexity theory (Øgland, 2006a, chapter 2.2-2.3) plus ISO 9000 theory (ibid, chapter 2.4-2.8) in order to see whether the COBOL research could be integrated with the research interests of the ISD researchers at UiO and aligned with the ISO 9000 strategies of NTAX.

Table 22 gives a summary of how the problem formulation evolved during the first BA control iteration of the third AR cycle. The outcome of the COBOL study during the second cycle was an attempt to understand the socio-technical dynamics of COBOL standardisation as a system of nine differential equations describing the stocks and flows of how each software package deviated from the programming standard (complex-unitary). The coefficients in the matrix describing the relationship between the equations were empirically estimated by use of curve fitting methods. By disregarding the effect of internal benchmarking, short term trends were predicted by exponential regression curves. As the focus of the research was on producing solutions that would include the effect of feedback by use of benchmarking, no analytical or numerical solution was yet found.

SOSM problem contexts	Solve problem (unitary)	Formulate problem (plural)	Evaluate solution (coercive)
Well-posed problem (simple)	5. ISO 9000 theory	4. "What gets measured gets done" model	
Ill-posed problem (complex)	1. Dynamic systems and control theory	3. Biological metaphor and brain metaphor	2. Poor fit with the interests of the academic research network

Table 22: Development of problem formulation during first turn around the Monopoly board

While this formulation of the problem might have been useful when trying to enrol in an actor-network of scientists interested in statistical quality control and dynamical process control, it matched less well with ISD research (complex-coercive). As a result of this, it seemed better to replace engineering theories with social theories. As mentioned by Flood (1993), the biological metaphor and brain metaphor are supposed to capture the ideological context of system dynamics and control theory. These two metaphors were consequently used in the action research evaluation report with ANT and complexity theory fitting with the biological metaphor and the cybernetics of ISO 9000 fitting with the brain metaphor (complex-plural).

The operational model used for studying the effects of how to improve audit strategies in an environment of socio-political complexity was based on the principle "what gets measured gets done" (simple-plural). The principle had been presented to NTAX through article in the NTAX magazine (Øgland, 2001) as background theory and a basic belief motivating the research conducted during the second cycle. In the preface for the first internal action research publication of the third AR cycle, the management theory behind the principle "what gets measured gets done" became a major aspect for motivating the research (Øgland, 2006a, p. ii).

As shown in the fifth and final step in the evolution of the problem formulation in table 22 (simple-unitary), what was originally an ill-posed problem of differential equations ended up as a well-posed problem about the use of ISO 9001:2000 self-assessments for improving audit strategies for helping the COBOL community in their quest for making software comply with democratically developed programming standards.

Round 2 – January 2006 to May 2007

On the 14th of February 2006 a letter to the COBOL community was written with the purpose of discussing a formal strategy for collecting data by way of receiving documents containing error statistics and conducting interviews. The strategy was formulated both verbally and with a flowchart, and the letter explained how the data collection and feedback process was designed to be predictable, controllable and certifiable as part of the overall ISO 9000 strategy at NTAX. Part of the learning from the second cycle of action research was to make sure the third cycle was designed in a manner which would make it difficult for the organization to terminate the research even though they would not be happy with the findings.

As DNV was working on how to improve the quality management system for the IT function at NTAX for the purpose of certifying it against the ISO 9001:2000 standard, designing the COBOL action research as part of this quality management system could be a way of not only preventing NTAX from destroying the action research in the future but also making sure that the research had impact on the organisational QMS.

With the research design looking reasonable from a practical point of view, the next challenge was how to align with academic interests. The approach for doing this was by writing a paper about the use of ISO 9001 for developing theory for the SWEBOK as a way of "improving the software improvement process as part of doing action research" and submitting it to the European Conference for Information Systems research (ECIS). The paper was rejected, however, assumingly because it was more suited for a SPI conference than an IS conference.

Having attended an IS workshop seminar at UiO in September 2005 that included a presentation of John Law's ANT story about Portuguese travellers, the initial challenge was to see whether the practical problems of TQM implementation at NTAX could contribute within the debates dominating IS journals and conferences. The final outcome of the "what gets measured gets done" situation as simple-unitary in table 22 was no longer valid. Further analysis and reformulation of the mess had to be done, as will be illustrated in table 23.

The TSI creativity process was used for turning Latour's (1988) use of Tolstoy's account of the Napoleon's battles in "War and peace" as a metaphor about the progress of science into a game model based on the logic of the ISO 9000 standards. The general idea was to define a control game between the COBOL programming community and the action researcher monitoring the community by thinking about this in terms of supply-chain management. From the viewpoint of the AR auditor the COBOL community was a supplier in terms of presenting him with quality control statistics, and the COBOL community was a customer when he returned trend statistics based on progress analysis made from the quality control statistics.

The output of the TSI choice process was then to use ISO 9001:2000 for self-improvement of the AR audit strategy. By focusing on ISO 9001 the action researcher would develop a quality management system for handling the actions of the AR player, gradually make the QMS for the audit function compliant with the ISO 9001:2000 standard and continue to improve by following the ISO 9004:2000 guidelines.

SOSM problem contexts	Solve problem (unitary)	Formulate problem (plural)	Evaluate solution (coercive)
Well-posed problem (simple)	3. Using ISO 9000 theory.	2. Supply-chain game model.	4. Small but promising signs of improvement in implementation success (Øgland, 2007a).
Ill-posed problem (complex)		1. Use of Napoleonic War metaphor for understanding conflict between ideologies	

Table 23: Development of problem formulation during second turn around the Monopoly board

The outcome of the TSI implementation process was an evaluation report that suggested this might be a viable approach (Øgland, 2007a).

Round 3 – May 2007 to January 2008

During the third turn around the Monopoly board the action researcher started landing on properties and monopolies owned by the other player.

- Reorganization resulting in the split between SKD and the IT function by the creation of SITS (Skatteetatens IT- og servicepartner)
- The software engineer responsible for the COBOL quality management system went into retirement but a backup-person continued the process of supporting output from the COBOL software quality control.
- The iteration produced a conference publication at IRIS 30 about strategies for integrating action research with software process improvement (Øgland, 2007b) and a conference publication at UKSS-2007 about implementing quality management systems when there is minimal management commitment to TQM, the latter being improved and made into a journal publication (*paper 6*).
- ISO 9001 was more deeply integrated into the evaluation report (Øgland, 2008, chapter 4.6-4.10), and the report included reflections, based on the paper published at IRIS 30, about whether the focus on ISO 9000 strategy would make it more relevant to frame the research as design science research making contributions to outlets similar to IEEE's Software Engineering Book of Knowledge (SWEBOK) rather than action research (ibid, p. 1).
- The focus on "what gets measured gets done" was articulated through the use of a double loop learning model (ibid, p. 5).
- Previous comments about ANT were replaced with references to the sociological systems theory of Niklas Luhmann (ibid, p. 5).

Round 4 – February 2008 to February 2010

Reorganization at NTAX caused serious problems for the survival of the COBOL process. The new organisational structure placed the action researcher outside the IT department (research was internal to SKD but external to SITS), which changed the nature of the research from a QMS research process into a QMS audit research process. Natural choices for designing the audit approach could be chosen in relation to frameworks like ITIL, ISO 9001 and CobiT.

- After the splitting of SKD into SKD and SITS, the person responsible for providing results from COBOL software quality control hesitated, and the process broke down in April 2008.
- A formal letter was written on the 11th of May 2008 asking for permission to continue the research. After a long period of negotiations, a contract was written in September 2008, but it was not until May 2009 before the research could continue where it had left off.
- Using motivational theory based on the principle "what gets measured gets done" resulted in an award-winning publication at the IRIS 31 conference (*paper 4*) and the acknowledgement from the academic community stimulated further elaboration on this theory as part of the practical action research design (Øgland, 2010a, chapter 2.2.2).
- The ISO 9001 requirements were integrated into the research by formulating compliance hypotheses based on the five major modules of the ISO 9001:2000 standard, and there were attempts to frame the action research as design science research by focusing on the design of the QMS and the audit strategy.
- The splitting of SKD and SITS made the quality function of SITS into the natural customer of the action research COBOL evaluation report.

Round 5 – February 2010 to September 2010

There were problems with getting in touch with the newly established quality management department at SITS. Although there were written documents explaining how SKD should carry out quality audits, the quality department at SITS refused being audited and refused taking action based on the audit findings presented by the action researcher.

- The evaluation report delivered at the end of the fourth iteration of the BA control loop did not result in any response.
- Based on the experience of feeling powerless in trying to audit SITS, despite having clarified all relevant RCA issues both formally and informally, the situation felt like being a environmental activist trying to make a powerful polluting industry comply with environmental laws and regulations (Øgland, 2010b, chapter 1.1).
- The environmental activist metaphor was supported with game theory models known from supply-chain theory (ibid, chapter 2.1).
- The empirical results by iterating once more through the BA control loop indicated that improvement trends towards COBOL standardisation slowed down after making SITS into a separate unit. This observation was used for requesting the SITS quality function for comments and permission to look more deeply at the formal quality system supporting the COBOL software development practice.

Round 6 – September 2010 to February 2011

Insights from reflecting upon the action research study as a whole by writing papers and attending conferences was starting to pay off in terms of seeing how game theory would exemplify that "nothing is as practical as a good theory" (Lewin, 1997, p. 288).

- At the end of the previous iteration through the BA control loop, the SITS quality function had responded by saying that they did not recognize the authority of the

COBOL evaluation report and thus refused taking corrective action. They also refused to share plans and methods with the action researcher, and the dialogue broke down when they stopped responding to mails.

- This kind of response supported the game model developed during the fifth round, but there was confusion about how to articulate the research. The evaluation reports had grown to a size of 200 pages and was pushing the 250 limit set by the print office. The size of the evaluation reports made them costly to maintain.
- Statistics from ISO 9001 self-assessments started to accumulate, but so far they indicated improvement in the audit process while the performance quality of the QMS being audited appeared to be systematically deteriorating. The situation was similar to the early stages of EFQM assessments of the second action research cycle. The research instrument had to be sufficiently tested and calibrated before results could be trusted.
- The COBOL evaluation report defining the end of the iteration (Øgland, 2011) tried to put pressure on the SITS quality function to take action based on audit results by making elaborate references to NTAX rules, regulations and contracts which explained the authority of the COBOL assessment process, plus sending a copy of the evaluation report to more powerful parts of the TQM actor-network.

Endgame – February 2011 to June 2011

After the publication of the action research report in February 2011, a new iteration of data collection and interventions started. The last visit to NTAX was in June 2011, just before they temporarily moved from Helsfyr to Tøyen in order to renovate the office structure at Helsfyr. At this stage the general plan was to continue collecting data for the seventh iteration of the BA control loop, but for reasons such as part of the COBOL programming community refusing to give out more error statistics, the BA reached a stage where it was no longer possible to continue.

Based on data collection and interventions carried out during the six months before the algorithm terminated, the terminal state could be characterised as follows:

- Statistical trends showed that not much had happened with the COBOL practice itself. Those who were motivated to standardise had continued in the same positive way, and from last years trends it was expected that the PSA group would have reached a state of no defects this year. Those who ignored the standards were still ignoring, and the software continued to grow worse by each year. Others said that they had no more time for COBOL audits and indicate that they would refuse to give out error statistics.
- The SITS quality function had formally accepted some kind of agreement on how to collaborate on making the QMS more compliant with ISO 9000 requirements, but it was still unclear what the agreement would mean in practice.

The most recent developments of the problem formulation are described in table 24. When the NTAX action research report was published in February 2011, the "what gets measured gets done" situation was in the state described as complex-unitary. Using an environmental activist metaphor for understanding the conflict between the problem solver and the environment was not sufficient for having a mathematically well-posed problem, but using the written experience of environmental activists as inspiration for trying to make the SITS quality department accept the idea of collaborating for the purpose of solving the COBOL quality problem was nevertheless a way of trying to find a solution.

SOSM problem contexts	Solve problem (unitary)	Formulate problem (plural)	Evaluate solution (coercive)
Well-posed problem (simple)		3. The current understanding of the problem needs to be simplified by use of a relevant game theory model that implies the ISO 9001 strategy being a Pareto efficient solution.	2. The strategy appears to create sufficient power and authority for making it possible to conduct quality audits on parts of the SITS quality management system
Ill-posed problem (complex)	1. Search for optimal solution for the control game by looking at formal aspects of organizational politics		

Table 24: Development of problem formulation during seventh turn around the Monopoly board

As the SITS quality function accepted to collaborate, even though the actual meaning of this acceptance never became quite clear, this meant that the problem could be reformulated to fit with the solution. One possibility might be to interpret the environmental activist metaphor as a game of "chicken" in the sense of two cars driving towards each other both determined to win by making the other change course ("chicken out") while trying to avoid the situation where nobody changes course and both cars collide. By empirically defining utility values for this game, this is a mathematically well-posed problem with known solutions. In other words, the "what gets measured gets done" situation could by this model be characterised as simple-coercive.

What would have to be the main concern within the seventh iteration of the BA control loop would be to investigate how the utilities in the chicken game could be improved by using ISO 9001 as an artefact for creating collaboration between quality audit and quality management. The purpose of this "simple-plural" process would then be to change relationship between the quality audit and quality managers from the zero sum game of chicken into a collaborative game that would provide Pareto efficient win-win solutions.

4.3.4 Evaluation

The purpose of the third action cycle was to investigate whether the use of "what gets measured gets done" as an operational research hypothesis would solve the problem of creating sufficient trust between the action researcher and organisation being researched for making efficient action research on how to use the BA for implementing TQM in a technically complex and socially distrustful setting.

The stability hypothesis (RH1)

As described in the action narrative, it took a lot of effort to make sure that the COBOL process stayed in a state of statistical control in the sense of publishing an action report every year for a period of six years after the TQM programme of the second action research cycle had been completed.

The fact that the COBOL process was constantly on the verge of breaking down supports the hypothesis that it makes sense to work with a network of processes rather than just a single project. The only reason the COBOL project survived as long as it did had to do with the fact that it was defined as necessary for the action research carried out as part of the PhD research. This is explicitly stated in the contract between Skattediretoratet (SKD) and the NTAX service department (SITS).

117

The outcome from testing the first hypothesis is that it was possible to implement and manage the BA in a state of statistical control even though the BA was only applied to a "network" of one single node. As explained in the action narrative, at the planning stage it was expected that the COBOL improvement project would be fairly unproblematic as it had been one of the most successful improvement projects during the second research cycle, the researcher was on friendly terms with the individual who was the main architect behind the QMS, and there was management acceptance that the process could be used as part of the PhD research. Soon, however, there were organisational changes. The QMS architect retired. The head of the IT department, who was the main source of power for getting data access to data and being allowed to do interventions, got a different job. Some of the best COBOL programmers moved to other jobs. The improvement project got in jeopardy, but through the use of negotiations and formal contracts it was possible to continue the research. Rather contrary to the outcome of the hypothesis that it was possible to run the BA in a state of statistical control, the learning from the experiment was that the earlier BA design that focused on a network of projects rather than a single project was a more robust approach.

Although the action hypothesis "what gets measured gets done" was not the main reason why the BA remained stable, the reason the BA survived as long as it did can be explained by the fact that the COBOL audit was designed as part of a PhD action research project defined by a contract between NTAX and UiO.

The impact hypothesis (RH2)

As DNV was using the ISO 9001:2000 standard for assessing the organisation, the corresponding ISO 9004:2000 assessment standard was used for evaluating the audit procedure. Although there are some improvements in the ISO 9004 score in terms of how the action research managed to make use of the ISO 9004 framework, there was minimal improvement among the COBOL programmers in their ability to adjust programming practice to fit with the NTAX programming standard, as shown in figure 30.

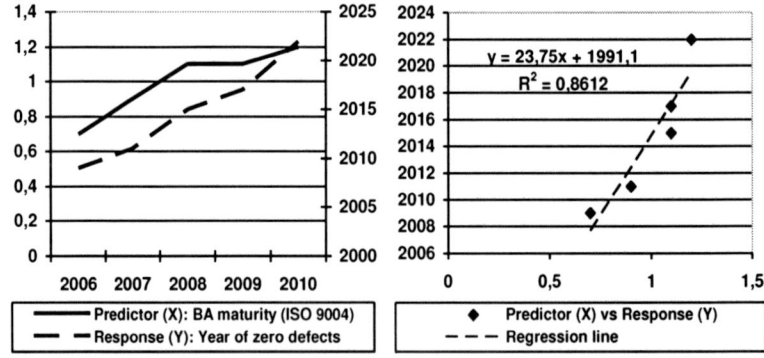

Figure 30: Visual comparison and correlation for BA maturity and COBOL year of zero defects

The diagram on the left side in figure shows a steady increase in BA maturity of the control approach and a steady increase in the expected period of time before all defects have been eliminated from the COBOL software. The diagram on the right side indicates a correlation of $R = 0.9280$ between technical productivity and research productivity. Given the sample size of $n = 5$, the correlation is big enough to reject the null hypothesis of population correlation $r = 0$ and sample correlation $R \neq 0$ at a 5% level of significance.

This does not mean that the BA was not working properly. It was quite evident that the results would have been even worse if there had been no monitoring of the COBOL process. There were improvements among those who had been actively responsible for the development of the standard in the first place, and there were continued improvement among those who had been among the most active improvers during the second action research cycle. Among those who had been performing below average during the second action research cycle, the performance was even worse now.

Although the COBOL action research reports were redesigned from year to year in order to make use of insights produced through the reflective nature of the action research, the tendency among the COBOL programmers was to deviate more and more from the programming standard rather than complying with them.

The optimality hypothesis (RH3)

The format of the COBOL report changed from year to year, trying to make it fit with the standards of action research. Although this change may reflect an increase in the maturity in the design of action research, gradually reaching for optimality, there were few improvements in terms of causing change among the COBOL programmers. Although the idea of self-improvement by use of ISO 9004 might have contributed to making the BA process optimal in the long run, when the BA was terminated NTAX had not implemented TQM and thus the BA was not optimal.

4.3.5 Reflection

The purpose of the third action cycle was to investigate whether the use of "what gets measured gets done" as an operational research hypothesis would solve the problem of creating sufficient trust between the action researcher and organisation being researched for making efficient action research on how to use the BA for implementing TQM in a technically complex and socially distrustful setting.

The experiment was successful in the sense of the researcher being allowed to continue for six years despite disputes and organisational attempts to terminate the research. The action research seemed to have some impact on TQM performance, although less than anticipated. In comparison with running the BA-driven TQM implementation from within the organisation, as was done in the second cycle of action research, the approach was less efficient and consequently not optimal.

Several issues can be considered when trying to explain the outcome of the cycle. A bullet list of five possible explanations is to be discussed.

- The new BA design was less efficient because the action researcher no longer represented management and "what gets measured gets done" is based on the assumption that workers follow what they believe managers focus on.
- The new BA design was less efficient because research procedures come as an additional cost to the cost associated with the already existing problem solving procedures.
- The new BA design was less efficient because the previously hidden assumptions about "what gets measured gets done" were being made more explicit and caused resentment as nobody likes being monitored and controlled.

- The new BA design was less efficient because the situation where it was employed had changed; change in personnel, the COBOL code was more mature and continual change consequently became more costly, some of the old software was to be replaced with new software and people were reluctant to spend time improving what would soon be obsolete.
- The new BA design was less efficient because the descriptive sociological theories used in the diagnosis part of BA action research were of limited use in trying to develop normative design theories for the treatment part of BA action research.

The first explanation, focusing on the lack of formal power for making people follow rules and regulations is consistent with the action narrative. Processes that worked fairly easy during the second action research cycle suddenly became complicated and people would not deliver error lists and respond to email until an action research contract had been made. It took more than a year to get such a contract accepted, and the contract itself was filled with all sorts of precautions. After the contract was established, communication remained difficult. While people would no longer have formal reasons to refuse answering emails, it could take several months before they answered an email. Although the lack of formal power defined by the organisational hierarchy made the situation more difficult than it had been, this was also an expected premise of the research design. While the issues addressed in the explanation are valid, the reason the BA design did not compensate sufficiently for this lack of power may be better understood as an insufficient BA design than something inherently problematic with the situation. As the research carried on, the organisational resistance was used as part of the research design in terms of measuring how long it would take before people responded to email requests and so on. The politics of the situation explain some of the difficulties, but as the purpose of the BA was to compensate for these expected political challenges, the situation itself cannot be used for explaining the outcome of the BA experiment.

Considering the second explanation, focusing on how action research creates additional cost in terms of research procedures makes sense in the way that spending too much time reflecting on the BA approach allows less time for running the BA. The narrative also supports this interpretation, and it is also supported by related research stating that the effect of action research may be that practical problem solvers have to "give up some level of speed to completion in favour of a more careful and deliberate approach to the problem" (Kohli & Hoadley, 2007, p. 249), but although this may have been valid for this particular action research, it does not seem like a valid statement from a general perspective. By streamlining the action research by keeping a narrow focus on research problem, theory, data collection, data analysis and related research, there seems to be no reason why the literature review, measurements, interviews, observations, discussions should go beyond what should be necessary for solving the problem by use of the high standard TQM work practice.

The third explanation addresses the usual resistance people have towards having their work processes evaluated and the evaluation results published to a wider audience. As commented upon in related research, one of the implications for practical problem solvers when getting involved in action research is that they may have to "give up their privacy in failure, preferring instead to learn from their shortcomings and allow others to learn as well" (Kohli & Hoadley, 2007, p. 249). Not all may feel equally comfortable with this. However, the ethical aspects of the research design had been a controversial issue already with the second action research cycle. The early action research reports had been written in a style to make the worst performers anonymous, while occasionally quoting from interviews with named people who represented best practice or interesting ideas. However, not all felt comfortable with this approach, so later reports were written in a style that treated all individuals in an anonymous manner. Although the research design itself may have caused frustration in the organisation, the research design in the third cycle was a direct continuation of the design from the second cycle and was made even more formal and with a lesser distribution of findings, so it seems unlikely that the political or ethical problems associated with the "what gets measured gets done" should have increased or have created greater resistance to change.

The fourth explanation draws attention to the fact that there were changes in the socio-technical network that defined the installed base in the second research cycle when moving to the third cycle. Certain key figures left the network and new people with limited knowledge about the COBOL quality management system joined. In a relatively early criticism of action research within educational field (Hodgkinson, 1957), it is pointed out that the validity of action research to a large degree depends on doing cycles of research on a homogeneous social structure in the sense of a teacher doing action research on how to teach students from a homogeneous group in terms of parameters like age, gender balance, and socio-economical background. If the population from which the classroom represents a sample is changed from year to year, what may have been success factors in one cycle may turn out to be the reason for failure in the next. Although the COBOL study was not homogeneous over time, with the NTAX reorganisation in 2007 being an important environmental change, the result of change was, however, that people who had been resistant to quality management in the second cycle had now moved onto organisational positions with more power and thus influencing a larger part of the network. In other words, this was a kind of change that had little to do with the redesign of the BA action research, and becomes as such an unreliable explanation of why the BA performance of the third cycle was less optimal than what was observed during the second cycle.

The fifth explanation addresses a general debate about the use of theory in how to design information systems action research (e.g. Davison et al., 2004; Baskerville, 2007; Järvinen, 2007). The idea behind the fifth explanation is to say that there was no significant difference in performance in how the BA worked on the COBOL problem in the second and third cycle. The only difference is that the practical challenges in running the BA, discussed as part of the four first explanations, became more pronounced in the third cycle and made it evident that descriptive social theory without support in mathematical models is not sufficient when trying to learn from the execution of action plans.

During the third cycle of action research the theoretical perspective developed by starting with the general systems perspectives associated with Parsons (1951) and Luhmann (1984), it was then modified due to having discussions with information systems researchers more focused on the network theories (e.g. Latour, 1999; Brunsson and Jacobsson, 2000), before the theoretical perspective evolved in the direction of developing a theory of quality control based on comparing the TQM implementation with social control theory used by environmental activists (e.g. EIN, 1997; Burns, 2007). The conceptual model for thinking about TQM implementation as environmental activism was useful for getting ideas on how to intervene, but it was not sufficient for learning about the consequences of the interventions. In order to do so it would be necessary to develop precise mathematical models explaining the design logic of environmental activism and then systematically test and revise the decision trees in practice when dealing with TQM implementation. In the final years of the third cycle there were some attempts at rewriting parts of the environmental activist model in the language of game theory and then design the action research as experimental game theory

(Camerer, 2003). The cycle was terminated before this approach was sufficiently developed.

The "research wheel" model in figure 21 (chapter 3.7) illustrates the reasoning behind the action research carried out in the third cycle. The action researcher investigates a phenomenon such as the TQM implementation process at NTAX by collecting process data in the shape of SPC charts and other methods by testing the "what gets measured gets done" hypothesis. Data models in the shape of statistical population models are created to make sense of the sample data as a way of understanding, predicting and giving control signals on when to intervene with the behavioural phenomenon. In order to be able to learn from situations where the empirical outcome does not fit with the predictions, like when there is a system of measurements and feedback but still nothing gets done, the data models have to be understood in the context of a theoretical model from sociology such as the theory of TQM implementation in hypocritical organisations (Brunsson & Jacobsson, 2000).

In the figure, Brunsson's thoughts about the social reality of TQM implementation are represented as a map where the TQM designer (mouse) is trying to establish TQM culture (find cheese) while avoid being terminated by actors inside the organisation who benefit from having a non-TQM culture (eaten by the cat). In the language of the Stag Hunt model from chapter 1, the cat and mouse game is played for the purpose of establishing a culture based on trust, long-term goals and scientific reasoning (mentality of the mouse) while driving out a mentality based on suspicion, changing goals and inability to admit mistakes (mentality of the cat). The cat and mouse game is an extreme simplification of the Monopoly game in the sense that all the decisions having to do with buying, selling, trading, developing and getting out of Jail are now represented as the decision points of the maze game. According to Simon (1996), however, the maze is the basic model for understanding all decision problems, and what Davison et al (2004) say about the importance of developing action research theory in the shape of "in situation S with salient features F, G and H, the outcomes X, Y, Z are expected from actions A, B and C" fits with the idea of using a cat and mouse maze game as the theoretical model that all other models and theories have to relate to.

The diagram in figure 31 illustrates different ways of formulating social theory. The cat and mouse game represents a precise mathematical game model for representing a social theory such as the Stag Hunt representation of Brunsson's theory of organisational hypocrisy. The Hamlet drama represents the social theory the way it is often presented in literature as a non-mathematical model abstracting general patterns from examples, like the way Brunsson and Jacobsson (2000) develop Brunsson's theories of organisational hypocrisy in the context of TQM and ISO 9000. The third type of theory represents a middle position between mathematical and non-mathematical theory, like how Axelrod (2002) uses mathematical ideas and concepts like the Monopoly game for reasoning in a non-mathematical manner about empirical data. Devlin (2009) refers to this as "soft mathematics" and argues that the mathematical way of thinking is such a powerful way that, when applied in a soft manner, it can lead to considerable advances in the understanding of various phenomena in the social realm of people.

The arrows in figure 31 suggest that the way to extract mathematical games from non-mathematical drama theory, or to understand the wider drama theoretical implications when analysing the outcome of game theory experiments, goes by the way of soft mathematics in order to identify the mathematical concepts needed for making communication precise and meaningful.

The problem with using the type of descriptive theory that Brunsson suggests as a theory in action research ("drama theory" in figure 31) is that such theories are verbal abstractions of case studies rather than mathematical theories mapping out the decision trees needed for solving the TQM implementation problem. In other words, Brunsson's theory is helpful for understanding why there is a 80% failure rate in TQM implementation due to the complex maze and the many cats the mouse has to consider in the search for cheese, but it has little advise to offer in terms of how the mouse might take advantage of this knowledge for the purpose of making better decisions in a manner that reduces the failure rates.

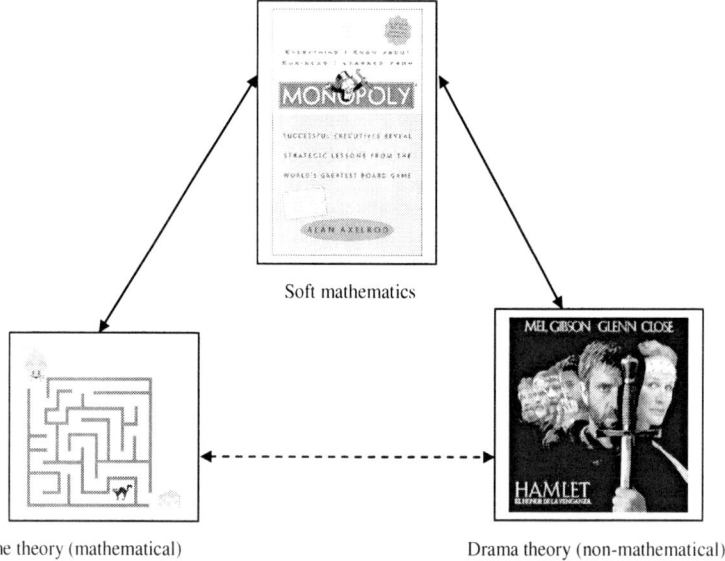

Soft mathematics

Game theory (mathematical)   Drama theory (non-mathematical)

Figure 31: Three types of theory for understanding BA and information infrastructure dynamics

When using this type of theory for deducing action plans to be implemented and tested, it becomes a problem what to do when the action plan fails. As the theory can only be used for explaining without predicting, no matter what the outcome of the experiment might be, the most natural result will be an interpretation of the outcome as another example confirming the ideological perspective embedded in the theory. In the context of the research wheel in figure 21 the situation is indistinguishable from not having any theoretical model at all as the only theoretical concept systematically tested and modified is the data model. As can be seen from the narrative part explaining the first years of action in the third cycle, the lack of a proper and relevant mathematical model for predicting and interpreting outcome of actions stalled learning because it was always possible to make social interpretations in the style of Brunsson no matter what the outcome of the SPC charts were. Later on, however, as the Brunsson way of explaining failure was supported with the game model derived from environmental activism ("game theory" in figure 31), it became easier to design and test strategies, which would result in a modification of the decision space as a consequence of how the strategies succeeded or failed.

The insight from the final action research cycle in the BA study are similar to those expressed by Elster (1982) when arguing that Marxism has to be understood from a game theoretical perspective rather than a dialectical perspective in order to be scientifically meaningful. The main insight from this reflection is that a principle like "what gets measured gets done" fitting with 90% of the data (*paper 4*) is less important than figuring out why it did not fit in the remaining 10% when testing an idea about how to "design quality management systems with minimal management commitment" (*paper 6*). It is not the confirmation of an idea or an ideology about oppression that should be the centre of action research but rather how to improve the strategy of liberation. In order to understand the 10% failure in the "what gets measured gets done" experiment it is necessary with game models for understanding why some people will not change their behaviour despite being systematically evaluated and having the evaluation results distributed to various interest groups.

The fifth explanation of the outcome of the third action research cycle is the most convincing. The new BA design was less efficient because the descriptive sociological theories used in the diagnosis part of BA action research were of limited use when trying to develop a treatment. Although the Monopoly game diagnosis was maintained from the previous cycle, the actual focus of the third cycle was on the use of the "what gets measured gets done" principle used as property development tactic in Monopoly and not on the larger game of Monopoly itself. Given this narrow focus the mistake could be described as failure by attempting to use BA in a situation where BA was not warranted (non-optimal solution in table 5). The reason for the mistake was getting carried away by social and psychological theories without making proper game theoretical interpretations of the theories in the manner suggested by figure 31.

5. ANALYSIS AND DISCUSSION

The purpose of this chapter is to analyse the results, showing contribution to knowledge and pointing out weaknesses and limitations. The analysis starts with an overview of how the individual papers contribute to the study as a whole (section 5.1). This is followed by looking at the whole through sequences of problem formulation (section 5.2), solution deduction (section 5.3) and solution implementation (section 5.4). Reliability and validity are discussed in section 5.5.

5.1 The individual papers and the study as a whole

The literature review in chapter 2 was structured around an OR/SA model (figure 7) that was used for guiding the review towards the formulation of research questions (section 2.5) supporting the research hypotheses that had been used for defining the study. As pointed out in that section, the individual papers listed in table 6 were written to explore each of the questions. In figure 32 the contributions from the papers are presented in the context of how they fit in with the OR/SA model.

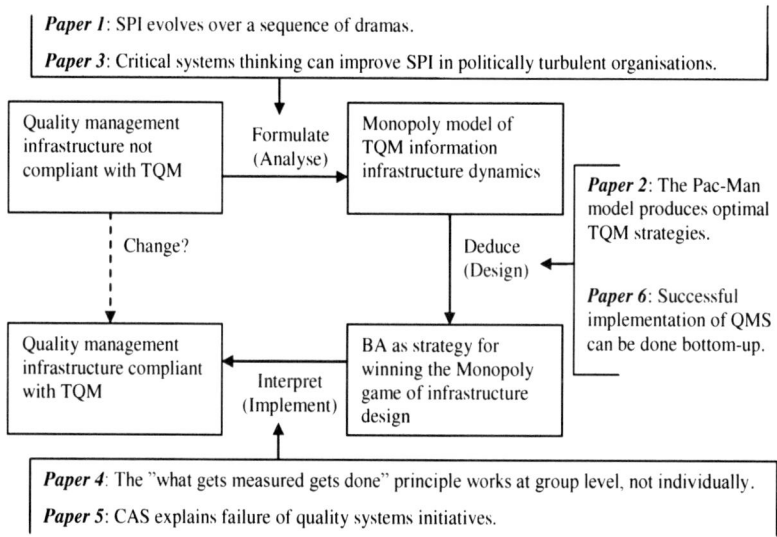

Figure 32: How the individual papers relate to the OR/SA model

Both **paper 1** and **paper 3** contribute to the kernel theory of understanding quality management infrastructure dynamics. The insight that SPI or TQM evolves over a sequence of dramas (**paper 1**) is formulated through the use of evolutionary game theory. In the context of the overall research this can be seen as a generalisation of the Monopoly model of information infrastructure in the sense that it emphasises the repeated playing of games in a Monopoly tournament that makes the BA into an evolutionary stable strategy. The idea that critical systems thinking can improve SPI or TQM in politically turbulent organisations (**paper 3**) stresses the importance of the TSI design as a part of using BA through canonical action research (CAR) or reflexive practice.

In **paper 2** and **paper 6** the main contributions relate to the design theory of how to implement TQM. The idea that the Pac-Man model produces optimal TQM strategies (**paper 2**) deals with how the TQM designer should make decisions for the purpose of getting management commitment to TQM. That successful implementation of QMS can be done bottom-up (*paper 6*) deals with the issue of motivating the workforce to follow quality standards and procedures in situations when it is uncertain whether management is sufficiently committed to TQM.

The main contributions in *paper 4* and *paper 5* relate to the understanding of how the BA works in practice. The insight that the "what gets measured gets done" principle works at group level and not individually (*paper 4*) explains why the way the BA was implemented according to design principles in *paper 2* and *paper 6* occasionally failed although it work well in most cases. Using CAS to explain failures of quality management initiatives (*paper 5*) is a type of explanation that focuses on how even robust strategies like the BA can fail for small reasons when the complexity becomes sufficiently large.

Table 25 gives an overview of how the papers are related to the OR/SA model by how they answer research questions designed to explore aspects of the BA hypotheses.

OR/SA model	Hypothesis	Question	Answer
Formulate/analyse (section 5.2)	**RH2**: The response to the BA treatment is performance improvements measurable by TQM assessments	**RQ2.1**: How can one use EGT for understanding TQM information infrastructure dynamics?	***Paper 1***: SPI evolves over a sequence of dramas.
		RQ2.2: How can one use CST for understanding TQM information infrastructure dynamics?	***Paper 3***: Critical systems thinking can improve SPI in politically turbulent organisations
Deduce/design (section 5.3)	**RH3**: The BA is optimal for implementing TQM in complex environments	**RQ3.1**: How should one design the details of the BA to optimise the interaction between TQM designer and management?	***Paper 2***: The Pac-Man model produces optimal TQM strategies.
		RQ3.2: How should one design the details of the BA to optimise the interaction between TQM designer and workforce?	***Paper 6***: Successful implementation of QMS can be done bottom-up.
Interpret/implement (section 5.4)	**RH1**: The BA can be implemented and managed in a state of statistical control	**RQ1.1**: How can one use the "what gets measured gets done" principle for explaining success and failure of quality management initiatives?	***Paper 4***: The "what gets measured gets done" principle works at group level, not individually.
		RQ1.2: How can one explain the success and failure of quality management initiatives on a systemic level?	***Paper 5***: CAS explains failure of quality systems initiatives.

Table 25: How the individual papers relate to the OR/SA model

The table also indicates the structure of how the analysis and discussion will be carried out in the next three sections. The purpose of the analysis is to explain the overall outcome of the BA hypotheses testing by commenting on the outcomes of the hypotheses testing for each of the three action cycles and what is described in the individual papers. In each of the three sections the analysis is followed by a discussion where the contribution to knowledge is made explicit in context of theory and related research. The research questions and answers given by the individually published papers are handled as part of the discussion.

5.2 Impact hypothesis (RH2): The Monopoly diagnosis

Part of the method used for evaluating the impact hypothesis at the end of each action research cycle in chapter 4 was to analyse the linear correlation between predictor variables representing the maturity of how the BA implementation and response variables assessing the TQM level for the organisation were BA is being applied. In the two first cycles, the correlation analysis supported the impact hypothesis but the results were not statistically significant. In the third cycle, the results were statistically significant but supported the "illogical" conclusion that the time it would take to standardise the COBOL software increased with the maturity of the audit approach. The statistics are summarised in table 26.

	Regression line	Correlation coefficient	Significant at 5% level
First action cycle	$y = 0.1630x + 16.493$	$r = 0.84$	No
Second action cycle	$y = 0.6501x + 73.382$	$r = 0.80$	No
Third action cycle	$y = 23.750x + 1991.1$	$r = 0.93$	Yes

Table 26: The impact of the BA approach on TQM implementation results

The way these statistical facts will be used for arguing in favour of the impact hypothesis will follow the same line of argument as done by Hanseth and Lyytinen (2004). What Hanseth and Lyytinen did was to look at one successful case of information infrastructure implementation and one unsuccessful case and show how the successful case matched with the BA principles while the unsuccessful case did not. In this study the first two cycles are interpreted as potentially successful cases of TQM implementation following the BA design principles while the third cycle is interpreted as an unsuccessful case having ignored BA design principles.

The statistics in the table can be seen as consistent with such a conclusion, but the lack of statistical significance in the two first correlation analyses makes it necessary to add supplementary explanations. It is necessary to explain in deeper detail how the action research outcome as a whole supports the idea that the design perspective provided by the BA has a significant impact on TQM implementation success in complex environments.

5.2.1 Using the Monopoly game model for explaining impact

The way the explanation will be carried out is by use of the Monopoly representation of the TQM implementation game from chapter 2. In order to structure the explanation, Seidman's (2011) analysis of how to win at Monopoly by breaking gameplay into four phases will be used. The four phases consist of (1) acquire properties, (2) negotiate and trade properties, (3) develop properties, and (4) game effectively over. As each phase of the game requires use of different strategies, explanations of what worked well when applying the BA approach for implementing TQM in the individually published papers are consequently structured according to which phase it belongs to. As shown in figure 33, *paper 3* will be related to the first phase of gameplay, *paper 1* to the second phase, the *papers 2, 4* and *6* to the third phase and *paper 5* to the fourth phase.

Paper 3 deals with issues of chance and strategy in buying properties in terms of TQM standards and organisational areas to apply such standards. *Paper 1* makes use of the Hamlet stage play for explaining strategies on how to negotiate and trade properties in terms of getting management commitment and how the timing of quality control procedures can influence the dynamics of the game. *Paper 2, paper 4* and *paper 6* deal with property development in the sense of cultivating organisational behaviour to comply with a given standard once that standard has been established. Finally, *paper 5* discusses TQM implementation at a stage when the consequences of earlier decisions and gameplay are locking in trajectories for further play in terms of dominating outcome of the game as a whole.

Acquire properties: **Paper 3**

Game effectively over: **Paper 5**

Negotiate and trade properites: **Paper 1**

Develop properties: **Paper 2, 4 & 6**

Figure 33: How the individual papers relate to the Monopoly board game model

5.2.2 Phase 1: Acquire properties (paper 3)

According to Seidman (2011, p. 30), what is important during the first phase of the game is to be aggressive about acquiring properties. If a player lands in Jail during this phase, he should immediately pay to get out. A player cannot afford to sit in Jail turn after turn while others gain properties easily just by landing on them. There is not much else to do since the game is dictated by the roll of the dice.

In the context of TQM implementation, to acquire properties means to get access to solutions, users and practices. The paper "Measurement, feedback and empowerment: Critical systems thinking as a basis for software process improvement" (*paper 3*) illustrates the process of how to acquire properties by focusing on the use of Total Systems Intervention (TSI) as a part of the TQM implementation strategy. From the viewpoint of TSI, the process of getting access to solutions, users and practices consist of three steps that are repeated in a cyclic fashion.

When some random event makes it possible for the TQM practitioner to get access to a particular group of solutions, users and practices, the nature of the "mess" the group is struggling with needs to be identified. Secondly, a suitable method needs to be chosen in order to handle the mess, whether this would mean clarifying the problem, solving the problem or evaluating the current solution. In *paper 3* there is a particular focus on this final step of evaluating the current solution, as might be expected should be the case when dealing with a methodology like TSI that is based on critical theory.

In order to develop an efficient strategy for getting ownership to the situation, the paper makes use of metaphors suggested by Flood (1993, pp. 73-93) in suggesting that the quality department can align with the workers in the control game against management (figure 1) by thinking of how management is creating an illusion of excellence and quality perfection in order to prevent the workers from thinking and taking responsibility for their own welfare. From this perspective TQM can be used as a liberation process where bringing forth hidden facts makes it possible to create the level of debate that is necessary for people to participate in the making of quality standards and procedures, and take responsibility for their own work processes.

The case used in *paper 3* for illustrating the process is a story of anger and frustration, but as the purpose of the intervention is to design TQM as a "conflict machine" for stimulating debate and discussion rather than developing a false consciousness of by accepting Christmas speeches about unvalidated "excellence and continual improvement", the way the conflicts continued for several years and motivated the workers into changing standards and procedures shows that the approach succeeded in creating impact on the TQM implementation process.

The way the BA was implemented made an impact on the TQM implementation outcome in terms of how solutions, users and practices were selected and cultivated.

5.2.3 Phase 2: Negotiate and trade properties (paper 1)

According to Seidman (2011, p. 30), the way players adjust their property holdings for the best monopoly positions by negotiating to trade properties and cash with each other is critical and is often the largest determinant of the final outcome.

When translating this into the language of TQM implementation, the difference between phase 1 and phase 2 is whether it is possible to get access to solutions, users and practice to start process improvement by some random event or whether access can only be achieved through some process of deliberate negotiations.

The paper "The game of software process improvement: Some reflections on players, strategies and payoff" (*paper 1*) focuses on the introduction of TQM standards as something that has to be negotiated. Once an organisation has committed to a certain standard, like ISO 9001, ISO 15504 or CMM, it is typically part of the job description of the quality department to make sure that the QMS supporting such standards is working properly and audits are carried out. Although the cultivation of solutions, users and practices based on a selected standard or TQM framework may also require continual negotiations as part of process improvement ("property development"), it is necessary to get general agreement on which standards should be used as norm to measure against when the improvement starts.

As discussed in *paper 1*, negotiating the right standards can be a complex problem. Along with the technical challenge of finding quality standards that are suited for the solutions, users and practices at hand, there are also social and political issues to consider. As the story from NTAX illustrates, negotiating standards can be a game that involves many people with different interests. People developing internal regulations for information security management were against ISO 9000 because use of international standards might put constraints on the development of the internal regulatory system. People with interests in outsourcing were interested in CMM as the development of a QMS based on this framework could be aligned with outsourcing strategies that were being considered. People from the human relations department were interesting in assessment models like Balanced Scorecard (BSC), the Common Assessment Framework (CAF) and EFQM as such models would strategically fit with the idea of aligning quality management with the department of finance and human relations. The Internal Audit, on other hand, argued the case of the CobiT audit standards as developing the QMS to fit with those would have strategic advantages vis-à-vis the national auditor general.

As the story in *paper 1* goes, the quality department ended up experimenting with all sorts of standards depending on which groups seemed useful to collaborate with. Some of these collaborations paid off, like enrolling the internal audit as part of the TQM network by focusing on CobiT, using the EFQM format for sharing results with the tax administrations in Denmark and Sweden and becoming part of Statkonsult's national network for quality management in the public sector, and becoming part of the ISO 9000 professional and consultancy network. As pointed out in the paper, the ISO 9000 strategy was a strategy that had a lasting impact on the TQM implementation because the standard was politically useful for the projects department. When the second action research cycle ended in failure with the TQM implementation process being terminated, ISO 9000 survived in the shape of an ISO 9000 implementation project. At the planning stage of the third action research cycle, ISO 9000 was an interesting standard that could be made use of when looking for new solutions, users and practices for starting the BA from scratch.

The way the BA was implemented made an impact on the TQM implementation outcome in terms of how TQM frameworks were negotiated and committed to.

5.2.4 Phase 3: Develop properties (paper 2, 4 and 6)

According to Seidman (2011, pp. 30-31), once a player has a monopoly or monopolies he must develop houses on them aggressively, erring on the side of spending too much money to do so, rather than saving money.

In the Monopoly game, having a monopoly in the sense of having collected a complete series of properties of the same colour is something that is done before property development can commence. In the TQM implementation game a monopoly is achieved when a player gains control over a complete network of activities. In the paper "Designing quality management systems with minimal management commitment" (*paper 6*) the series of "properties" discussed are the COBOL programming activities. The goal of the property development is to make sure that the COBOL programmers follow programming standards and take responsibility for the continual improvement of the standards. In order to achieve this a strategy is explained that includes a series of activities, like having the programmers themselves design the standards, develop the software needed for checking whether the standards are being followed and make sure the programmers are able to run these control programs whenever they need to. The standards also have to be sanctioned by management, but a complete monopoly is not established until management is committed to the activity or the programmers behave as though there is management commitment.

The paper "Software process improvement: What gets measured gets done" (*paper 4*) deals with the practicalities of motivating COBOL programmers to follow standards by establishing a system of monitoring and wide scale feedback by not only informing the programmers themselves about the progress they are making but also making sure that programmers see that managers and other shareholders are getting this feedback information. Regardless of how much management commitment there actually was to the COBOL standardisation issue, in *paper 4* it can be seen that for nine out of ten groups of COBOL programmers a trend of software getting individualised and less compliant with common standards was changed and followed with a four year period of continuous improvement.

The paper "The Pac-Man model of total quality management: Strategy lessons for change agents" (*paper 2*) argues that getting sustainable management commitment to TQM is wishful thinking. What may be possible, however, is to get short bursts of management commitment that can be used for making sure that COBOL programmers and others find it rational to follow the rules and expectations of TQM. The empirical part of *paper 2* consists of describing five years of TQM implementation at NTAX as though it was a session of Pac-Man gameplay where different events during TQM implementation at NTAX are interpreted through the strategy sets and payoffs of the Pac-Man game. The evolution of the Pac-Man score is then compared with the actual EFQM scores that were used by the quality department for keeping score of the design game.

The way the BA was implemented made an impact on the TQM implementation outcome in terms of influencing the control game played between management and workforce by adding structures and practice of measurements and feedback that would modify existing mechanisms of regulation and incentives to become more compatible with the ideals of TQM.

5.2.5 Phase 4: Game effectively over (paper 5)

According to Seidman (2011, p. 31) the game of Monopoly is effectively over when one player maintains a clearly superior and significantly larger expected cash flow than anyone else. Once this phase is identified there is typically nothing that can be done to change the outcome. The game usually ends quickly. If one is the winning player, one is likely to win soon. If one is a loosing player, one is likely go bankrupt soon. The only instances where the situation might be reversed are through a series of lucky rolls in favour of the losing player, provided the loosing player still owns at least one expensive monopoly with lots of houses or hotels for the winning player to land on.

When using the Monopoly game as a business model, Axelrod (2002, p. 184-191) argues that most players view the endgame as flying on automatic pilot without much opportunity or need for input, but this is a mistake as a combination of luck and strategy may turn the tables through a process of making endgame deals. Orbanes (2007, p. 123), on the other hand, argues that the most important issue when the game is effectively over is to behave as a good looser or a person that other players do not mind loosing to, to avoid reducing the chances of being invited to further gameplay.

In none of the three games of TQM implementation described by the series of action cycles in this study was TQM successfully implemented in the sense of having the organisation in question win the European EFQM excellence award or achieving something similar. On the contrary, the story told in the paper "Designing quality management as complex adaptive systems" (*paper 5*) deals with how the two first cycles of TQM implementation failed and how insights from those failures could be used for making the third cycle a success. The problem was not that the BA did not have an impact on TQM implementation, but rather how neglect of important issues or political mistakes turned the tables and caused the TQM implementation process to be quickly terminated.

Although the use of the Monopoly model for understanding TQM implementation turns the implementation process into a zero sum game, it would nevertheless be interesting to rank the non-winners for seeing how a non-winning BA approach might compare with alternative approaches. However, as Darzinksis (1987, p. xii) found in one of his Monopoly computer simulation studies, although the winner of a Monopoly game was predictable, the order of going bankruptcy for the loosing players was not. The final standings of the losers are due to blind luck. When talking about skill in Monopoly, there are only two meaningful standings: the winner and the non-winner. Second place is no more meritorious than fourth place.

In other words, the fact that *paper 5* describes the TQM implementation at NTAX in terms of saying that the impact of the BA approach started out good and got exponentially better with each year does not make it any better than any randomly chosen implementation strategy from the TQM literature when using the Monopoly game as an explanatory frame of reference. In fact, the way the zero sum structure of Monopoly makes it difficult to compare strategies beyond the classes of winning and non-winning strategies correspond with how Hanseth and Lyytinen (2004) analyse the design principles of the BA by using it for interpreting one successful and one failed attempt at developing an information infrastructure. In the successful case they recognize how the BA principles have been met, and in the unsuccessful case they show how one or more of the BA principles have not been met. However, following this kind of logic, the CAS-driven TQM approach described in *paper 5* would not be seen as a BA because the characteristic of a BA, implied by Hanseth and Lyytinen, is that it always succeeds. On the other hand, any successful approach, regardless of how it is defined, would probably be seen as a BA as the language in table 3 is written in a way that makes it possible to embrace any type of development method.

However, as Darzinskis only mentions his four-player Monopoly experiment without explaining in detail how it was designed, like how strategies for each of the players were chosen and what the strategies were like, it is difficult to understand exactly how to interpret his results. For instance, if one of the players was assigned with a strategy designed for loosing as quickly as possible, doing things like never buying property, it seems reasonable to expect that such a player would end fourth place in most games. In other words, Darzinskis' observation must be based on how Seidman described the game being effectively over when one player maintains a clearly superior and significantly larger expected cash flow than anyone else. Because of increasing returns on the winner's investments, what Darzinskis says about the way the other players being eliminated in random order seems reasonable, but he did not communicate that the focus of the experiment was on players who had survived up to this stage. What is relevant for the BA study is the distinction between strategies that allow a player to survive until the endgame sets in and strategies that forces the player out of the game before the endgame starts.

Another issue that needs to be taken into consideration is a point made by Axelrod (2002, p. 26) when he says that every player in Monopoly starts on an equal footing with 1,500 dollars while in real life there are always many differences. This is particularly relevant when dealing with TQM implementation in technically complex and socially distrustful environments where it may be much easier for the organisation to accept the "fake TQM" approach than doing TQM for real (Brunsson and Jacobsson, 2000).

Considering the way the CAS-driven TQM implementation processes in *paper 5* are described as starting out good and getting exponentially better with time while surviving as long as 6-7 years in TQM hostile environments, this supports the impact hypothesis even though the TQM implementation approach is not a perfect BA approach in the sense that it did not result in successful TQM implementation. If the TQM designers had played along with the "fake TQM" ideology they might have survived even longer, but the way *paper 5* explains how the process broke down gives more credibility to the impact hypothesis in pointing out how things like applying a "real TQM" approach within the quality department stirred up emotions which started a chain of motions that resulted in the termination of the TQM implementation process.

The way the BA was implemented made it have an impact on TQM implementation by starting out good and becoming increasingly more successful up until the stage of where the endgame started.

5.2.6 The Monopoly model as a contribution to knowledge

In the analysis above, *paper 1* and *paper 3* were used along with the other papers for using the Monopoly model to explain the impact of the BA strategy by looking at specific phases of game play. The main outcome of the analysis is that the Monopoly model is a useful model for understanding information infrastructure dynamics in a manner that is helpful for planning ways to detail the BA pseudo-code into practice and to reflect upon the results. However, as explained in section 5.1, these two papers also make specific contributions to knowledge by answering research questions related to how the Monopoly model should be formulated.

The literature review in section 2.2 was structured around the idea of showing how the Monopoly game could be used as a model of information infrastructure dynamics in situations dealing with TQM implementation. It was shown how the Monopoly model matched the way scholars within the research community talked about information infrastructure design as a "world domination" game, and it was suggested how different key concepts in information infrastructure dynamics could be represented through Monopoly game mechanics. The inclusion of the Monopoly model into the theory of information infrastructure dynamics does not contradict or challenge existing theory, as existing theory is founded in dynamics systems theory by use of concepts like nonlinearity, positive feedback, attractors and on so (e.g. Ciborra, 2000), but it adds the opportunity for more detailed analysis by identifying a specific model from the dynamic systems literature, the Monopoly model (Luenberger, 1979, chapter 7), that provides a logical connection between the understanding of the information infrastructure dynamics and the BA as a method of controlling the dynamics in terms of the BA as a Monopoly strategy.

Among information systems scholars looking at design theories like those needed for investigating the BA, there are those who argue that a kernel theory like information infrastructure dynamics is not essential because the focus of research should be whether the BA works and how well it works rather than why it works (Venable, 2006). In this study, however, kernel theory is of great importance because of the need to understand the reasons why specific instantiations of the BA do not work and how to learn from this kind of failure. Due to the nature of how ANT is being used in information infrastructure theory, evolutionary game theory (EGT) and critical systems thinking (CST) were of particular interest for analysing the relationship between the diagnosis of the information infrastructure dynamics and the design of the BA treatment. Two research questions were defined in section 2.5.2:

- **RQ2.1**: How can one use EGT for understanding TQM information infrastructure dynamics?
- **RQ2.2**: How can one use CST for understanding TQM information infrastructure dynamics?

The contribution of the Monopoly model to the literature of TQM and information infrastructure dynamics is partly in using the Monopoly game as a standard dynamic systems model to represent information infrastructure dynamics and partly the way the Monopoly model can be seen to model the politics of information infrastructure dynamics at a macro level by CST and at a micro level by EGT. Politics at the macro level, represented by how Brunsson and Flood interpret the game of TQM in grand sociological narratives based either on social networks or class struggle, is discussed in *paper 3*. Politics at the micro level in terms of how the Monopoly game of TQM implementation is made up of repeated trading and cultivation games and how the Monopoly game of TQM implementation itself should be viewed in the context of TQM tournament gaming is discussed in *paper 1*.

The usefulness of the Monopoly model for TQM implementation beyond the specific cases investigated in this study can be illustrated in several ways. For example, the way Legge (2002) tells a story about TQM implementation by emphasising the role of politics could be retold by use of the Monopoly model, which would provide a narrative comparable to what has been presented in this study. However, in order to show how the Monopoly models used for understanding the TQM information infrastructure in this study are examples of how the Monopoly model can be used for understanding TQM information infrastructure dynamics in general it is useful to return to the historical roots of TQM implementation, as was done in chapter 2.3.1, by commenting on how scientific management bootstrapped itself into world dominance.

The "simulation" of TQM mechanism design by observing Taylor's career can be seen to consist of three periods of Monopoly game play. There were early years of developing scientific management by use of engineering theory and getting data from practicing as workman and manager in various organisations in Pennsylvania and Maine, then were the mature years of elaborate experiments with scientific management at Bethlehem Steel until conflicts with management forced him to leave, and then there were the final years after being awarded the degree of Doctor of Science and working as a professor at Dartmouth College while writing, lecturing and consulting on scientific management.

The different stages in Taylor's career correspond to different stages in the development of the information infrastructure used for supporting scientific management. At the early stage the main focus was on "buying properties" in terms identifying and cultivating installed bases of scientific management either by doing manual labour himself or working as a supervisor to do small scale task improvement experiments. The second stage was "trading properties" and obtaining acceptance to do large scale scientific studies at Bethlehem Steel. Getting acceptance and management commitment allowed him to move to the third stage of "develop properties" in terms of doing large scale experimental studies, publish results, give scientific management momentum and cash in on the increasing returns in terms of global interest in industrial engineering, while standards and technology for doing scientific management provided path-dependency and lock-ins. At this end-game stage he could withdraw from the practical experimental work and focus on writing, lecturing and consulting.

In order to understand the unfolding of the Monopoly game of scientific management mechanism design, a useful manner of describing the career of Taylor would be by use of actor-network theory, in the same manner as Latour (1988) described the career of Pasteur. In other words, not only is the Monopoly model an important contribution to information infrastructure theory from the viewpoint of practice and action research, it is also an important contribution from a detached theoretical perspective in the sense that it provides a natural link between dynamic systems theory and actor-network theory. The usefulness of the Monopoly model for both diagnosing and planning for a treatment of the situation supports the viewpoint of Gintis (2009) that game theory should be viewed as basis for a unified theory of social and behavioural science.

5.3 Optimality hypothesis (RH3): Design of BA treatment

As explained in chapter 2, the purpose of the BA optimality hypothesis was not first of all to prove that the BA is optimal but rather to provide a norm for analysing how the implementation of the BA in the study went wrong and how it could be improved for further use. Based on observations in each of the individually published papers, the BA optimality hypothesis will be challenged by looking at the BA step by step, and adjustments in how the BA is formulated will be suggested in order to make it easier to implement in an optimal manner. An overview is presented in table 27.

Bootstrap Algorithm	Challenge with respect to TQM implementation
Start with • simple, cheap, flexible solution • small network of users that may benefit significantly from improved communication with each other only • simple practices • non-critical practices • motivated users • knowledgeable users	*Paper 6*: Because management commitment is critical for making TQM work, it is difficult to identify an installed base if there is no management commitment. What can be done, however, is to start with the illusion of having an installed base and then cultivating from that perspective.
1. Repeat as long as possible: Enrol more users	*Paper 3*: The illusion of excellence as a mental prison and the liberation process. The paper deals with the process of finding people imprisoned by false consciousness defined by "fake TQM" and liberating them by enrolling them into the "real TQM" network.
2. Find and implement more innovative use; go to 1	*Paper 1*: Selecting quality standards for getting management commitment
3. Use solution in more critical cases; go to 1	*Paper 5*: Critical cases are cases that may cause breakdown of the whole TQM implementation process. Three critical cases relate to star topology, controlling the controllers and getting into trouble with QMS owners.
4. Use solution in more complex cases; go to 1	*Paper 2*: The way to learn to play the political Pac-Man game between designers and managers is to start with simple cases before moving onwards to the more complex. At each level of game play the tension gets larger, everything moves quicker, the bonus fruits and power pellets last shorter, and in the end it is a game about survival.
5. Improve the solution so new tasks can be supported; go to 1	*Paper 4*: Few people seem to doubt the principle of "what gets measured gets done", but when tested out in practice it only worked in 9 out of 10 cases. How to improve the QMS to make it support new tasks is a research question for design science.

Table 27: How the failures discussed in papers relate to different steps in the bootstrap algorithm

5.3.1 BA step 0: Starting conditions (paper 6)

The logic of the BA asks the practitioner to identify an installed base of solutions, users and practices before starting to cultivate and expand this into an information infrastructure. In order to make sure the actor-network of solutions and users linked together by practices provide a fertile ground for growth and development, the initial step of the BA states that the solutions should be simple, cheap and flexible, the practices should be simple and non-critical, and the users should be motivated and knowledgeable.

The paper "Designing quality managements systems with minimal management commitment" (*paper 6*) addresses the problem that it may not always be possible to meet the ideal expectations of the initial BA step. *Paper 6* deals specifically with a situation where the QMS is a simple, cheap and flexible solution, the practice of quality control of COBOL software as part of the annual maintenance cycle is simple and non-critical, the COBOL programmers as a network of users would benefit significantly if they all followed the same standards, and at least among some of them there is knowledge and motivation for following the standards of

135

the QMS. What is missing, however, is sustainable management commitment for regulating and creating incentives for the QMS to work.

In order to deal with this situation, the idea in *paper 6* is that management commitment is observed through the eyes of those being managed, so whether the commitment is illusory or real may not necessarily be of fundamental importance. From the viewpoint of the initial step in the BA, the idea suggests that the lack of motivation from the management side of the user group can be compensated by temporarily forgetting about management and rather try to control the remaining users by trying to create an illusion of management commitment, and a method for doing this is presented and validated by referring to seven years of success in an organisational setting.

While trying to manipulate the work force into believing that management is committed to TQM, it is also suggested in *paper 6* that it might be a good idea to try to manipulate management into believing that the work force is performing better against the TQM standards than they really are. The reason for suggesting this is based on the "no news is good news" culture of NTAX where unfortunate trends related to error statistics shown to management might more likely result in management destroying the QMS and hiding the statistics rather than trying to do something about the situation.

Although there are no logical inconsistencies found in the initial step of the BA, a problem with how the statement is formulated is that it can give the impression that it is just a question of finding an installed base of solutions, practices and users matching the requirements and then start the process of growth and development. What is suggested in *paper 6* is that the initial requirements of the BA may sometimes never be met. In such a case the only option may be to focus on a fragile actor-network of solutions, practices and users that one hopes will be sufficiently strong for making it possible to continue with the remaining steps of the BA. An alternative way of expressing the initial step of the BA could perhaps be to extend the initial "start with..." into "start with a population where each individual is an actor-networks made up of..." in order to emphasise that the fragility of individual actor-networks may be compensated by focusing on a population of such networks rather than just one.

5.3.2 BA step 1: Enrol more users (paper 3)

The first step of the control loop within the BA gives the termination criterion for the loop as "as long as possible" and defines the first task for cultivating information infrastructure as enrolling more users into the current base of solutions, users and practices.

The paper "Measurements, feedback and empowerment: Critical systems thinking as a basis for software process improvement" (*paper 3*) can be seen to interpret the first step of the BA in the context of TQM implementation by discussing how to enrol users from the "fake TQM" network into the "real TQM" network. By focusing on the ideology of critical systems thinking (CST) used in the TSI-way of doing TQM (Flood, 1993), the "fake TQM" network is described as a mental prison and the process of enrolling users into the "real TQM" network is described as a liberation process.

Although the case story in *paper 3* exemplifies that the TSI approach can be used effectively for breaking the illusion of what users believe about organisational excellence by confronting them with facts and thus creating conflict and debate, it is also noticed how this approach is not without problems. When being confronted with the fact that practice did not correspond with standards, what the users wanted to do was to rewrite the standards to make the standards fit with practice rather than the other way around. In many cases this may be the right thing to do, but as pointed out in this particular story, the changes the users insisted on doing were changes that would cause fewer defects when being audited without actually having to change any of the work practices. Unfortunately when viewing some of these changes in local standards and procedures from the CMM perspective, the change resulted in movements downwards the maturity ladder rather than upwards.

In the paper this fact is downplayed by saying that the major contribution of applying the TSI approach consisted of making the QMS visible, breaking the illusion of how the QMS was an integral part of daily work practice, and motivate the users to debate the issues among themselves and find solutions that would make sense for them. In other words, the use of TSI stimulated a process of greater democracy on the workplace, but in retrospect one might wonder for how long the users will be part of the "real TQM" network by following their newly created standards or whether they will simply drift back to the "fake TQM" of pretending to be using standards and procedures while the practices evolve without any regard to what QMS says.

Although a statement like "enrol more users" is relevant, a problem with a statement like this is that it gives the impression that once a user has been enrolled there is nothing more to worry about. In order to avoid the less fortunate aspects of the situations described in *paper 3*, it is possible that a statement like "enrol more knowledgeable users" would encourage the BA practitioner to focus on enlightening the users in order to liberate them from the mental prison of "fake TQM". The purpose of enrolment is to strengthen the "real TQM" network by including knowledgeable users who will then contribute in making the QMS solution ready to deal with more complex and critical practices.

5.3.3 BA step 2: Find and implement more innovative use (paper 1)
When dealing with TQM implementation, the second step of the BA control loop is to grow and develop the QMS by keeping focus on how to "find and implement more innovative use". One way of expanding the use of quality control is to make use of standardised TQM frameworks such as ISO 9000, CMM and EFQM as meeting the requirements of such frameworks typically means that new local quality standards and procedures need to be developed.

The paper "The game of software process improvement: Some reflections on players, strategies and payoff" (*paper 1*) deals with the challenge in selecting such frameworks. In this paper the selection of such frameworks is described as a dilemma between finding framework standards that fit with the technical needs of the domain where quality problems are to be solved and the politics attached to the choice of standards. The technical quality of the standards are important for addressing the right problems in a right manner, but the politics are important for getting the management commitment necessary for implementing the standards.

The story in *paper 1* deals with a long series of negotiations and experiments in trying to find TQM frameworks that can solve the dilemma. Although the process results in innovation by changing the focus of how the QMS can be used in ways that meet new needs, unarticulated needs or old needs in new ways, the constant focus on innovation gave less time for exploring each framework in the level of detail needed to optimise the individual QMS processes. In the end the ISO 9000 framework was the only framework to survive, and as an external assessment showed, the organisation was still a long way away from meeting the basic ISO

9001:2000 requirements.

Although a statement like "find and implement more innovative use" is important and relevant, a challenge with a statement like this is that it does not distinguish between the context of critical and non-critical practice. In *paper 1* the Hamlet play involves the introduction of technical standards and frameworks like ISO 9000, CMM and EFQM, but as each such framework is also part of a political network, part of the reason the TQM implementation breaks down is because of the protagonist's inability to differentiate between critical and non-critical practice when these frameworks are applied. A way to articulate the second step in the BA to emphasis the importance of practice might be something like "find and implement more innovative use while keeping practice non-critical".

5.3.4 BA step 3: Use solution in more critical cases (paper 5)

As explained in chapter 2 and illustrated in chapter 4, the way the term "critical cases" is interpreted in this TQM implementation study is by referring to cases that may cause a breakdown of the TQM implementation process. The paper "Designing quality management systems as complex adaptive systems" (*paper 5*) first shows how the QMS design used at DNMI and NTAX fitted the CAS principles described as "the nine laws of God" (Kelly, 1994), and then discusses reasons why the TQM processes broke down in spite of the TQM implementation process following a CAS design.

The paper explains the breakdown as a combination of three reasons. The first reason has to do with the typical star topology of quality management systems. The second reason has to do with paradoxes of attitudes towards process improvement and quality control. The third reason has to do with ownership of the quality management system.

The critical nature of QMS topology

By viewing the QMS as an information infrastructure, *paper 5* identifies both the QMS design at DNMI and the QMS design at NTAX as having star topologies like the centralised network configuration in figure 10.

In both the DNMI case and the NTAX case, the general idea was to encourage a distributed TQM system that would be developed through a process of organisational democracy where individuals or organisational units developed their own standards and procedures and such items were coordinated through some kind of peer-review process similar to how scientific communities work and how internet encyclopaedias like Wikipedia develop (Hanseth, 2004; Tapscott & Williams, 2006). The role of the quality department was thus to make sure that the peer-review system was working properly, but this required use of monitoring and feedback which is in itself a quality control activity, and this quality control activity became the central and crucial node in the QMS topology.

The central monitoring and feedback activity for controlling the local peer-review quality control systems was crucial for making the total QMS work because lack of regulation and incentives caused the agents to play games that bypassed the peer-review quality control ideas. Both at DNMI and NTAX there were models, standards and procedures being developed, but without mechanisms enforcing the use of such tools, they ended up as shelfware without impact on how work was carried out.

At DNMI the approached used for strengthening the QMS network was to mechanise the central monitoring and feedback by automating it as part of the KLIBAS climate database system. By automating and integrating the monitoring and feedback as part of the system being developed and maintained, the monitoring and feedback would in principle not depend on any particular person and one might then expect that the central node keeping the QMS together would not be vulnerable to changes in personnel and technology. However, as explained in *paper 5*, automating the process did not help much when nobody maintained and used it for the purposes it was designed for. As a consequence of this the QMS broke down.

At NTAX the information infrastructure was not sufficiently integrated to make it possible to automate the central node for giving feedback on the peer-review quality control practice, but in order to strengthen the network and make it less reliant on the central node there were attempts to establish quality circles and to encourage people into developing monitor and feedback systems that would decentralise the way the peer-reviews were motivated by central monitoring and feedback. This approach did not work either (Øgland, 2009a).

When discussing the QMS topology towards the end of *paper 5*, the role of the central monitoring and feedback is compared with the role of the ant queen in an ant colony. While removing one worker ant in the ant colony may have little consequences for the ant colony as a whole, this may not be the case if we remove the queen ant. Complex adaptive systems in nature seem to contain special components that if they do not behave as leaders of the system at least they have an important role in how the system is coordinated. Kelly (1994, p. 5) suggests that an important part of the resilience of such systems has to do with the role of the queen ant or the queen bee are passive but important parts of the system. In a similar way it appears important to protect the central node in the QMS by making sure it does not come under attack.

The critical nature in attitudes towards improvement and control

The second reason in the explanation of the breakdown of the CAS-based QMS in *paper 5* had to do with how it became increasingly difficult to protect the central node of the QMS from internal attack. The story is told from the perspective of how the quality department wanted to apply TQM principles in a self-reflective manner for the purpose of controlling and improving the processes used by the quality department internally and when interacting with others. In addition to being more efficient in carrying out quality audits and quality coordination, it seemed like a good idea to test out new quality improvement methods internally before applying them in the more critical context of dealing with others.

What the quality manager (writer of this thesis) tried to do in order to improve the performance of the quality department was to make the quality coordinators themselves suggests how they wanted their work to be measured in order to focus on process improvement. Nevertheless, all attempts, whether they were based on individual suggestions, international standards on how quality management should be done, or if it was simply to measure individual performance in relation to what the group as a whole was trying to achieve, all such efforts were met with hostility. Regardless of what was done in order to improve the monitoring and feedback system in order to increase both happiness and efficiency, the hostility only got worse and eventually played a relevant part in how the whole TQM process broke down.

In order to understand why the situation spiralled out of control, a questionnaire study supported by in-depth interviews were carried out with quality management personnel at a national ISO 9000 conference. The investigation showed a similar negative attitude towards eating one's own medicine, giving the impression that what had happened at NTAX was not an extraordinary event.

In *paper 5* there are some speculations about why quality personnel seem to have such a negative view on applying tools of their own trade on themselves, but what is perhaps more important in the context of discussing optimal use of the BA is the importance of protecting the central node of the QMS topology by avoiding actions that might cause internal friction and stress.

The critical nature of QMS ownership

The third reason used for the breakdown of the TQM process had to do with the worldview of those having the power to terminate the process. ISO 9000 and TQM literature in general (e.g. Deming, 1986; Juran, 1989; Beckford, 2002) emphasise the importance of having the quality department organised in manner which makes it report directly to the top manager. This is important for TQM because the system view of the organisation should represent the view of the top manager and not the manager of some specific department, although that doesn't mean that the quality department is always organised in this manner.

Within the IT function of NTAX, the quality department was organised as a part of the projects department responsible for IT development. This department tended to see everything as projects in the sense of complex activities bounded in time, cost and functionality. The measure of whether the department was successful or not was to which extent it was capable of delivering projects according to such criteria. Problems were often related to other departments not being able to respond in time and provide clear input to the projects. Once a project was completed in terms of having delivered a solution, whether the solution worked adequately was a concern for other departments, like the production department or the maintenance department.

The case study in *paper 5* tells a story of how networking and designing quality management processes into vital steps of business processes helped drive through improvement in areas that were outside the scope of responsibility for the projects department. Nevertheless, not aligning quality management with the specific interests of the projects department also made the quality department less important for the projects department and ultimately expendable.

Paper 5 provides some reflections on how the quality department could have aligned in a better manner with the projects department and thus made the quality department less expendable, but the general input in the context of an optimal use of the BA is how the central node of the QMS got increasingly vulnerable while the QMS solution was being put to increasingly more critical use while controlling and expanding the network outside the responsibility area of the projects department.

The relevance of the third control step for making the BA optimal

In the action research study, the statement of "use solution in more critical cases" was used in terms of trying to make sure that improvement processes were chosen in a manner to fit with the ideology of the QMS owners, trying not to agitate the quality coordinators while improving the quality department by eating one's own medicine, and there were attempts to build the QMS in a decentralised manner by utilising existing TQM standards and TQM practice rather than introducing a totally new design. Ultimately, however, the TQM process broke down as the sum of critical events became too much to handle.

Although a statement like "use solution in more critical cases" is relevant, a problem with a statement like this is that it gives the impression that the designer is in control of how the solution is being used. In order to avoid the situations described in ***paper 5***, it is possible that a statement like "use solution in more critical cases through use of risk analysis" would encourage the BA practitioner to focus on designing methods for handling risk rather than trying to control something that is potentially uncontrollable (Iversen, Mathiassen & Nielsen, 2004).

5.3.5 BA step 4: Use solution in more complex cases (paper 2)

In the context of TQM implementation, the fourth step of the BA control loop is to grow and develop the QMS by keeping focus on how to "use solution in more complex cases". Starting with simple quality management processes that work and gradually expand the QMS is typical of the kaizen (continuous improvement) method of quality control development (Imai, 1986).

The paper "The Pac-Man model of total quality management: Strategy lessons for change agents" (***paper 2***) describes the kaizen process through the lens of a maze-chase conflict between TQM designers and managers that gets more complex and intense with each level of game play. Reaching a perfect score of 3,333,360 points resulting from perfect game play is virtually impossible. With the score resulting from the interpretation of TQM implementation at NTAX resulting in a fraction of the score, an easier way of understanding the nature of games like Pac-Man is to measure success by how long one manages to survive rather than whether some ideal has been reached or not.

Although a statement like "use solution in more complex cases" is important and relevant, a challenge with a statement like this is that it doesn't take into consideration the possibility that the solution may eventually be so complex that it becomes impossible to manage. The way increase in complexity is handled in ***paper 2*** is by saying that increase of complexity in an environment does not necessarily result in a more complex algorithm for searching the environment. In the case of the Pac-man game the users Blinky, Pinky, Inky and Clyde become more erratic, the solution becomes more complex in the sense that power pellets do not last as long as earlier and bonus fruits appear less frequently, but the strategy Pac-Man has to use for handling the gradually more complex situations is still the same basic strategy only with more skill and precision. As the BA distinguishes between the complexity of the solution and the complexity of practice, an alternative way of expressing the BA statement could be to say something like "use solution in more complex cases without increasing the complexity of practice".

5.3.6 BA step 5: Impr. solution so new tasks can be supported (paper 4)

The final step in the BA control loop is central to TQM. In order to design a QMS that meets with the requirements of ISO 9001 it is necessary to have self-reflective mechanisms that makes the maintenance of the QMS focus on improving the solution so new tasks can be supported (Hoyle, 2006).

The paper "Software process improvement: What gets measured gets done" (***paper 4***) deals with the continual improvement of a QMS designed for making COBOL programmers follow standardised procedures when developing software. The mechanism design for the QMS is based on the idea of "what gets measured gets done" by measuring performance and giving feedback not only to the programmers themselves but also to other shareholders in order to motivate the programmers to follow the standards. During the period covered in ***paper 4*** the approach worked in 9 out of 10 cases, so there was a need for improving the solution in order to make it work in all 10 cases as the COBOL programming task was a small but important part of the quality management of the general system engineering life-cycles.

The narrator in *paper 4* tried to investigate and figure out why the approach did not work in the tenth case. By interviewing different people, the result was that management and external shareholders seemed to have a confused understanding of the situation while the programmers themselves were allowed to decide for themselves whether they would follow standards or not. There was no proper regulation and the incentives created by the QMS did not work because the programmers in the tenth case had noticed that line management did not care sufficiently about whether COBOL standards were being followed or not.

Although a statement like "improve solution so that new tasks can be supported" is important and relevant for implementing TQM, a challenge with a statement like this is that it may give the impression that practices can be changed by improving solutions without paying sufficient respect to user psychology. The story in *paper 4* illustrates the problem of changing practice by focusing on the solution when the bottleneck of the system had to do with relationship between users. As the story continued to develop after the events reported in *paper 4*, the QMS performance of COBOL standardisation changed for the worse with every year despite the fact that the QMS solution itself was continually improved. A possible way of rephrasing the final statement in the BA control loop to make it easier to use could perhaps be to formulate it along the lines of "improve solution and motivate users so that new tasks can be supported".

5.3.7 The revised BA design as a contribution to knowledge

In the analysis above, *paper 2* and *paper 6* were used along with the other papers for challenging the formulation of specific steps of the BA and suggesting alternative formulations. The main outcome of the analysis, however, is that the BA framework based on TSI and GA is a useful framework. However, as explained in section 5.1, these two papers also make specific contributions to knowledge by answering research questions related to how the revised BA should be formulated.

Based on the review of BA literature in section 2.3 a revised BA approach was suggested in section 2.4. The revision did not change the pseudo-code formulation of the BA in table 3, but it suggested a way of interpreting the pseudo-code by use of total systems intervention (TSI) and genetic algorithm (GA). TSI was used in the context of how the BA could be seen as prototype development (section 2.4.1). The GA was used for how the BA could be seen as programme management (section 2.4.2). An additional challenge when using BA in the context of TQM is the way the users in the BA formulation refer both to management and workforce (section 2.5.3), resulting in the follow research questions:

- **RQ3.1**: How should one design the details of the BA to optimise the interaction between TQM designer and management?
- **RQ3.2**: How should one design the details of the BA to optimise the interaction between TQM designer and workforce?

The contribution of the revised BA to the literature of TQM and information infrastructure dynamics is partly in using TSI and GA to formulate the BA and partly the idea that the users in BA has to be handled with different tactics depending on whether they are representatives of management or workforce. The tactics for dealing with management is explained in terms of strategies for winning the Pac-Man video game. The tactics for dealing with workforce is explained as a bottom-up strategy of QMS implementation based of deconstruction (undoing of understanding by suggesting alternative understandings). The exact nature of these tactics and how the tactics relate to theory and empirical research is explained in *paper 2* and *paper 6*.

The role of TSI as part of BA could be seen as an attempt to include into the current vogue a way of political thinking that was dominant in Scandinavian IS research during the 1970s and 1980s (Aanestad & Olaussen, 2010). The political nature of *paper 2* and *paper 6* fit with the way TSI is based on a kind of critical systems thinking (CST) that was prominent in Scandinavian IS research during those decades (Bansler, 1989). In a similar way to how Elster (1982) argued the need for reformulating Marxist theory in the language of game theory, there were debates within the Scandinavian IS community about game theory and dialectical materialism as alternative ways of understanding conflict (Øgrim, 1993). As pointed out in *paper 2*, there appears to be no trace of similar debates in the CST literature that the TSI builds upon. The critical theory used in CST is based on thinkers from the Frankfurt school of sociology and elsewhere without any attempt to translate the verbal theories into the mathematical language used by practitioners of systems theory and operations research.

When using the BA as an action research strategy in association with the health information systems programme (HISP), research is being carried out in a political context. Although it has been explained that HISP can be seen as a prolongation of earlier political Scandinavian IS research (Braa, 2009), and still makes use of slogans like "power to the users" (Braa & Sahay, 2012), it is less explicitly political and makes no explicit use of game theory for diagnosis and treatment. One way the BA used in this study makes an important contribution to knowledge is by the way TSI and the philosophy of CST has been successfully implemented through game theory for the purpose of having a framework that makes it possible both to mathematically deduce solutions from problem formulations and to make such solutions subject to falsifiable tests.

The other important contribution to knowledge made by the BA in section 2.4 has to do with the role of the GA. Hanseth and Lyytinen (2010) refer to Holland's (1995) book on genetic algorithms and complex adaptive systems (CAS) when discussing the design theory of dynamic complexity of information infrastructures, of which the BA is an important part, but they do not make any explicit references to the GA as part of the design theory. On the contrary, they refer to CAS as the kernel theory rather than design theory for the BA and related methods, and then they refer to concepts from dynamic systems theory like non-linear dynamics, positive feedback and attractors as examples of how CAS is being used. In other words, when they are referring to CAS as kernel theory they are actually referring to dynamic systems theory while pointing out that dynamic systems theory can be understood as the kernel theory for CAS design theory, giving BA the same status as GA without making any explicit references to GA. How the revised BA in this study makes an important contribution to knowledge, however, is in the way it goes beyond Hanseth and Lyytinen in making an explicit reference to GA and arguing how this reference is important for the practitioner and action researcher because it allows the BA to be seen as part of an already existing mathematical theory.

It should also be mentioned that Holland (2006) has been explicitly critical of the way scholars like Hanseth and Lyytinen interpret his book on genetic algorithms and complex adaptive systems by focusing primarily on the aspects of kernel theory (dynamic systems theory) that is used for explaining complexity and motivating the needs for search methods the GA. Although there is nothing wrong about ideas like the butterfly effect, bifurcation, fix points, attractors and so on, they only explain the premise of why prediction and control is fundamentally difficult without providing any input in terms of how to handle the situation. The focus of CAS, as he sees it, is in concepts like the GA and how such concepts can be seen as part of a unified theory of complex adaptive systems. This view is shared in this study by the effort to make the BA part of CAS design theory rather than an independent design theory that makes use of the same kernel theory as CAS does.

5.4 Stability hypothesis (RH1): Administering the BA treatment

The individual outcomes from testing the stability hypothesis in each of the three action research cycles were recorded and analysed in the results section. The purpose of the sections 5.4.1 to 5.4.4 is to compare the outcomes and give an overall analysis by reflecting upon how the different outcomes contributed to a unified understanding of the stability of the bootstrap algorithm (BA). How the outcome of the analysis compares with theory and related research is discussed in section 5.4.5. The SPC diagram in figure 34 shows the number of improvement processes managed by the BA during the complete action research run.

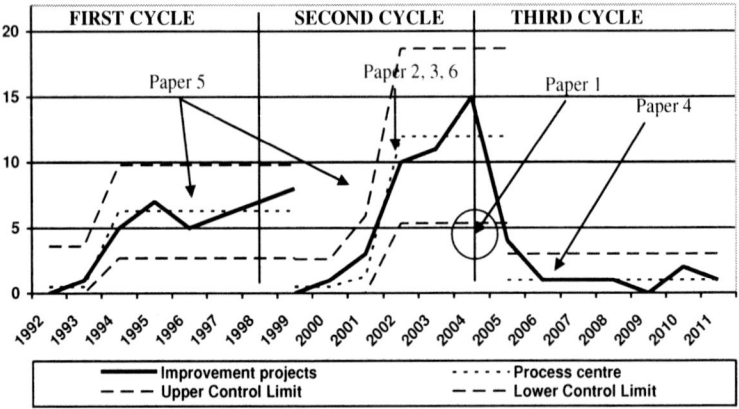

Figure 34: The number of improvement processes managed by the BA

As each of the individually published papers listed in table 6 deals with particular aspects of the action research, the stability hypothesis will be discussed by using the papers for discussing stages of BA of transitions from instability to stability (*paper 5*), maintaining stability over longer periods (*paper 2, 3* and *6*), transitions from stability to instability (*paper 1*) and special cases of running the BA in a state of forced stability (*paper 4*).

5.4.1 Stages of instability and stability in running the BA (paper 5)

In the first cycle it took three years before the BA was running in a state of statistical control with the average population of six improvement projects each year, and there was no sign of instability when the first cycle was terminated. In the second cycle it took four years before the BA was running in a state of statistical control with an average population of twelve improvement projects each year.

The paper "Designing quality management systems as complex adaptive systems" (*paper 5*) starts by discussing Lewin's unfreeze-change-freeze idea of change management (French & Bell, 1995) and how this principle of stabilising processes before attempting to change them is of fundamental importance in TQM literature building on the statistical process control (SPC) (Deming, 1986; 1994). However, the organisational reality that quality managers have to deal with is often significantly different from ideal assumptions of organisational stability.

One of the purposes of *paper 5* is to show how quality management systems can be designed as complex adaptive systems (CAS) in order to operate in a stable manner in unstable environments. While there are several CAS frameworks, the "nine laws of God" (Kelly, 1994) was used for explaining the design principles and evaluating the results in this particular paper as this was the framework used when designing the QMS first at DNMI and then at NTAX.

At DNMI the QMS started out as an improvised way of getting things done in an environment characterised by technical challenges and social tensions. The KLIBAS project had been designed for the purpose of developing a new climate database system by following a water-fall development model, and certain influential people within the organisation had invested prestige in making the project succeed, but at a stage it was clear that it would not be able to deliver what was expected. At this stage the development strategy changed into prototype development, and the BA approach emerged out of the need for controlling the prototype development process. Due to the moderate failure of the water-fall approach, the BA started with a situation that was unpredictable and how to carry out the prototype development was done by more or less random identification of solutions, users and practices that were expected to be useful for developing a KLIBAS network of systems and applications.

As the BA was used more like a hermeneutical tool for understanding the development process in retrospect than an algorithm that was strictly being followed, the early stages of formal information systems development by use of project management and water-fall models was a period of instability from the BA perspective in the sense that it was unclear whether progress was being made or not. When the CAS approach was developed and put to work, the BA stabilised in the sense of control parameters used for monitoring the development and maintenance of the growing network of KLIBAS solutions becoming stable (figure 34).

As explained in *paper 5*, the approach used for TQM implementation at NTAX was based on the CAS design from DNMI, but the initial instability at NTAX had more to do with the difficulty in finding solutions, users and practices that would satisfy the starting conditions for the BA. After seeding several attempts that did not catch on, a quality control routine designed for the purpose of making sure that software was developed according to common standards became the first stable practice. Having met the initial criteria of the BA, it was possible to expand the network. All the time new opportunities for defining improvement projects were seized upon, and many such projects failed, but following the logic of the BA by expanding the network of improvement projects by considering issues like complexity, criticality, innovation and maintenance many projects continued to stay alive. As illustrated in figure 34, the average population size consisted of 12 improvement projects each year.

Unlike the BA at DNMI, which showed no sign of instability once it had entered the control loop characterised by the BA steps 1 to 5, the BA at NTAX worked in a state of statistical stability for several years until it suddenly turned instable. Much of the focus in *paper 5* consists of explaining the reason for turning instable and how the BA could have been implemented in a different manner to have prevented this from happening. In other words, the reason the BA turned instable had more to do with the fact that the BA had not been implemented in an optimal manner, something that was discussed in section 5.3, and not something to do with the statements in the BA itself. On the other hand, when Hanseth and Aanestad (2003) introduced the BA there was no discussion of stability. The fact that it was possible to run the BA in a state of statistical control in this action research study does not mean that it is necessarily easy to reach and maintain a state of statistical control. Especially in the NTAX case it took a lot of trial and error until a set of solutions, users and practices were found to satisfy the initial conditions of the BA, and it continued to take time and effort to continue the development of the QMS from this basis while making sure that it did not break down.

5.4.2 Running the BA in a state of control (paper 2, 3 and 6)

In the previous section it was stated that it took time and effort to make sure that the BA stayed in a state of statistical control while the QMS was developing. Three of the individually published papers explain this in more detail.

The triangle model in figure 1 was used for presenting TQM mechanism design as a game played for the purpose of changing the control games played within an organisation. The challenge of running the BA in a state of control is to make sure that the design game interferes sufficiently with the control game to create change but not so much as to make the process instable. The revised triangle model in figure 35 shows how strategies described in *papers 2, 3* and *6* were developed to meet the challenge.

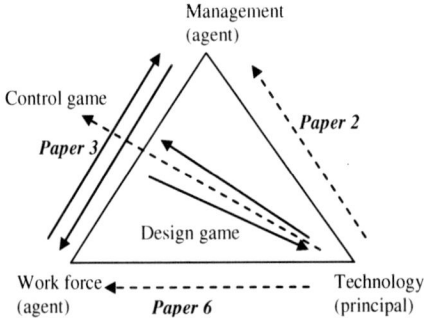

Figure 35: Trying to make the TQM design game stable

The paper "Measurements, feedback and empowerment: Critical systems thinking as a basis for software process improvement" (*paper 3*) looks at the design game from an overall perspective of how the QMS designer may influence the control game played between management and workforce. The control game is understood from the viewpoint suggested by Braverman (1974) as the objective of management being to optimise profits and productivity through exploitation of workers through oppression and alienation. The workforce may either fight back or give in by developing false consciousness. Flood (1993) sees TQM as an approach for fighting back. The message in *paper 3* consists partly of identifying the "fake TQM" strategy of pretending to be doing TQM while not actually doing so (Brunsson and Jacobsson, 2000) as a strategy that primarily serves management, and partly of the "real TQM" strategy suggested by Flood (1993) as means of liberation by improving productivity and social conditions at the same time.

The paper "Designing quality management with minimal management commitment" (*paper 6*) deals specifically with mechanism design for motivating the workforce for rejecting the "fake TQM" ideology that may prove fatal in the long run and accepting the "real TQM" ideology that will give them more power over their own work practice. The challenge, however, is that there may be limited management commitment to following standards and procedures. Without management involvement there is a risk that the workforce develops a false consciousness in terms of accepting management's "fake TQM" understanding of the world in terms of believing that the organisation is doing TQM when it is not. What *paper 6* suggests is a strategy for fighting false consciousness by developing quality control routines based on monitoring and feedback giving the impression that there is management commitment regardless of whether such commitment exists or not.

The paper "The Pac-Man model of total quality management: Strategy lessons for change agents" (*paper 2*) deals with the tensions between management and QMS designers. Based on insights from relationships between managers and scientists in operational research, managers and QMS designers are described as "natural enemies" (Beer, 1968). Using the Pac-Man video game as a lens for describing the relationship as it develops along the TQM implementation process, specific strategies for getting temporarily management commitment to the TQM implementation process are discussed.

What the study suggests is that it is possible to keep the BA in a continual state of statistical control by redesigning the control game (*paper 3*) through a process of playing games with the workforce in trying to make them believe management is committed to TQM (*paper 6*) while at the same time playing games with management in order to make them commit to TQM for periods of time (*paper 2*). As the purpose of TQM is to change how an organisation behaves, changing the work practice of the workforce is the main goal, but as this is difficult to do without changing management mentality, both games have to be played continuously until the organisation eventually reaches the stage where management is sustainably committed to TQM and the work force is sustainably working according to the models, standards and procedures and ideals of TQM.

5.4.3 The BA process turning unstable (paper 1)

In the SPC diagram in figure 34 the final observation in the second action cycle is marked with a circle as it is below the lower control limit. The paper "The Game of software process improvement: Some reflections on players, strategies and payoff" (*paper 1*) explains how the BA turned unstable by showing how the BA can be stable without necessarily being robust.

The way this is explained in *paper 1* is by telling the story of TQM implementation at NTAX in the style of a Hamlet-like drama that maximises issues of distrust, manipulation, hidden agendas, politics and conflict in order to clarify that the BA could break down any time, despite the fact that it was running in a stable manner. In fact, the central message of the paper is to consider TQM implementation not as a single-shot game but rather as a tournament of TQM implementation gameplaying. The fact that the BA turned unstable was not a surprise or something that could be easily avoided, but rather a natural consequence of how the TQM implementation game works.

Although the drama presented in *paper 1* ended with all the players stabbed, drowned or poisoned, the end of one game can be the start of another game. In figure 34 this is illustrated by the way the TQM implementation line continues from the second cycle into the third cycle where a new version of the TQM implementation game is being played.

5.4.4 Running the BA in a state of forced stability (paper 4)

When looking at the visual representation of the stability of the BA in figure 34, the way the

BA was running in the third cycle looks somewhat similar to how it was running at the very beginning of the first cycle and second cycle. The reason they look similar is because they were designed in a similar way. At the beginning of the first cycle, the mode of running the KLIBAS development process was in the style of a conventional IT project following a water-fall model. Work was broken down in time, cost and functionality, progress reports were written as the work went on and each milestone in the development resulted in analysis and design documents describing different aspects of the system. From a BA perspective the situation can be described as trying to cultivate the solutions, users and practices associated with one single node in the network, the node representing the KLIBAS project by itself.

The paper "Software process improvement: What gets measured gets done" (*paper 4*) deals with the COBOL improvement process that was used for bootstrapping the "real TQM" network during the second cycle. The process was the only process to survive into the third action cycle, and the paper represents a reflection on the process at an early stage in the third cycle. While the stability of the BA in the earlier cycles followed from the fact that the BA focused on a population of process improvement projects where the least promising projects were removed from the population while new projects were added, at the stage when *paper 4* was written the main focus was on trying to understand why the COBOL standardisation project had proved useful as a starting point for bootstrapping the TQM information infrastructure, and how one could most efficiently start the bootstrapping process from scratch now that a new TQM implementation game had been defined.

The hypothesis in *paper 4* is that the success with the COBOL standardisation can be explained by the way measurements and feedback have been aligned with the motivational theory of "what gets measured gets done". Although this theory had been taken for granted in the second cycle, when looking more critically at a COBOL project where empirical observations did not fit with the theory, a mixture of a single individual COBOL programmer being extremely reluctant to follow the standard and no real management incentives motivating the individual to follow the standard explained the situation. This kind of situation is sometimes described in game theoretical terms as "the tragedy of the commons" (Hardin, 1968; Binmore, 2007, p. 66) in the sense that following the practices that are good for the community (following standards that makes the software understandable and maintainable not only by the individual who created it) may conflict with what is perceived as optimal practice from the perspective of the individual members of the community.

At the stage when *paper 4* was written nine out of ten COBOL projects were making good progress, but due to various changes that happened over the next few years, the situation changed. In 2011 the action cycle was forced to close as the programmers would no longer cooperate on the process improvement project.

Paper 4 supports the stability hypothesis in the sense that it illustrates the relevance of the GA logic for creating BA stability by focusing on a population of process improvement projects rather than a single project. The single project described in *paper 4* was kept stable for more than ten years, but in the later years it took more and more effort to keep it stable, and in the end it was no longer feasible to do so. When implementing the BA by use of the GA such behaviour would be expected and would not have any consequences for the stability of the BA. When the stability of the BA was dependent on the stability one particular project, however, it had a fatal consequence for the stability of the BA.

5.4.5 BA implementation strategy as a contribution to knowledge

In the analysis above, *paper 4* and *paper 5* are used along with the other papers for explaining the stability and robustness of the BA as the process unfolded during 20 years of action research. However, as explained in section 5.1, these two papers also make specific contributions to knowledge by answering research questions related to how the BA should be implemented.

Despite having a good Monopoly model of the information infrastructure dynamics (section 2.2) and a good BA solution design (section 2.3 and 2.4), TQM may still fail to emerge if the implementation strategy is poor. In the analysis of BA stability it was suggested that it does not necessarily take a lot of effort to make the BA perform in a stable manner. It has been specifically designed to operate in unpredictable environment by trading off adaptability with efficiency. Nevertheless, this does not mean that the BA can be implemented in a totally mindless manner. Even though there are examples of successful use of the BA (Hanseth & Lyytinen, 2004), analysis of the BA from a design theory perspective (Hanseth & Lyytinen, 2010), and suggestions on how the BA can be used as a basis for doing action research (Braa et al, 2004), this type of literature has little to say about BA failure and how to learn from BA failure. In section 2.5.1 the following two research questions were formulated:

- **RQ1.1**: How can one use the "what gets measured gets done" principle for explaining success and failure of quality management initiatives?
- **RQ1.2**: How can one explain the success and failure of quality management initiatives on a systemic level?

The study makes a contribution to BA implementation strategy by arguing the need for action research to make use of game models to support theory and by suggesting specific game mechanisms that are important for TQM implementation success. The game mechanism associated with the "what gets measured gets done" principle is based on the idea of using the principle as a hypothesis in action research and use observed failures in meeting the expectations of the principle as a driver for carrying out interviews and investigations (*paper 4*). The other game mechanism is associated with the way CAS is a theory for dealing with complex environments and the idea is then to test the robustness of BA designs and use unexpected failure as a driver for investigation and reflection (*paper 5*).

Where this study diverges from earlier BA studies and other change management studies is in the emphasis on game theory and game theory models as a basis for linking diagnosis with treatment. Game theory is important because it makes it possible to deduce treatments from the diagnosis, meaning that a failed treatment will automatically challenge the diagnosis.

The error tree in figure 8 described the logic of analysing causes for why there is an 80% failure in TQM efforts by first questioning implementation strategy, then questioning solution designs and finally questioning how the problem was formulated. In the experience of Argyris and Schön (1978), the fact that organisations are aware of the importance of asking questions in such a looped manner is not sufficient for making them resist the urge to improve the solution designs and start asking questions about the problem formulation. They tend to get stuck in the single loop learning shown in figure 36 where the BA implementation strategy fails because the TQM designer spends all his time on the BA design without questioning the validity of the current version of the Monopoly model.

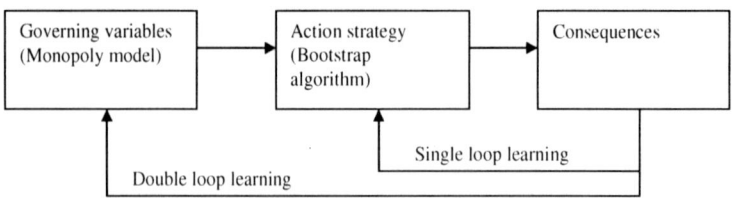

Figure 36: Viewing the BA from the perspective of double loop learning

What this study contributes in terms of BA implementation strategy is to say that the link between the governing variables and the action strategy in the figure should be made explicit through the use of game theory. In fact, by using the Monopoly model for representing information infrastructure dynamics and thinking about the BA as a Monopoly strategy, the overall game theoretical structure is given. What needs to be specified in each particular case, however, is the exact nature of the Monopoly game board and how to interpret specific components of the Monopoly game, such as buying, trading and developing property, through game theory models that make empirical sense for the given change management situation.

5.5 Weaknesses and limitations

The canonical action research (CAR) approach creates some weaknesses and limitations to the results and analysis in the sense that an action research study is only a partially controlled experiment and there are limits to how much knowledge can be generalised from observing the BA in three different settings. As methodological weaknesses and limitations of this sort have already been discussed in chapter three, the focus on this section is to discuss to which extent the five CAR principles have been followed in each of the research cycles.

5.5.1 The principle of the researcher-client agreement (RCA)

According to Davison et al (2004), a well-constructed RCA should provide a solid basis for building trust among the various stakeholders and contribute to the internal validity of the research. When one of the aims of the study is to investigate the impact of BA on TQM implementation, if the relationship between the researcher and client should develop in the direction of conflict rather than collaboration, rival explanations for the change in the dependent variables may arise. Table 28 shows how each of the CAR criteria for the researcher-client agreement were met in each of the three action research cycles.

CAR criteria for the researcher-client agreement (RCA)	First action cycle	Second action cycle	Third action cycle
1a. Did both the researcher and the client agree that CAR was the appropriate situation?	When joining DNMI in 1992 the writer was given the formal title of 'research scientist'. There were no discussions about research methods.	When joining NTAX in 1999 the writer was expected to implement TQM, not to do research. There were no discussions about research methods beyond the 'scientific method' of PDCA.	In 2005 the writer was given the formal title of 'research scientist' at NTAX. The 2006 contract between NTAX and UiO mentions action research but not CAR.
1b. Was the focus of the research project specified clearly and explicitly?	The emergent focus on programme management started in 1995 as the KLIBAS development project ended and the maintenance and	When becoming director of quality management in 2000, a formal job description was written and used as a mandate for TQM implementation.	The 2005 job description gave a broad outline of the expectations of quality management research. The 2006 contract with UiO made

	improvement process started.	There was no explicit research agenda.	this more concrete through the research proposal and research plan.
1c. Did the client make an explicit commitment to the project?	The monthly KLIBAS status reports were signed and approved by management, along with all other formal publications. The researcher was asked to represent DNMI in Nordic and European quality control research groups.	There was an explicit management commitment to TQM in the IT strategies and other important documents, but there was no explicit management commitment to the implicitly defined research agenda on how to do TQM programme management.	The formal agreement between UiO and NTAX documents commitment to the research project.
1d. Were the roles and responsibilities of the researcher and client organization member specified explicitly?	The role as action researcher emerged in order to handle the responsibilities of managing the KLIBAS programme and was not formally specified.	The role of action researcher was informally embedded in the role of quality manager. All practical issues related to the role of quality manager were specified explicitly, but without any reference to research.	In 2008 a formal contract was established between the researcher and parts of the organisation in order to make action research possible.
1e. Were project objectives and evaluation measures specified explicitly?	The needs for researching and improving the KLIBAS programme emerged out of the situation. There were no explicitly defined objectives and evaluation measures beyond what emerged as the format of the monthly publications evolved. By 1999 the process was sufficiently mature to be presented at the EUMETNET conference.	Project objectives and evaluation measures for quality control and process improvement were explicitly specified through plans and documents, but there were no objectives and evaluation measures related to the process of challenging and revising existing TQM implementation theory.	As the action research was a continuation of a specific process from the second cycle, objectives and evaluation measures remained the same as had been described in the annual process improvement report published since 2001. Objectives and evaluation measures related to theory development were made more explicit.
1f. Were the data collection and analysis methods specified explicitly?	The software used for collection and analysis of data for the KLIBAS programme was documented in the same formal manner as all KLIBAS software. The first report was published in 1997.	Observations, document studies, interviews and the collection and statistical analysis of numerical data needed for the research were identical to what was needed for the TQM implementation practice.	Methods for collection and analysis of data had been specified in the methodology chapter in each of the annual process improvement reports.

Table 28: CAR criteria for the researcher-client agreement

One of the challenges in framing the TQM implementation game as a three-player game between management, workforce and TQM designer (figure 1) is that the role of the client may become somewhat difficult to explain. On one hand one might say that it is the management part of the organisation that finances the research, and should thus be seen as client by default. On the other hand, when the challenge is to implement TQM in a "fake TQM" environment, the Monopoly game describes the relationship between management and researcher as a zero-sum game of total conflict. From the viewpoint of TSI the moral client of research is the oppressed workforce, but if the workforce has accepted the "fake TQM"

151

ideology by developing a false consciousness, the game between the researcher and the client is still a zero-sum game as the researcher plays the Monopoly game to deconstruct the false consciousness of his client.

A third alternative is to think of the researcher and the client as the same person. This makes sense if one thinks of action research from the perspective of a practitioner researching how to improve his own practice (McNiff & Whitehead, 2006). As the question of the stability and impact of the BA on TQM implementation cannot be understood without taking the action researcher running the BA and evaluating the impact on TQM into consideration, this same-person perspective can be argued to be a natural choice, but it will nevertheless raise a challenge if the explanations for changes in TQM levels given by the TQM designer are subject to rival explanations from management and workforce.

Regardless of how one interprets the client in the RCA relationship, the way the CAR criteria for the RCA are described to have been met in table 28, it should show that different forms of researcher-client agreements have been met in the different cycles, depending to a large degree on different degrees of formality, and the RCA is often supported by documents developed by the client for the research to agree with rather than the other way around.

5.5.2 The principle of the cyclical process model (CPM)

According to Davison et al (2004), the unpredictability of testing an action hypothesis in a real environment may make it necessary to repeat the experiment through cycles that will make the repeated experiment spiral towards more predictability and controllability. Table 29 shows how each of the CAR criteria for the cyclical process model were met in the study. How the criteria 2a and 2g were met can only be answered by looking at the study as a whole, but the meeting of the other criteria will be answered individually for each of the three cycles.

CAR criteria for the principle of cyclic process model (CPM)	First action cycle	Second action cycle	Third action cycle
2a. Did the project follow the CPM or justify any deviation from it?	Initially the research was not conceptualised to follow a CPM, but in retrospect the CPM can be used for describing how the same BA experiment was repeatedly carried out in different organisational settings.	Not applicable.	Not applicable.
2b. Did the researcher conduct an independent diagnosis of the organizational situation?	The period spanning the KLIBAS development project from 1992 to 1995 was used for conducting the informal diagnosis used for the treatment to follow.	The introductory period at NTAX before the researcher became director of quality management was used for diagnosing the organisation.	The period between being given the title of research scientist at NTAX and getting accepted at the PhD programme at UiO was used for diagnosing the new situation.
2c. Were the planned actions based explicitly on the results of the diagnosis?	The BA was implemented in a manner to deal with the technical complexity of the quality management system.	The BA was implemented in a manner to deal with the political complexity of the quality management system.	The BA was implemented to first manage a single politically complex improvement process and then to gradually expand the control span by enlarging the population of processes.

152

2d. Were the planned actions implemented and evaluated?	Implementation and evaluation of actions is documented by monthly progress reports published between March 1995 and August 1999.	Implementation and evaluation of actions is documented by monthly progress reports published between June 2000 and August 2004.	The COBOL process was evaluated on an annual basis. There was no additional evaluation of the TQM programme as it only consisted of managing this single project.
2e. Did the researcher reflect on the outcomes of the intervention?	A general reflection about the usefulness of the BA was written and presented at a EUMETNET conference in 2000.	The director of the IT department wanted and was given a "lessons learnt" verbal presentation. Many of the core reflections from this presentation were later elaborated into papers presented at conferences and journals between 2006 and 2009.	The final communication with the NTAX programming community was in June 2011. At this stage it was not clear whether communications could be re-established, so there was no immediate reflection on the cycle as a whole beyond the parts of this document dealing specifically with the third action cycle.
2f. Was this reflection followed by an explicit decision on whether or not to proceed through an additional process cycle?	As the outcome had been a success, the decision was to try the same BA experiment in another setting.	As the outcome had been a BA failure, the decision was to try the same BA experiment in the same organisation but this time working more closely with the scholarly action research community.	With the time limit defined in the contract between NTAX and UiO being reached, it would not be possible to add further cycles, but ending of the final cycle leaves food for further research to be commented on in section 6.4.
2g. Were both the exit of the researcher and the conclusion of the project due to either the project objectives being met or some other clearly articulated justification?	Not applicable.	Not applicable.	Testing the main BA hypothesis (RH) through three cycles of action research has not been sufficient for formally rejecting or failing to reject the associated null hypothesis, but it provides enough data for discussing the practical use of the BA in real-life situations.

Table 29: CAR criteria for the principle of the cyclic process model

Although the table shows that the action research design was not planned at the beginning in 1992, but rather something that evolved over time as a consequence of how the reflective practice got increasingly focused on scholarly ways of doing action research, the logic behind reflective practice matches the logic of the CPM used in CAR. One reason behind this match has to do with the similarities between the cyclic PDCA model used in TQM and cyclic action research models like the CAR model. In fact, both models have a common ancestor in the cyclic model used in scientific management (Ishikawa, 1985; Gold, 1999, pp. 295-296).

Whenever some kind of technical project intervening with the social world is carried out, stages of diagnosis, planning, action, evaluation and reflection should be easy to identify. The challenge has to do with the quality of work committed to each of the five steps. Despite having an RCA and a CPM that meets most of the CAR requirements, an action research study is often a type of study where the action researcher defines the problem, provides the theory, designs the experiment, evaluates the results, and explains how the study contributes to theory. Unless the study makes extensive use of triangulation and statistical methods for objectifying the facts it may be challenging to convince a positivist audience of information systems researchers of the validity and reliability of the research (Koch et al, 1997; DeLuca & Kock, 2007). What has proved useful in this context is that several independent consultants did organisational assessments at NTAX at various stages while the action research was going on. In terms of sharing or providing a similar diagnosis they all identified the IT function of NTAX as a technically and politically challenging organisation with great need for implementing TQM (Wipro, 2001; Statskonsult, 2002; DNV, 2005; Gartner, 2010).

The Wipro study was a combined ISO 9001:1996 and SEI-CMM v1.0 assessment of the IT function as a whole where a quality expert from Bangalore spent two weeks doing interviews and document reviews at the NTAX offices at Helsfyr. The outcome was a report showing how organisational practice failed to meet the requirements of the standards supported by recommended actions for filling the compliance gaps. The Statskonsult study was more focused on organisational issues. Using Mintzberg's (1983) classification of organisational structures, it argued that parts of NTAX designed as a machine bureaucracy were gradually developing into an administrative adhocracy as control and decision making was increasingly being carried out by the IT department instead of those with the formal NTAX authority to do so (Statskonsult, 2002, p. 43).

The DNV study was an ISO 9001 assessment, similar to the Wipro study, but now using the revised ISO 9001:2000 standard and being executed with a larger team of assessors. The outcome of the study was similar to the Wipro study in terms of showing that the compliance gap was significant but this time also overlapping some of the findings of the Statskonsult study by commenting on cultural issues. As already mentioned in chapter 4.2.1, the Gartner study shared a similar perspective with the DNV study by addressing the NTAX dilemma of how the organisation was in need of TQM while organisational culture made TQM implementation difficult.

Another aspect that aided the study in complying with the requirements of the CAR cycle was the way the process had been extensively documented since the beginning in 1992. A total of 574 documents were published. Most of these documents were published as Klima reports, KLIBAS reports, NTAX reports and as articles in the NTAX journal, but 121 reports from the firsts cycle are accessible through the Norwegian library systems BIBSYS and a total of 14 papers related to the second and third cycle were published in peer-reviewed scholarly outlets.

5.5.3 The principle of theory
Davison et al (2004, p. 74) start the discussion of the theory principle by saying that "action research without theory is not research", and then discuss at which stage it is necessary to make use of explicit theory in the CPM and what kind of theory is meaningful for understanding and designing action. Table 30 shows how the criteria for the principle of theory in CAR have been met within each of the three cycles.

CAR criteria for the principle of theory	First action cycle	Second action cycle	Third action cycle
3a. Were the project activities guided by a theory or set of theories?	Total quality management (TQM) (Mitra, 1993) and Complex adaptive systems (CAS) (Kelly,	TQM + CAS + Critical systems thinking (CST) (Flood, 1993)	TQM + CAS + CST + game theory and mechanism design theory (Binmore, 2007)

	1994)		
3b. Was the domain of investigation, and the specific problem setting, relevant and significant to the interests of the researcher's community of peers as well as the client?	Domain of quality control and climate database development was received as interesting for the climate research community and led to enrolment in Nordic and European networks and projects.	The domain of investigation and specific problem setting led to enrolment in the national network of quality management for the public sector and presentation of results at a conference held by this network.	Several of the papers listed in table 6 were well received in peer reviews or when presented at conferences. One paper won a best paper award.
3c. Was a theoretically based model used to derive the causes of the observed problem?	Following the ideas of Kelly (1994), images of bee hives, ant colonies and algorithmic representation of natural evolution were used for thinking about TQM implementation, but such models were not explicitly used in scientific publications at the time.	Following the ideas of Flood (1993), different models were used for addressing different types of situations. The dominant model was the cybernetic control-loop ("unitary-complex") situation in the language of TSI), but rich pictures ("plural") and loose models based on game theory ("coercive") were used.	Following the ideas of Gintis (2009), game theory can be used for unifying the behavioural sciences. CST provided a way of opening TQM to all types of potentially incompatible sociological theories, and game theory suggested a way uniting such theories by sharing the same mathematical models.
3d. Did the planned intervention follow from this theoretically based model?	Computer programming and social interventions were done in the ad hoc manner suggested by the theoretical models.	Audits and other interventions were done with the aim of improving the models used for representing the various situations.	The PDCA used for improving the audit system for interacting with the COBOL standardisation evolved more and more into becoming a framework for doing experimental game theory.
3e. Was the guiding theory, or any other theory, used to evaluate the outcomes of the intervention?	Statistical quality control methods explained by Mitra (1993), primarily simplified methods of SPC, were used for evaluating the outcome of interventions.	Statistical quality control methods were used in the same manner as in the first cycle although now with more experience and a better theoretical understanding of TQM. Due to the social nature of the problems the CST perspective was used for explaining why the interventions succeeded or failed.	Evaluations were carried out as in earlier cycles although with an increasing focus on the use of game models for articulating the conflict perspectives from CST in a manner that would lead to falsifiable tests in further action research cycles.

Table 30: CAR criteria for the principle of theory

Although there are weaknesses displayed in the table, such as the study starting more or less as grounded research before the arrival of the CAS perspective, and how the final cycle was terminated before the PDCA process had been capable of producing an outlet to be peer-reviewed and accepted within the experimental game theory community, it should nevertheless show that the action research had been theoretically driven to the extent of what is required by CAR.

5.5.4 The principle of change through action

A possible threat to validity in action research is that there may be alternative explanations to an observed changed beyond the planned intervention (Argyris & Schön, 1989). The fourth principle of CAR may prove helpful for identifying challenges to the research outcome by focusing on the relationship between action and change. Table 31 shows how the criteria related to the CAR principle have been met within each of the three cycles.

CAR criteria for the principle of change through action	First action cycle	Second action cycle	Third action cycle
4a. Were both the researcher and client motivated to improve the situation?	The researcher was part of the KLIBAS project development team and it was vitally important for the client and organisation to develop the technology and social practice that was needed to compensate for the old climate database system that was being replaced.	The researcher was working in the position as director of quality management with the specific aim of implementing TQM.	Learning from the outcome of the previous cycle, there was a strong focus on making sure that client, i.e. owner of the audit system used for intervening with the COBOL standardisation practice, had no problems with the researcher trying to improve this system.
4b. Were the problem and its hypothesized cause(s) specified as a result of the diagnosis?	The diagnosis consisted of applying a CAS perspective on the environment where system development was taking place and thus seeing it as complex.	The diagnosis was the same as what had been the case in the first cycle, although at NTAX the political component of the complexity was much larger.	The problem of finding out how to make the programmers use their own quality management designs was understood as part of the political complexity used for diagnosing the NTAX culture as a whole.
4c. Were the planned actions designed to address the hypothesized cause(s)?	The BA prototype followed from the CAS-based diagnosis.	The BA prototype followed from the CAS-based diagnosis.	The planned action focused on the initial conditions of the BA in the sense of identifying and understanding the installed based of TQM within the COBOL programming community and its environment.
4d. Did the client approve the planned actions before they were implemented?	The organisation questioned the ad hoc approach of CAS and generally preferred a more structured project management approach, but did not intervene as long as the KLIBAS system was improving.	There was no specific approval of the BA approach as a formal NTAX method, but the opportunistic logic implied by the BA caused problems with the organisation that were solved by the client (head of IT department) understanding and accepting the nature of the BA approach.	The client (owner of the audit system) was helpful in negotiating access to data as the organisation was initially unwilling to implement the part of their own QMS that specified use of external quality audits.
4e. Was the organization situation assessed comprehensively both before and after the intervention?	There were no comprehensive EFQM-like assessments before and after the BA intervention, but the outcome reports of the KLIBAS project worked as an assessment and gap description that was used	Different assessment methods such as ISO 9004, ISO 15504, CMM, CobiT, CAF and EFQM were used. The dominant methodology emerged through the EFQM approach but the annual assessments with monthly	Continuing the process improvement practice from the second action cycle, annual assessments were carried out in terms of measuring error volumes, calculating change rates and predicting the year of

	for directing further development.	updates were based on what data was available as there was never enough time and resources for doing complete EFQM assessments.	zero defects. ISO 9004 self-assessments were introduced for understanding and improving the audit process aspect of the control game.
4f. Were the timing and nature of the actions taken clearly and completely documented?	All actions were systematically documented through technical reports, status reports and research reports.	All actions were systematically documented (see 3.6).	Annual action research reports were written and distributed among shareholders within the organisation (see 3.6).

Table 31: CAR criteria for the principle of change through action

A challenge about trying to confirm the BA hypothesis is that the BA is a political process which aims at making use of all kinds of organisational dynamics available for creating change. Although the way the CAR criteria are being met in table 31 should indicate that the research was driven by planning and taking action to change the current situation and its unsatisfactory conditions, it would in principle be possible to ask to which extent the BA was responsible for those aspects of the study that could be described as TQM implementation success. After all, the BA was a method for managing the TQM programme, not a method for designing the process improvement projects themselves.

In this study, however, alternative explanations of change do not represent a real problem as the most natural outcome when dealing with the complexity in all of the three action cycles would be no change at all. The outcome is also moderate in the sense that it is not claimed that the organisation changed forever as a consequence of using the BA for a period. What is stated is that the BA had an impact on TQM implementation while it was in action. When the BA was terminated the TQM practices collapsed. There is little reason to expect that quality management standards are being explicitly followed when it has no immediate consequence for the user of those standards (e.g. COBOL programmer) whether a standard is being followed or not. It may have severe consequences for the community of COBOL programmers, but as long as nobody is taking overall responsibility by managing a proper regulation mechanism, it would be surprising if actors would break habits that benefit them as individuals in order to comply with the needs of the community as a whole.

5.5.5 The principle of learning through reflection

As the focus in action research is on creating change and improvement, there is a risk that pressure to keep up with current challenges does not give sufficient time to reflect and learn from past failures. There is also the issue that writing and reflecting about failures and what went wrong in public may not be popular with the organisation. Although the RCA was created for the purpose of minimising such problems, there is also the practical issue of implementing the RCA in terms of developing practice that makes it possible to learn through reflection. Lack of learning through reflection could represent a threat to reliability and validity when commenting on the outcome of the overall BA hypothesis test.

As mentioned in chapter 3.6, the BA study has been extensively documented through progress reports, action research reports and the fact that the researcher has been writing research diaries. Table 32 shows how the practice of documentation, reflection and learning used in the study matches the CAR criteria for learning through reflection.

157

What should be read out of table 32 is that the way the study has been focused on continual writing and distribution of quality improvement reports as part of the way the BA was implemented makes it reliable in the sense that it easy to repeat in new settings in the same way as has already been carried out in three cycles of action research. Whether the outcome of the BA experiment would remain the same in all such settings is another question as there are issues beyond the format of writing and pattern of distributing improvement reports that matters for making the process predictable.

CAR criteria for learning through reflection	First action cycle	Second action cycle	Third action cycle
5a. Did the researcher provide progress reports to the client and organizational members?	The researcher wrote and distributed several progress reports related to the KLIBAS project from 1992 to 1995. From 1995 a series of monthly status reports were written to describe the progress of the BA approach for implementing TQM.	The researcher provided the client and organisational members with monthly progress reports from June 2001 to October 2004.	The researcher provided the client with monthly progress reports.
5b. Did both the researcher and the client reflect upon the outcomes of the project?	To the extent the client refers to project owner in the sense of being somebody who can terminate the project, the main strategy was to feed the client with information in order to prevent him from making thoughts about terminating the project.	The client wanted a change of approach and suggested that the researcher changed organisational position from assistance director to research scientist and got enrolled in a PhD programme for improving the action research.	Both researcher and client reflected on the outcome of the project, but did not express any shared view of how to interpret the outcome of the failed change management project.
5c. Were the research activities and outcomes reported clearly and completely?	A total of 295 KLIBAS reports were written to cover all aspects of methods, systems and processes. There was no feedback indicating that the writing was unclear.	A total of 39 action research reports describing activities and outcomes are listed in chapter 3.6.2.	The six action research reports written during this part of the study should be seen as part of the total series of ten reports describing COBOL research activities and outcomes.
5d. Were the results considered in terms of implications for further action in this situation?	With the system development being done as prototype development, the results were always considered in terms of implications for further action.	The 19 reports focusing specifically on business process improvement were used as input for a formal NTAX decision process (N7). Other reports were designed to create action by other means.	The COBOL action research reports were written and distributed to create change based on ideas explored and discussed in paper 4 and 6.
5e. Were the results considered in terms of implications for action to be taken in related research domains?	Sometimes progress on one type of system could produce ideas on how to improve another type of system. Documented experiments were conducted on how to integrate the various systems.	Once a given research approach seemed to work, similar attempts were done in related domains. For example, the experiments with PSA improvement led to similar experiments with FOS, LFP and other business processes.	The general idea was to make the COBOL study as a starting point for managing a population of improvement projects, but the difficulties with the COBOL process made this impossible.

5f. Were the results considered in terms of implications for the research community (general knowledge, informing/re-informing theory)?	The publication and presentation of the overall assessment of the CAS method at the EUMETNET conference in 1999 informed the research community about the usefulness of BA for implementing TQM.	Publication and presentation of overall results of the cycle in academic outlets was carried out between 2006 and 2009, after the second cycle had formally ended.	Some of the publications and presentations for academic outlets between 2006 and 2009 dealt specifically with the COBOL process, but the evaluation of the BA as TQM programme management during the third cycle has so far only been described in this document.
5g. Were the results considered in terms of the general applicability of CAR?	Although the research process can in retrospect be seen to meet with the requirements of CAR, it was not explicitly defined as a CAR process at the time it was carried out.	The research design during the second cycle was motivated by the idea of viewing the PDCA improvement cycle of TQM as an action research process similar to the action research method used for developing TSI.	Especially during the final years of the third cycle, the idea of using mechanism design and game theory to formulate control design hypotheses in a feedback control system has become the dominant way of understanding how to implement CAR.

Table 32: CAR criteria for learning through reflection

Although the extensive writing and distribution of research reports was useful for making formal diagnosis of the different situations, search out treatments, carry out the action, evaluate the results and reflect on the outcome, the challenge in creating reliability and validity had more to do with how to write action research reports than the practical issues of writing them. This issue was brought up in section 5.4.5 as the issue of how the theoretical framework influences reliability and validity of the results was discussed.

It should also be mentioned that many of the documents referred to in table 32 are documents describing action research associated with the individual process improvement projects rather than documents describing the management of the TQM programme as a whole. In a strict sense the only documents that are of relevance for answering the criteria in table 32 are the progress reports listed in chapter 3.6.1 and research documents summarising the outcome of running the BA for years in a particular setting, but it was the action research reports related to the individual improvement projects that were of prime interest to the client. The challenges in how to manage the TQM programme was more or less only interesting to the researcher himself and the community of practitioners and scholars interested in managing TQM programmes.

6. CONCLUSION

The purpose of this chapter is to describe main lessons learned from the study and what future research should be conducted. The description starts by commenting on the structure of the thesis argument (section 6.1). This is followed by commenting on the outcome from testing of the hypotheses (section 6.2), commenting on how these outcomes contribute to knowledge (section 6.3), and what this means in terms of implications for practice and directions for future research (section 6.4).

6.1 Structure of thesis argument

In the final section of the first chapter a Vee model was used for explaining how the BA can be studied as part of an action research design (figure 5). The Vee model in figure 37 will be used for commenting on the outcome of the study.

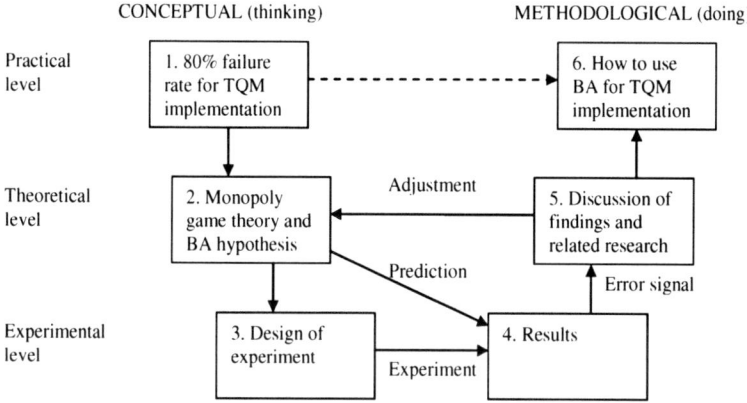

Figure 37: A Vee model of how the BA was studied as part of an action research design

The model consists of a conceptual left leg and a methodological right leg mapping out the three first and three last chapters of the thesis (kappa). The movement down the left leg represented planning of the BA research by discussing the practical problem (chapter 1), model development and refinement of hypotheses (chapter 2), and design of action research experiment (chapter 3). In chapter 1 the model was used for presenting the BA study from the perspective of the left leg in the sense of suggesting some of the premises for the outcome to be presented at the corresponding levels of the right leg of the model.

When revisiting the Vee model in this conclusion, it will be used in a symmetrical way by focusing on the right leg, making use of the conclusion chapter for commenting on how the outcome on each of the three levels corresponded to expectations on the corresponding levels on the left leg. Section 6.2 will focus on the experimental level in terms of commenting on the outcomes of hypothesis testing. Section 6.3 will comment on what the outcomes contribute to theory. Section 6.4 will focus on what the study suggests in terms of implications for practice and what could be useful directions for future research.

6.2 Research hypotheses

The investigation of the bootstrap algorithm (BA) as an approach for implementing total quality management (TQM) in complex environments was made more precise through the following hypothesis.

RH: The BA is an optimal mechanism design for implementing TQM

The testing of the hypothesis implied looking both at whether it was possible to make the BA run in a state of statistical control and whether the BA would have an impact on changing the control games in the organisation by making the games more compliant with requirements and expectations of TQM. For the purpose of testing the RH, three supporting research hypotheses (RH1-3) were used.

RH1: The BA can be implemented and managed in a state of statistical control

RH2: The response to the BA treatment is performance improvement measurable by TQM assessments

RH3: The BA is optimal for implementing TQM in complex environments

While RH1 and RH2 were needed for making sure that the BA would actually work, the purpose of RH3 was to aid the study in asking critical questions about the practical BA implementation that might produce ideas for future improvement.

6.2.1 Outcome of testing

As was shown in table 6 in the final part of chapter 1, the thesis consists of six individually published papers and a cover document (kappa). While a chronological listing of papers with full reference details was practical for giving an overview in the introduction, in table 33 a similar overview is created for the purpose of commenting on the research conclusions by sorting the papers thematically in relation to the research hypotheses and how the theory, method and contribution of the individual papers related to the theory, method and contribution of the kappa.

The first row in the table summarises the theory, method and contribution from the kappa. The way the study has been focusing on TQM, information infrastructure and game theory was presented in broad terms in chapter 1 with more specific details for the purpose of developing exploratory research questions related to each of the research hypotheses in chapter 2. In the theory column the individual papers are narrower in their theoretical focus. Rather than addressing TQM theory in general, they focus on specific issues like SPI, TSI, EFQM or double loop learning. Rather than addressing the theory of information infrastructure dynamics in general they discuss specifics like systems theory and complex adaptive systems. Rather than discussing game theory in general they focus on specifics like evolutionary game theory and use of game theory in game design. In a similar way the method column shows how different research methods have been applied in the papers for the purpose of supporting the overall canonical action research (CAR) used in the kappa. The way theory and methods in the individual papers related to the theory and method of the kappa is shown by the listing of hypotheses and references to CAR in the first column.

In table 33 the CAR approach is seen as consisting of the three steps of making the diagnosis, deciding the treatment and administering the treatment. As these three steps can be compared to the operations research (OR) and systems analysis (SA) steps of analysis, design and implementation, the literature review in chapter 2 was structured around this three-step approach although the research design in chapter 3 applied the five steps used in the cyclical process model (CPM) in CAR. The five steps of the CPM were also used for narrating the results of hypotheses testing for each of the three cycles in chapter 4. The narration covered twenty years of Monopoly diagnosis and BA treatment at DNMI, NTAX and NTAX/UiO. Each cycle started by conducting a diagnosis of the existing TQM information infrastructure by constructing a Monopoly game board to represent the information infrastructure dynamics. This board was then used for deciding on a BA treatment in terms of how the pseudo-code of the BA should be written out for the specific context. The BA was then executed while performance was being measured and monitored. The next step was then to make use of the data for evaluation by use of statistical methods at the end of the cycle. The final step of the CPM consisted on reflecting upon elements of success and failure during the period of execution.

Hypothesis	#		Theory	Method	Contribution
RH Canonical action research (CAR)	Kappa	Mechanism design for total quality management: Using the bootstrap algorithm for changing the control game	TQM, information infrastructure, game theory	Action research	The bootstrap algorithm is an effective strategy for TQM implementation
RH2 CAR: Making a diagnosis by use of the Monopoly game model	1	The Game of Software Process Improvement: Some reflections on players, strategies and payoff.	Software Process Improvement (SPI), Evolutionary game theory	Case study	SPI evolves over a sequence of dramas
	3	Measurements, Feedback and Empowerment. Critical systems theory as a foundation for Software Process Improvement.	Total Systems Intervention (TSI)	Design research	Critical systems thinking can improve SPI in politically turbulent organisations
RH3 CAR: Deciding a treatment based on the BA framework	2	The Pac-Man model of total quality management: Strategy lessons for change agents.	TQM, EFQM, Game theory (in games)	Case study	The Pac-Man model produces optimal TQM strategies
	6	Designing quality management systems with minimal management commitment.	TQM, systems theory	Design research	Successful implementation of QMS can be done bottom-up
RH1 CAR: Administering the BA treatment	4	Software process improvement: What gets measured gets done.	Double-loop learning	Design research	The "What gets measured gets done" principle works at group level, not individually
	5	Designing quality management systems as complex adaptive systems.	Complex adaptive systems	Case study	Explaining failure of quality systems initiatives

Table 33: Research hypotheses and publications

Although the CPM narration in chapter 4 allowed for producing statistical facts and interpretations of the meanings of these facts for each of the three cycles, a unified analysis and discussion of the total outcome was presented in chapter 5. Despite having the statistical hypotheses testing suffer from poor data quality and too short time series, the outcome was not in conflict with the overall picture in table 33 of how the findings from the individual papers support the research hypotheses.

6.2.2 Reflections on methodology

The listing of publications in table 33 indicated a range of theories and methods that were used for investigating particular events and phenomena described in individual papers within the overall action research study using theories and methods described in the kappa. In commenting on the table, a broad picture was given on how these specific theories and methods aimed to support the overall issue of TQM, information infrastructure and game theory for showing how the bootstrap algorithm is an effective strategy for TQM implementation. In chapter 2 and 3 it was explained in more detail why and how the theories and methods have been mixed, focusing on the practical concerns of how they were to be used in the context of action research. In chapter 5 these issues were once again addressed when using the CAR criteria for commenting on reliability and validity of the results. As the aim of this research has been driven by practical rather than philosophical concerns, philosophical debates concerning CAR, the nature of individual theories and methods used and the validity of mixing them by use of the CAR framework have not been addressed. In the context of summarising the outcomes from hypothesis testing, however, such a reflection on methodology by way of philosophical debates could be relevant.

Dahlbom and Mathiassen (1993), for instance, argue that the systems developer is caught inside a dialectic process where the quality of his practice depends on the ability to find a balance between the thesis of mechanistic rationalism and the antithesis of interpretive romanticism. If this kind of conflict-oriented perspective on systems development includes research traditions and research communities to exemplify how the two different worlds are manifested, the idea of synthesising these two worlds may not seem obviously feasible. The two worlds are different to the extent that they can be seen to represent incommensurable paradigms of science.

There are two schools of research practice addressed in this study. In the research tradition of ISO 9000, TQM and statistical process control (SPC), the aim of research is to address problems like how to ensure that millions of Toyotas are produced exactly identical. In the research tradition of information infrastructure and CAS the aim of research is on how to explain (and possibly influence on) the non-linear trajectories of complex systems. The first type of research is often characterised by use of hypotheses, experiments and statistical analysis. The second type of research is often more focused on qualitative data and verbal reasoning.

Researchers within these two types of schools are not always on the best of terms with each other. There have for instance been systems thinkers from the qualitative school who have been vocal against the dominant "hard systems thinking" tradition of control engineering and operations research by saying that such methods often lead to efficient solutions for the wrong problems (e.g. Churchman, 1968; Checkland, 1981; Flood & Jackson, 1991; Flood, 1993; Ackoff, 1999). A response from the school of hard systems science is that soft system methods tend to be intangible, not easy to understand, not easy to use, often created and propagated by believers who want to change the world and use the scientific press for attacking non-believers, tending to focus more on the people involved in the problem than the problem itself and thus claiming success when "they all agreed on the way forward and committed to it" even though this may be an absolute disaster in terms of understanding and solving the problem (Beasley, 2004).

Sometimes, however, scholars from interpretive tradition borrow from the hard systems tradition by making use of mathematical models and concepts. In the theory development described through this study, and the information infrastructure tradition it is built upon, mathematical concepts like non-linear dynamics, positive feedback, attractors and algorithms are important, although the concepts are used more metaphorically than they would be used in a book on engineering control. From the viewpoint of natural scientists like Sokal and Bricmont (1998), this metaphorical use of ideas from physics and mathematics in the socially oriented sciences is a cause for worry. Metaphors of this kind, they argue, may be causing more harm than help in that they are often used by scholars who do not fully understand the concepts, writing to an audience that may be illiterate in terms of natural science. Rather than developing insights about complex phenomena, this kind of scholarly practice leads to academic confusion at best and dangerous actions in the real world at worst. In the final chapter of the book they refer to Chomsky's laments about the poor effect postmodernist philosophy has on universities in the third world where researchers focus on contextually irrelevant problems in order to get published in journals that expect them to relate their discourses to the latest intellectual fashions from Paris (ibid, pp. 189-90).

Much of the theory used in this study is, nevertheless, of the type criticised by Sokal and Bricmont, including the actor-network theory by Latour who they specifically attack in their book, and the reason for doing so has to do with the way the Monopoly model and other models have been used in the study. In the CAR framework it is recommended that action research theory should relate to hypotheses formulated in the style of "in situation S with salient features F, G and H, the outcome X, Y and Z is expected from action A, B and C" (Davison et al., 2004, p. 74). As the hypothesis is to be related to a theory of how to achieve change in a situation involving more than one decision maker, the hypotheses can be interpreted as a game strategy and the theory as game theory. The purpose of testing the statement is to validate a certain aspect of the game model against an empirical situation involving social conflict.

The CAR diagram in figure 38, based on the simplified three-step version of CAR used in the first column of table 33, shows the role of game models in action research as a way of communicating insights between interpretive diagnosis and positivist administering of treatment. The fact that interpretive and positive research can sometimes be seen as two worlds of theories, methods and language means that an action researcher has to put constraints on how he involves in both traditions as his research paradigm depends on being able to circle through sequences of making diagnoses and administering treatments until both the diagnosis and the treatment can be seen to make empirical sense.

The critical point in developing these models, that are supposed to communicate knowledge back and forth between the interpretive and the positivist worldview, is that the model conclusions to be tested can be mathematically deduced from the model. In the study the diagnosis was carried out by designing Monopoly game boards. The Monopoly game is used for understanding the information infrastructure from a dynamical systems perspective in the sense of trying to capture the cash flow (measured in TQM currency) as a dynamic consequence of how the Markov process representation of the game is being executed (Luenberger, 1979).

The BA treatment, on the other hand, relates to the problem of how to influence the non-linear trajectories of the complex system represented by the Monopoly board and is thus deduced from analysing the Monopoly board and is represented as the model conclusion. Model conclusions for the Monopoly model are mathematically represented as subsets of the run tree for the algorithms in the Monopoly strategy space (Frayn, 2005).

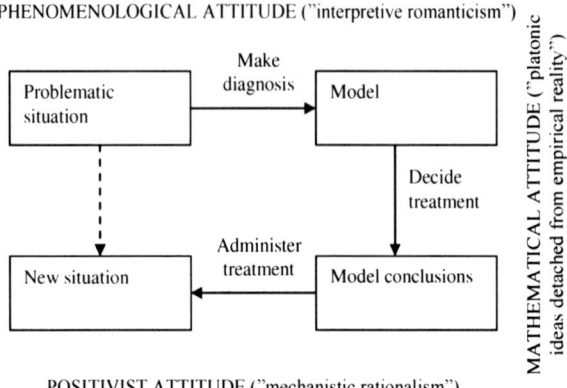

Figure 38: The scientific model as mediator between epistemological traditions

Once the interpretivist has been able to develop the model, it is up to the positivist to validate it. As indicated in the diagram, the main focus is on the solution space (model conclusions) as this is where the BA treatment (intervention) is represented as a Monopoly strategy. If the treatment should fail, this may either be because of poor BA game play (model conclusions) or it may be because the design of the Monopoly game board failed to capture important aspects of the information infrastructure dynamics (model). The positivist approach makes an explicit test of the model conclusions, but if the model conclusions have been mathematically deduced from the model, the outcome of the test should also have consequences for trust in the model.

Contrary to what Sokal and Bricmont say about the dangers of misrepresenting concepts from mathematics and physics in the social sciences, the basis for the reasoning above, based on a model-centric philosophy of science (van Fraassen, 1980; Creager et al, 2007; Øgland, 2009c), the use of concepts from mathematics can be highly useful for improving the quality of social research. British mathematician Keith Devlin, for instance, argues the importance of "soft mathematics" for thinking in domains that are inherently non-mathematical (1997). Checkland (2009) makes the same argument in describing the conceptual reasoning conducted through the use of rich pictures, control diagrams and other conceptual aspects of soft systems methodology (SSM) as indistinguishable from mathematical reasoning.

From the viewpoint of how this study was conducted, it was important that the BA was defined as an algorithm and it was important that the information infrastructure (II) was defined through the language of dynamical systems theory. Without such specific references to mathematical theory, the choice of models for linking the interpretive and positivist aspects of CAR practice would be much more random. The way this study has been making use of BA and II definitions has been in the same manner as how Kuhn (1996) describes the relationship between normal science and revolutionary science. In order for this normal science action research study to have meaning it depends on the paradigm from the revolutionary science of BA and II dynamics to provide the conceptual framework ("soft mathematics") that can be used for developing scientific models for the purpose of studying concrete situations ("hard mathematics").

Although the synthesis of interpretive and positivist research by use of game theory is another way of understanding science and research than the conflict-oriented view expressed by Dahlbom and Mathiassen, the insights expressed in their book are still valid and important in the context of this study. The practitioner or action researcher has to relate to two types of reality. On the one hand he has to make sure that his design ideas are tested in a mechanistically rational manner, but, on the other hand, he also has to make use of romantic interpretivism when trying to understand why the designs fail. What makes the logic of the reasoning in this study different from how Dahlbom and Mathiassen reason is that the conflict between the romantic and mechanistic view is not represented as a conflict of perspective but rather modes of thinking that relate to whether the object in study is a system to be understood or a control strategy to be evaluated. What prevents these two perspectives from being in conflict with each other is the way game theory and game theory models are being used to mediate between the world of systems and the world of control. From an empirical perspective systems theory is used descriptively and game theory is used normatively, but from a mathematical perspective both theories are integrated in feedback and control systems theory (DiStefano et al, 1990; Weinberg & Weinberg, 1988, p. 243).

To conclude the reflection it should also be mentioned that total systems intervention (TSI) was developed for the purpose of showing how the practitioner or action researcher may synthesise and integrate different epistemologies and research streams in the purpose of implementing TQM (Flood & Jackson, 1991). TSI was chosen as part of the framework for the study for this reason and was used for managing the process of how to change different theories and methods depending on whether the nature of research dealt with formulating the problem, solving the problem or validating the solution. TSI also made the distinction between simple and complex scenarios for each situation, as explained in chapter 2 and illustrated through examples in chapter 4. The main difference between TSI as defined by Flood and Jackson and the way it has been used in the study was on how the study kept a more explicit focus on system models and game models as explained above.

6.3 Reducing the knowledge gap in TQM-related BA research

The BA research hypotheses (RH1-3) were designed for confirming implicit assumptions about the BA that had previously not been discussed or made explicit in BA literature. The outcome of the testing of each of the hypotheses should consequently reduce the knowledge gap in TQM-related BA research that was presented in chapter 1.2.

6.3.1 Lessons about BA stability and robustness

The way Hanseth and Lyytinen (2010) analyse the bootstrap strategy for designing information infrastructure, they use non-linear dynamics for describing the growth and development of information infrastructure and a list of principles and criteria for describing the control strategy. Although their use of mathematical control theory is strictly metaphorical, in the sense that they only discuss the phase portraits and attractors of the implied systems without commenting on how the models should be constructed, they do not address the fundamental control theory questions about stability, sensitivity and robustness. For the information infrastructure designer, however, it is of fundamental importance that the bootstrap strategy is stable and robust in the sense that using such a strategy will be of practical use of designing information infrastructure and not simply drive the information infrastructure dynamics into a state of chaos and catastrophe.

What this study contributes to the design community about the stability and robustness of the

BA approach is a rich description of what TQM implementation by use of BA looks like from the designer perspective. In the action research narrative covering three cycles and spanning twenty years of TQM implementation, the BA was in a state of statistical control most of the time. The only exception was the breakdown of the TQM implementation process at the end of the second action cycle. When the stability hypothesis (RH1) was analysed and discussed in detail, several aspects of the BA and how it intervenes in a complex environments were identified. The outcome of the analysis and discussion in section 5.4 can be summarised in four bullet points.

- The BA may start in an instable manner but will quickly become stable
- The stability of the BA can be explained by how it relates to the GA
- The BA thrives on conflict and disequilibrium
- The BA is not robust

Although these four findings are specific to the concrete BA designs used for implementing TQM in this particular study, they can also be seen to correspond with related research concerning general aspects of complex adaptive systems (CAS) (Kelly, 1994).

Holland's (1995) description of CAS, based on his research on genetic algorithms (GA), makes him see CAS as systems that are made up of autonomous agents with the ability to adapt according to a set of rules in response to other agents' behaviour and changes in the environment. Hanseth and Lyytinen (2010) make explicitly use of this CAS definition when discussing design principles and design rules related to the BA, but do not mention the GA itself. An aim with this research, however, has been to aid the TQM designer in understanding how to implement the BA by making the connection between the BA and GA more explicit.

Based on the various difficulties experienced in how to make use of the BA for making practical mechanism designs, the analysis and discussion in section 5.4 resulted in adding comments to each of the command statements of the BA. In figure 39 the revised version of the BA is represented in the shape of a GA. The boxes and arrows are drawn to represent the GA logic in table 9. As the purpose of the research was to show that the BA is an optimal approach for implementing TQM in environments characterised by technical complexity and social distrust, the GA representation of the BA does not conflict with the logic of the original BA, but it reframes it in a perspective that may make it easier to reach an optimal practical BA design.

The most important change when comparing the revised BA in figure 39 with the original BA in table 3 is that the installed base in the initial step is described as a population where each individual is an actor-network. This does not contradict the original BA definition, and it is indeed also possible to run the new BA by focusing on a population consisting of only one individual, but in terms of what was experienced in the study it was of vital importance to focus on several individuals at the same time to create stability.

Another important change in perspective, when viewing the BA through the lens of the GA, is that the control structure of the algorithm becomes more evident. In the original BA the only explicit use of a conditional statement is in the termination criterion. In the revised version the response to individual cultivation failure is made explicit through the use of fitness measurements and how to maintain the population by selecting individual process improvement projects with high fitness scores. In practice, however, the fitness evaluation and selection may not be as much a consequence of conscious decision making as it may be the consequence of how individual improvement efforts fail for political or other reasons. Nevertheless, the GA structure of the revised BA makes this aspect of information infrastructure design explicit and makes the number of individuals maintained by a population into a useful indicator for analysing BA stability.

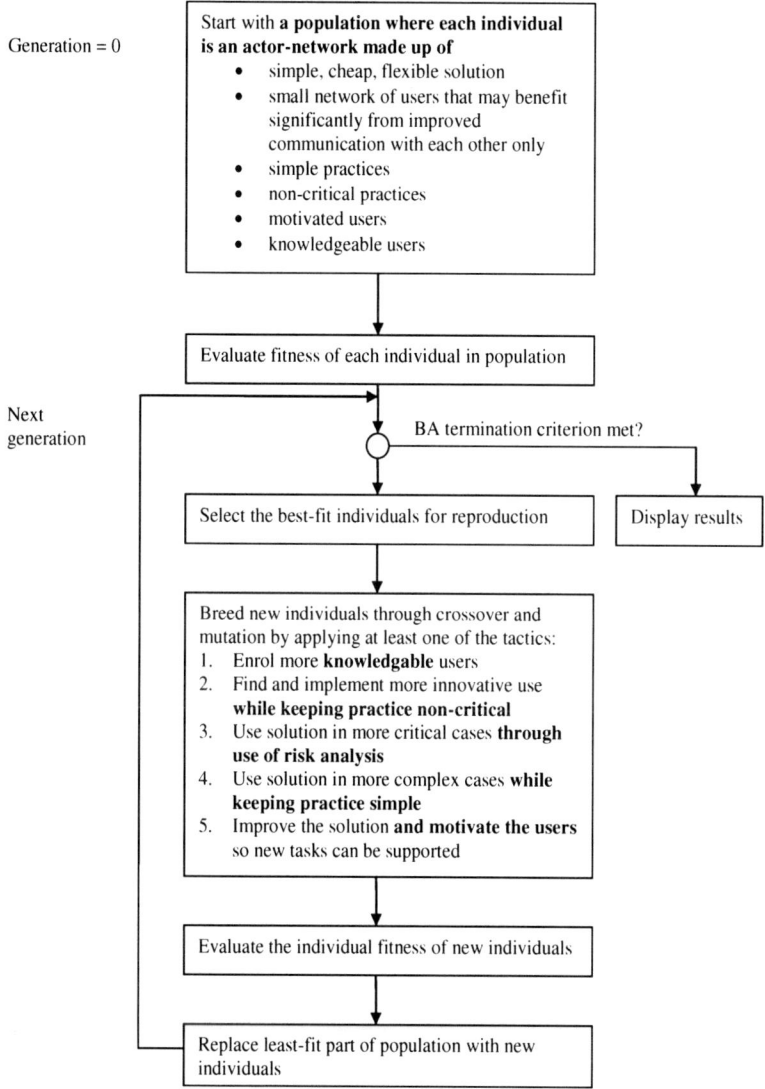

Figure 39: Representing the BA in the shape of a GA

While one of the characteristics of the GA is the way it simulates the robustness of biological evolution (Louis & Rawlins, 1993), one of the bullet points summarising the outcome of analysis and discussion of the BA said that it was not robust. The paradox created by these statements has to do with the fact that the GA is designed to be executed on a computer while the BA is a set of instructions to be used by a designer (principal) for the purpose of intervening in the control game played by management and workforce (agents). Even though the execution of the BA itself may be carried out in a stable manner, both the principal and the agents are part of the actor-network being acted upon and if the principal should be removed from the network this could be comparable to unplugging the computer running the GA. It is consequently important to maintain good political relationships and make sure that the location from where the BA is being executed is protected.

6.3.2 Lessons about BA impact on TQM implementation success

The TQM implementation process can be seen as a two-player zero sum game between the TQM designer (principal) and the management and workers (agents) playing the organisational control game (Flood, 1993). A typical mechanism in such control games, seen from the viewpoint of the Frankfurt school of sociology, is the way management tries to manage organisational culture by cultivating false consciousness among the workers to prevent them from questioning authority (Marcuse, 1964). Brunsson and Jacobsson (2000) suggest that this effect may be better understood by looking at society from a networks perspective rather than a class perspective. Different diagnosis may result in different treatments. The problem for the TQM designer is to adjust behaviour among the agents in the organisation by redesigning the control game in a way that makes it compliant with the ideals of TQM.

As illustrated in figure 40, the impact of the BA on TQM implementation is based on the idea that the Monopoly game of information infrastructure dynamics can be understood as a game of mechanism design that changes the payoff structure of the Stag Hunt game and thus influences whether the TQM designer and organisation will be playing the "real TQM" or the "fake TQM" equilibrium. Unless the "real TQM" equilibrium is being played, the Matching Pennies game will not be a good representation of the "what gets measured gets done" logic that is the reason for doing audits and quality controls.

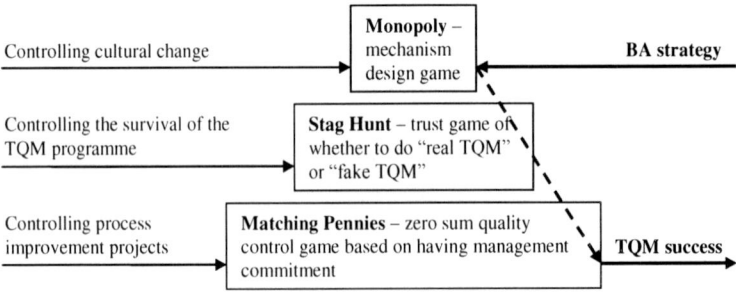

Figure 40: Monopoly changes payoff in Stag Hunt to make Matching Pennies align with TQM

Similar to the game of TQM mechanism design, Monopoly is a game of strict conflict in the sense that winning the game is equivalent to everybody else loosing. When using Monopoly to represent the game of TQM mechanism design, the Monopoly properties are interpreted as users and solutions while the colouring of the properties represent practices that group the users and solutions together in natural units. A Monopoly rule says that it is necessary to have a complete colour monopoly of properties before the properties can be developed by erecting houses and hotels. In the world of TQM implementation this is used for representing the idea that process improvement by educating users and redesigning solutions should be done with a focus on business processes goals.

170

According to Seidman (2011), analysing strategies for winning Monopoly starts with dividing the game into the four consecutive phases of (1) acquiring properties, (2) negotiating and trading properties, (3) developing properties, and (4) the game reaching a state where it is effectively over. As illustrated in figure 41, the initial step of the BA can be identified with the first phase of Monopoly play while the five steps of the control loop are used for playing Monopoly through the next two phases. When the game reaches a stage where one player is starting to take the lead, either the principal or the agents, there is not much more to do for the BA apart from observing how the rich get richer and the poor get poorer until game play ends in TQM implementation success or TQM implementation failure.

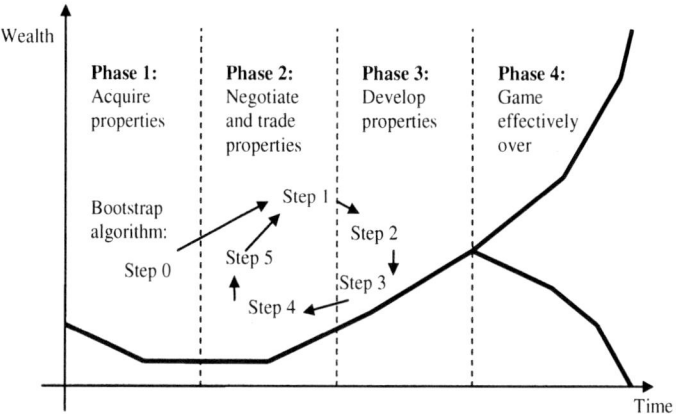

Figure 41: Using the BA for playing the Monopoly game of TQM implementation

The figure illustrates how the BA interacts with the four phases of TQM implementation. The BA is represented by having the steps visualised in a cyclic pattern. The initial step is associated with the first phase of Monopoly while the next five steps describe the sequence of tactical moves that has to be carried out in a thoughtful manner during the next two phases until the final phase runs on auto pilot.

The graph in the time series diagram illustrates the impact the BA has on TQM implementation. As the curve mirrors the "rich getting richer" dynamics mentioned in Monopoly simulation studies (Eastwood, 2009), the label "wealth" is used for representing the TQM maturity level. The behaviour of the curve in relation to the four phases is based on Seidman's (2011) verbal descriptions.

The initial step of the BA represents a period of investments with little or no return, so the impact line is pointing slightly downwards. As soon as properties have been acquired, however, process improvement can start and the impact line moves upwards. If the phases of trading and developing properties have been skilfully carried out, the hope is that sufficient momentum has been created for making TQM implementation drive itself exponentially towards completion through the law of increasing returns.

Each of the action research cycles in the study show BA/GA designs, summarised in figure 39, having impact on TQM maturity development that corresponds with patterns in figure 41. In the first cycle the TQM implementation process was abandoned after it was seen to be following the path upwards in the fourth phase. In the second cycle the TQM implementation was locked in on the downward spiral as the fourth phase was reached. The third cycle only managed to reach phase two before it was terminated.

The lessons learned about how the BA impacts on TQM implementation through the understanding of the Monopoly model is summarised in table 34.

Phase	Bootstrap algorithm	Monopoly model
1	Find suitable practices, solutions and users at the initial stage of TQM implementation when the BA is primarily driven by chance	Make investments in terms of buying properties
2	During the early stages of TQM implementation, the focus of the BA control loop should be on using task improvement activities for negotiating access to complete business processes	Trade properties in order to gain monopolies
3	During the more mature stages of TQM implementation, the focus of the BA control loop should be on improving practice by redesigning solutions and educating users	Develop monopolies by erecting houses and hotels
4	Once a critical stage in the TQM implementation game has been reached, the law of increasing returns sets in and the BA will rapidly lead towards either success or failure	Game effectively over

Table 34: Using the BA for playing the Monopoly game of TQM implementation

A difference between the BA approach to TQM implementation and conventional TQM implementation methods know from textbook literature is that the BA approach is an opportunistic bottom-up approach while the conventional methods are usually more preplanned and top-down driven (e.g. Oakland, 1999; Masing, 1999; Juran & Godfrey, 2000; Dale, 2003). Even with the TSI approach, which tries to implement TQM in the context of critical theory to improve social conditions from a workforce perspective, the way TSI makes use of Viable Systems Methodology (VSM) for constructing a network of control loops is based on the idea of aligning with top management and implementing TQM in an essentially top-down manner (Flood, 1993, chapter 9).

As pointed out in relation to table 4 when discussing impact in the introductory chapter, how the TQM designer aligns the BA strategy with the interests of management and workforce may have positive and negative consequences for TQM implementation success. An important and interesting aspect of the BA approach is that it is politically aligned with technology rather than labour nor capital. As pointed out in their essay on the history of information systems research in Scandinavia, Aanestad and Olaussen (2010) identify a change of political orientation as the ethnographically oriented studies of the last few decades have clarified the role of technology as a political actor while earlier sociologically oriented studies were more concerned with the conflict between labour and capital.

To make sure the BA has an impact on TQM implementation it is necessary to align with management and workforce whenever this can be useful for making the QMS grow and develop, but it is also necessary to observe when such alliances work against the interests of the TQM designer as a political actor. In reference to the political alignment dilemma in table 4, where some TQM implementation philosophies align with the management perspective (Beckford, 2002) and others with the workforce perspective (Flood, 1993), the BA approach suggests that such alignments have to be negotiated and renegotiated all the time, depending on what is useful for the growth and development of the QMS as a political perspective in itself. The way the BA and information infrastructure makes use of actor-network theory is important both for understanding how to make the BA impact on TQM implementation and why it impacts or fails to do so (Hanseth & Monteiro, 1998).

172

6.3.3 Lessons on how to make optimal use of the BA

In the introduction chapter it was suggested that a reasonable explanation for the high failure rates in TQM implementation could be found when using the stag hunt game model for representing what Brunsson and Jacobsson (2000) said about difficulties organisations have with walking the TQM talk. The basin of attraction for the Nash equilibrium of neither the organisation nor the TQM designer walking the TQM talk was greater than the basin of attraction for the Nash equilibrium where both the organisation and the TQM designer walk the talk. Without applying a mechanism design strategy taking the imbalance of the two basins of attraction into consideration it is understandable why most TQM implementation projects fail or end up pretending to be doing TQM rather than actually doing it.

The framing of the study started with the idea of using Monopoly board game theory for understanding the problem of how a TQM designer (principal) should redesign the organisational quality management system (QMS) in order to make the control game carried out between management and workforce (agents) comply with the requirements and expectations of TQM. It was argued that the bootstrap algorithm (BA) for growing and developing information infrastructure could be viewed as a Monopoly strategy, but in order to make optimal use of the BA it was necessary with a deeper analysis of the TQM mechanism design game by looking at the games discussed in the individually published papers. How these individual games can be seen as subgames of the Monopoly game of TQM mechanism design is illustrated in figure 42.

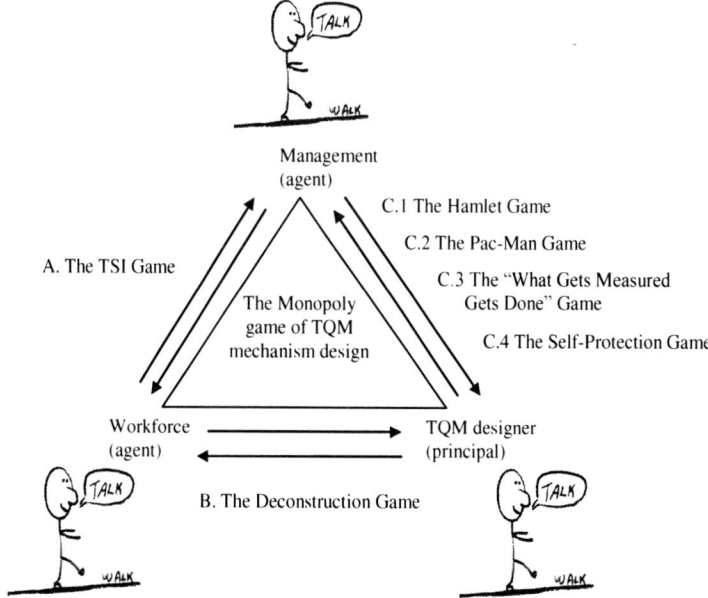

Figure 42: How to make use of all the games and strategies in the study for optimising the BA

Along the axis between management and workforce what was previously described as the control game has been relabelled as the TSI game. The TSI game is an interpretation of the conflict between capital and labour seen from the perspective of system designers wanting to implement TQM for the joint purpose of improving business and liberating the oppressed (Flood, 1993). The way this game is represented in *paper 3*, the focus is on how labour is accepting oppression by developing false consciousness of "fake TQM" in the sense of believing that the organisation is doing TQM when it is not (Brunsson and Jacobsson, 2000), and the liberation strategy then becomes to confront the illusion of doing TQM with facts derived from quality audits.

The deconstruction game at the bottom axis between workforce and technology is a game of trying to break down false consciousness ("fake TQM") and replace it with a liberating belief in real TQM. In a "fake TQM" environment, where there is no real management commitment to TQM, there are no incentives for the workforce to comply with standards created by the workforce community and instead they pursue individual goals. The example used in *paper 6* is the that it may be good for the individual software developer to have maximum flexibility in how to design software but from the viewpoint of the community it is better to have standards to make sure the software stays maintainable. In the deconstruction game (*paper 6*) the TQM designer tries to convince members of the workforce into believing that management is committed to TQM while the members may respond with counter-strategies based on whether they are convinced or not.

Along the axis between technology and management there are four games. In order to prevent the deconstruction game from becoming pointless, in the sense of only having a single Nash equilibrium consisting of the pair of strategies where the TQM designer tries to bluff the workforce about management commitment and the workforce calls the bluff, three of the games along the management axis deal with the issue of getting different levels of management commitment to TQM. The fourth game deals with the situation of how to act as principal when the agents are capable of having the principal eliminated.

The Hamlet game is concerned with getting management commitment to a TQM framework based on standards like EFQM, CMM and ISO 9000. The framework will be used for defining which areas and processes within of the organisation to audit, what level of audit detail is necessary in such areas and processes, and how to measure TQM maturity levels. While the TQM designer wants to select standards that are suited for the organisation and can be used for aligning with a network of other organisations using the same framework, management may have other reasons for preferring one standard to another or not wanting any standard at all. In *paper 1* the game play is narrated in the style of Hamlet in order to focus on themes like moral corruption, appearance and reality, and mortality. Although the game may be challenging to win from the TQM designer point of view, the overall aim is to find a compromise which combines the political goal of getting management commitment and the technical goal of getting a formal but useful TQM framework.

Even though it may be possible to find a TQM framework that creates management commitment at a high level, there may still be a challenge to make managers commit to quality when there are other priorities to be made. The Pac-Man game (*paper 2*) describes a conflict between a yellow mouth (Pac-Man) eating its way through a maze filled with dots, fruits and power pellets while being chased by four monsters. If Pac-Man eats one of the four power pellets the monsters temporarily turn into ghosts and may be chased and eaten by Pac-Man. This game is used for modelling the central idea that managers and TQM designers are "natural enemies" (Beer, 1968, pp. 22-23), meaning that managers tend to see the TQM designer as stirring up problems by making hidden problems visible through statistics and graphs but are nevertheless grateful for quality audits in those rare situations where audits and quality control are needed for purposes like convincing a third party. The purpose of the game from the TQM design perspective is to identify and exploit these rare situations of "power pellets" to gain temporary commitment to TQM that can be further used in the deconstruction game.

While the Hamlet game is played against top-level management and the Pac-Man game played against mid-level management, the "what gets measured gets done" game in *paper 4* is primarily thought of as a game for getting low-level management commitment. The game consists of the TQM designer confronting management with statistics and error trends showing lack of progress and asking whether they can explain. Management may then choose to make up excuses and forget about it or investigate and do something. If something is done about the situation, this may provide important input for the deconstruction game. Otherwise the TQM designer has to take note of the excuses and carry out further investigations and audits to show that the excuses are absurd while producing more evidence of how statistics and error trends continue to point in the wrong direction.

The final game on the axis between management and technology deals with the conflict of how to create sufficient provocations for creating organisational change while avoiding to be considered a problem or a threat. The self-protection game is depicted on management/technology axis because the formal power to remove the TQM designer comes from management, although the reason for removing him may have to do with how he interacts with each of the three corners of the diagram. The way the game is described in *paper 5*, the TQM designer has to be careful in selecting interventions that encourage quality control along workforce processes, he has to be careful in how he creates commitment to TQM at the different management levels and he has to be careful in how he makes sure that the TQM design team stays up to date with the rest of the organisation by practicing self-reflective TQM. In all of these three corners there may be limits to what can be done before somebody in power gets convinced that the TQM designer is part of the problem rather than the solution.

As the overall purpose of the diagram is to illustrate how these six games represent different aspects in making the BA optimal for playing the Monopoly game of TQM mechanism design, the six arrows surrounding the triangle are used for representing the Monopoly game as a whole. The BA strategy is conceptualised as the actual mechanism design used by the TQM designer for playing the Monopoly game, represented by the two arrows going out from the TQM designer to balance the strategies represented by the remaining four arrows. As a consequence of this, the way the six individual games are connected to the Monopoly board game consists of the four games played against management, these games being typical of the phase with primary focus on negotiating and trading properties, while the game played against workforce is more characteristic of the phase focusing on property development. The TSI game associated with the control game played by management and workforce is supposed to be understood in the context of the design of the Monopoly board and equipment such as cards, deeds, dice and tokens.

At the three corners of the TQM mechanism design game model there are cartoons illustrating the stag hunt game of what happens when there are different matches and mismatches between talking and doing TQM. As was mentioned in the introduction, playing the payoff dominant Nash equilibrium (both organisation and TQM designer taking TQM seriously) and the risk dominant Nash equilibrium (both organisation and TQM designer pretending to be doing TQM) are evolutionary stable strategies for repeated plays of stag hunt. If the organisation had serious intents about implementing TQM and found a serious TQM designer there would be no problems. The situation is worse if the organisation had no serious commitment to TQM or the chosen TQM designer would not have the sufficient skill, knowledge or motivation for doing serious TQM. As the risk dominant Nash equilibrium has a greater basin of attraction than the payoff dominant equilibrium, the expected result would be as Brunsson and Jacobsson (2000) predict in terms of the TQM implementation process converging towards the risk dominant equilibrium. However, the difference in size between the two basins depends on the payoff structure of the game, and the payoff structure is a mechanism that depends on the level of trust in the culture (figure 40).

What this study suggests is that optimal use of the BA will influence the payoff structure of the stag hunt game by making it more obvious to management that there is more to be gained by taking TQM seriously (increase the utility for hunting stag) and influence the rules and incentives of the organisational control game to make it less attractive to carry out individual actions that work against the interest of the community (decrease the utility for hunting hare). Unless the changes in utilities changes the nature of the game from no more being a stag hunt game, there will still be a difference in the size of the basins of attractions, making the fake TQM equilibrium more likely than the serious TQM equilibrium, but the difference is expected to be less when using the optimal BA than when using a more conventional TQM implementation method.

When gaps concerning knowledge about optimal use of the BA were introduced in the first chapter, two problematic issues concerning use of BA and non-BA strategies in complex and simple environments were addressed through the use of table 5. Firstly, the use of non-BA strategies in complex environments was identified as a problem for exactly the same reasons that the BA evolved in the first place. Conventional TQM methods are based on operations research and cybernetics, which is important for dealing with problems that can be understood through such frameworks, but may cause problems when the environment is of such a complex nature that they can only be understood from a CAS perspective. Secondly, by using CAS as a default perspective on problematic situations, regardless of level of complexity, there is a risk that the TQM designer jumps to the conclusion of applying the BA strategy before having properly formulated the problem.

It was suggested that the total systems intervention (TSI) framework might be able to manage the process of changing between BA and non-BA strategies as the problematic situations were interpreted as simple or complex. As pointed out in this study, BA and TSI can be well-integrated as a TQM implementation approach by thinking about individual process improvement through the perspective of TSI and the management of the process improvement programme from the perspective of BA.

When looking at the different games in figure 42 from the perspective of the non-BA strategy for dealing with a simple QMS, there are only three games that matter. The TSI game describes the control game between management and workforce, but only the upper half of the SOSM matrix (figure 14) is in use because of the simplicity of the situation. Of the four games defined along the axis between management and TQM designer, the "what gets measured gets done" game is the only game that has to be kept in focus in order to maintain the management commitment that is already embedded in the simple situation. This means that the deconstruction game between workforce and TQM designer can be played more or less on auto-pilot as a part of the "what gets measured gets done" game. As the situation grows more complex, however, the TSI needs to address the lower parts of the SOSM and all the games in figure 42 have to be played in a more intense manner. However, as the purpose of the TSI is to reduce complexity, the focus of TQM implementation may alter between simple situations and complex ones, and the TSI will help deciding when to use BA strategies and when to use non-BA strategies.

As a final comment on optimality, perhaps of more importance for the TQM designer than the particular games listed in figure 42 is the general idea of using game theory in as a normative theory for understanding organisational change. Although game theory was presented with great promise as part of systems theory and elsewhere in the fifties and sixties (McDonald, 1950; Churchman et al, 1956; von Bertalanffy, 1968), it became less fashionable in the seventies and eighties (Colman, 1995). By the time Flood and Jackson (1991) developed TSI as a method of systems development based on critical theory, it may be that certain parts of the systems community had lost faith in game theory as there is no mention at all of game theory in their writing. With the advancement of computer technology in the period that followed, however, game theory continues to develop and has become an important part of economics, psychology, sociology, biology and computer science with strong connections to the theory of CAS in general (Axelrod & Cohen, 2000; Nisan et al.,2007; Gintis, 2009).

6.4 The TQM challenge and need for further research

The motivation for the study was based on the observation that TQM is important but often difficult to implement. This was illustrated by examples from the nuclear power industry where the consequences of poor quality management and plant failure can be quite dramatic. In Perrow's (1984) analysis of the Three Mile Island disaster in 1979 he concludes that accidents in complex and tightly-coupled systems like nuclear power plants should be expected as a consequence of the nature of the systems. No matter how much TQM is applied for reducing the probabilities of serious failure, he argues, the consequences of failure can be so dramatic that one should ask whether society can accept the risk of living with such systems. The kind of systems indirectly addressed through this study, the climate system and the financial system, are also complex and tightly-coupled systems but in this case it is not a question of whether society can live with the costs of system failure or not. Breakdown and failure in these large systems may have disastrous consequences for national and international infrastructure and deployment of TQM by use of control technology seems to be the only way of preventing ultimate chaos and disaster (Beniger, 1986).

What complicates the issue further, however, is the "tragedy of the commons" in the sense of nobody wanting chaos and disaster while playing by the rules of a game that makes individual rationality conflict with what is rational for the community at large (Hardin, 1968). In the case of wanting to implement TQM, the TQM designer may find himself in a world where everybody is talking about the importance of TQM while nobody is doing anything about it (Brunsson and Jacobsson, 2000). What needs to be done is to redesign the rules of the game people are playing, what is known as mechanism design in game theory literature. By reviewing information infrastructure literature it seems like the bootstrap algorithm (BA) for designing information infrastructure could be a useful approach for mechanism design, if we choose to represent the TQM information infrastructure dynamics by a mathematical dynamic systems model such as the Monopoly game board.

6.4.1 Using the BA to control TQM implementation programmes

From the TQM practitioner perspective, the single most important idea from this study may be the idea of integrating systems theory and game theory as an overall unified theoretical framework for understanding TQM implementation, as illustrated in figure 43.

In the diagram the black sleeve represents the controller (principal) trying to regulate the information infrastructure development to support a cultural basis for playing a control game based on "real TQM" (system input), and the checker patterned sleeve represents forces within the organisational (agents) wanting a cultural basis that aligns with "fake TQM" (system dynamics). From a descriptive perspective the information infrastructure (system) is understood as a Markov chain representation of the Monopoly game model. At the interface between the principal and agents (system input and output) the information infrastructure is understood as a mechanism design game in the shape of strategies and solution concepts for playing Monopoly.

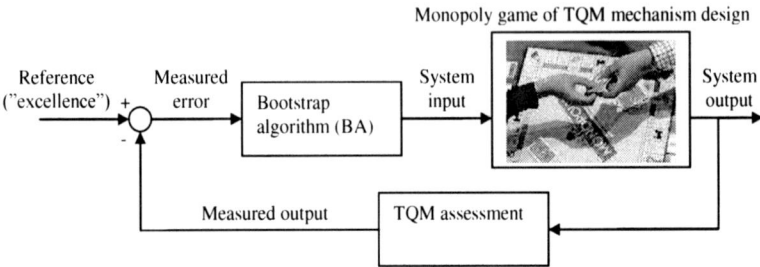

Figure 43: Thinking about control design from the viewpoint of game theory

Given this conceptual description, the purpose of this study has been to use the Monopoly game as tool for turning the BA in table 3 into a practical strategy for winning the Monopoly game defined by the diagnosis of the organisation's QMS information infrastructure. While the pseudo-code representation of the BA in table 3 can be seen as an optimal strategy for playing information infrastructure Monopoly from a theoretical point of view, in the empirical situation a specific Monopoly model has to be diagnosed and the BA has to be formulated to work as an optimal strategy for that particular version of the Monopoly game.

By viewing the TQM mechanism design problem in the context of systems theory, in the manner exemplified in figure 43, the problem is reformulated into a design problem within the theory of feedback and control systems. This systems perspective on a game theoretical problems means that it is not sufficient to select a BA implementation that is optimal or close to optimal, but it also has to be stable and robust. For the community of TQM practitioners and action researchers represented by Flood (1993) and those responsible for the case studies of TSI-based TQM implementation in his book, this integrative perspective on using systems theory for diagnosing, game theory for deciding treatment and then again systems theory for administering treatment is missing but would be expected to be helpful for practice, if it were included, in the same way as it has been helpful for practice in this study.

Another way of explaining the practical importance of integrating systems theory and game theory as an overall unified theoretical framework for understanding TQM implementation is by thinking about the control loop in figure 43 through the perspective of double loop learning. By thinking about the control loop in figure 43 as single loop learning in the manner illustrated by figure 36 in section 5.4.5, the set point (reference) to the far left in figure 43 defines "excellence" in terms of how the instantiation of the BA performs in the empirical case modelled by the Monopoly game, but it does not challenge the Monopoly representation. The purpose of double loop learning is to challenge the governing variables in the sense of how the current version of the Monopoly model seems to represent reality and then make adjustments in the model when needed. The way the Monopoly model can be analysed, both from a dynamic systems perspective through its Markov chain representation and from a game perspective through its game tree representation, makes it possible to question the validity of the Monopoly model whenever a BA strategy does not perform as expected. Single loop learning comes from designing and testing the BA treatment. Double loop learning comes from making and validating the Monopoly diagnosis.

In other words, by making use of the Monopoly model, which allows integrating systems theory and game theory, the TQM practitioner or action researcher can formulate his BA design (control design) by use of game theory and then use systems theory for learning about why the control design succeeded or failed. The fact that the Monopoly model is both a dynamic systems model and a game model means that it can used for analysing both systemic and political aspects of a socio-technical phenomena, similar to how actor-network theory deals simultaneously with politics (actors) and systems (networks), but with the benefit of being a normative rather than descriptive theory.

6.4.2 What future research should be conducted

The study makes important contributions to the problem of how to use the BA as a mechanism design for growing and developing a QMS that changes the organisational control game towards compliance with TQM. The nature of the contributions consist partly of illustrating challenges in how to use the BA for implementing TQM and partly of creating some hypotheses on how such challenges can be overcome. Action research can be used for testing strategies in real-world environments, describing in rich detail how a TQM implementation approach like the BA may fail in a specific environment, but it is difficult to generalise from a specific case in order to say something about what to expect from the BA in a more generalised context.

Just like a phenomenological case study is often used as the first step in a positivist research design, a natural next step to follow up on the findings from this BA study would be to carry out BA driven TQM laboratory experiments on a large scale. Unlike the positivist TQM researcher who collects his data from questionnaires, polling the opinion of people on what they believe or have experienced as success factors for TQM implementation, further research would benefit more from laboratory experiments concerned with the practical outcome of running the BA and less with distributions and patterns in peoples' opinions about BA practice. The kind of studies used in experimental game theory would be a natural reference (e.g. Colman, 1995; Camerer, 2003; Ariely, 2008). However, laboratory testing by giving one part of a population a BA treatment and another part of the population a different treatment, for aligning with standard procedures of double blindfold to prevent placebo effects and observer bias, can be difficult to carry out.

A more realistic agenda for further research could be to expand on the current action research by developing a 'networks of action' programme for managing action research projects aimed at testing out the BA approach in different organisational settings. While this will not be a perfect research design for comparing and contrasting the BA with alternative methods, it can at least be used as an approach for researching how to optimise BA designs for different types of complex organisations.

REFERENCES

Aanestad, M. & Olaussen, I. (eds.), 2010: *IKT og samhandling i helsesektoren: Digitale lappetepper eller sømløs integrasjon?*, Tapir Akademisk Forlag: Trondheim.

Abt, C.C., 1970: *Serious Games*, Viking Press: New York.

Ackoff, R.L., 1999: *Ackoff's Best: His Classic Writings on Management*, Wiley: New York.

Albertarelli, S., 2000: "1000 ways to play Monopoly," *International Journal for the Study of Board Games Studies*, Vol. 3, pp. 117-121.

Albertos, P. & Mareels, I., 2010: *Feedback and Control for Everybody*, Springer Verlag: Berlin.

Araya, J.L. and Alfaro, E.J., 2008: "Prueba e implementación de algoritmos de control de calidad de datos de temperatura superficial del aire en un contexto operative", *Tecnología en Marcha*, Vol. 21, No. 3, Julio-Setiembre 2008, pp. 47-61.

Araya, J.L., 2010: "Capacity building at the National Meteorological Institute: Training personnel to apply quality control tools", *WMO Technical conference on meteorological and environmental instruments and instruments and methods of observation (TECO-2010)*, Helsinki, Finland, 30 August - 1 September 2010.

Argyris, C. & Schön, D.A., 1978: *Organizational Learning: A Theory of Action Perspective*, Addison-Wesley: Reading, Massachusetts.

Argyris, C. & Schön, D.A., 1989: "Participatory action research and action science compared: A commentary," *American behavioral scientist*, Vol. 32, No. 5, pp. 612-623.

Ariely, D., 2008: *Predictably Irrational: The Hidden Forces that Shape Our Decisions*, Harper: London.

Ash, R.B. & Bishop, R.L., 1972: "Monopoly as Markov Process", *Mathematics Magazine*, Vol. 45, No. 1, pp. 26-29.

Auriol, E. & Benaim, M., 2001: "Convergence and oscillation in standardization games," *European Journal of Economic and Social Systems*, Vol. 15, No. 1, pp. 39-56.

Avison, D., Lau, F., Myers, M. & Nielsen, P.A., 1999: "Action Research," *Communications of the ACM*, Vol. 42, No. 1, pp. 94-97.

Axelrod, A., 2002: *Everything I know about business I learned from Monopoly: Successful executives reveal strategic lessons from the world's greatest board game*, Running Press: Philadelphia, Pennsylvania.

Axelrod, A., 2009: *RISK: The Decision Matrix – Strategies That Win*, Sterling Publishing: New York.

Axelrod, R. & Cohen, M.D., 2000: *Harnessing Complexity: Organizational Implications of a Scientific Frontier*, Basic Books: New York.

Bang, S., Efsen, S., Hunderborg, P., Janum, H., Mathiassen, L. & Schultz, C., 1991: *Kvalitetsstyring i Systemutvikling*, Teknisk Forlag: Copenhagen.

Bansler, J., 1989: "Systems development research in Scandinavia: Three theoretical schools," *Scandinavian Journal of Information Systems*, Vol. 1, No. 1, pp. 3-20.

Baskerville, R., 2007: "Educing theory from practice," in Koch, N. (ed.): *Information Systems Action Research: An Applied View of Emerging Concepts and Methods*, Springer: New York, pp. 313-326.

Beasley, J.E., 2004: "Soft OR," *OR-Notes*, http://people.brunel.ac.uk/~mastjjb/jeb/or/softor.html (downloaded on April 12th, 2013)

Beck, U. & Willms, J., 2000: *Conversations with Ulrich Beck*, Polity Press: Oxford.

Beckford, J., 2002: *Quality*, Second edition, Routledge: London.

Beer, S., 1959: *Cybernetics and Management*, Unibooks: London.

Beer, S., 1968: *Management Science: The Business Use of Operations Research*, Doubleday: New York.

Beer, S., 1972: *Brain of the Firm*, Penguin Press: London.

Beer, S., 1974: *Designing Freedom*, CBC publications: London.

Beniger, J.R., 1986: *The Control Revolution: Technological and Economic Origins of the Information Society*, Harvard University Press: Cambridge, Massachusetts.

Bennett, P., Bryant, J. & Howard, N., 2001: "Drama theory and confrontation analysis," in Rosenhead, J. & Mingers, J. (eds.): *Rational Analysis for a Problematic World Revisited: Problem Structuring Methods for Complexity, Uncertainty and Conflict*, Second Edition, Wiley: Chichester, pp. 225-248.

Berlinski, D., 1976: *On Systems Analysis: An Essay Concerning the Limitations of Some Mathematical Methods in the Social, Political and Biological Sciences*, The MIT Press: Cambridge, Massachusetts.

Bewersdorff, J., 2007: *Glück, Logik und Bluff: Mathematik im Spiel – Methoden, Ergebnisse und Grenzen*, 4. Auflage, Vieweg Verlag: Wiesbaden.

Bhattacharyya, G.K. & Johnson, R.A., 1977: *Statistical Concepts and Methods*, Wiley: New York.

Binmore, K., 2007: *Game Theory: A Very Short Introduction*, Oxford University Press: Oxford.

Bjerknes, G., Ehn, P., & Kyng, M. (Eds.), 1987: *Computers and democracy – a Scandinavian challenge*, Aldershot: Avebury.

Boddy, D., Boonstra, A. & Kennedy, G., 2005: *Managing Information Systems: An Organisational Perspective*,

Second Edition, Prentice-Hall: Harlow, England.

Boje, D.M. & Winsor, R.D., 1993: "The resurrection of Taylorism: Total quality management's hidden agenda," *Journal of Organizational Change Management*, Vol. 6, No. 4, pp. 57-70.

Brady, M., 1978: *The Monopoly Book: Tactics and strategy of the world's most popular game*, Hale: London.

Brandreth, G., 1985: *The Monopoly Omnibus*, Willow Books: London.

Braverman, H., 1974: *Labor and Monopoly Capital: The Degradation of Work in the Twentieth Century*, Monthly Review Press: New York.

Brunsson, N., 1989: *The Organization of Hypocrisy: Talk, Decisions and Actions in Organizations*, Wiley: New York.

Brunsson, N. & Jacobsson, B. (Eds.), 2000: *A World of Standards*, Oxford University Press: Oxford.

Braa, J., 2009: "Action research in HISP," panel debate positioning at: *17th PhD Workshop in Information Systems*, September 17th 2009, University of Oslo.

Braa, J., Monteiro, E. & Sahay, S., 2004: "Networks of Action: sustainable health information systems across developing countries", *MIS Quarterly*, Vol. 28, No. 3, pp. 337-362.

Braa, J., Hanseth, O., Heywood, A., Mohammad, W. & Shaw, V.: 2007: "Developing health information systems in developing countries: The flexible standards strategy", *MIS Quarterly*, Vol. 31, No. 2, pp. 381-402.

Braa, J. & Sahay, S., 2012: *Integrated Health Information Architecture: Power to the Users*, Matrix Publishers: New Delhi.

Burnes, B., 2010: "Call for papers for Journal of Change Management. Special issue on Why Does Change Fail and What Can We Do about It", http://www.egosnet.org/jart/prj3/egosnet/data/uploads/CfP/CfP_JCM.pdf (downloaded on September 22nd 2011)

Burns, D., 2007: *Systemic Action Research: A strategy for whole system change*, Policy Press: Bristol.

Börgers, T., 2013: *An Introduction to the Theory of Mechanism Design*, unpublished book, http://www-personal.umich.edu/~tborgers/LectureNotes.pdf (downloaded on April 15th, 2013).

Camerer, C.F., 2003: *Behavioral Game Theory: Experiments in Strategic Interaction*, Russell Sage Foundation: New York.

Checkland, P., 1981: *Systems Thinking, Systems Practice*, Wiley: Chichester.

Checkland, P., 2005: Video interview, UK systems society, http://www.youtube.com/watch?v=Pq90qS5FvBg (downloaded April 18th 2013)

Checkland, P., 2009: Keynote, *the 13th UK Systems Society International Conference (UKSS-13): "Systems Research: Lessons from the Past - Progress for the future"*, 1-2 September 2009, Oxford, UK.

Checkland, P. & Holwell, S., 1998: *Information, Systems and Information Systems: Making sense of the field*, Wiley: Chichester.

Churchland, P.M. & Hooker, C.A. (eds.), 1985: *Images of Science: Essays on Realism and Empiricism with a Reply from Bas C. van Fraassen*, The University of Chicago Press: Chicago.

Churchman, C.W., 1968: *The Systems Approach*, Dell Publishing: New York.

Churchman, C.W., Ackoff, R.L. & Arnoff, E.L., 1956: *Introduction to Operations Research*, John Wiley & Sons, New York.

Ciborra, C.U., 1998: "Crisis and Foundation: an inquiry into the nature and limits of models and methods in the information systems discipline", *Strategic Information Systems*, Vol. 7, No. 1, pp. 5-16.

Ciborra, C.U. (ed.), 2000: *From Control to Drift: The Dynamics of Corporate Information Infrastructure*, Oxford University Press: Oxford.

Clark, T.J., 1999: *Success Through Quality: Support Guide for the Journey to Continuous Improvement*, ASQ Quality Press: Milwaukee, Wisconsin.

Clegg, S., Kornberger, M. & Pitsis, T., 2005: *Managing and Organizations: An Introduction to Theory and Practice*, SAGE Publications: London.

Cockburn, A., 2002: *Agile Software Development*, Addison-Wesley: Boston.

Coghlan, D. & Brannick, T., 2001: *Doing Action Research in Your Own Organization*, SAGE: London.

Cole, R.E., 1999: *Managing Quality Fads: How American Business Learned to Play the Quality Game*, Oxford University Press: Oxford.

Cole, R.E. & Scott, W.R., (eds.), 2000: *The Quality Movement & Organization Theory*, SAGE Publications: Thousand Oaks, California.

Collis, J. & Hussey, R., 2003: *Business Research*, Second edition, Palgrave Macmillan: London.

Colman, A.M., 1995: *Game Theory and its Applications in the Social and Biological Sciences*, Routledge: London.

Concerning Learning, 2011: "The Hypocrisy of Learning", http://concerninglearning.blogspot.com/2011/08/hypocrisy-of-learning.html (downloaded on September 6th 2011).

Cordella, A., & Shaikh, M., 2003: "Actor network theory and after: What's new for IS research?" *Proceedings* *of the 11th European Conference on Information Systems*, Naples, pp. 496-508.

Creager, A.N.H., Lunbeck, E. & Wise, M.N. (eds.), 2007: *Science without Laws: Models systems, cases, exemplary narratives*, Duke University Press: Durham.

Crocco, F., 2011: "Critical gaming pedagogy", *Radical Teacher*, Vol. 91, No. 1, pp. 26-41.

Crosby, P.B., 1979: *Quality is Free: The Art of Making Quality Certain*, McGraw-Hill: New York.

Csikszentmihályi, M., 1990: *Flow: The psychology of optimal performance*, Harper & Row: New York.

Dahlbom, B. & Mathiassen, L., 1992: "Systems development philosophy," *ACS SIGCAS Computers and Society*, Vol. 22, No. 1-4, pp. 12-23.

Dahlbom, B. & Mathiassen, L., 1993: *Computers in Context: The Philosophy and Practice of Systems Design*, Blackwell: Oxford.

Dale, B.G., 2003: *Managing Quality*, Fourth edition, Blackwell: Oxford.

Darzinskis, K., 1987: *Winning Monopoly: A complete guide to property accumulation, cash-flow strategy, and negotiating techniques when playing the best-selling board game*, Harper & Row: New York.

Darzinskis, K., 2007: "Superb presenter of mathematics," *Amazon.com customer review*, http://www.amazon.com/Luck-Logic-White-Lies-Mathematics/product-reviews/1568812108/ref=cm_cr_dp_see_all_btm?ie=UTF8&showViewpoints=1&sortBy=bySubmissionDateDescending (downloaded on May 30th 2013).

Davison, R., Martinsons, M.G. & Kock, N., 2004: "Principles of Canonical Action Research", *Information Systems Journal*, Vol. 14, No. 1, pp. 65-86.

del Castillo, E., 2002: *Statistical Process Adjustment for Quality Control*, Wiley Series in Probability and Statistics, Wiley-Interscience: New York.

DeLuca, D., 2005: "Using action research for positivist research," *AMCIS 2005 Proceedings*, Paper 501. http://aisel.aisnet.org/amcis2005/501

DeLuca, D. & Kock, N., 2007: "Publishing information systems action research for a positivist audience," *Communications of the AIS*, Vol. 19, No. 10, pp. 1-39.

Deming, W.E., 1986: *Out of the Crisis*, MIT Press: Cambridge, Massachusetts.

Deming, W.E., 1994: *The New Economics for Industry, Government, Education, Second Edition*, MIT Press: Cambridge, Massachusetts.

Devlin, K., 1997: *Goodbye, Descartes: The End of Logic and the Search for a New Cosmology of the Mind*, John Wiley & Sons: New York.

Devlin, K., 2009: *Soft Mathematics*, http://www.maa.org/devlin/devlin_10_09.html (downloaded June 16th 2013)

DiMaggio, P., Hargittai, E., Neuman, W.R., & Robinson, J.P., 2001: "Social implications of the internet", *Annual review of sociology*, pp. 307-336.

DiStefano, J.J., Stubberud, A.R. & Williams, I.J., 1990: *Feedback and Control Systems*, Second Edition, McGraw-Hill: New York.

DNV, 2005: *Kvalitetsarbeid i IT-funksjonen, Vurdering av systemet for kvalitetsstyring i IT-funksjonen i Skattedirektoratet*, Rapport unntatt offentlighet, 03.10.2005, Det Norske Veritas: Høvik.

Dooley, K.J., 1997: "A complex adaptive system model of organizational change," *Non-linear dynamics, psychology, and life sciences*, Vol. 1, No. 1, pp. 69-97.

Dooley, K.J., Johnson, T.L. & Bush, D.H., 1995: "TQM, chaos & complexity", Human Systems Management, Vol. 14, No. 4, pp. 287-302.

Dresher, M., 1981: *The Mathematics of Games of Strategy: Theory and Applications*, Dover: New York.

Drucker, P.F., 1950: *The Effective Executive*, Harper & Row, New York.

Drucker, P.F., 1974: *Management: Tasks, Responsibilities and Practices*, Harper & Row, New York.

Eastwood, D.C., 2009: "A random walk down Monopoly Lane", *Giant Battling Robots: The mathematics and statistics of games*, http://giantbattlingrobots.blogspot.no/2009_01_01_archive.html (downloaded April 14th 2013)

EIN, 1997: *The Control Game: A reference guide for recognizing political/social control tactics by power brokers, large corporations, public relation firms and government entities*, Environmental Information Network (EIN), http://www.actionpa.org/activism/controlgame.html (downloaded June 16th 2013)

EIPA, 2012: "CAF – Common Assessment Framework", http://www.eipa.eu/en/topic/show/&tid=191 (downloaded January 25th 2012)

Elster, J., 1982: "Marxism, functionalism, and game theory: The case for methodological individualism," *Theory and Society*, Vol. 11, No. 4, pp. 453-482.

Flood, R.L., 1991: "Implementing Total Quality Management through Total Systems Intervention: A creative approach to problem solving in Diagnostic Biotechnology (PTE) Ltd", *Systems Practice*, Vol. 4, No. 6, pp. 565-578.

Flood, R.L., 1993: *Beyond TQM*, John Wiley & Sons: Chichester.

Flood, R.L., 1999: *Rethinking the Fifth Discipline: Learning within the unknowable*, Routledge: London.

Flood, R.L., 2004: "The relationship of 'systems thinking' to action research," in: Reason, P. & Bradbury, H.

(eds.) *Handbook of Action Research*, SAGE: London, pp. 117-128.

Flood, R.L. & Isaac, M., 1993: "Supplier development strategy for small and medium sized companies: The case of Cosalt Holiday Homes," *International Journal of Quality and Reliability Management*, Vol. 10, No. 6, pp. 25-41.

Flood, R.L. & Jackson, M.C., 1991: *Creative Problem Solving: Total Systems Intervention*, John Wiley & Sons: Chichester.

Frayn, C.M., 2005: "An evoluationary approach to the strategies for the game of Monopoly", *Proceedings for the IEEE Symposium on Computational Intelligence and Games*, Essex University, Colchester, Essex, UK, 4-6 April, 2005, pp. 66-72.

French, W.L. & Bell, C.H., 1995: *Organizational Development: Behavioral Science Interventions for Organization Improvement*, Fifth Edition, Prentice-Hall: Englewood Cliffs, New Jersey.

Gartner, 2010: *Root cause analysis - en rapport for Skatteetaten. Version 1.1, February 4th 2010*, internal publication, Skatteetaten.

Giere, R.N., 1988: *Explaining Science: A Cognitive Approach*, Chicago University Press: Chicago.

Gintis, H., 2009: *The Bounds of Reason: Game Theory and the Unification of the Behavioural Sciences*, Princeton University Press: New Jersey.

Gitlow, H.S., 2001: *Quality Management Systems: A Practical Guide*, St. Lucie Press: New York.

Goggin, G., 2006: *Cell Phone Culture: Mobile Technology in Everyday Life*, Routledge: New York.

Gold, M., 1999: *The Complete Social Scientist: A Kurt Lewin Reader*, American Psychological Association: Washington.

Goldberg, D.E., 1989: *Genetic Algorithms in Search, Optimization, and Machine Learning*, Addison-Wesley Professional: New York.

Goldberg, D.E., 2000: "The Design of Innovation: Lessons from Genetic Algorithms, Lessons for the Real World," *Technological Forecasting and Social Change*, Vol. 64, pp. 7-12.

Goldstein, J., 1994: *The Unshackled Organization: Facing the Challenge of Unpredictability through Spontaneous Reorganization*, Productivity Press: Portland, Oregon.

Grant, R.M., Shani, R. & Krishnan, R., 1994: "TQM's challenge to management theory and practice," Sloan Management Review, Vol. 35, No. 2, pp. 25-35.

Green, S.M., 1992: "Total Systems Intervention: Organizational Communication in North Yorkshire Police", *Systems Practice*, Vol. 5, No. 6, pp. 585-599.

Green, S.M., 1993: "Total Systems Intervention: A Practitioner's Critique", *Systems Practice*, Vol. 6, No. 1, pp. 71-79.

Greenbaum, J. & Kyng, M., 1991: *Design at Work: Cooperative Design of Computer Systems*, CRC Press: Boca Raton, Florida.

Grol, R., Baker, R. & Moss, F., 2004: *Quality Improvement Research: Understanding the Science of Change in Health Care*, BMJ Books: London.

Gross, E., 2005: "Comment #23", In Quiggen, J.: *What's wrong with game theory*. http://johnquiggin.com/2005/10/13/whats-wrong-with-game-theory/, (downloaded on September 27th 2011)

Hacking, I., 1999: *The Social Construction of What?* Harvard University Press: Cambridge, Massachusetts.

Hannemyr, G., 2009: Personal communication at Department of Informatics, University of Oslo.

Hanseth, O., 2001: "Gateways – just as important as standards: How the internet won the 'religious war' over standards in Scandinavia", *Knowledge, Technology & Policy*, Vol. 14, No. 3, pp. 71-89.

Hanseth, O., 2002: "From systems and tools to networks and infrastructures – from design to cultivation. Towards a theory of ICT solutions and its design methodology implications", *Unpublished manuscript*, http://heim.ifi.uio.no/oleha/Publications/ib_ISR_3rd_resubm2.html (downloaded on April 16th, 2013)

Hanseth, O., 2004: "Knowledge as infrastructure," in Avergou, C., Ciborra, C. & Land, F. (eds.): *The Social Study of Information and Communication Technology: Innovation, Actors and Context*, Oxford University Press: Oxford, pp. 103-108.

Hanseth, O. & Ciborra, C.U. (eds.), 2007: *Risk, Complexity and ICT*, Edward Elgar Publishing: Cheltenham.

Hanseth, O. & Lyytinen, K., 2004: "Theorizing about the design of information infrastructures: Design kernel theories and principles", *Sprouts: Working Papers on Information Systems*, Vol. 4, No. 12, pp. 208-242.

Hanseth, O. & Lyytinen, K., 2010: "Design theory for dynamic complexity in information infrastructures: The case of building the internet", *Journal of Information Technology*, Vol. 25, No. 1, pp. 1-19.

Hanseth, O. & Monteiro, E., 1997: "Inscribing behaviour in information infrastructure standards," *Accounting, management and information technologies*, Vol. 7, No. 4, pp. 183-211.

Hanseth, O. & Monteiro, E., 1998: *Understanding Information Infrastructure*, unpublished book, http://heim.ifi.uio.no/oleha/Publications/bok.pdf (downloaded April 14th, 2013).

Hanseth, O. & Aanestad, M., 2003: "Design as bootstrapping: On the evolution of ICT networks in healthcare", *Methods of Information in Medicine*, Vol. 42, No. 4, pp. 384-391.

Hansson, N., 2009: "Actor-Network Theory and Culture", *Machine assemblages – Just another WordPress*

Weblog, http://machinicassemblages.wordpress.com/2009/08/27/actor-network-theory-and-culture/ (downloaded on September 27th 2012)

Hamblin, S. & Hurd, P.L., 2007: "Genetic algorithms and non-ESS solutions ot game theory models", *Animal Behaviour*, Vol. 74, No. 4, pp. 1005-1018.

Hardin, G., 1968: "The Tragedy of the Commons," *Science*, Vol. 162, pp. 1243-1248.

Harding, N., 2003: *The Social Construction of Management*, Routledge, London.

Hildebrandt, S., Kristensen, K., Kanji, G. & Dahlgaard, J.J., 1991: "Quality Culture and TQM", *Total Quality Management*, Vol. 2, No. 1, pp. 1-16.

Hodgkinson, H.L., 1957: "Action research – a critique," *Journal of Educational Sociology*, Vol. 31, No. 4, pp. 137-153.

Holland, J., 1995: *Hidden Order: How adaptation builds complexity*, Addison-Wesley: New York.

Holland, J., 2006: "Studying complex adaptive systems," *Journal of Systems Science and Complexity*, Vol. 19, No. 1, pp. 1-18.

Holeman, R., 1995: "The Software Process Improvement Game", in: Ibrahim, R.L. (1995): *Proceedings for Software Engineering Education: 8th SEI CSEE Conference*. New Orleans, LA, USA, March 29 - April 1, 1995, pp. 261-262.

Hoyle, D., 2006: *ISO 9000 Quality Systems Handbook*, Fifth Edition, Butterworth-Heinemann: London.

Hevner, A.R., March, S.T., Park, J. & Ram, S., 2004: "Design science in information systems research", *MIS Quarterly*, Vol. 28, No. 1, pp. 75-105.

Humphrey, W.S., 1989: *Managing the Software Process*, Addison-Wesley: Reading, Massachusetts.

Huysmans, J.H.B.M, 1970: *The Implementation of Operations Research: An Approach to the Joint Consideration of Social and Technological Aspects*, Wiley: New York.

Iivari, J. & Venable, J.R., 2009: "Action research and design science research - Seemingly similar but decisively dissimilar". *ECIS 2009 Proceedings*. Paper 73. http://aisel.aisnet.org/ecis2009/73

Imai, K., 1986: *KAIZEN: The Key to Japan's Competitive Success*, McGraw-Hill: New York.

Innomet, 2007: "Developing TQM culture using EFQM", www.innomet.ee/innomet/ERPKoolitus/4.TQM.ppt (downloaded on September 21st 2011).

Ishikawa, K., 1985: *What is Total Quality Control? The Japanese Way*, Prentice-Hall: Englewood Cliffs, New Jersey.

Iversen, J.H., Mathiassen, L. & Nielsen, P.A., 2004: "Managing risk in software process development: An action research approach," *MIS Quarterly*, Vol. 23, No. 8, pp. 395-433.

Jackson, M.C., 2000: *Systems Approaches to Management*, Kluwer Academic: New York.

Jackson, M.C., 2003: *Systems Thinking: Creative Holism for Managers*, Wiley: Chichester.

Juran, J.M., 1964: *Managerial Breakthrough*, McGraw-Hill, New York.

Juran, J.M., 1989: *Juran on Leadership for Quality: An Executive Handbook*, Free Press: New York.

Juran, J.M. & Godfrey, A.B., 2000: *Juran's Quality Handbook*, Fifth edition, McGraw-Hill: New York.

Järvinen, P., 2007: "Action research is similar to design science," *Quality & Quantity*, Vol. 41, No. 1, pp. 37-54.

Kelly, K., 1994: *Out of Control: The rise of neo-biological civilization*, Addison-Wesley: New York.

Kendall, K.E. & Kendall, J.E., 1988: *Systems Analysis and Design*, Prentice-Hall: Englewood Cliffs, New Jersey.

Kennedy, R. & Waltzer, J., 2004: Monopoly: *The story behind the world's best-selling game*, MJF Books: New York.

Kjensli, P.O. & Moe, M., 1992: *Kvalitetsstyring for Prosjektarbeid. Delprosjekt 5*. Report no. 45/92 KLIMA, The Norwegian Meteorological Institute.

Kock, N. (ed.), 2007: *Information Systems Action Research: An Applied View of Emerging Concepts and Methods*, Springer: New York.

Kock, N.F., McQueen, R.J. & Scott, R.L., 1997: "Can action research be made more rigorous in a positivist sense? The contribution of an iterative approach," *Journal of Systems and Information Technology*, Vol. 1, No. 1, pp. 1-23.

Kohli, R. & Hoadley, E.D., 2007: "Healthcare: Fertile ground for action research," in Koch, N. (ed.): *Information Systems Action Research: An Applied View of Emerging Concepts and Methods*, Springer: New York, pp. 241-253.

Kotrik, R., 2012: "Searching for a strategy of Monopoly game using cognitive and artificial intelligence approach", *The Sixth Middle European Conference on Cognitive Science Conference*, June 22-23, 2012, Bratislava.

Koury, K., 2012: *Monopoly Strategy: How to win the world's most popular board game*, Lulu Press: Raleigh, North Carolina.

Krick, E.V., 1969: *An Introduction to Engineering and Engineering Design*, Second Edition, Wiley: New York.

Kuhn, T.S., 1996: *The Structure of Scientific Revolutions*, Third Edition, The University of Chicago Press: Chicago.

Kvalobs, 2011: "Open Source Software for the Quality Control of Geophysical Observations", *Kvalobs open source software project (kvoss)*, https://kvalobs.wiki.met.no/doku.php?id=kvoss:system:qc2:requirements:algorithms:diptest03 (downloaded on March 6th 2012)

Lash, S., Giddens, A. & Beck, U., 1994: *Reflexive Modernization: Politics, Tradition and Aesthetics in the Modern Social Order*, Polity Press: Oxford.

Latour, B., 1987: *Science in Action: How to follow scientists and engineers through society*, Harvard University Press: Cambridge, Massachusetts.

Latour, B., 1988: *The Pasteurization of France*, Harvard University Press: Cambridge, Massachusetts.

Latour, B., 1999: *Pandora's Hope: Essays on the Reality of Science Studies*, Harvard University Press: Cambridge, Massachusetts.

Latour, B., 2005: *Reassembling the Social: An Introduction to Actor-Network Theory*, Oxford University Press: Oxford.

Latour, B. & Woolgar, S., 1979: *Laboratory Life: The Social Construction of Scientific Facts*, SAGE: London.

Legge, K., 2002: "On knowledge, business consultants and the selling to total quality management", in: Clark, T. & Fincham, R. *Critical Consulting: New Perspectives on the Management Advice Industry*, Blackwell Business: Oxford, pp. 74-90.

Lemke, J. 2000: "Material sign processes and emergent ecosocial organization", in: P.B. Anderson et al (eds.): *Downward Causation*, Aarhus University Press, pp. 181-213.

Lewin, K., 1920: "Die Sozialisierung des Taylor systems", *Praktischer Sozialismus*, Vol. 4, pp. 3-36.

Lewin, K., 1946: "Action research and minority problems", *Journal of Social Issues*, Vol. 2, No. 4, pp. 34-46.

Lewin, K., 1997: *Resolving Social Conflicts & Field Theory in Social Science*, American Psychological Association: Washington, D.C.

Levine, D.K., 2009: "What is Game Theory?" *Economic and Game Theory*, http://levine.sscnet.ucla.edu/general/whatis.htm (downloaded on May 29th 2013)

Lilienfeld, R., 1978: *The Rise of Systems Theory: An Ideological Analysis*, Wiley: New York.

Loffredo, N., 2008: "Agent based simulation, negotiation and strategy optimization of Monopoly", *Computer Systems Lab Senior Research projects 2007-2008*, Thomas Jefferson High School for Science and Technology, Alexandria, Virginia, p. 83.

Louis, S.J. & Rawlins, G.J., 1993: "Syntactic analysis of convergence in genetic algorithms", *Foundations of Genetic Programming*, Vol. 2, pp. 141-151.

Lucas, H.C., 1981: *Implementation: The key to successful information systems*, Columbia University Press, New York.

Lucas, H.C., Ginzberg, M.J. & Schultz, R.L., 1990: *Information Systems Implementation: Testing a Structural Model*, Ablex Publishing, Norwood, New Jersey.

Luce, R.D. & Raiffa, H., 1957: *Games and Decisions: Introduction and Critical Survey*, Wiley: New York.

Luenberger, D.G., 1979: *Introduction to Dynamic Systems: Theory, Models & Applications*, John Wiley & Sons: New York.

Luhmann, N., 1984: *Soziale Systeme. Grundriss einer allgemeinen Theorie*, Suhrkamp: Frankfurt am Main.

Luhmann, N., 1990: *Die Wissenschaft der Gesellschaft*, Suhrkamp: Frankfurt am Main.

Lyytinen, K. & Robey, D., 1999: "Learning failure in information systems development," *Information Systems Journal*, Vol. 9, No. 2, pp. 85-101.

McDonald, J., 1950: *Strategy in Poker, Business & War*, W.W. Norton & Company: New York.

McGregor, D., 1960: *The Human Side of the Enterprise*, McGraw-Hill: New York.

MacKay, J. & Marshall, P., 2007: "Driven by two masters, serving both: The interplay of problem solving and research in information systems action research projects," in: Kock, N. (ed.): *Information Systems Action Research: An Applied View of Emerging Concepts and Methods*, Springer: New York, pp. 131-158.

McNiff, J. & Whitehead, J., 2006: *All You Need to Know About Action Research*, SAGE Publications: London.

March, S.T. & Smith, G.F., 1995: "Design and natural science research on information technology", *Decision Support Systems*, Vol. 15, No. 4, pp. 251-166.

Marcuse, H., 1964: *One-Dimensional Man: Studies in the Ideology of Advanced Industrial Society*, Beacon Press: Boston.

Masing, W., (Ed.), 1999: *Handbuch Qualitätsmanagement*, 4. Auflage, Hanser Verlag: München.

Mastilak, C., 2012: "First-day strategies for millennial students in introductory accounting courses: It's all fun and games until something gets learned", *Journal of Education for Business*, Vol. 87, No. 1, pp. 48-51.

Mehregan, M.R., Kahreh, M.S. & Yousefi, H., 1998: "Strategic planning by use of Total Systems Intervention towards the strategic alignment," *International Journal of Trade, Economics and Finance*, Vol. 2, No. 2, pp. 166-170.

Miller, J., 2003: *Game Theory at Work: How to Use Game Theory to Outthink and Outmanoeuvre Your Competition*, McGraw-Hill: New York.

186

Mintzberg, H., 1983: *Structures in Fives: Designing Effective Organizations*, Prentice-Hall: Upper Saddle River, New Jersey.

Mitra, A., 1993: *Fundamentals of Quality Control and Improvement*, Macmillan: New York.

Moe, M., 1995: *KLIBAS – The DNMI Climatological Database System*, DNMI Report no. 22/95 KLIMA, The Norwegian Meteorological Institute.

Monteiro, E., 2006: Informal comments to students while lecturing the course "INF 5210 information infrastructures", October 10th, 2006,
http://www.uio.no/studier/emner/matnat/ifi/INF5210/h06/undervisningsplan.xml

Morgan, G., 1997: *Images of Organization*, SAGE: London.

Nielsen, P.A., 2007: "IS action research and its criteria," in: Kock, N. (ed.): *Information Systems Action Research: An Applied View of Emerging Concepts and Methods*, Springer: New York, pp. 355-375.

Nisan, N., Roughgarden, T., Tardos, É. & Vazirani, V.V. (eds.), 2007: *Algorithmic Game Theory*, Cambridge University Press: New York.

Nordlie, P.Ø. & Øgland, P., 1995: *Data-kontroll for Aanderaa-stasjoner: PD-rutinen*, DNMI Rapport nr. 22/94 KLIBAS, The Norwegian Meteorological Institute.

Novak, J.D. & Gowin, D.R., 1984: *Learning how to learn*, Cambridge University Press: Cambridge.

Nygaard, K., 1996: "Those were the days or heroic times are here again?" *Scandinavian Journal of Information Systems*, Vol. 8, No. 2, pp. 91-108.

Oakland, J.S., 1999: *Total Organizational Excellence: Achieving world-class performance*, Butterworth-Heinemann: Oxford.

Øgland, P., 1993a: *Theoretical analysis of the dip-test in quality control of geophysical observations*, DNMI Report no. 24/93 KLIMA, The Norwegian Meteorological Institute.

Øgland, P., 1993b: *A method of weighted linear estimation applied to quality control of precipitation values*, DNMI Report no. 42/93 KLIMA, The Norwegian Meteorological Institute.

Øgland, P., 1994a: *Innlasting av synoptiske data til arbeidslager*, DNMI Rapport nr. 40/94 KLIBAS, The Norwegian Meteorological Institute.

Øgland, P., 1994b: "Some recent developments regarding quality control of precipitation data in Norway", *Det 19nde Nordiske Meteorologimøte*, 6.-10.6.1994, Kristiansand, Norway, pp. 179-184

Øgland, P., 1995a: *Kvalitetskontroll av automatstasjonsdata februar 1995*, DNMI Report no. 12/95 KLIMA, The Norwegian Meteorological Institute.

Øgland, P., 1995b: *Fremdriftsrapport for automatstasjonene mars 1995*, DNMI Notat nr. 02/95 KLIBAS, The Norwegian Meteorological Institute.

Øgland, P., 1995c: *Eksperimentell innlasting av METAR*, DNMI Rapport nr. 24/95 KLIBAS, The Norwegian Meteorological Institute.

Øgland, P., 1995d: *Driftsrapport juni 1995*, DNMI Notat nr. 09/95 KLIBAS, The Norwegian Meteorological Institute.

Øgland, P., 1997a: *Automatic interpolation of SYNOP weather observations: Interpol1 and Interpol2*, DNMI Report no. 61/97 KLIBAS, The Norwegian Meteorological Institute.

Øgland, P., 1997b: *Automatic correction of SYNOP weather observations: Control1, Control2 and Interpol3*, DNMI Report no. 62/97 KLIBAS, The Norwegian Meteorological Institute.

Øgland, P., 1997c: *Evaluation of a meteorological radial interpolation method by statistical experiments*, DNMI Report no. 23/97 KLIMA, The Norwegian Meteorological Institute.

Øgland, P., 1997d: *Evaluation of a double exponential correlation weighted interpolation method by statistical experiments*, DNMI Report no. 25/97 KLIMA, The Norwegian Meteorological Institute.

Øgland, P., 1998: *Towards an ISO 9000-standard for systems development by DRIFT*, DNMI Report no. 47/98 KLIBAS, The Norwegian Meteorological Institute.

Øgland, P., 1999a: *Automatic update of NORDKLIM project plans by DRIFT v.1.1*, DNMI Report no. 25/99 KLIBAS, The Norwegian Meteorological Institute.

Øgland, P., 1999b: *Using AANDERAA_INN v.1.1 for monitoring AWS data collection*, DNMI Report no. 30/99 KLIBAS, The Norwegian Meteorological Institute.

Øgland, P., 1999c: *Monitoring KLIBAS system mail by MAILSTAT v.2.1*, DNMI Report no. 35/99 KLIBAS, The Norwegian Meteorological Institute.

Øgland, P., 1999d: *Improving system monitoring of kabase with CHECK_MAIL v.1.3*, DNMI Report no. 49/99 KLIBAS, The Norwegian Meteorological Institute.

Øgland, P., 1999e: *HIRLAM v.1.3: Interpolating in TELE with forecast data*, DNMI Report no. 65/99 KLIBAS, The Norwegian Meteorological Institute.

Øgland, P., 1999f: *Computer assisted systems engineering (CASE) with KAPO v.1.2*, DNMI Report no. 69/99 KLIBAS, The Norwegian Meteorological Institute.

Øgland, P., 1999g: *Interpolasjon og kvalitetskontroll i KLIBAS*, DNMI Report no. 17/99 KLIMA, The Norwegian Meteorological Institute.

187

Øgland, P., 1999h: *Software process improvement with DRIFT v.1.2*, DNMI Report no. 73/99 KLIBAS, The Norwegian Meteorological Institute.

Øgland, P., 1999i: *Quality Control of Meteorological Observations from the DNMI – Airport Weather Stations: The ALF/METAR Routine*, DNMI Report no. 26/99 KLIMA, The Norwegian Meteorological Institute.

Øgland, P., 1999j: *Quality Control for the DNMI – Automatic Weather Stations: The AWS Routine*, DNMI Report no. 30/99 KLIMA, The Norwegian Meteorological Institute.

Øgland, P., 1999k: *NORDKLIM Quality Control at DNMI. Status August 1999*, DNMI Note no. 17/99 KLIBAS, The Norwegian Meteorological Institute.

Ogland, P., 2000: "Quality Assurance of Data Flow and Systems Management at DNMI" in Moe. M. (ed.): *Eumetnet ECSN Project: Climate Databases. Proceedings from the Oslo workshop 11.-12. October 1999*, DNMI Report no. 05/00 KLIMA, Norwegian Meteorological Institute, pp. 56-62.

Ogland, P., 2001: "Personlig kvalitet – personlige ambisjoner", *Skattebladet*, No. 10, 2001, pp. 12-13.

Øgland, P., 2004: *Bruk av uavhengig revisjon i IT-funksjonen (Cobit-M4)*, SKD 2004-009, Internal Publication, The Norwegian Tax Administration.

Øgland, P., 2006a: *Opprydding og standardisering av COBOL-programvare*, Internal report, January 24th 2006, Skattedirektoratet: Oslo.

Øgland, P., 2006b: "Using internal benchmarking as strategy for cultivation: A case of improving COBOL software maintainability," *29th Information Systems Research Seminar in Scandinavia (IRIS 29): "Paradigms Politics Paradoxes"*, 12-15 August, 2006, Helsingør, Denmark.

Øgland, P., 2007a: *Opprydding og standardisering av COBOL-programvare*, Internal report, January 18th 2007, Skattedirektoratet: Oslo.

Øgland, P, 2007b: "Improving Research Methodology as a part of doing Software Process Improvement," *30th Information Systems Research Seminar in Scandinavia (IRIS 30): "Models, Methods and Messages"*, 11-14 August, 2007, Tampere, Finland.

Øgland, P., 2008: *Opprydding og standardisering av COBOL-programvare*, Internal report, January 27th 2008, Skattedirektoratet: Oslo.

Ogland, P., 2009a: "In search of a Ciborra strategy for CMM-based software process improvement," in Molka-Danielsen, J. (ed.): *Proceedings of the 32nd information Systems Research Seminar in Scandinavia, IRIS 32, Inclusive Design*, 9-12 August 2009, Molde University College, Molde, Norway.

Øgland, P., 2009b: "Implementing continuous improvement using genetic algorithms," *12th International QMOD and Toulon-Verona Conference on Quality and Service Sciences (ICQSS)*, 27-29 August 2009, Verona, Italy.

Ogland, P., 2009c: "Action Research and Design Science Research - More similar than dissimilar", in Krogstie, J. (ed.): *Proceedings for Norsk konferanse for organisasjoners bruk av informasjonsteknologi, NOKOBIT 16*, Institutt for datateknikk og informasjonsvitenskap NTNU, 23-25 November 2009, Trondheim, Norway, pp. 171-184.

Øgland, P., 2010a: *Standardisering av COBOL-programvare for ligningsår 2007*, Internal report, February 22nd 2010, Skattedirektoratet: Oslo.

Øgland, P., 2010b: *Standardisering av COBOL-programvare for ligningsår 2008*, Internal report, September 21st 2010, Skattedirektoratet: Oslo.

Øgland, P., 2011: *Tilsyn med kvalitetssikring og intern kontroll ved standardisering av COBOL-programvare for ligningsår 2009*, Internal report, January 31st 2011, Skattedirektoratet: Oslo.

Øgland, P. & Førland, E.J., 1993: *Klimastatistikk for værstasjon 8711 Andøya 1981-1991*, DNMI Rapport nr. 05/93 KLIMA, The Norwegian Meteorological Institute.

Øgland, P., Hellsten, E., Jacobsson, K., Madsen, H., Rissanen P. & Vejen, F., 1999: *Human Quality Control (HQC) in the Nordic countries*, DNMI Report no. 32/99 KLIMA, The Norwegian Meteorological Institute.

Øgrim, L., 1993: *Ledelse av systemutviklingsprosjekter: En dialektisk tilnærming*, Dr Scient thesis, December 1993, Research Report no. 183, Department of Informatics, University of Oslo.

Orbanes, P., 2002: "Everything I know about business I learned from Monopoly", Harvard Business Review, Vol. 80, No. 2, pp. 51-57.

Orbanes, P., 2007: *The Monopoly Companion*, Third Edition, Sterling Publishing: New York.

Orbanes, P., 2013: *Monopoly, Money, and You*, McGraw-Hill: New York.

Page-Jones, M., 1988: *The Practical Guide to Structured Systems Design*, Second Edition, Prentice-Hall: Englewood Cliffs, New Jersey.

Palmberg, K., 2009: *Beyond Process Management: Exploring Organizational Applications and Complex Adaptive Systems*, PhD Thesis, Luleå University of Technology.

Parsons, T., 1951: *The Social System*, Free Press: New York.

Perrow, C., 1984: *Normal Accidents: Living with High-Risk Technologies*, Basic Books: New York.

Peters, T.J. & Waterman, R.H., 1982: *In Search of Excellence: Lessons from America's Best-Run Companies*, Warner Books: New York.

Peterson, M., 2009: *An Introduction to Decision Theory*, Cambridge University Press: Cambridge.

Phillips, D.T., Ravindran, A., & Solberg, J., 1976: *Operations Research: Principles and Practice*, Wiley: New York.

Poppendieck, T. & Poppendieck, M., 2003: *Lean Software Development: An Agile Toolkit*, Addison-Wesley: Boston.

Power, M., 1997: *The Audit Society: Rituals of Verification*, Oxford University Press: Oxford.

Reason, P. & Bradbury, H., 2006: *Handbook of Action Research: The Concise Paperback Edition*, SAGE: London.

Rose, J., Aaen, I. & Nielsen, P.A., 2008: "Managerial and Organizational Assumptions in the CMMs," in *Software Processes & Knowledge: Beyond Conventional Software Process Improvement*, P.A. Nielsen, P.A. and K. Kautz (eds.), Software Innovation Publisher, Aalborg, pp. 9-28.

Rosenhead, J. & Mingers, J., 2001: *Rational Analysis for a Problematic World Revisited: Problem Structuring Methods for Complexity, Uncertainty and Conflict*, Second Edition, Wiley: Chichester.

Rowntree, D., 1981: *Statistics without tears*, Penguin: London.

Rudestam, K.E. & Newton, R.R., 1992: *Surviving your dissertation: A comprehensive guide to content and process*, SAGE: London.

Salen, K. & Zimmerman, E., 2004: *Rules of Play: Game Design Fundamentals*, The MIT Press: Cambridge, Massachusetts.

Schein, E., 1985: *Organizational culture and leadership: A dynamic view*, Jossey-Bass: New York.

Schön, D., 1983: *The Reflective Practitioner: How Professionals Think in Action*, Basic Books: New York.

Seddon, J., 1992: *I want you to cheat! The unreasonable guide to service and quality in organisations*, Vanguard: Buckingham.

Seddon, J., 1997: *In Pursuit of Quality: The case against ISO 9000*, Oak Tree Press: Dublin.

Seidman, G., 2011: *Winning Monopoly*, Author-House: Bloomington, Indiana.

Sein, M.K., Henfridsson, O., Puaro, S., Rossi, M. & Lindgren, R., 2011: "Action Design Research," *MIS Quarterly*, Vol. 35, No. 1, pp. 37-56.

Seirawan, Y., 2005: *Winning Chess Tactics*, Gloucester Publishers: London.

Senge, P., 1990: *The Fifth Discipline: The Art and Practice of the Learning Organization*, Currency Doubleday: New York.

Senge, P., 1999: *The Dance of Change*, Currency Doubleday, New York.

Shewhart, W.A., 1931: *Economic Control of Quality of Manufactured Product*, Van Nostrand Company: New York.

Shewhart, W.A., 1938: *Statistical Method from the Viewpoint of Quality Control*, Dover: New York.

Shingo, S., 1987: *The Sayings of Shigeo Shingo: Key Strategies for Plant Improvement*, Productivity Press: Portland, Oregon.

Simon, H.A., 1996: *The Sciences of the Artificial*, Third Edition, The MIT Press: Cambridge, Massachusetts.

Sokal, A. & Bricmont, J., 1998: *Intellectual impostors*, Profile Books: London.

Statskonsult, 2002: *Organisering av IT-funksjonen i skatteetaten*, Rapport 2002: 13, Statskonsult: Oslo.

Stewart, I., 1996a: "How fair is Monopoly?" *Scientific American*, Vol. 274, No. 4, pp. 104-105.

Stewart, I., 1996b: "Monopoly Revisited," *Scientific American*, Vol. 275, No. 4, pp. 116-119.

Susman, G.I. & Evered, R.D., 1978: "An assessment of the scientific merits of action research," *Administrative Science Quarterly*, Vol. 23, No. 4, pp. 582-603.

Tapiero, C.S., 1996: *The Management of Quality and its Control*, Chapman & Hall: London.

Tapscott, D. & Williams, A.D., 2006: *Wikinomics: How Mass Collaboration Changes Everything*, Portfolio: New York.

Tarbuck, E.J. & Lutgens, F.K., 1994: *Earth Science*, Seventh Edition, Macmillan: New York.

Taylor, F.W., 1911: *The Principles of Scientific Management*, Harper & Row: New York.

Taylor, F.W., 1947: *Taylor's Testimony before the Special House Committee*, Harper: New York.

Tikhonov, A.N. and Arsenin, V.Y., 1977: *Solutions of Ill-Posed Problems*, New York: Winston.

Tostado, K., 2010: *Under the Boardwalk: The Monopoly Story*, Documentary film, Rhino Films: Los Angeles, California.

Tsoukas, H., 1993: "The road to emancipation is through organisational development: A critical evaluation of Total Systems Intervention," *Systems Practice*, Vol. 6, No. 1, pp. 53-70.

Ulrich, W., 1983: *Critical Heuristics of Social Planning: A New Approach to Practical Philosophy*, Verlag Haubt: Bern.

Vejen, F., Jacobson, C., Fredrikson, U., Moe, M., Andresen, L., Hellsten, E., Rissanen, P., Pálsdóttir, T. y Arason, T., 2002: *Quality Control of Meteorological Observations. Automatic Methods Used in the Nordic Countries*. NORDKLIM, Nordic Co-operation within Climate Activities, DNMI Report No. 08/02 KLIMA, The Norwegian Meteorological Institute.

Venable, J., 2006: "The role of theory and theorising in design science research," *Proceedings of the 1st*

International Conference on Design Science in Information Systems and Technology (DESTRIST 2006). February 24-25, 2006, Claremont, California.

van Fraassen, B.C., 1980: *The Scientific Image*, Clarendon Press: Oxford.

van Fraassen, B.C., 2002: *The Empirical Stance*, Yale University Press: London.

van Fraassen, B.C., 2008: *Scientific Representation*, Oxford University Press: Oxford.

von Bertalanffy, L., 1968: *General System Theory: Foundations, Development and Applications*, George Brazillier: New York.

Walls, J.G., Widmeyer, G.R. & El Sawy, O.A., 1992: "Building an information systems design theory for vigilant EIS", *Information Systems Research*, Vol. 3, No. 1, pp. 36-59.

Wang, G., 1996: *The Programmer's Job Handbook: The Skills You Need for Long-Term Job Security and Programming Success*, McGraw-Hill: Berkley.

Weinberg, G.M. & Weinberg, D., 1988: *General Principles of Systems Design*, Dorset House: New York.

Wheeler, D.J., 1993: *Understanding Variation: The Key to Managing Chaos*, SPC Press: Knoxville, Tennessee.

Whitehead, J., 1993: *The Growth of Educational Knowledge: Creating Your Own Living Educational Theories*, Hyde Publications: Dorset.

Wipro, 2001: *Analysis Report for Software Development Process: Skattedirektoratet, Helsfyr*, Wipro Technologies: Bangalore, India.

Wright-Maley, C., 2013: "Deficit Crisis Simulation: Using Monopoly to Teach About the Deficit Debate", *Social Studies Research and Practice*, Vol.8, No. 1, pp. 89-101.

Wuffle, A., 1978: "Monopoly is a capitalist plot: A hegemonic view of games as instruments of economic indoctrination," *Simulation and Gaming*, Vol. 9, No. 2, pp. 252-254.

Yasumura, Y., Oguchi, K. & Nitta, K., 2001: "Negotiation strategy of agents in the Monopoly game", in: *Proceedings for IEEE international Symposium on Computational Intelligence in Robotics and Automation*, pp. 277-281.

Yilmaz, M. & O'Connor, R.V., 2012: "A market based approach for resolving resource constrained task allocation problems in a software engineering process," In: O'Connor, R.V., Pries-Heje, J. & Messnarz, R., *Systems, Software and Service Process Improvement*, Springer: Berlin, pp. 25-36.

Zahran, S., 1998: *Software Process Improvement: Practical Guidelines for Business Success*, Addison-Wesley: Harlow, England.

APPENDIX

I.   Øgland, P., 2009. The Game of Software Process Improvement: Some reflections on players, strategies and payoff. Krogstie, J. (Ed.): *Proceedings for Norsk konferanse for organisasjoners bruk av informasjonsteknologi, NOKOBIT 16*, Institutt for datateknikk og informasjonsvitenskap NTNU, 23-25 November 2009, Trondheim, Norway. ISBN 978-82-519-2493-1, pp. 209-222

II. Øgland, P., 2009. The Pac-Man model of total quality management: Strategy lessons for change agents. *Systemist*, Vol. 31, No 2&3, pp. 82-103.

III. Øgland, P., 2009. Measurements, Feedback and Empowerment. Critical systems theory as a foundation for Software Process Improvement. *The 17th European Conference on Information Systems (ECIS-17): "Information Systems in a globalising world; challenges, ethics and practice"*, 8.-10. June 2009, Verona.

IV. Øgland, P., 2008. Software process improvement: What gets measured gets done. *31st Information Systems Research Seminar in Scandinavia (IRIS 31): "Challenging the Future: Context, Participation and Services"*, 9-12 August 2008, Åre, Sweden. (Awarded best paper)

V.   Øgland, P., 2008. Designing quality management systems as complex adaptive systems. *Systemist*, Vol. 30, No 3, pp. 468-491.

VI. Øgland, P., 2007. Designing quality management systems with minimal management commitment. *Systemist*, Vol. 29, No 3, pp. 101-112.

THE GAME OF SOFTWARE PROCESS IMPROVEMENT: SOME REFLECTIONS ON PLAYERS, STRATEGIES AND PAYOFF

Petter Øgland, Department of Informatics, University of Oslo, P.O. Box 1080 Blindern, 0316 Oslo, Norway, petterog@ifi.uio.no

Abstract

When starting the software process improvement (SPI) journey, there are many SPI standards to select from. Selecting good SPI standards can be a technical problem from a software engineering point of view, but it can also be a political problem, some standards fitting more with internal political agendas than others. As it is well-known that SPI without management commitment can have disastrous effects on SPI, so can also be the consequence of selecting standards that are technically unfit. The dilemma on how to select SPI standards provides a picture of SPI as a political game played out between managers, software engineers and SPI people. Starting with SPI from the viewpoint of control theory, the paper identifies different conflict situations within the control theory framework, and suggests using game theory and drama theory for finding optimal control strategies. Drama theory is further explored through a SPI case study that illustrates how SPI standards stabilize in spite of conflicts and social disaster. The contribution of the paper consists of introducing the concept of 'evolutionary drama theory' (derived from evolutionary game theory, EGT) as a tool for describing and analysing how an artefact like a SPI standard evolves towards equilibrium (evolutionary stable strategy, ESS) by looking at repeated dramas where equilibriums may not necessarily be found or, if found, may not necessarily fit with the ESS.

Keywords: Software process improvement, standards, control theory, game theory, drama theory

1   INTRODUCTION

In the software process improvement (SPI) literature there are numerous SPI models, such as ISO 9000, ISO 15504, CMM, V-model, Bootstrap (e.g. Zahran, 1998; Hoyle, 2006), CMMI (Chrissis et al., 2003), various agile methods (Schwaber, 2004; Cockburn, 2002), attempts at balancing discipline and agile (Boehm & Turner, 2004), general overviews based on best practices and/or research findings (e.g. Dybå et al., 2002; Sommerville, 2001) or models focusing on social issues and critical theory rather than technical guidelines (e.g. Nielsen & Kautz, 2008). How should we choose?

As most quality management systems require a process of quality audits, a way of improving the system that is already integrated in the design of the system is to go with an audit driven improvement approach (e.g. Schlickman, 2003). The diagram in figure 1 illustrates the concept of audit driven approach as a simple closed-loop control system, the main dynamics of the system being the relationship between process assessments $y(t)$ made by the quality control team and the control signal $u(t)$ given by line management to software engineers. The concept of audit driven improvement in this context means that, while the software engineers may produce quality and productivity indicators $x(t)$ as a part of running the software process, it is the role of quality control to audit $y(t)$ whether the current practice is in compliance with the quality standards $r(t)$ and make sure that the result of the comparison $e(t)$ is communicated to management.

The logic of the control system in figure 1 stresses the need for having quality standards (process standards) in order to do process improvement, and as pointed out by Legge (2002), the success or failure of process improvement depends to a large degree on "selling the models and methods" to management, creating management commitment. It is often argued in quality management literature that the single most important issue for succeeding with quality management is management commitment (e.g. Beckford, 2002). Nevertheless, according to Seddon (1997), selecting the wrong process improvement standards may have disastrous consequences for the organization.

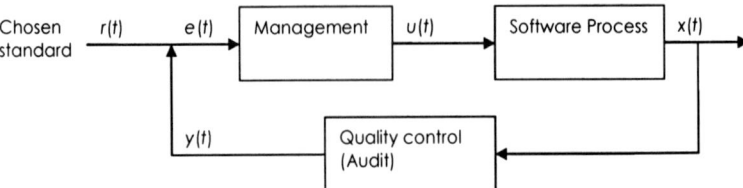

Figure 1. The basic configuration of a simple closed-loop control system (DiStefano et al, 1990, p. 16)

The purpose of the study documented in this paper is to investigate the dilemma of how to select a SPI framework that fits with the requirements of doing measurement driven SPI and also fits with organizational culture and management style inherit in the organization. More precisely, the hypothesis of the study is that SPI can be understood as a game (conflict) between managers, software engineers and auditors, a game about software production, knowledge management and management commitment, where the best way to ensure stability in the control system, represented in figure 1, is to make sure that the choice of process standards can be interpreted as "Nash equilibrium" for the game, i.e. that choice of SPI standards produces a situation where neither management, engineers nor auditors benefit from moving from the strategy implied by the standards into different strategies. Drawing upon the theory of Evolutionary Game Theory (Alexander, 2009) and Drama Theory (Howard, 1971), a new concept of 'evolutionary drama theory' will be introduced.

In section two there will be a literature review covering some elementary aspects of game theory and the "soft extension" of game theory into drama theory, including the introduction of the new concept of 'evolutionary drama theory', arguing the relevance of such theories in the case of SPI. Section three explains methodology for empirical research designed for analysing the hypothesis more properly, using data from a longitudinal action research-driven SPI study conducted by the author. The results are reported in the shape of a drama theoretical case study narrative in section four. In section five, the narrative is discussed with respect to the model in figure 1, trying to give meaning to the politics of selecting SPI standards through the perspective of game theory and drama theory. The study concludes, in section six, by summarising how the new concept of 'evolutionary drama theory' puts the question on how to select SPI standards in a new perspective, emphasising the long-term importance of having an evolutionary stable strategy and how local or temporal conflicts should be solved with this in mind.

2 LITERATURE REVIEW

Game theory is a mathematical theory for analysing models of conflict and cooperation, drawing insights from games like Chess and Bridge with applications in economy, sociology, biology, and computer science, among others, using the concepts of players, strategy and payoff as framework for analysis (Bicchieri, 2004). The aim of this literature review is first to address the topic of social research in SPI and then focus on the two axes of conflict in the SPI game in figure 2.

2.1 Social aspects of software process improvement in general

Sommerville and Rodden (1995) comment that from the very beginning of SPI literature in the late 1980s, influential SPI writers were aware of human, social and organizational considerations which affect software processes and the introduction of software technology, but given the scientific background of most people working in the area of software engineering, continued research in software process technologies has paid little attention to these problems. There are, however, examples of software process researchers who have focused on issues like the importance of qualitative observations and ethnographic research, understanding how cultures work, the importance of involving users etc. (Conradi & Fughetta, 2002; Dybå et al. 2002). Nevertheless, there is little advice on how to handle situations where the organization say they are following SPI standards while not actually doing it (Brunsson et al., 2000), or what do to when there are obvious conflicts due to SPI challenging the knowledge/power structure of the organization (e.g. Beer, 1968).

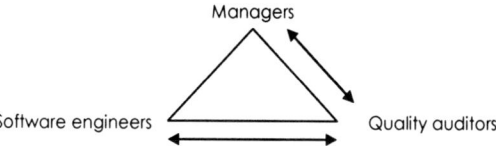

Figure 2. The SPI game represented by the groups of players as seen from the auditors' perspective

Some political issues are addressed by Scandinavian researchers from the information systems community suggesting SPI standards like CMM may be biased towards American management styles, making organizational assumptions that do not necessarily fit with Scandinavian organizational reality (e.g. Nielsen & Kautz, 2008), but even if this kind of research motivates the image of SPI as a political game, there are not so many insights on how to play this game in a successful way.

2.2   The game played by quality auditor and software engineer

If the quality control personnel can be seen as the extended arm of management, meaning that the management function in figure 1 automatically transforms the error signal $e(t)$ into a control signal $u(t)$, figure 3 illustrates a simple game theoretic model of the quality control game played between quality auditors and software engineers. For both the auditor and the engineer the four outcomes (payoffs) in figure 3 are ranked as 4 = best, 3 = second best, 2 = second worst and 1 = worst. The payoffs for the auditor are designed in the manner to fit with the aim of quality control, namely that the auditor wins if the software engineer follows the process standards, but gets no payoff if the software engineer chooses to ignore. As following standards has no value per se for the software engineer, he wins by following standards while being controlled and looses, the variable $k = 1$, if not following while being controlled. If there is no control, the software engineer prefers following his own standards rather than being forced into some framework.

		Software Engineer	
		Ignore	Comply
Quality auditor	Ignore	(2, 4)	(3, 2)
	Audit	(1, k)	(4, 3)

Figure 3. Normal-form representation of the game played by quality auditors and software engineers

Initially, in figure 3, the software engineer's best strategy appears to be to comply, in order to avoid the outcome of audit ("minimax"). However, in repeated games, if the auditor assumes the engineer is basing his strategy upon this assumption, he may ignore to audit, as he expects the engineer to comply. But, as this may result in the engineering evolving the belief that there will be no audit, he may choose to ignore instead. Consequently, if the auditor acknowledges that he has to maintain the belief that he is going to audit, he may either decide on repeated auditing or develop a random strategy, alternating between the two strategies, thus forcing the engineer to choose the comply strategy.

A Nash Equilibrium specifies players' actions and beliefs such that (i) each player's action is optimal given his beliefs about other players' choices, and (ii) players' beliefs are correct (Bicchieri, 2004). In the case of the game in figure 3, audit and comply appears to be a Nash Equilibrium.

The assumption so far was that the auditor was able to function as an extended arm of management, thus setting the variable k equal to one. If this is not the case, if management does not transform $e(t)$ into $u(t)$, then the variable k may be equal to four, meaning that there are no negative consequences for the engineer, regardless of what strategies the auditor chooses, thus making the strategy of ignoring an optimal choice for the engineer, and as there is no point in auditing if auditing has no impact, this makes the joint strategy of ignore-ignore into a Nash equilibrium.

2.3   The game played by quality auditor and management

One of the most fundamental criteria for succeeding with quality control and process improvement is to have management commitment (Deming, 1986; Humphrey, 1989; Beckford, 2002). As argued in the section above, the quality control game of making software engineers follow standards is a game that is determined by management. If there is strong management commitment, there is a Nash equilibrium in auditing and complying, but if there is no management commitment, there is a Nash equilibrium of no control and no compliance. According to McClelland and Burnham (1976), for managers, particularly those in complex organizations, increasing power may be a much more important motivator than improving results. In other words, while the control loop in figure 1 may represent the world as seen by the SPI practitioner (quality auditor), it may not correspond with the way management sees it.

Consequently, in order to win the game of making people following standards, it is necessary for the quality control people to take part in the political game of trying to attain management commitment to the SPI system. In the world of politics, however, it may not be so obvious what the alternative strategies are and how they will play out against each other. In fact, for messy problems of this kind there is a body of literature called Problem Structuring Methods (PSM) (Rosenhead & Mingers, 2004), with drama theory being a "soft" extension of game theory for the purpose of simulating and analysing messy game-like situations (conflict and cooperation).

The history of drama theory appears to have started with Goffman's (1959) ideas of applying game theory through the metaphor of the theatre in sociological research, with Howard (1971) linking it more deeply with game theory and leading the development of drama theory into how it is being used in PSM today. Drama theory allows for meaningful analysis of different game-like situations, often using classical game theory examples such as Chicken and Prisoner's Dilemma as part of the vocabulary for classifying episodes within the drama. In fact, drama theory consists of a large and systematic set of concepts, tools and methods (Bennett et al., 2004), but it is beyond the scope of this paper to go into this.

However, we now define the new concept 'evolutionary drama theory' to represent the viewpoint taken by Evolutionary Game Theory (Alexander, 2009) to be used in drama theory. The concept is intended for analysing how an artefact like a SPI standard evolves towards equilibrium (evolutionary stable strategy, ESS) by looking at repeated dramas where temporal equilibriums may not necessarily be found, or, if found, may not necessarily fit with the ESS. In other words, what this concept signifies is the drama theory equivalent of not only analysing a single game of, say, Prisoner's Dilemma, but what are the winning strategies for populations playing endless sequences of this game.

3   METHODOLOGY

In order to provide insights on how to select SPI standards and get management commitment, in the context of the model in figure 1, the author will be using his own experience with SPI in a large public sector organization during the period 1999 to 2005. Also, some of the prehistory from working with SPI in another public sector organization 1992-1999 will be used, and the style of narrating the story will be that of a play, using an exemplary play from drama theory as guideline (Howard, 2004).

As the purpose of the research method is on trying to explicate conflict and drama, organizations and individuals are made anonymous, and as those who know the author may still be able to identify some of the models behind the play, characters, places and events from Shakespeare's Hamlet have been used in order to provide further disguise.

The organization where the SPI study takes place will thus be named Elsinore, run by the present king Claudius, while the experience from the older organization Wittenberg will be explained through Hamlet's conversations with the ghost of his father. Although the narrative of the play did not unfold exactly like the narrative of Hamlet, there are some similarities, so the overall structure of Hamlet will be used as a rough guide. The characters and their formal relationships are shown in table 4.

Claudius	Director of IT department	Elsinore, Denmark
Laertes	Director of projects management	Reporting to Claudius
Guildenstern	Director of information systems	Reporting to Claudius
Rosenkrantz	External ISO 9000 auditor	England
Polonius	Head of information security	Reporting to Claudius
Hamlet	Director of quality management	Reporting to Laertes
Horatio	Quality coordinator	Reporting to Hamlet
Ophelia	Quality coordinator	Reporting to Hamlet
Fortinbras	Director of HR department, future CEO	Norway
Ghost of Hamlet's father	Manager at organization where Hamlet used to work	Wittenberg

Table 4.Dramatis personae

Despite this elaborate pretence, the purpose of the play is to investigate real problems experienced by the author in trying to design and implement model-based SPI.

4   CASE STUDY - THE PLAY

4.1   Act I

Scene 1. Hamlet meets the ghost of his former employer. They discuss ISO 9000, and we have an exposition of what will lead to the development of the tragedy.

GHOST: How are you doing in your new job at Elsinore?

HAMLET: After having worked for seven years with SPI from an engineering perspective, I find it fascinating to work with social issues, but, as Osterweil famously states; "software processes are software too".

GHOST: Beware of your stubbornness, Hamlet.

HAMLET: The most important things I learned at Wittenberg were the mathematical principles of measurement, abstraction and generalization, and the general values of academia; intellectual integrity, community of peers and respect for knowledge.

4.2 Act II

Scene 1. Hamlet is supposed to help Polonius, head of the information security unit, in working with quality control and process improvement. Polonius' formal background is in legal informatics. He is highly competent in this field, and is deeply focused on developing rules and regulations for information security.

POLONIUS: The first I want you do to is to read what we have written about process improvement and quality control, the way we have integrated this in the part of the security regulations dealing with information integrity, and after you are beginning to feel comfortable with this, I would like to have you as a part of a committee working on how to improve and expand this part of the legal system.

HAMLET: I see, but what about audits? Are we certain that people are following rules and standards without auditing or doing some kind of control?

POLONIUS: Hmmm, as I said, what we need to improve upon is how these internal policies, strategies and standards are defined.

HAMLET: And you want me to look at the standards from the perspective of, say, ISO 9000?

POLONIUS: No, no, no. We have already looked at ISO 9000. What we need to do is to set up a committee. As your formal position in the organization is that of an advisor, you should only speak with people who are below the level of assistant directors. If we could assemble an interdisciplinary group of ...

HAMLET: Sorry to interrupt, but, in your estimation, how long do you think it will take until we have done sufficient analysis to start implementing and improving the quality management system?

POLONIUS: Well, in the case of the security management system, it took six years to analyse what we need, so we are actually only starting to look at what the system will do in practice.

HAMLET: Six years?

POLONIUS: And perhaps even longer, as I expect the quality management system is much larger and more complex than the information security system.

HAMLET: In my seven years of experience with this sort of thing, what I have done is much more test-driven; starting quality control and improvement as quickly as possible, in order to get a feel of what are the strengths and weaknesses of the current system, and then to systematically improve from there, building upon existing practice, existing standards etc.

POLONIUS: In your experience, yes. Well, you see, in the information security department, I am in charge, and the way we do things here is by committees and policy development.

HAMLET: Even if this is contradictory to TQM, SPI, experts like Deming, Juran etc.?

POLONIUS: I am no expert in TQM and SPI. That is your field of expertise. The only thing I am saying is that formal competence ranks higher than real competence. You may not be aware of how bureaucracy works, so let me explain: Even though your real competence as an expert in SPI tells you that SPI should be implemented according to certain principles, being your boss, my formal competence is higher than yours, so regardless of what you believe is the best approach, it is my judgement that is final, and I have already explained my opinion in these matters.

HAMLET: I see.

POLONIUS: So what do you think of the quality strategies and policies we have so far?

HAMLET: Well, it is a bit difficult to say without knowing how they relate to practice...

4.3   Act III

Scene 1. Hamlet continues to work according to Polonius terms, feeling he is not utilizing his expertise in a productive manner, so when Polonius leaves the castle, thanks to king Claudius, head of the IT department, Hamlet gets promoted to director of quality management.

HAMLET: Thank you very much. It's nice to talk to somebody who understands.

CLAUDIUS: Congratulations, and best of luck. Now we need to figure out where to place you in the organization.

HAMLET: Hmmm, yes. In ISO 9001 there is a requirement about the person being responsible of TQM and SPI should report to the top manager, which would be you in this case.

CLAUDIUS. Well, you see, there are already so many people reporting to me, so I think we have to think of some other way.

HAMLET: Of course, although the intension of that particular ISO 9001 clause is, naturally, to stress the importance of management involvement. As most of us know, without management involvement, things like TQM and SPI are difficult to get to work.

CLAUDIUS: Yes, indeed. In our case, however, we have to go for second best.

HAMLET: Then perhaps I could work with Laertes, head of project management. The theory of project management is in many ways linked with the theory of quality management, and it is always good to solve quality related problems as early on in the life cycle as possible.

Scene 2. Hamlet starts working with Laertes. Mostly this works quite well, although it becomes gradually obvious that project management and quality management often work in two different directions.

LAERTES: The guy working as quality coordinator on project X just left. We need somebody to take his place. Would it be possible for you to do that?

HAMLET [avoidingly]: Well, that could be an interesting experience, but now that I have started auditing and improving the business processes, that would mean that I would have to leave what is important in the long run in order to do fire fighting.

4.4   Act IV

Scene 1. Claudius and Laertes are working out strategies.

CLAUDIUS: Your idea, Laertes, about outsourcing the Y2K problem to India was a brilliant idea. We got lots of good publicity that way, even the prime minister was impressed.

LAERTES: Heh heh. I'm lucky to have a friend working as a consultant in the outsourcing business. Let's see if we can find further use of him.

CLAUDIUS: One thing that impresses many people concerning these Indian software factories is that they are often certified against something called CMM level 5. Perhaps we could use them in finding out whether we could get a similar certificate? Hah hah. At least I know of quite a few people who would be impressed if we managed that!

LAERTES: Good idea. I will talk to Hamlet.

Scene 2. Hamlet works with an Indian CMM assessor. The result of the assessment is that the organization is on level one, so Claudius and Laertes loose interest. Due to the discrete maturity ladder of CMM, Hamlet does not find the model particularly useful for measuring continuous improvement and gets external help for doing an ISO 15504 assessment. This results in an even lower maturity level score, creating even less enthusiasm. Hamlet, however, continues testing different models, EFQM, CAF, ISO 12207, CobiT and ISO 9004, trying to convince Claudius on the importance of using international SPI standards for benchmarking and continuous improvement. Laertes and Claudius meet and assess the situation.

CLAUDIUS: This idea about using people from India in helping us reach CMM level five didn't work out.

LAERTES: The problem is the line management. Nothing is documented. There is no discipline. Each time one of my projects delivers a new information system, the organization is totally unprepared to handle it, and we have long periods of chaos until they get the hang of it.

CLAUDIUS: Yes, I know. We are dealing with layers and layers of incompetence, but perhaps we could use the people from India for documenting the systems? Hamlet has been working with Rosenkrantz on doing an ISO 9000 assessment of the SPI system. He says the way towards CMM, EFQM and such starts with reaching compliance with ISO 9000.

LAERTES: He does? Hmmmm. What if we hired Rosenkrantz to work directly for us instead, designing the project in a way that will give it the proper prestige it deserves? It seems to me that we might have a quick win here.

Scene 3. Hamlet is gaining momentum in process improvement and is granted his request for two assistants, Horatio and Ophelia, to help him doing audits and measurements. Horatio turns out to be of tremendous help while Ophelia quickly becomes a source of problems.

OPHELIA: This ISO 9004 model doesn't work. It is impossible to know whether a process is on level one, two, three or five. Besides, people only get annoyed when I try to fill out these numbers.

HAMLET: The ISO 9004 model is perfectly simple. We have gone through this several times, and you have lots of examples to look at. I also experience people resenting being evaluated, but you must remember that we are in the business of measuring continuous improvement. Without measurements, it is impossible to apply statistical process control.

OPHELIA [angrily]: I don't believe statistical process control works. With statistics you can prove anything, but it doesn't mean that it is right. You never explain anything to me, you just complain. Last week you complained about how I simplified the EFQM model, the week before that you corrected the way I was using CobiT. As far as I can tell, none of these models fit together, and, besides, I don't think quality can be measured in the first place. I think we should focus on meeting people on their own terms.

4.5   Act V

Scene 1. Laertes is focused on getting projects completed and sees Hamlet's audits and measurements as disturbance. As he observes Ophelia's similar dislike for audits and general distrust in numerical SPI methods, he ponders how to remove Hamlet without causing too much organizational havoc. He asks Hamlet to enter his office.

LAERTES: Have you ever thought about doing research?

HAMLET: Research? Yes, I used to be a research scientist once. That was an interesting period of my life. Now, however, I enjoy being director of quality management.

LAERTES: Well, you see, I've had some complaints, and I have been thinking, perhaps you would enjoy life better as a research scientist, doing research related to quality management, of course.

HAMLET: Complaints?

LAERTES [opens a large folder]: Yes, you see, this is where I collect everything about you, every mail you write etc. There are several complaints here, people complaining about your quality management methods.

HAMLET: Is there something wrong with my methods? I just measure practice against process, giving people feedback in an objective manner, in order to help them improve.

LAERTES: Well, over a long period a series of complaints have piled up, I will not go into that...

HAMLET: I still don't understand. If people object to what I am doing, why don't I hear anything? During our last development conversation, only a few months ago, I cannot remember any talk about problems?

LEARTES [getting irritated]: Well, I think you should consider what I have explained to you during this conversation. Think about it, and then we will talk more.

Scene 2. After a few days there is another meeting, now with Claudius also present.

CLAUDIUS: I hear there have been some complaints?

HAMLET: People are always complaining about quality management, that is the nature of the work I do. If only I could get more specific feedback, somebody telling me what the problem is.

LAERTES: To be frank, Guildenstern addressed me last week and said he was not too happy with Hamlet upsetting the software engineers.

HAMLET: Guildenstern? I have regular meetings with him every month. I can't remember there being anything problematic there?

LAERTES: Well, he told me there were serious problems.

CLAUDIUS: It seems to me that the next thing to do is for you, Hamlet, to visit Guildenstern and find out what these problems are.

Scene 3. Hamlet visits Guildenstern.

HAMLET: I have this feeling that Claudius and Laertes want to get rid of me, but I don't understand what is behind it. I feel our conversations have always been easy going. Perhaps you could give me some advice on what to do. Laertes says that you have complained to him about my behaviour?

GUILDENSTERN: Claudius and Laertes have decided that they want to get rid of you? Well, to tell you the truth, I don't think our monthly conversations have been all that good. Besides, as I have told you earlier, I think you focus too much on auditing my software engineers. It causes stress, and sometimes it isn't possible to follow standards. You pointing out how various processes deviate from standards is simply not very useful.

HAMLET: But that is my work!!! That is what I'm paid to do!

GUILDENSTERN: Actually, I often have problems understanding Claudius and Laertes, but they are the two most powerful people in the organization. I don't want to get my nose rubbed against those two guys.

HAMLET: So there is no hope for me?

GUILDENSTERN: I didn't say that. There is always hope. I only said to Laertes that doing quality audits while we were developing new standards and methods is causing problems.

Scene 4. Hamlet has another meeting with Claudius and Laertes.

HAMLET: Well, now I have spoken with Guildenstern in order to find out what the problems were.

CLAUDIUS: Yes?

HAMLET: He mentioned to Laertes that it was causing distress among the software engineers being measured against standards that they were already considering rewriting. Clearly he was frustrated in this respect, but he didn't frame any serious complaints. Besides, in order for me to measure continual improvement, the basic idea is to measure all the time. I don't see what he finds so difficult in this, as this is a topic we have discussed several times, but I do understand that he dislikes his engineers getting stressed. Perhaps I could discuss more with him how to solve this.

CLAUDIUS: No, no. Forget about Guildenstern. What we want you to do now is to write a formal letter where you state that you want to change job description. You no longer want to be director of quality control; you want to become a research scientist.

HAMLET: But that is not what I want. My whole life and personal identify has now been interwoven with what I am doing now. I am part of a professional community. I have achieved more dramatic SPI results in this organization than what most people would believe were possible.

CLAUDIUS [angry]: You write this letter, or else!!!

Scene 5. Laertes, as head of project management, gets the idea that ISO 9000 could be a high prestige project, makes sure that those within the organization who are competent at ISO 9000 are kept away and hires consultant to do the analysis and implementation, as consultants are easier to handle. However, the consultants turn out to be incompetent. The project is costly and makes no progress. With the arrival of Fortinbras as a new CEO, there is a total reorganization, many of those until now in power being removed or given other jobs.

HORATIO: I was asked to become quality manager after Hamlet was asked to leave, but the politics of the organization made me frustrated. I am now doing projects management instead.

FORTINBRAS: Every reorganization and change is difficult, but even though people are changed, ideas remain. I want new people to continue working on what has already been done.

4.6   Analysis

Similar to Shakespeare's Hamlet, this version of Hamlet is divided into five acts and the characters behave in a slightly similar manner as known from the classic drama. In the first act, Hamlet uses the conversation with the ghost of his father to contemplate the importance of standards and also reflect on SPI as pure engineering science without any understanding of the politics involved. The second act is focused on misalignment of interests in terms of introducing a SPI framework. Polonius is developing a security management system based on domestic strategies, policies and standards (SPS) for security and quality management, deliberately avoiding international standards and scientific methods. For Hamlet this strategy is not optimal, but in lack of anything else he uses the SPS for auditing purposes and tries to figure out how the SPS fits with international standards such as ISO 9000.

In the third act, Polonius is no longer part of the game, and Hamlet's conflicts are primarily related to working with Laertes who is head of the projects department. From the viewpoint of SPI, a project is just one single dot on a run chart, while the aim should be to predict how projects behave in the long run and what can be done in order to achieve process improvement. For Laertes, however, power, influence and prestige is tied up with each particular project, meaning that the rise to power comes form being involved in the right committees, right contacts, doing things that looks impressive etc., rather than doing what is necessary on a long term perspective in the sense of what is required of the ISO 9000 and CMMI standards. For Laertes, Hamlet means problems, and, through the influence of Ophelia, who has her own reasons for being in conflict with Hamlet, Laertes decides to have Hamlet removed. Although following SPI models is not in the interest of Laertes, he is nevertheless aware of the prestige in complying with ISO 9001 and CMMI/5, so at various stages he tries establishing CMM- and ISO 9000 projects.

The fourth act is focused on the scheming of Laertes and Claudius, and on the domestic conflicts between Hamlet and his assistant Ophelia, contrasted with the harmonious relationship between Hamlet and his other assistant, Horatio. The conflict with Ophelia is based on Ophelia being good at handling people but poor at handling statistics and the technical sides of SPI, making her uncomfortable in the role of auditing various groups and processes through the use of numerical assessment methods. Despite the conflict, it is useful for Hamlet and the quality management department to receive the frustrated criticism from Ophelia as incentives for improvement, but eventually the conflict drives her destructively mad.

In the fifth act, the sum of all previous episodes has produced two kinds of results. On the one hand, the SPI activities have risen to a maturity level never before experienced within the organization, but on the other hand, the efficiency of the SPI also makes processes more transparent and several people are feeling uncomfortable by having what was previously unknown or only known to a few become public knowledge in terms of improvement trends or lack of trends etc. The sum of forces in favour of having Hamlet removed becomes greater than those keeping him, so he is asked to resign. This results in the SPI system collapsing, and shortly after, other political games result in total reorganization and a fall-down of the empire as it was defined.

In the epilogue, however, it is suggested that despite people coming a going, some of the ideas and structures, like those of ISO 9000, were strengthened, meaning that the organization today may be more ideally suited for SPI development.

5   DISCUSSION

5.1   Use of drama theory for understanding the dynamics of the SPI game

As suggested by drama theory, presenting the case study as theatrical episodes makes it possible to think more clearly about the situation, exploring more fully some of the more dramatic aspects of the story, possibly also making it possible to enter the mind of the theatre critic, comparing a play constructed in this manner with the classics from world drama, Shakespeare, Ibsen, Chekhov etc., using the catalogue of exemplary dramas from drama theory for comparing and contrasting in order to see what is special about the particular case of SPI implementation and how similar cases have been given the PSM treatment and turned into more structured problems that can be analysed by the use of game theory.

As explained in the methodology chapter, the play was written in the style of Hamlet as the real story behind the play is a story of intense conflict, on many levels, partly in order to go more deeply into such aspects of conflicts, and partly in order to make the real people in the organization anonymous. A challenge in using this model, however, is that Hamlet is a rather complex play, and rather than telling a story about, say, a hero scientist fighting against the stupidity of the bureaucracy (Latour, 1993), it becomes a story about one event that leads to another, following the logic of tragedies where the solution at the end of the play is hinted at in the very beginning. From this perspective, the narrative becomes more like the narratives of "systems archetypes" used in dynamical systems theory (e.g. Senge, 1990) than a rational investigation of mappings between decision and payoff.

What the story is supposed to ask, however, is whether there is anything to learn about process improvement and organizational politics by using Hamlet as a theoretical lens. In order to answer this question properly, on a general basis, a thorough review of the literature on Hamlet is needed, and unless the SPI researcher happens to be an expert in literature theory, perhaps already having done PhD studies in Hamlet, the comparison between the real case and the model case can easily become shallow if the researcher has only a shallow understanding of the model. If the SPI researcher is interested in drama, however, drama theory can be an interesting approach. As pointed out by Kott (1974), in his analysis of Shakespeare in the context of Eastern Europe in the fifties and sixties, it is remarkable how rich and insightful Shakespeare can be if one manages to make a good match between the right play and a contemporary political situation.

One common way to interpret Hamlet is to think of it as an existential play (Kott, 1974), something that turns the story about SPI in the bureaucracy into a story about life and death, a story similar to Kakar's analysis of Fredrick Taylor (1970), where the message is that there is a deep connection between Taylor's enthusiasm with control and process improvement and how he had difficulties in coping with certain aspects of social life. Kakar has later been accused of misrepresenting Taylor, making him more neurotic that he actually was (Kanigel, 1997), but the idea of trying to go beyond the surface of his model in order to search for phenomenological explanations is an interesting approach that fits very well with most of the PSM styles, like, for instance, soft systems methodology (SSM) (Checkland, 1981). Although Kakar may have provided a distorted model of Taylor, Kakar's caricature could perhaps give sufficient ideas about SPI psychology for hypothesizing solutions for the SPI game. Similarly, there are different interpretations of Hamlet giving the SPI researcher flexibility in comparing his analysis of the SPI drama with different type of Hamlet interpretations.

The question remains, nevertheless, whether using Hamlet versus Claudius, the main conflict in Shakespeare's play and main conflict in the SPI play in section four, as a model for understanding what Beer (1968, p. 22) calls the "natural enemies" of process improvement scientists (quality auditors) and managers in an organization is a useful model. Bram (1994) provides a game theoretical analysis of the conflict between Hamlet and Claudius, using his own mathematical expansion of game theory ("theory of moves") for illustrating how the underlying rationality of the conflict can be understood. However, as the mock-Hamlet in the SPI case study is not an exact replica of Shakespeare's Hamlet, the arguments presented by Bram do not seem to fit in this particular case.

In order to bring insight on what to do if there appears to be little or no connection between $e(t)$ and $u(t)$ in figure 1, resulting in the quality game in figure 3 reaching a Nash equilibrium in ignore-ignore rather than audit-comply, does a hermeneutical understanding of the collaboration between Claudius and Laertes, or a phenomenological understanding of the managers hiding between these masks, provide guidance on how to link $e(t)$ with $u(t)$? Although the case study as reported in section four does not answer this, it is the belief of the author that there are some general insights to be found from this approach. Much of the success of the SPI in the reported case study had specifically to do with a persistent attempt to try to understand each and every person in power. As Checkland (1981, p. 351) points out, a system owner is defined by the person able to destroy the system. From a SPI perspective, the system owners are the most important people in the organization, and although there are theories of motivation and behaviour in general, when it comes to real life SPI, it is necessary to get a deep phenomenological understanding of how certain people think, feel and behave, in order to make the proper "game moves" that prevent the SPI system in getting destroyed.

5.2   Establishing agreement on rules for playing SPI games

In figure 5, the PSM-based phenomenological approach towards SPI is put in a greater explanatory picture that makes a map out of the sciences, in the style of Burrell and Morgan (1979), by putting the "hard" sciences on the right hand side of the matrix and the "soft" sciences on the left hand side, and having sciences where the researcher is a part of the system being investigated at the top ("action"), while the bottom represents research done by a distant researcher ("perception"). In the case of the SPI problem presented in figure 1, the problem was an engineering problem belonging in the world of the stick man at the upper right corner of the model in figure 5. However, as the SPI engineering solution did not work according to theory, it was necessary to open the black boxes of conflict and negotiations in figure 1, moving the focus in figure 5 from engineering to psychology. Although there are motivational theories, like those of McClelland and Burnham (1976), suggesting that getting management commitment may be reached more efficiently if we assume that management is motivated by power than if we were to assume they were motivated by achievement, this makes it necessary to understand what kind of social reality we are dealing with. Social reality, the nature of the organization that breeds certain types of psychological behaviour, is a social science research theme belonging in the lower left corner of the model. Although drama theory is primarily a psychological research tool, it can also be seen as a sociological tool in the way that it is linked with Goffman's ideas of applying the theatre as a lens for understanding society.

The fact that drama theory is an extension of game theory also makes it into an extension of a positivist perspective of society, thus the arrow from social science to physics in the lower right corner of the model. Although drama theory is not a mathematical science, the aim of the approach is to investigate episodes in the same way as game-like situations are analysed in game theory, searching for optimal strategies, equilibriums and such. Even though one should be of the persuasion that strategies and equilibriums are phenomena that exist in reality, the language of game theory and natural science is a social construct (van Fraassen, 1980), thus finally leading us back to the engineering position at the upper right corner of the diagram were we started, i.e. mathematical models and their extended verbal models as engineering constructs.

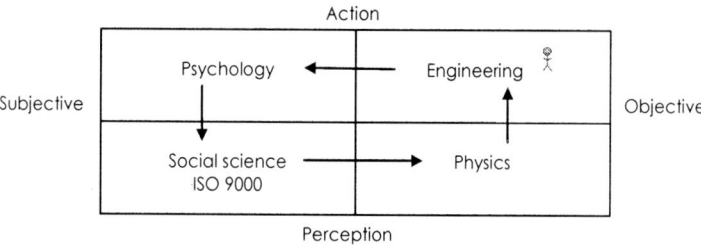

Figure 5. Circle of explanation along paradigms of science (adapted from Burrell and Morgan, 1979)

Relating the model in figure 5 with the case study, the ISO 9000 standards have been placed in the lower left corner of social science rather than the upper right corner of software engineering. This is done in order to illustrate the major point about the case study in terms of how the SPI standards were chosen by management in order to fit with the politics of the organization. As illustrated in the case story, several standards, such as CAF, EFQM, BSC, ISO 9001, ISO 9004, ISO 12207, ISO 15504, CMM, CobiT and ITIL were discussed and implemented for test purposes, some models more useful and promising than others. What finally and gradually emerged as an equilibrium strategy was a cluster of standards, using ISO 9001:2000 as a core and interpreting the others in compliance with this.

In this particular case, as explained in act five, the game between SPI and management resulted in the SPI people being thrown overboard; first Hamlet being asked to resign, then Ophelia leaving the organization, and finally Horatio giving up. The fact that a new castle was built after Fortinbras burned the old one down could be subject for further empirical research, supporting narrative for a new play. Returning from PSM to game theory, the equivalent to investigating how a SPI strategy evolves over a sequence of dramas corresponds with evolutionary game theory (Alexander, 2009), and what appears to be the key insight from this particular case study is that engineers, auditors and managers may come and go, but the evolutionary SPI game is played out through many generations, in this case indicating that the ISO 9000 strategy may represent an equilibrium in the long run.

6   CONCLUSION

The starting point for this study was the observation that there are many methods, models and standards for doing software process improvement (SPI). From the perspective of the people in charge of SPI, it is important to select the SPI standards that fit the purpose of the improvement activities, while also making sure that management gets sufficiently committed to the framework. Using control theory (DiStefano et al., 1990) for analysing the problem of SPI design, the model in figure 1 assumes the role of management being that of responding to the difference $e(t)$, between accepted performance $r(t)$ and perceived performance $y(t)$, in developing and communicating control signals $u(t)$ to the software engineers. Without management commitment to SPI standards, it is unlikely that the error signals will be efficiently transformed into control signals.

Referring to organizational literature (e.g. Legge, 2002) and looking at a narrative produced by a SPI case study, getting and maintaining management commitment can be a challenge. There may be perfectly rational reasons why the level of management commitment required in SPI theory may be difficult to achieve in practice. What was suggested in this paper, however, was to look at social tension between the three boxes in the control theory model in figure 1 as a three-player game of engineers, managers and quality auditors in figure 2 and then focus on the conflict between engineers and auditors in figure 3. The equilibrium in this latter model depends on management commitment.

As pointed out by Brunsson et al (2000), there is a fundamental difference between management saying they are committed to ISO 9000 and management being committed to ISO 9000. When game-like situations are too complex or obscure to define a mathematically well-defined problem, the literature of problem structuring methods (PSM) (e.g. Rosenhead and Mingers, 2004) suggests drama theory as an extension of game theory. Using the tragedy of Hamlet as a template for analysing a particular SPI case study, it is suggested that single SPI projects can be seen as repeated games in the context of evolutionary game playing (Alexander, 2009), with the ISO 9000 standards emerging as equilibrium SPI strategies.

The key contribution to the theory of social aspects of SPI lies in the PSM perspective on SPI as an evolutionary game, the new concept of 'evolutionary drama theory'. As illustrated by the case study, engineers, managers and auditors may come and go, but the SPI game continues from generation to generation, paving its way towards strategic equilibriums. For the organization as a whole, as represented by management, the idea is to have good auditors involved in the SPI game, watching how long they survive, and then replace them to make sure the SPI game continues without end.

References

Alexander, J.M. (2009). Evolutionary Game Theory, Stanford Encyclopedia of Philosophy, http://plato.stanford.edu/entries/game-evolutionary/, Accessed on July 6th, 2009.

Beckford, J. (2002). Quality. 2nd Edition. Routledge, London.

Beer, S. (1968). Management Science. Aldus, London.

Bennett, P., Bryant, J. and Howard, N. (2004). "Drama theory and conflict analysis," in: Rational analysis for a problematic world revisited: Problem structuring methods for complexity, uncertainty and conflict. Second edition (Rosenhead, J. and Mingers, J. Eds.), pp. 225-248, Wiley, Chichester.

Bicchieri, C. (2004). "Game Theory: Nash Equilibrium," In: The Blackwell Guide to the Philosophy of Computing and Information (Floridi, L. Ed.), pp. 289-304, Blackwell, Oxford.

Boehm, B. and Turner, R. (2004). Balancing Agility and Discipline, Addison Wesley, Boston.

Bram, S.J. (1994). Theory of Moves, Third Edition, Cambridge University Press, Cambridge.

Brunsson, N. et al. (2000). A World of Standards, Oxford University Press, Oxford.

Burrell, G. and Morgan, G. (1979). Sociological Paradigms and Organizational Analysis, Ashgate, Aldershot, Hants.

Checkland, P. (1981). Systems Thinking, Systems Practice. Wiley, Chichester.

Chrissis, M.B., Konrad, M. and Shrum, S. (2003). CMMI – Guidelines for Process Integration and Product Improvement, Addison Wesley, Boston.

Cockburn, A. (2002). Agile Software Development, Addison Wesley, Boston.

Conradi, R. and Fuggetta, A. (2002). "Improving Software Process Improvement," IEEE Software, Vol. 19, No. 4, pp. 92-99.

Deming, E.W. (1986). Out of the Crisis, MIT University Press, Cambridge, Massachusettes.

DiStefano, J.J., Stubberud, A.R. and Williams, I.J. (1990). Schaum's Outline of Feedback and Control Systems. Second Edition. McGraw-Hill, New York.

Dybå, T. Dingsøyr, T. and Moe, N.B. (2002). Praktisk prosessforbedring: En håndbok for IT-bedrifter, Fagbokforlaget, Bergen, Norway.

Goffman, E. (1959). The Presentation of Self in Everyday Life, Doubleday, Garden City, New York.

Howard, N. (1971). Paradoxes of Reality, MIT Press, Cambridge, Massachusetts.

Howard, N. (2004). "The M&A Play: Using Drama Theory for Mergers and Acquisitions," in: Rational analysis for a problematic world revisited: Problem structuring methods for complexity, uncertainty and conflict. Second edition (Rosenhead, J. and Mingers, J. Eds.), pp. 249-265, Wiley, Chichester.

Hoyle, D. (2006). ISO 9000 Quality Systems Handbook. Butterworth-Heinemann, Amsterdam.

Humphrey, W. (1989). Managing the Software Process, Addison-Wesley, Boston.

Kakar, S. (1970). Frederick Taylor: A Study in Personality and Innovation, MIT Press, Cambridge, Massachusetts.

Kanigel, R. (1997). The One Best Way: Frederick Winslow Taylor and the Enigma of Efficiency, Penguin, New York.

Kott, J. (1974). Shakespeare our contemporary, Second Edition, Norton, London.

Latour, B. (1993). The Pasteurization of France, Harvard University Press, Cambridge, Massachusetts.

Legge, K. (2002). On Knowledge, Business Consultants and the Selling of Total Quality Management. In Critical Consulting: New Perspectives on the Management Advice Industry (Clark, T. and Fincham, R. Ed.), pp. 74-90, Blackwell, Oxford.

McClelland, D.C. and Burnham, D.H. (1976). "Power is the great motivator," Harvard Business Review, 25, pp. 159-166.

Nielsen, P.A. and Kautz, K. (2008). Software Processes & Knowledge: Beyond conventional software process improvement, Software Innovation Publisher, Aalborg.

Rosenhead, J. and Mingers, J. (2004). Rational analysis for a problematic world revisited: Problem structuring methods for complexity, uncertainty and conflict. Second edition. Wiley, Chichester.

Schlickman, J.J. (2003). ISO 9001:2000 quality management system design, Artech House, Boston.

Schwaber, K. (2004). Agile Project Management with Scrum, Microsoft Professional, Redmond, Washington.

Seddon, J. (1997). In Pursuit of Quality: The Case against ISO 9000, Oak Tree Press, Dublin.

Senge, P. (1990). The Fifth Discipline: The art and practice of the learning organization, Currency Doubleday, New York.

Sommerville, I. and Rodden, T. (1995). Human, Social and Organizational Influences on the Software Process, Cooperative Systems Engineering Group, Technical Report CSEG/2/1995, Lancaster University, Computing Department, Lancaster.

Sommerville, I. (2001). Software Engineering, 6th Edition, Addison-Wesley, Harlow, England.

van Fraassen, B.C. (1980). The Scientific Image, Oxford University Press, Oxford.

Zahran, S. (1998). Software Process Improvement: Practical Guidelines for Business Success. Addison-Wesley, Harlow.

II

The Pac-Man model of total quality management: Strategy lessons for change agents

Øgland, Petter

Department of Informatics, University of Oslo, Norway

Abstract

Organizational development frameworks like total quality management (TQM) can create conflicts between change agents and managers. Some researchers believe that playing video games has an impact on how people make decisions and handle conflicts. The purpose of this paper is to identify and investigate a Pac-Man model for aiding change agents in developing optimal TQM strategies. An empirical study of a five year TQM development project is analysed by using the Pac-Man video game as a theoretical lens. The results are presented as simulations of game play, suggesting four implications on how Pac-Man strategies can be used as TQM strategies. The four strategies consist of (1) never stop "eating dots" in terms of continuous quality auditing, (2) find and follow the "patterns" in the organizational maze that can be audited without upsetting management by understanding "ghost" psychology, (3) eat "power pellets", getting management commitment when the organization is in a receptive mode, and (4) eat "bonus fruits" of management appreciation whenever it appears. In conclusion the study suggests elaboration of critical systems theory (CST) by applying ideas and concepts from game theory.

Key words: Total quality management, Pac-Man, game theory, critical systems theory

Introduction

In his analysis of management science (operational research, OR) in business use, Beer (1968, pp. 22-23) describes the conflict between managers and scientists as a conflict between "natural enemies". Scientists want to use a scientific approach for solving business problems, but know less about business from a practical perspective. Managers, on the other hand, see a threat to dominion in the shape of the scientists. As a response to this problem, management science has expanded beyond the positivist framework of operational research and systems analysis in applying theories from psychology, sociology and philosophy for improving the ways of analyzing political conflicts (Checkland, 1981; Jackson, 2000; Mingers, 2006). In order to succeed with OR frameworks like total quality management (TQM), a technical education in OR is not sufficient, it is also necessary to develop political skills.

Game theory has since its conception been seen as an integrated part of operational research and systems theory, providing systems models for modelling conflict situations (Churchman et al, 1957; von Bertalanffy, 1968; Rapoport, 1986). While game theory has made impact on the type of systems thinking that is sometimes referred to as problem structuring methods (PSM) (e.g. Bennett et al, 2001), other PSMs dealing specifically with politics, such as critical systems thinking (CST) (Ulrich, 1994; Flood & Jackson, 1991; Flood, 1993; Jackson, 2000), have, perhaps somewhat surprisingly, no references to game theory. Beck and Wade (2006) argue that people growing up with computers and video games have developed certain political skills and ways of seeing the world that is radically different from that of an older generation.

While game theory is only one of many theoretical perspectives used by game designers, game theory is used for analysing strategies for serious and non-serious games (Salen & Zimmerman, 2004). Abt (1969, p. 9) defines serious games as games that "have an explicit and carefully thought-out educational purpose and are not intended to be played primarily for amusement". As observed by Axelrod (2002), also non-serious games, like the Monopoly board game, can be interpreted as a serious game by viewing it as a model of the real world, and then see, for instance, whether optimal strategies for winning at Monopoly carry over into the world of real estate speculations or business in general. Expanding on the research carried out by Beck and Wade (2006), the idea of using the non-serious Pac-Man video game as a serious game and a model for understanding the politics of implementing TQM is the purpose of this paper.

The hypothesis of the study is that the Pac-Man model produces optimal TQM implementation strategies ("quality plans") in complex organizations.

In order to investigate this, the remains of the paper have been structured in five parts. First there is a literature review bringing more detail to the hypothesis in terms of explaining what is meant by complex organizations in the context of TQM, some comments on game theory and a short explanation of the Pac-Man video game and what is meant by a Pac-Man model of organizational conflict. Next there is a methodology section explaining how the Pac-Man model has been used for interpreting the dynamics and results of a five year long TQM project within a Scandinavian public sector organization. The methodology section is followed by a results section narrated in the style of game simulation. Then there is a discussion section using the simulation results for evaluating the Pac-Man model and the strategies developed through the model. The final section concludes the paper by summarizing how the Pac-Man model is an effective model for capturing certain core dynamics of the TQM game, providing simple strategies on how change agents should play to maximize payoff. Concerning the debate of how systems theory can learn from the past and prepare for the future, the position articulated through this paper is that game theory should be more explicitly used and further developed within systems research domains like PSM and CST.

Literature review

The literature review is written with the aim of clarifying the hypothesis in terms of first reviewing literature on the game of TQM in complex organizations, as this is the context of the moderator variable in the hypothesis. This is followed by reviewing the literature on TQM assessment methods, as the hypothesis states that the Pac-Man model is able to produce optimal TQM strategies. The final part of the section consists of reviewing literature used for formulating the Pac-Man model.

The game of total quality management (TQM)

Use of game metaphors in TQM literature

Crosby, one of the gurus of the quality movement in the 1980s, had been active in sports and used metaphors from games and sports extensively in his writing (Crosby, 1979; 1984; 1999), "quality is ballet, not hockey" being a typical example. In his final interview before his death in 1993, Deming, the most well-known TQM guru, told the interviewer that "the legacy he wanted to leave was systems thinking and win-win" (Schultz, 1995, p. 152), a reference to the theory of positive-sum games.

While Berry (1991) uses metaphors about baseball and golf for giving inside suggestions on how to implement TQM, Cole (1999) gives an outside analysis of the quality movement in terms of how a series of different "quality fads" changed the quality game but helped the industry grasping key insights from different ideas as they were highlighted through each fad.

The political game of TQM is indirectly pointed out by Beckford (2002, p. 311) when he says "management commitment is the single most critical issue in the pursuit of quality. Without it, the program will fail – as so many do." Legge (2002) interprets statements like these to mean that the TQM practitioner is recommended to play the game of persuading management into buying some TQM framework and then continue manipulating and persuading them into staying committed to the framework. What is not touched upon in this account of the political TQM game, is what Beer (1968) describes as managers and scientists (TQM practitioners) being "natural enemies", meaning that persuasion and manipulation can sometimes be a never-ending process.

The idea of the Pac-Man model is to take all these game aspects into consideration when using the Pac-Man game as a model for learning about TQM implementation in practice ("serious game"). Within the literature on TQM, there are serious games focused on role playing, simulations and different types of serious games used as part of training (e.g. Caroselli, 1995), but no serious games for training TQM practitioners on handling the ongoing conflict with management.

Concerning the point in systems theory where this paper aims to make a contribution, the award winning book "Beyond TQM" (Flood, 1993) articulated a mixed methods approach towards designing TQM founded in critical systems theory (CST) without referring to game theory. The Pac-Man model aims at showing how this approach can be elaborated further through explicit use of game theory.

Action research and scientific management – the game of science

Some anthropologists and sociologists contributing to the theory of science and technology studies (STS) describe science more or less like a game of scholars developing strategies for convincing other scholars (e.g. Latour 1979, 1987; Sismondo, 2004), emphasizing the role of power and politics in such games. Contrasting the descriptions of the scientific process from the outside, Sindermann (2001) uses the game metaphors for giving inside advice on how to "win the game of science", stressing the importance of understanding the rules and ethics of the game. Although he mentions game theory in the introduction of his book, the advice is given in conventional prose. Bonilla (2006), on the other hand, shows how game theory can be explicitly used for describing the social aspects of doing scientific research, both from the inside and the outside.

Action research (Reason & Bradbury, 2004; Collis & Hussey, 2002) is a methodology used in organizational science for investigating how various socio-technical parameters can have an impact on organizational performance. For epistemological reasons, knowledge is sometimes defined through the researcher's ability to understand his research subjects in being able to identify with their beliefs. This kind of research has to be explicitly political, and can in this sense be seen not only as a scientific game of convincing others but also a political game of trying to influence decisions and actions.

When stressing the technological parameters rather than the social parameters for the purpose of researching how to improve organizational performance, the research design is sometimes called design science (Simon, 1996; Cross, 2008). In such cases, the research is often less politically explicit, but, following the reasoning of STS, it is can still be seen as a political game. Scientific management (Taylor, 1911), quality control (Shewhart, 1938), operational research (Beer, 1968), total quality management (Deming, 1986) etc., are all variations of the same theme, what Cole (1999) would call different game variations within the total game of management science.

TQM and game theory

Reyniers and Tapiero (1995) explain how game theory can be used for developing audit strategies for supplier-producer contracts. If the situation is quality sensitive, game theory may highlight how each party is developing strategies for maximizing profits and minimizing quality control costs.

This same approach could be used for analyzing the scenario described by Beer (1968) with scientists and managers being natural enemies. In this context, the strategies are not formulated in an audit contract but in the quality plans developed by the quality department. To elaborate on Beer's concept of "natural enemies", the conflict can be seen to consist of managers and quality coordinators playing two different types of games. While the managers may find it useful to hide knowledge, being able to use bluff as a strategy for maintaining and building power (a game of imperfect information, like Poker), the nature of quality improvement is to make knowledge explicit and visible through use of measurements, graphs and feedback in order to stimulate process improvement (a game of perfect information, like Chess).

Being involved in two different games, the scientists and managers become "natural enemies". As it is the managers who are formally in power, the TQM game challenge for the scientist is to try to stimulate process improvement by auditing processes and present results, speculating on when to present the results, to whom, knowing when to keep silent, and when the organization may respond positively to being audited.

In addition to chase and scatter behaviour in management, due to the relationship between knowledge and power, it is important not to forget the importance of management commitment (Beckford, 2002; Legge, 2002), meaning that whenever it should happen that the scientist's "natural enemy" in management should actually be happy or thankful for work well done, something that happens rarely and lasts only for short intervals, this is a moment to celebrate.

In game theoretic terms (von Neumann & Morgenstern, 1953, pp. 48-60), the game of TQM politics can be thought of as a $n+1$ player game consisting of one scientist and n managers. The allowed moves of the scientist consists of auditing the organization, but having to avoid management until a series of audits relevant to some particular quality control practice that involves management happens. While management would normally be sceptical of the auditing process making knowledge and sources of power visible, at the time of formal decision making such knowledge is needed. Credit is given to the scientist when submitting quality reports for the right people at the right time. The more managers the scientist manages to commit to process improvement at such times, the better.

Evaluating TQM strategies through payoff functions

In wanting to investigate the effect of applying Pac-Man strategies in the real world of total quality management, it is necessary to have a somewhat precise mapping between the payoff function $f(s)$ for playing strategy s in a game of Pac-Man and the payoff $f'(s')$ when we interpret the Pac-Man strategy s as the TQM strategy s' and the Pac-Man payoff f as TQM payoff f'.

There are many ways of measuring the TQM level of a given organization, with different assessment methods and models for different industries. In the software development industry, for instance, organizations can be measured on a level from 1 to 5 according to the CMM model (Humphrey, 1989) or on a continuous scale from 0 to 5 according to the ISO 15504 model (Zahran, 1998). The assessment model ISO 9004:2000 uses a similar five level model, making it possible to start the journey towards TQM by first developing a quality management system that complies with the requirements of ISO 9001:2008 and then improve this system step by step as it rises up the five step ladder.

For organizations participating in the international game of TQM, however, there are annual TQM competitions and TQM awards based on three regional standards. In Japan they have the Deming Award, in the United States they have the Malcolm Baldrige Award and in Europe we have the EFQM Excellence Award, based on the results of the EFQM assessment model, where an organization can score between 0 and 1000 points (0.0 to 100.0%). In this context, one aspect of the hypothesis means that a Pac-Man strategy *s* producing the maximum Pac-Man score of 3,333,360 points should correspond with a TQM strategy *s'* that produces an EFQM score of 1,000 points.

While the Pac-Man score is fairly easy to calculate, as will be explained later, the EFQM assessment model is highly complex. When applying for the EFQM Excellence Award, an application report has to be written and a team of experts are brought in for doing the evaluations. Although it is possible to use the EFQM model for doing self-assessments, it is costly and as much of the assessments depend on subjective judgements, the score is not as precise as that of eating dots, ghosts and bonus fruits.

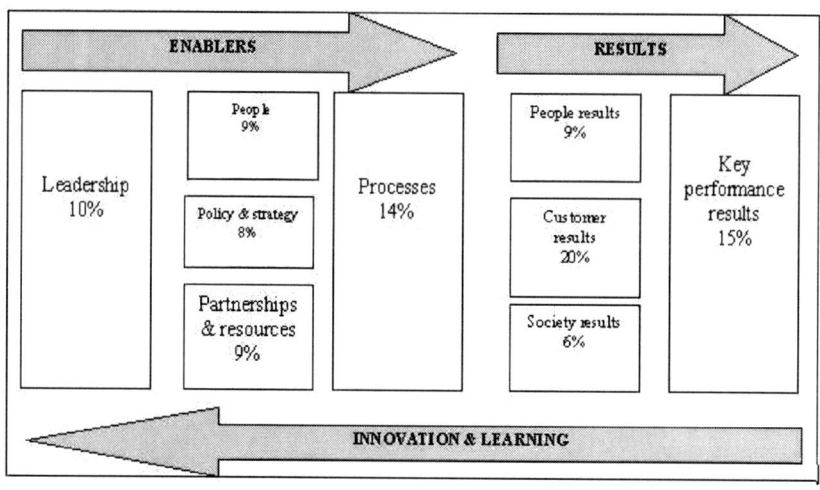

Figure 1: The EFQM Excellence Model

At the most abstract level, the EFQM Excellence Model divides organizational excellence into nine categories (figure 1); four categories for evaluating the excellence in terms of results indicating excellence and five categories implying that excellence has to be enabled in a certain way. Each of these nine boxes is evaluated by going through questions and checkpoints on a deeper level.

Due to the complexity of the model, a simplified version Common Assessment Framework (CAF) has been developed for the public sector, primarily as a motivational tool for getting started with EFQM-like self-assessments and improvements. The EFQM model can be used for the whole organization or for a single department. One way of developing excellence within the quality department might be to do annual self-assessment by use of models like the EFQM model or the CAF model.

The Pac-Man model

The video game Pac-Man was developed and released in Japan in 1979 and became a surprise success when released in the US in 1980, now being considered among scholars of game studies as one of the most important games in the history of video games (Loquidice & Barton, 2009).

Pac-Man can be played as a single-player game ("puzzle") against the computer, or it can be played as a two-player game as two people can compare scores in trying to solve their own Pac-Man puzzles (figure 2). In this two-player version, the game can be described in game theoretic terms as a two-player positive-sum game of perfect information. However, when using the Pac-Man game for modelling the politics of TQM, the game theoretic interpretation of the single-player version of Pac-Man is to see it as a five-player game (Pac-Man and the four ghosts Blinky, Inky, Pinky and Clyde) of imperfect information as the novice player does not know all details of the artificial intelligence running the behaviour of the ghosts.

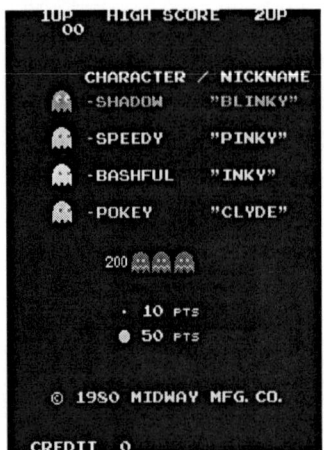 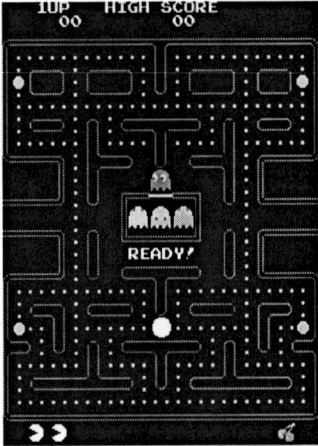

Figure 2: Title screen (left) and start of game (right)

As pointed out by Salen & Zimmerman (2004, p. 245), in order to apply the game theoretic approach, it is necessary that (1) time in the game takes place in turns or other discrete units, (2) players make a finite number of clear decisions that have knowable outcomes, and (3) the game is finite in terms of not being able to go on forever.

Although the Pac-Man game appears to be running in continuous time, by conceptualizing the game as if it were running at a very slow pace, it can be seen to meet the first requirement. Requirement number three represents a potential challenge in the way that Pac-Man was not intentionally designed to be a finite game. When one board has been completed, a new board is prepared at a slightly more difficult level, and so it goes on level after level. However, due to a technical malfunction in the original software, after 255 levels the board structure breaks down. It is a finite game. The second requirement, about players making a finite number of clear decisions that have knowable outcomes, is a consequence of requirements one and three having been met.

In game theory, each strategy (sum of all choices defining a game play) is associated with a payoff function. In the case of Pac-Man this translates to the total score reached at the end of the game. The score is updated as the game progresses, as Pac-Man eats dots, power pellets, ghosts and bonus fruits, some of the scoring mechanisms described on the left side of figure 2, with a more detailed score board to be presented later. A perfect Pac-Man game occurs when the player achieves the maximum possible score on the first 255 levels (by eating every possible dot, power pellet, fruit, and ghost) without losing a single life. The maximum possible score is 3,333,360 points.

The first contributions for developing a theory of Pac-Man consisted of describing strategies for winning the game (e.g. Zavisca & Beltowski, 1982; Editors of Consumer Guide, 1982). Although more recently (e.g. Thompson et al, 2008), simulation studies by use of the theory of complex adaptive system (CAS) has been used for finding strategies for achieving perfect game, the strategies described in the books written in the early 1980s were developed by endless hours of human game play.

In order to find an optimal strategy for Pac-Man, it is necessary to understand how the ghosts operate. The behaviour of the ghosts is defined through algorithms of artificial intelligence (AI), each ghost behaving in its own characteristic manner.

Ghost	Behaviour (AI)
Shadow (Blinky)	When the ghosts are not patrolling their home corners, Blinky will attempt to shorten the distance between Pac-Man and himself. If he has to choose between shortening the horizontal or vertical distance, he will choose to shorten whichever is greatest. For example, if Pac-Man is 4 grid spaces to the left, and 7 grid space above Blinky, Blinky will try to move up before he moves to the left.
Speedy (Pinky)	When the ghosts are not patrolling their home corners, Pinky wants to go to the place that is four grid spaces ahead of Pac-Man in the direction that Pac-Man is facing. If Pac-Man is facing up, Pinky wants to go to the location exactly four spaces above Pac-Man. He does this following the same logic that Blinky uses to find Pac-Man's exact location.
Bashful (Inky)	Bashful has the most complicated AI of all. When the ghosts are not patrolling their home corners, Bashful considers two things: Shadow's location, and the location two grid spaces ahead of Pac-Man. Bashful draws a line from Shadow to the spot two squares in front of Pac-Man, and extends that line twice as far. Therefore, if Bashful is alongside Shadow when they are behind Pac-Man, Bashful will usually follow Shadow the whole time. But if Bashful is in front of Pac-Man when Shadow is behind him, Bashful tends to want to move away from Pac-Man (in reality, to a point very far ahead of Pac-Man).
Pokey (Clyde)	Pokey has two basic AIs, one for when he's far from Pac-Man, and one for when he is near to Pac-Man. When the ghosts are not patrolling their home corners, and Pokey is far away from Pac-Man (beyond 8 grid spaces), Pokey behaves very much like Blinky, trying to move to Pac-Man's exact location. However, when Pokey gets within 8 grid spaces of Pac-Man, he changes his behaviour and goes to his home corner in the bottom left of the maze.

Table I. Verbal description of the ghosts' behavioural patterns (StrateWiki, 2009)

As the ghosts represent managers when using the Pac-Man model for understanding the politics of TQM, it could be interesting to place each of the ghosts within a managerial grid model (Blake & Mouton, 1964) as the managerial grid model has served as inspiration for conflict management style inventories such as the Thomas-Kilmann inventory (Womack, 1988).

As Blinky is aggressively seeking Pac-Man, his behaviour could be described as high concern for people and high concern for production, the upper right ("team leader") on the grid in figure 3. Pinky has a similar concern for production, but as he aims four steps ahead of Pac-Man rather than straight at Pac-Man, one could say that he represents the "produce or perish"-type manager at the bottom right of the grid. Clyde is the least dangerous, always avoiding direct confrontation, and seems to fit in the "impoverished" category of the grid, while Inky is clearly the most social of the ghosts in having a strategy that focuses on the behaviour of the others, the "country club" manager.

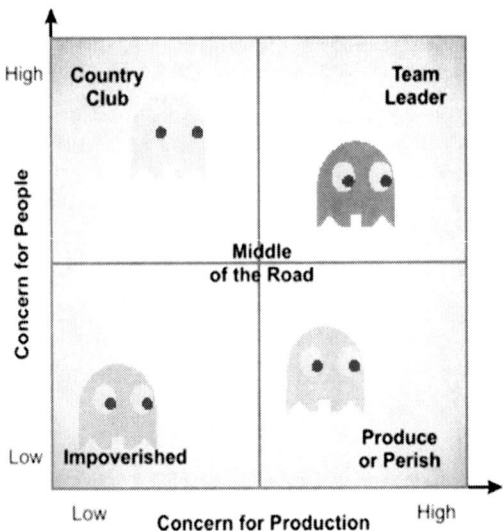

Figure 3: Placing the ghosts on the managerial grid model (Blake & Mouton, 1964)

Due to the fact that the AI algorithms for the ghosts do not include elements of random behaviour, it is possible to find patterns for Pac-Man to move within each board that makes it possible to eat all the dots without being chased down by the ghosts. Although some of the best Pac-Man players in the world prefer to play the game in a more intuitive manner, manipulating the ghosts around the maze, identifying and utilizing the patterns makes it possible for less experienced players to achieve high scores. However, when eating power pellets, it is useful to have all the ghosts within short reach as long as they are in scared mode, meaning that manipulating them into a cluster at the right moments is also an important skill.

Methodology

In order to investigate the Pac-Man model in an empirical TQM setting, the idea has been to make the author reflect upon his own five year experience as a quality manager within the IT-function of a

Scandinavian public sector organization, using the Pac-Man model as a device for narrating the story in a way that emphasizes some of the political aspects.

The TQM implementation was extensively documented through plans, progress reports, assessment reports and other documents (table II). When using the Pac-Man model in order to search for TQM strategies, not all aspects of the video game are equally simple to convert into an organizational setting. For instance, when playing Pac-Man the move from one level to another happens when all 244 dots have been eaten. A new board is then prepared, looking exactly like the previous, with a few game-play parameters changed in order to make the new level more challenging. Each level in the organizational setting, on the other hand, is defined by the annual budget cycles and production cycles. This means that it is not necessary to eat a given number of dots (e.g. do a given number of audits or verifications) in order to move from one level to another, as the change of level is time driven rather than event driven.

Pac-Man phase	Period	Administrative	TQM documents	Other documents
Insert coin	November 1st, 1999	-	-	-
Level 1	2000	6	-	1
Level 2	2001	15	2	4
Level 3	2002	16	9	4
Level 4	2003	13	10	1
Level 5	2004	10	12	-
Game over	January 25th, 2005	-	4	-

Table II. Count of documents produced during each year of the TQM process

In order to tell the story of TQM politics in the language of the Pac-Man model, table III assigns the Pac-Man scoring mechanisms onto TQM activities. As it is already shown in table II that the particular Pac-Man simulation studied here only lasted five levels, only bonus fruits for the first five levels are included in table III.

What happens when Pac-Man eats a power pellet is that the ghosts turn from aggressive chasing into scarred scattering, and Pac-Man can chase them down and eat them, producing scores as shown in table III. In a TQM context, the translation done in this study is to define the power pellets as quality reports that are aligned with the parts of the quality management system that is already institutionalized, using the reports as input for decision processes where managers are already committed to making signatures and thus using the report as a "management review" (ISO 9001, chapter 5.6; Hoyle, 2006) for trapping them into taking responsibility for defects and make sure process improvement is commenced or sustained.

Although a document verification is a simpler task than a quality audit (which may typically include document verifications), for the purpose of keeping as close as possible to the rules of Pac-Man, both these activities give the same amount of points.

In Pac-Man, the bonus fruits (cherry, strawberry, lemon and apple) appear randomly and quite seldom. A TQM change agent getting positive feedback for work well-done is perhaps even more rare and random, especially as the game levels rise, and conflict levels rise accordingly, but it is an important event that should be given proper score.

Pac-Man food	Level	Points	TQM activity
Dot	All	10	Document verification
Dot	All	10	Quality audit
Dot	All	10	Quality report not part of a management decision process
Power pellet	All	50	Quality report as part of management decision process
1st Ghost	All	200	Impact on manager
2nd Ghost	All	400	Also impact on a second manager
3rd Ghost	All	800	Also impact on a third manager
4th Ghost	All	1600	Impact on four managers or more
Cherry	1	100	Positive feedback
Strawberry	2	300	Positive feedback
Lemon	3+4	500	Positive feedback
Apple	5	700	Positive feedback

Table III. Assigning the Pac-Man score board onto TQM practice

Case study presented as a simulation experiment

Insert coin

Describing the quality management experience in the IT-function of a Scandinavian public sector organization as a Pac-Man simulation, the starting point was as the author entered the organization in November 1999. The first months consisted of being handed over a large document ("game manual") explaining the strategies, policies and standards of quality management of the organization. These documents were written as a part of the strategies, policies and standards for information security (i.e. the opposite of conventional ISO 9001 practice where security management, environment management etc are defined as special cases of quality management).

Furthermore, the author was also given instructions in game play, primarily focusing on the principle of formal authority overruling competence authority, and then having this illustrated by the head of information security stating he had no competence in TQM but nevertheless wanted it implemented in a such-and-such way. This resulted in quality being managed consistently with how information security was managed, although conflicting with basic ideas and principles of TQM such as continuous improvements, customer satisfaction, process approach etc.

To the author, these first few months provided good learning experiences in terms of understanding the organizational culture and the explicit conflict between a managerial approach (doing things in order to maintain and increase power) and a scientific approach (doing things in order to learn and improve).

First two levels of game play

In February 2000, after the head of the Information Security Department left the organization, the author was appointed director of quality management, and the real game was ready to commence. Consistent with the logic of Pac-Man, the author started running through the maze, eating dots in terms of doing document verifications and quality audits, working as closely as possible with the IT professionals in order to avoid stepping into the political schemes of the managers. However, as verifications consist of measuring products and processes against the standards set by the organization, it quickly became visible that there was close to no focus on compliance with standards, and as the managers were being reminded of this the chase was on.

Several strategies were used for traversing this first level of the game, few of them resulting in documents that generated scores according to table III. The most important idea was to start some kind of repeatable activity that would result in demonstrating the principle of continuous improvement, producing a success project that could be used as an example for starting more and more ambitious improvement projects. As a cause of a near accident, due to lack of standardization in the COBOL software development process having created some management attention, a measurement system for monitoring compliance between existing software and organizational standards was designed and implemented. However, as the final report ("management review") was presented early next year, this process did not contribute to the first level score, but generated 10 Pac-Man points at the beginning of level two. Unfortunately, no ghosts were caught as the COBOL process was not integrated with any of the institutionalized routines that required management signatures.

The second result in 2001, according to the counting in table III, was an initial attempt at describing parts of the existing quality management system within the framework of ISO 9000, as ISO 9000 was mentioned in both the information security policies and the IT strategy document. This was an attempt to go for the strawberry bonus fruit, hoping to get positive management feedback and commitment to a TQM strategy that would allow for a more systematic approach. As no such response was achieved, this resulted in zero score.

A better result was achieved when publishing articles about TQM and progress on the TQM project in the internal journal. By writing the articles in a way that made the IT function seem professional, focused on standards and continuous improvement, the initiative was acknowledged by the head of the IT function as a positive signal, regardless of the less convincing results produced by actual verifications and audits. The author was given positive feedback on all four journal publications (table II), corresponding to eating four bonus strawberries, increasing the score with 1200 points.

Level three

With a total score of 1,210 at the beginning of level three, it seemed like a good idea to continue writing articles. Of the four articles written in 2002, the first three resulted in positive feedback, producing 1,500 points of eating lemons, but in the case of the forth article, the author was told that some manager had taken offence, and the strategy of writing articles was effectively terminated for good.

On the other hand, writing journal articles was time-consuming, and even though they were aligned with IT management politics and could perhaps have some minor cultural impact, a better way to impact real organizational improvement would probably be do to the usual things that TQM professionals do, such as introduce ISO 9000, EFQM assessments, statistical quality control, audits, measurement feedback, improvement projects etc.

During the course of 2002, nine quality reports were written. Three of these were aligned with institutionalized practice, thus making them into power pellets and producing a score of 150 points. The first of the "management reviews" involved only one manager (200 points), but with the two others involved two managers each (400 points x 2 = 800 points). Among the other reports, there was one TQM evaluation of the IT function, using the CAF public sector quality assessment model. This report did not create any signatures (10 points), but the author was asked to give a TQM presentation at a management meeting which resulted in positive feedback (bonus fruit = lemon, 500 points).

Another report showed results from TQM assessments using the CMM model and the ISO 15504 model, resulting in 30 points of dot-eating. Each of the assessment were carried out by external experts, resulting in management presentations, but not resulting in positive feedback that could be used for using either of the models for general TQM implementation frameworks. A new COBOL evaluation report produced 10 points.

As a part of the TQM process, the author had been collaborating with the Internal Audit, and the Internal Audit was interested in trying out the CobiT audit model for auditing the IT function. The author was invited by the Internal Audit to participate in the national CobiT forum, for discussing best practices in applying CobiT audits. As a first approach for trying out the model, the author wrote a quality report focused on the M4 audit process, evaluating the process of doing quality audits and internal audits. This, however, resulted in turning a friendship into conflict as the manager of the audit team got upset by being audited and started chasing the scientist in the style of the "Clyde" ghost (i.e. keeping distance). As the report included a total of five audits, the total dot-score for the report was 60 points.

Another report was politically motivated by an IT manager who wanted to exercise power over a unit outside the IT domain, and the author was asked to write a quality report. As the author was not invited to explain the report, it is unclear whether it was used as part of a decision process (although a decision was made), but at least the report included four audits, producing a score of 50 points.

As a part of the success so far, the author was granted an extra life in terms of having an industrial engineering student working for him during summer. The student helped out in conducting quality audits, and quality report evaluating project management according to the CobiT standard was produced, including results from seven audits (8 x 10 points = 80 points). A "Pinky"-type manager (aggressive and manipulative) tried to convince the "Blinky" top-manager (aggressive and confrontational) to prevent more interference from students doing quality audits.

As seen in table II, a part of the strategy for preventing management into interfering with TQM was to produce annual plans, monthly status report and annual self-evaluations. Although this was a Herculean task, it seemed to work in terms of preventing the managers in interfering. In the case of the 2002 evaluation report, the Balanced Score Card (BSC) assessment method was used, something that triggered positive feedback, as there had been some discussion on the top management level concerning BSC, and the report fitted with the political argument the IT department was trying to make (lemon = 500 points).

Level four

Having now been playing Pac-Man for some levels, a certain feeling for what were the best patterns for running through the maze, eating dots and ghosts started to emerge. Although not scoring many political points, focusing on the real problems of the organization and trying to contribute input at the time when the organization was ready to discuss (eating power pellets when the ghosts were close and close together) was a sustainable way of getting points. This approach resulted in another two lives in terms of having two students helping out with audits during summer and also being allowed to hire two quality coordinators to help out on a permanent basis.

Among the ten quality reports produced in 2003, six of them were "management reviews" (power pellets, 50 points each) that each resulted in four management signatures or more (3,000 points x 4 = 12,000 points), and where each report included an average six document verifications or quality audits (10 points x 6 x 4 = 240 points).

In an attempt to make the TQM implementation strategy more risk driven, a series of CobiT-PO9 quality audits were carried out. This process did not align with any institutionalized quality control practice, and no management signatures, but it resulted in 7 x 10 = 70 points of dot eating. As the department was later visited by the National Audit, wanting to do a total evaluation of the organization according to the CobiT audit standard, the PO9, PO10 and M4 reports were used as input for producing our own CobiT self-assessment report just ahead of the National Audit report. This resulted in another 30 points of dot eating.

The most important event this year, however, was that one of the quality coordinators, that we managed to get on a permanent basis, happened to have a "Inky" personality, meaning mediocre technical TQM skills but highly developed social skills. This resulted in creative tension within the quality department proving highly efficient in terms of stimulation for self-improvement. A self-evaluation report was written, 4 x 10 = 40 points.

Level five

What started out as creative tension on level four quickly evolved into aggression on level five. The quality coordinator "Inky" managed to manipulate and coordinate the managers "Blinky", "Pinky" and "Clyde". The author was chased down, in October 2004 there were obvious indications of "game over", and in January 2005 the author was formally removed from the position.

Despite quality coordinators following their own private agendas rather than working together as a unit, the measurable results of 2005 turned out to be better than ever. A total of seven power pellets were eaten, each time managing to capture more than four ghosts, resulted in a score of 7 x 3,050 = 21,350 points.

A COBOL evaluation resulted in 10 points. A revision of the total CobiT self-assessment resulted in 10 points. A long series of document verifications as input for a CobiT-AI4 audit resulted in 120 points.

Despite political turbulence within the quality department, a new EFQM self-assessment produced another 20 points. The year also consisted of establishing international network of quality management, the author being elected member on a national board of quality management, and more useful collaboration with the National Audit.

Game over

Due to the impetus created during the previous years, the first four weeks of 2005 resulted in eating two power pellets and a maximum number of ghosts, 2 x 3,050 = 6,100. A new COBOL report was written (10 points), and a CobiT-M2 audit was also completed (10 points).

Final reflections

The evolution of the Pac-Man score is plotted on the left side diagram in figure 4, the diagram on the right side presenting the results of the quality department doing EFQM Excellence self-assessments. Theoretically both the Pac-Man score and the EFQM assessments should be monotonously increasing curves. In practice, however, the EFQM score is seen to be increasing from 2001 to 2002, and then decreasing from 2001 to 2003 due to calibrations and difficulties in finding out how to measure in an exact way, until a baseline is found in 2003 and there is a slight increase in 2004.

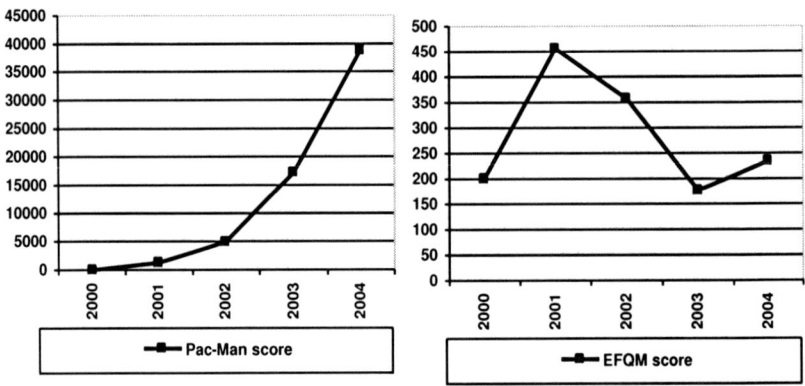

Figure 4: Pac-Man payoff from Pac-Man strategy (left) and EFQM payoff for same strategy (right)

The payoff from strategy used for five years of organizational play resulted in a score of 38,770 points. Although this only amounts to 1.2% of the score from performing perfect play, it is significantly better than the high score of 2,230 points achieved by a comparable Pac-Man simulation carried out in the streets of New York (Pac-Manhattan, 2004).

Discussion

Applying Pac-Man philosophy in the real world

Table IV summarizes three strategic insights that seem specific for Pac-Man, and that also seemed to work well as TQM strategies when working in a politically turbulent environment.

In order to answer whether optimal Pac-Man strategies also work as optimal TQM strategies, the literature review suggested that the performance of the quality department could be monitored by use of the EFQM Excellence model. When doing this in the empirical case, the points in the literature review about the model being complex and difficult to use is illustrated in figure 4, showing several years of adjustments before the TQM baseline is established and measurements of continuous improvements can commence.

	Pac-Man	TQM politics
Principle 1	Keep eating, and reflect in action (or between games). For each board level, there are behavioural survival patterns (Zavisca & Beltowski, 1982).	Keep auditing, measuring, analyzing and making improvements. Data collection, analysis, action and progress must never stop.
Principle 2	Understand ghost psychology, both on individual level and how they act as a swarm (Kelly, 1994; Holland, 1995).	Expect conflict, study management psychology and avoid irritating people unnecessarily.
Principle 3	Get energized and attack when the ghosts are clustered, before they manage to scatter in all directions.	Design "management review" (Hoyle, 2006) to fit with institutionalized quality control practice (annual budget process, annual production cycles etc.), get as much management commitment as possible.

Table IV. Transfer of insights that are specific to Pac-Man

Although this calibration phenomenon makes it difficult to perform statistical comparisons between the Pac-Man payoff function and the TQM payoff function, if the game had not been terminated at level five, there is reason to believe that both payoff functions would continue to rise as the baseline for the EFQM measurements was identified in 2003.

A major difference between the two payoff functions, however, is that the Pac-Man model insists on a conflict of interest between the scientists and managers while the module that is given the highest weight in the EFQM model is the module marked "customer satisfaction" (figure 4), in this case meaning management satisfaction. As illustrated at the beginning of the game, doing what is needed in order to improve processes ("eating dots") and doing what results in management satisfaction ("bonus fruits") may not necessarily be the same thing. In fact, trying to keep management satisfied without doing what is substantially needed for improving the organization can lead to the organization getting imprisoned into a mental state of "fake quality" (Ogland, 2009a).

Although not a problem with Pac-Man per se, a significant amount of TQM work needs to be done (244 dots eaten) before exiting one level and stepping up to the next, but the way the model was implemented in this empirical case, going through a level by just eating bonus fruits could be a highly successful approach for producing game score, while being a totally unsatisfactory approach from a TQM perspective.

Nevertheless, although it is difficult to say whether the resulting TQM strategies are optimal or not, the results of viewing the TQM politics from the Pac-Man perspective produces TQM strategies that fit with an energetic, fact oriented and generally sceptical and disillusioned approach that reflect values inherent in scientific work.

Evaluation of the Pac-Man model

While conventional TQM advice would be to get management commitment and measure, analyze and improve the organization on behalf of management, the Pac-Man model suggests a completely differ- ent reality based on the assumption assume that there is a constant conflict between the "natural ene- mies" of managers and scientists (Beer, 1968). In the case study, several conflict situations were pre- sented, providing context for illustrating various reasons why conflict between scientists and manag- ers may sometimes be the default scenario.

In figure 3, there was an attempt to create a mapping between the behaviour of the four Pac-Man ghosts and the five management styles defined by the managerial grid (Blake & Mouton, 1964). The case study illustrated challenges due to the scientist being chased by a swarm of managers. Although conventional wisdom might suggest handling one manager at a time, by looking at the conflict from the perspective of a Pac-Man game, the managers are applying a "swarm logic" (Kelly, 1994) in at- tacking the scientist, a tactic that is based on the managers partly acting in an individual manner and partly coordinating their behaviour with other managers.

Like Pac-Man gamers say they develop gaming skills through long periods of intense trial and error, the CAS-method of genetic algorithms (GA) has been used for developing strategies for winning the game of Pac-Man (Thompson et al, 2008). This approach can be carried over to quality management, using CAS-inspired rules and principles for handling the turbulent situation (Øgland, 2008) or, more ambitiously, designing quality control and continuous improvement as GA (Øgland, 2009b).

Game theory con- cepts	Pac-Man	Science	TQM
Players	Pac-Man, Blinky, Inky, Pinky, Clyde	Scientists	Change agent, managers, workers
Rules	Maze, scoring mecha- nism, framework defined by the computer	Methods and behaviour accepted by the commu- nity of practice	TQM standards and meth- ods, rules and behaviour accepted by the organiza- tion.
Strategies	Food, flight, fight.	Argumentation through theory and experimenta- tion	Improve organizational performance by measure- ments, analysis and rede- sign.
Payoff	Score at end of game	Established facts, strengthening theories, impact factors on publi- cations	Significant findings, suc- cessful improvements, re- sults from TQM assess- ments

Table V. Comparison of Pac-Man, science and TQM by use of game theory concepts

When using Pac-Man as a model for understanding the conflict between scientists and managers when implementing TQM, one way of making sense out of the game is to think of it in terms of food, fight and flight within an organizational labyrinth. The scientist Pac-Man eating dots can be seen as researching the organization, making trivial findings and continuously upsetting the four managers living within the main office at the centre of the labyrinth. Each according to his own psychology tries to track down the scientist in order to have him eliminated, while the scientist must learn the skills of manoeuvring efficiently around the organization while reading, interpreting and discovering patterns of psychological behaviour among the managers in order to avoid them.

If the scientist makes a substantial scientific finding (eats a power pellet), then the managers become scared and scatter. During this short period of confusion, the scientist can attack the managers and scores points for each manager he gets. This only works for a period of time, however, because soon the organizational climate returns to normal and the managers start preying on the scientist again.

If the scientist manages to audit the whole organization, he is promoted to the next management level where he meets the same managers behaving slightly more aggressively and intelligently, as they have learned from previous encounter with the scientist and are now even more concerned with not having management issues cluttered with objective facts and scientific rationality.

Comparing the serious game of Pac-Man with Axelrod's (2002) comment about Monopoly modelling business as a zero-sum game, winning the game of Monopoly being equivalent to making all others loose, in Pac-Man there is no way for the scientist to win. Payoff (score) is being measured by how long the scientist is able to survive in the organization. With each set of managers he gets to outsmart or track down, they will always re-emerge on a new and fiercer game level.

While the case study supports the Pac-Man model for understanding action research-driven TQM (table V), the least successful aspect of the model is probably the score board. It would be nice to maintain the score board exactly as it was in the video game version of Pac-Man, but the way some types of rather costly work is identified as a single dot, only producing 10 points, while a relatively more simple tasks may result in thousands of points, makes a challenge. If one should not tamper with the score board, then there is at least need for rethinking the relationship between TQM activities and Pac-Man scores (table III).

Conclusion

The Pac-Man model is a simplistic model. As a model for quality management and organizational change, the only quality improvement and changes in behaviour that are created by the Pac-Man game is the behaviour of the Pac-Man player. It is played like a game of survival, not a game about creating change. Nevertheless, by defining the maze in a way that paves way for performance improvement, the survival game may be sufficient for generating the behaviour that is needed for the quality manager (change agent) to operate effectively. This is the message of the case study.

The world of Pac-Man is non-stop action of instinct behaviour driven by impulses of food, fight and flight. Although the TQM strategies implied by the Pac-Man model are contrary to common wisdom about management commitment, quality awareness, quality culture, motivated workers etc., often such key premises are not present in organizations, and the quality manager has to choose whether to give up the TQM project or to try it anyway. The Pac-Man model suggests strategies for succeeding in conflictual, complex and unpredictable environments, implying strategies that comply with what Dooley et al. (1985) have described as a complex adaptive systems approach to TQM.

Looking at what may be interpreted as a systems debate within the field of problem structuring methods (PSM) on which systems frameworks to include and how to mix them (e.g. Flood & Jackson,

1991; Rosenhead & Mingers, 2001), this paper can be seen as an argument, along with Bennett et al. (2001), that game theory can and should be more explicitly used in PSM, for instance as a part of TQM-oriented critical systems thinking (CST) (Flood, 1993; Jackson, 2000).

References

Abt, C.C. (1969). *Serious Games*, Viking Compass Book, New York.

Axelrod, A. (2002). *Everything I know about business I learned from Monopoly: Successful executives reveal strategic lessons from the world's greatest board game*, Running Press, Philadelphia, Pennsylvania.

Beck, J.C. and Wade, M. (2006). *The Kids are Alright: How the Gamer Generation is Changing the Workplace*, Harvard Business School Press, Boston, Massachusetts.

Beckford, J. (2002). *Quality, Second Edition*, Routledge, London.

Beer, S. (1968). *Management Science: The Business Use of Operations Research*, Doubleday & Company, New York.

Bennett, P., Bryant, J. and Howard, N. (2001) "Drama theory and confrontation analysis", in: Rosenhead, J. and Mingers, J. (2001). *Rational analysis for a problematic world revisited: Problem structuring methods for complexity, uncertainty and conflict, Second Edition*, Wiley, Chichester, pp. 225-248.

Berry, T. (1991). *Managing the total quality transformation*, McGraw-Hill, New York.

Blake, R. and Mouton, J. (1964). *The Managerial Grid: The Key to Leadership Excellence*. Houston: Gulf Publishing Co.

Bonilla, J.P.Z. (2006). "Science Studies and the Theory of Games," *Perspectives on Science*, Vol. 14, No. 4, pp. 525-557.

Caroselli, M. (1995). *Quality Games for Trainers: 101 Playful Lessons in Quality and Continuous Improvement*, McGraw-Hill, New York.

Checkland, P. (1981). *Systems Thinking, Systems Practice*, Wiley, Chichester.

Churchman, C.W., Ackoff, R.L. and Arnoff., E.L. (1957). *Introduction to Operations Research*, Wiley, New York.

Cole, R.E. (1999). *Managing Quality Fads: How American Business Learned to Play the Quality Game*, Oxford University Press, New York.

Collis, J. and Hussey, R. (2003). *Business Research, Second Edition*, Palgrave Macmillan, New York.

Crosby, P.B. (1979). *Quality is Free: The Art of Making Quality Certain*, Mentor, New York.

Crosby, P.B. (1984). *Quality without tears: The art of hassle-free management*, McGraw-Hill, New York.

Crosby, P.B. (1999). *Quality and me: Lessons from an evolving life*, Jossey-Bass, New York.

Cross, N. (2008). *Engineering Design Methods: Strategies for Product Design, Fourth Edition*, Wiley, Chichester.

Deming, W.E. (1986). *Out of the Crisis*, MIT Press, Cambridge, Massachusetts.

Dooley, K., Johnson, T. and Bush, D. (1985). "TQM, Chaos and Complexity," *Human Systems Management*, Vol. 14, No. 4, pp. 1-16.

Editors of Consumer Guide (1982). *How to Win at Pac-Man*, Penguin, New York.

Flood, R.L. and Jackson, M.C. (1991). *Creative Problem Solving: Total Systems Intervention*, Wiley, Chichester.

Flood, R.L. (1993). *Beyond TQM*, Wiley, Chichester.

Holland, J.H. (1995). *Hidden Order: How Adaptation Builds Complexity*, Addison-Wesley, New York.

Hoyle, D. (2006). *ISO 9000 Quality Systems Handbook, Fifth Edition*, Butterworth-Heinemann, Amsterdam.

Humphrey, W. (1989). *Managing the Software Process*, Addison-Wesley, New York.

Jackson, M. (2000). *Systems Approach to Management*, Kluwer Academic, UK.

Kelly, K. (1994). *Out of Control: The New Biology of Machines, Social Systems, and the Economic World*, Addison-Wesley, New York.

Latour, B. and Woolgar, S. (1979). *Laboratory Life: The Construction of Scientific Facts*, Princeton University Press, Princeton, New Jersey.

Latour, B. (1987). *Science in Action*, Harvard University Press, Cambridge, Massachusetts.

Legge, K. (2002). "On Knowledge, Business Consultants and the Selling to Total Quality Management", in: Clark, T. and Fincham, R. (2002). *Critical Consulting: New Perspectives on the Management Advice Industry*, Blackwell Business, Oxford, pp. 74-90.

Loquidice, B., and Barton, M. (2009). *Vintage Games: An Insider Look at the History of Grand Theft Auto, Super Mario, and the Most Influential Games of All Times*, Focal Press, Burlington.

Mingers, J. (2006). *Realizing Systems Thinking: Knowledge and Action in Management Thinking*, Springer, New York.

Øgland, P. (2008). "Designing quality management systems as complex adaptive systems," *Systemist*, Vol 30, No 3, pp. 468-491.

Øgland, P. (2009a). "Measurements, Feedback and Empowerment: Critical systems theory as a foundation for Software Process Improvement," *The 17th European Conference on Information Systems (ECIS-17): "Information Systems in a globalising world; challenges, ethics and practice"*, 8-10 June 2009, Verona.

Øgland, P. (2009b). "Implementing continuous improvement using genetic algorithms," *12th International QMOD and Toulon-Verona Conference on Quality and Service Sciences (ICQSS)*, 27-29 August 2009, Verona, Italy.

Pac-Manhattan (2004). *High-scores*, http://pacmanhattan.com/highscores.php, accessed on May 29th 2009.

Rapoport, A. (1986). *General System Theory: Essential Concepts and Applications*, Taylor & Francis, New York.

Reason, P. and Bradbury, H. (2004). *Handbook of Action Research, Concise Paperback Edition*, SAGE, London.

Reyniers, D.J. and Tapiero, C.S. (1995), "Contract design and the control of quality in a conflictual environment," *European Journal of Operational Research*, Vol. 82, No. 2, pp. 373-382.

Rosenhead, J. and Mingers, J. (2001). *Rational analysis for a problematic world revisited: Problem structuring methods for complexity, uncertainty and conflict, Second Edition*, Wiley, Chichester.

Salen, K. and Zimmerman, E. (2004). *Rules of Play: Game Design Fundamentals*, MIT Press, Cambridge, Massachusetts.

Schultz, L.E. (1995). "Remove barriers to pride of workmanship", in: Voehl, F. (ed.), *Deming: The Way We Knew Him*, CRC Press, Boca Raton, Florida, pp. 145-154.

Shewhart, W. (1938). *Statistical Method from the Viewpoint of Quality Control*, Dover, New York.

Simon, H.A. (1996). *The Sciences of the Artificial, Third Edition*, MIT Press, Cambridge, Massachusetts.

Sindermann, C. (2001). *Winning the games scientists play*, Basic Books, New York.

Sismondo, S. (2004). *Introduction to Science and Technology Studies*, Blackwell, Oxford.

StrateWiki (2009). *PAC-MAN*, http://strategywiki.org/wiki/Pac-Man , accessed on May 12th, 2009.

Taylor, F.W. (1911). *The Principles of Scientific Management*, Harper & Row, New York.

Thompson, T., McMillan, L., Levine, J. and Andrew, A. (2008). "An Evaluation of the Benefits of Look-Ahead in Pac-Man," in: Hingston, P. and Barone, L. (eds.), *Proceedings for the 2008 IEEE Symposium on Computational Intelligence and Games (CIG'08)*, 15-18 December, Perth, Australia.

Ulrich, W. (1994). *Critical heuristics of social planning: a new approach to practical philosophy*, New York, Wiley.

von Bertalanffy, L. (1968). *General Systems Theory: Foundations, Development, Applications*, George Brazillier, New York.

von Neumann, J. and Morgenstern, O. (1953). *Theory of Games and Economic Behavior*, Princeton University Press, Princeton, New Jersey.

Womack, D.F. (1988). "Assessing the Thomas-Kilmann Conflict Mode Survey," *Management of Communication Quarterly*, Vol. 1, No. 3, pp. 321-349.

Zahran, S. (1998). *Software Process Improvement: Practical Guidelines for Business Success*, Addison-Wesley, Harlow.

Zavisca, E. and Beltowski, G. (1982). *Break a million at Pac-Man!* Delair Publishing Company, New York.

MEASUREMENTS, FEEDBACK AND EMPOWERMENT: CRITICAL SYSTEMS THINKING AS A BASIS FOR SOFTWARE PROCESS IMPROVEMENT

Øgland, Petter, Department of Informatics, University of Oslo, P.O. Box 1080 Blindern, 0316 Oslo, Norway, petterog@ifi.uio.no

Abstract

While organizations in software industry want to portray themselves as professional in terms of following standards and methods, they may also have needs for improvising and short-cutting when necessary. Such dilemmas of dual logics are sometimes internally resolved by evolving a false belief of what is done (practice) being in correspondence to what is said (standards), regardless of what an empirical investigation might show, something that can have poor business implications and also poor social implications. Particularly focusing on this latter point, the meta-methodology of total systems interventions (TSI) has been used for integrating critical systems theory with total quality management, improving social conditions in parallel with improving business processes. Although TSI is not designed for liberating organizations where nobody see themselves in need of liberation, the hypothesis of this paper is that it is possible to design quality management systems as "conflict machines", causing sufficient social tension for more or less automatically changing "fake quality" into "real quality". The hypothesis is investigated by applying design research in a Scandinavian public sector organization. The findings consist of statistical and interpretative evidence for the success of the approach, making a contribution to how TSI can be applied in the software industry.

Keywords: Software process improvement, total systems interventions, design research

1 INTRODUCTION

Selecting an effective strategy for designing software process improvement (SPI) systems can be a difficult problem, depending both on technical issues related to the complexity of production processes, software products, chosen set of SPI standards and practical engineering of the control system, and on social and cultural issues.

According to Brunsson et al (2000, p. 130), extensive research since the mid-1960s has shown that "there may be substantial differences between presentation and practice, between formal structures and actual operations, and between what people say and what they do. [...] Actors have dual systems which are decoupled from each other; they may argue that they follow a standard while not doing so in practice. This is a phenomenon which standardizers seldom appear to notice, or at least seldom discuss seriously in public".

Indeed, in many of the classic references on total quality management (TQM) and software process improvement (SPI) (e.g. Crosby, 1979; Deming, 1986; Juran, 1993; Humphrey, 1989), the main issue is on issues like explaining the importance of aligning quality control with business strategies, measuring customer satisfaction, implementing the methods in a technically sound manner, and getting sufficient management commitment for making sure that the system will be developed and sustained. The issue of organizations pretending to follow standardized principles of TQM or SPI just to win contracts or attract customers, and how this influences culture, is seldom addressed.

Primarily focusing on the internal politics of organizations along the vertical axis of management and labour, Flood (1993) has developed an approach to TQM based on systems thinking and critical theory. The idea is that TQM should be understood in a holistic perspective and it should be used for improving social conditions along with business processes. The idea of implementing TQM in this way was developed as an application of a more general framework called Total Systems Intervention (TSI) (Flood & Jackson, 1991; Jackson, 2000). TSI has been a topic for discussions in academic journals for systemic research (e.g. Tsoukas, 1993; Flood, 1994), has been used as a framework for doing action research (Green, 1992; Flood, 2006), and it remains an interesting topic among both researchers and practitioners in the area of TQM (Taiwo, 2001; Beckford, 2002; 2009).

However, as Beckford (2002, p. 301) points out, "the process of [critical thinking in TSI] is, of course, only useful where all parties are willing to contribute to the process and to make adaptations based upon the findings". This does not present TSI as a promising approach when we deal with organizational dualism, implying primarily external motivation for implementing SPI. On the other hand, a well-known challenge in knowledge management systems design is that knowledge is political, meaning that changing the flow and distribution of knowledge may have consequences for explicitly and implicitly existing organizational power structures (Davenport & Prusak, 1998).

The hypothesis in this research is that (1) a political SPI system, exploiting political tensions induced by creation and distribution of knowledge, can be designed to fit with the ideas and framework of TSI, and (2) this type of political knowledge management approach can create a stable SPI process (improvement process) in an environment where there is otherwise little support for making SPI work.

In section two, a more detailed theoretical presentation of the revised TSI model will follow. This is followed by a section three concerned with the design of empirical research for exploring and evaluating the model in an empirical context of looking at how SPI is practiced among software engineers, managers and administrative staff in a Scandinavian public sector organization. The results of this investigation are reported in section four, pointing out aspects of the SPI project that were successful and aspects that failed. Finally, in section five, the empirical findings are used for evaluating the model, summarising the research in terms of pointing out how the political analysis leads to political guidelines all aimed at creating tension along the vertical and horizontal axes of the organization and making sure that the critical approach can be maintained.

2   PROCESS IMPROVEMENT BY SYSTEMS INTERVENTIONS

As SPI can be seen as TQM applied in the area of software engineering (Humphrey, 1989), generic quality management standards, such as the ISO 9000 standards and guidelines, can be used as framework for SPI. In the ISO 9000 series, there is a difference between control and improvement (Hoyle, 2006), that corresponds with what Argyris & Schön (1978) refer to as single loop learning and double loop learning. Quality control is the task of making sure that processes are carried out in compliance with standards and regulations (single loop learning). Quality improvement deals with challenging and improving such standards and regulations (double loop learning).

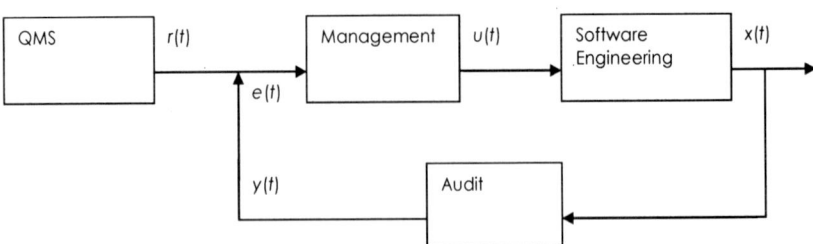

Figure 1. The basic configuration of a simple closed-loop control system (DiStefano et al, 1990, p. 16)

The diagram below illustrates the single loop learning of auditing a quality management system (QMS) used for defining a SPI system. The QMS contains all procedures and standards that describe how software engineering shall be carried out in a given organization, and this set of documents is used as a reference point $r(t)$ when doing audits $y(t)$. If there is a mismatch $e(t)$ between practice $y(t)$ and procedure $r(t)$, that should function as a point of action $u(t)$ for management.

Mathematical theory of control systems started in electrical engineering, but has later been used both metaphorically and technically for studying both technical and social systems (Berlinski, 1976). In order to study the audit control system in figure 1 from a mathematical perspective, one would typically need a description of the relationship between $u(t)$ and $y(t)$ in terms of differential equations, and areas to be looked into would typically be observability, controllability and stability of the system (DiStefano et al, 1990).

2.1   Total Systems Intervention (TSI)

TSI evolved as a method for solving two problems; how to apply critical social theory in management problems based on a systems approach, and how to select the best systems methodology depending on the nature of the management problem to be solved (Jackson, 2000).

Doing TSI consists of going through three phases. First there is a phase labelled "creativity" that consists of using metaphors for trying to see to which extent various metaphors may give insights on problems and perspectives of the organizations (Morgan, 1980). Secondly, there is a phase labelled "choice" that deals with choosing an appropriate systems-based intervention methodology to suit particular characteristics found through metaphor analysis. As the makers of TSI experienced some difficulty in getting managers to understand Morgan's way of linking metaphors and sociological paradigms, Jackson (2000) develop a simplified method called the "system of systems method". Thirdly there is the phase of "implementation" which means that the conventional implementation strategies of Viable Systems Methodology (Beer, 1972), Soft Systems Methodology (SSM: Checkland, 1981), Critical System Heuristics (CSH: Ulrich, 1983), or whatever systems approach chosen is implemented, given that the implementation of a chosen methodology or mix of methodologies is employed according to the logic of TSI (Jackson, 2000, pp. 368-370).

Although practitioners working with TSI as an approach for implementing TQM reported successful results, theoretical criticism came from academia, questioning the use of metaphors for framing problems, the way metaphors linked with methodologies, whether TSI practitioners could be expected to have the enormous amount of systems theory knowledge that seems to be needed, whether each of the methodologies catalogued by TSI are as different as the framework assumes etc. (Jackson, 2000, pp. 371-374). As a consequence of such questions, TSI theory keeps developing (e.g. Flood, 2006).

What TSI still seems to lack in its analysis, however, is that the people responsible for designing organizational interventions may neither represent the workers nor the managers, but could be considered a separate group. In his comments on the early days of Operational Research (OR), Beer (1968) points out that there were ongoing tensions between managers and scientists. The scientists developed an understanding of the organizational problems from a mathematical point of view, although with little practical understanding. The managers had a practical understanding developed through experience, but little conceptual understanding in terms of mathematical models. This resulted in mutual distrust.

Rather than trying to provoke labour and management through the kind of critical questions suggested by CSH, for an organization that is only pretending to be committed to SPI, it is an underlying assumption in the hypothesis stated in this paper that it may be better to design the SPI system as a kind of "conflict machine", a system that is not primarily designed for making people think less in order to work more efficiently but rather as system that contributes to the production and distribution of knowledge in ways that are likely to challenge current power structures. The idea is to build tension along the management/scientist and labour/scientist axes and use debate that results from this for making the organization focus on the management/labour axis.

In 1996, Flood and Romm redesigning TSI in the language of triple loop learning. Figure 2 illustrates the principle of how the nested loops are represented with different types of logic. The innermost loop of the system tries to answer the question of how to improve efficiency, how to reduce error rates, how to increate customer satisfaction etc. If a SPI problem is formulated in a clear and well-defined way, there is a large body of literature from OR that could and should be used. However, if the problem is neither clear nor well-defined, there is a body of literature on Problem Structuring Methods (PSM: e.g. Rosenhead & Mingers, 2001) that include various methods for organizations to reach mutual understanding of problems. SSM is one of the most used methodologies of this category. The aim of PSM is to address the question of what the problem is. Finally, there is a third loop that aims as questioning why are given problems focused in the first place. Whose interest are people serving by solving the given set of problems? Who is gaining power? Who is loosing power?

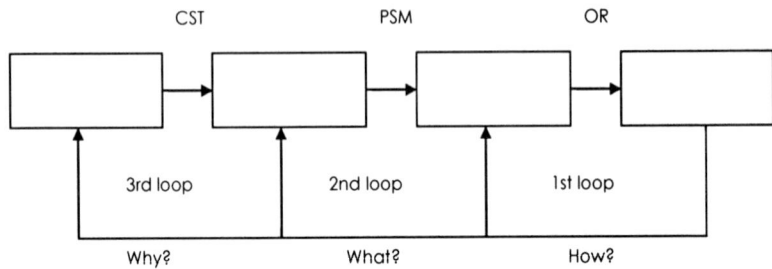

Figure 2. Triple loop learning as a way of describing TSI (Flood & Romm, 1996)

The control loop in figure 1 gives a more detailed description of the first loop in figure 2, suggesting mathematical notation and logic that fits with the rationality of OR. The single loop learning aspect of quality management can be a highly difficult problem from a technical point of view, but from a social point of view it is banal in the way that it simply consists of measuring whatever people are doing against the organizational standards of how it should be done.

Second loop learning in TQM is socially more challenging, as this loop consists of getting people in authority to interpret what is going on, try to make sense out of these interpretations and then choose targets for technical investigation and improvement. As Checkland (1981) argues, problem structuring methods such as SSM contain elements of critical thinking in the way that they challenge the views encoded in the single loop learning. Perhaps the problem being solved by the current OR loop is not the right problem to solve? An SSM analysis can bring in the perspectives of different people in the organization, producing a collective understanding of the organization and business, and cause radical changes in the understanding of what should being studied and improved.

For a SPI system to comply with the ISO 9001:2000 standard, the system must have elements of double loop learning. Not only do the ISO 9001 clauses require that process should fit with procedure, but procedures and all aspects of the QMS are to be audited and challenged on a regular basis (e.g. ISO 9001 clause no. 4.1; see: Hoyle, 2006). But, as argued by Brunsson et al (2000), the fact that an organization is required to practice double loop learning does not necessarily mean that it does, even if they are certified against ISO 9001 and being regularly checked.

The third loop in figure 2 is something that does not read naturally as a part of ISO 9001:2000, and something one would not expect to find in management consultant literature (Legge, 2002). From a business point of view, the aim of the organization may be issues like making a profit, or delivering services at high quality with low cost. On the other hand, there may be other agendas. The purpose of the third loop is to identify such agendas, help people to discover that they may be imprisoned by agendas they don't know, don't understand or may be unhealthy, and then to help in the process of liberation (Critical Systems Thinking, CST: Flood and Jackson, 1991), the socially critical aspect of TSI.

2.2   Adding the idea of a "SPI conflict machine" to TSI theory

As observed by Bénézech et al. (2001), the fact that the ISO 9001:2000 model can be interpreted as a double loop learning model means that a management system (or a SPI system) compliant with ISO 9001:2000 can be seen as a knowledge management system.

Although not explicitly stated by Flood (1993), one way of interpreting his use of critical theory as a foundation for TQM could be to say that quality management systems are not tools for managers to exercise command and control (e.g. Braverman, 1974), but they are rather tools for workers to gain knowledge and power over their own work situation, become experts and be able to challenge oppressive power structures.

In order to give people freedom, it is necessary that knowledge becomes visible and available. It is necessary that the implementation of TQM follows a strategy that is based on how knowledge about quality of processes and products affects the power structures of the organization. As pointed out by Davenport and Prusak (1998, p. 177), one of the main challenges in the implementation of knowledge management systems is that current power structures may be based on keeping people unaware, only letting an inner circle of people have knowledge that matters.

Reyniers and Tapiero (1995) discuss the design of contracts and the control of quality in a conflictual environment through the use of game theory. They model the situation between the supplier and producer as players in a nonzero-sum game, where the supplier can control the effort invested in the delivery of quality and the producer may or may not inspect incoming materials. In their paper, they state (p. 373) that the traditional approach to statistical quality control does not recognize that quality management often takes place in a conflictual environment.

The game design suggested in this paper, in order to make SPI work as a "conflict machine", is to regard the QMS as the rules of the game, use quality indexes (measurements of compliance with QMS standards) as payoff functions ("score"), turn the game from into a "perfect information game" (like chess, unlike the "imperfect information game" of bridge) by distributing the scores vertically and horizontally across the organization, aligning knowledge distribution strategies with power strategies as they may be identified through experience and analysis.

The most important design aspect of this SPI game design, however, is to make sure that the game is kept alive, in other words make sure that it does not challenge those who are capable of destroying the SPI system ("the owners of the system"; Checkland, 1981, p. 318).

3   METHODOLOGY

In order to investigate the effect of the revised version of TSI, the TSI method has been implemented and tested in an organizational setting, and a design research framework has been implemented (Simon, 1996; Hevner et al., 2004; Iivari, 2007). The design research approach is illustrated in figure 3, where the emphasis is on showing how the engineering cycle and the research cycle run in parallel through iterations of four stages, the engineering cycle applying theory while the research cycle aims at contributing theory. The ellipse marked "model" in the middle of the figure corresponds with the models discussed in the context of the theory in section 2 above with section 2.2 containing specifications for the design/artefact to be evaluated in the context of a TSI implementation.

In practical terms, the way the engineering cycle is used as a framework for research is by using the assumption of a successful design and statistically stable design process as hypothesis, considering the design process as an experiment, and look at the design evaluation as a test of hypothesis. This idea was originally formulated by Shewhart (1939) as a way of thinking about quality control in the field of mass production as a framework for scientific investigations, where he suggests the use of statistical process control (SPC) as a way of testing the hypothesis that the design process is statistically stable ("assignable causes have been eliminated"; Shewhart, 1939, p. 150).

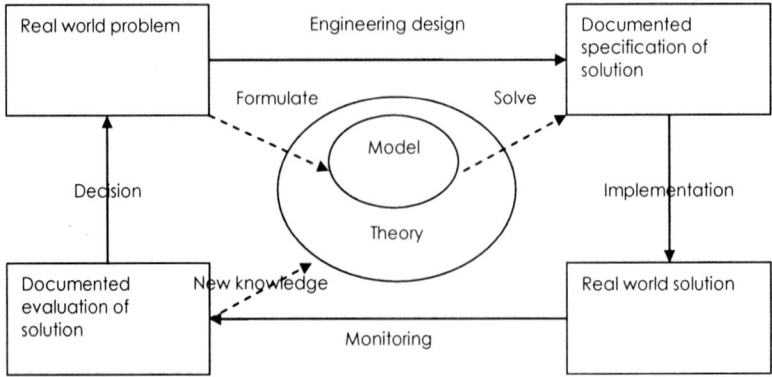

Figure 3. Design science in the context of the engineering design cycle (based on: Krick, 1969)

As the experiment is based on a short number of life cycle iterations, the X-MR chart will be used as SPC-design (Clark, 1999, pp. 86-90). In addition, as there are controversies among statisticians as to how SPC links with statistical hypothesis testing (e.g. Woodall, 2000), the testing of whether the SPI process is stable or not will be done by visual judgements (Interocular Traumatic Test, ITT) as suggested by Roberts and Sergesketter (1993, p. 64).

If the test should indicate that the SPI process is perfectly stable during TSI, this should indicate that similar designs should be carried out under other conditions, such as other units within the same organization or, preferably, other organizations. Otherwise, if the test should indicate problems, exploratory research needs to be carried out.

3.1   Population, research procedures, data collection and analysis

The setting for investigating the changed version of TSI is a software engineering unit within the IT department of a Scandinavian public sector organization. The unit to be discussed consisted of about 20 people, more or less equally distributed between males and females. The average age was about 40. Half of the people were systems designers who were also responsible for testing the system on large scale, while the other half were programmers that implemented the design in COBOL software and did detailed tests. The system followed an annual life cycle model, and all people were involved in writing and updating system documentation.

The initial version of the system was implemented in 1998, and the first few years consisted of making the solution fit with the original systems requirements. During the time of investigation, the system had reached a level of maturity where the life cycle work mostly consisted of making adjustments and improvements as requested by the ministry.

Although the TSI implementation was carried out through annual cycles between 2003 and 2005, aligned with the lifecycle model, earlier project documentation was also used. Three evaluation reports were produced during the TSI experiment, as decision support for management at the time of the annual life cycle when the system went into production. The reports were written by the author of this paper, then functioning in the role of quality manager being assisted by quality coordinators for doing audits and tests. The final analysis has been conducted after the TSI projected was completed, depending to a certain degree on retrospective reflection.

4   CASE STUDY

4.1   Evolution of the SPI system from a technical perspective

As a part of the design research approach, the tools for evaluating the design evolved as a part of the evolution of the software process improvement (SPI) system. In the context of this narrative, the SPI system consisted of the strategies, policies and standards that made up to documented part of the quality management system (QMS) and the QMS practices that were carried out in terms of checking whether the documented system was being followed, recording problems, and taking corrective and preventive action.

Prior to taking contact with the unit in question, some interviews were first carried out with IT top management and representatives of the internal audit. In both these cases, it was pointed out that the QMS for this particular unit was one of the better systems of the organization. People were following the rules, as they should, and there was organizational learning in terms of continuous improvement.

Reading the reports from internal audit and generating a general overview of the documented part of the QMS, it quickly became obvious that there were no independent quality audits, at least not in the way required by the general QMS. Perhaps the QMS worked perfectly within the unit, people following standards as they should, but there was no way of knowing this without establishing a practice of doing quality audits.

A quality audit system was easy to implement as the procedure V10 for doing audits was written and just waiting for being put into use. Separate audits should be done along the software development life cycle, including the phases (1) threat and risk assessment, (2) quality planning, (3) requirements analysis, (4) analysis, (5) implementation, and (6) test. As a final checkpoint on procedure V10, the audits should be summarized and presented to management as input for the acceptance procedure N7.

As there were detailed standards for how to document and carry out work within each of the phases above, it was easy to develop simple checklists that was then used for ticking off and producing quality indexes for measuring compliance on a scale from 0 to 100 percent, defining $e(t)$ in figure 1.

The diagrams in figure 4 show the final results of plotting the average of all quality indexes year by year. Indexes for the years 2000 to 2002 were constructed by performing quality control of old documents and old software, while the more recent indexes were computed along with the design process and used as immediate feedback. Control limits for X-MR are based on values 2001-2003.

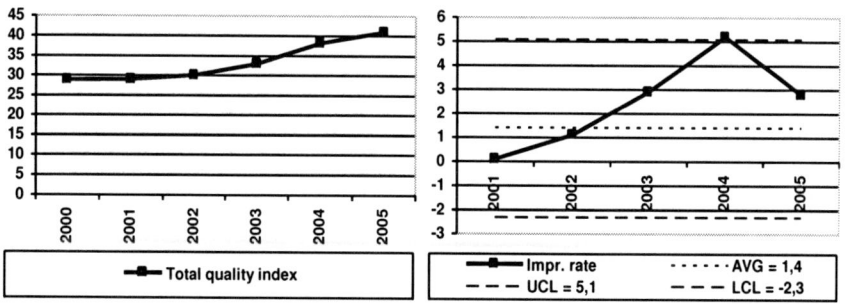

Figure 4.   Total quality index and improvement rate (annual increase in total quality index)

As the X-MR diagram on the right hand side in figure 4 goes slightly above upper bounds in 2004, the null hypothesis of instability due to assignable causes cannot be rejected. The assignable cause for the anomaly is that the QMS consists of procedures and practice, and much of the practice was carried out by the quality department through their SPI design research rather than be the people in the unit themselves, indicating that increase in improvement rates may be a direct cause of the TSI approach.

Using a t-test with four degrees of freedom for comparing improvement rates before and during TSI made it possible to reject the null hypothesis of no difference in sample average at a significance level of 0.022. Recalculating control parameters for separating the process prior to intervention and during intervention, the average improvement rates would first be 0.6 before TSI and 3.6 during TSI. A SPC design based on X-MR only for the TSI period showed no indication of instability.

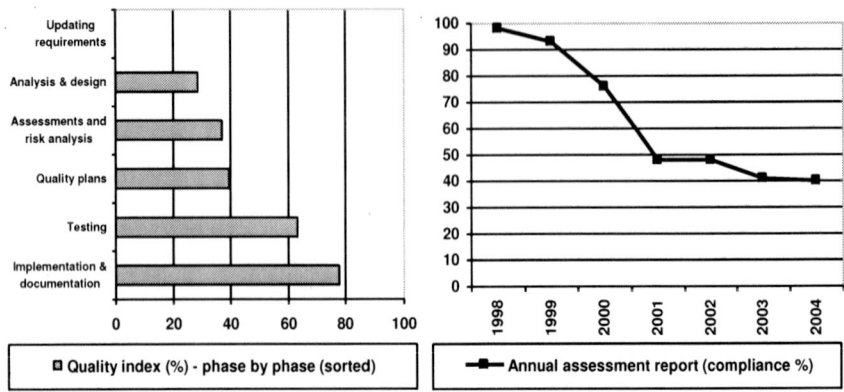

Figure 5.   Total quality index and improvement rate (annual increase in total quality index)

When decomposing the total quality index into what was measured (the final year) for each of the six phases of the software cycle, the left hand side of figure 5 shows how the compliance between different phases differ. The right hand side of the figure shows the development of the column marked "assessment and risk analysis" on the left hand side of the figure, showing how the practice in this part of the life cycle got less and less compliant with the standard. Another indicator systematically evolving in the wrong direction (not included in the diagrams here) was a process capability indicator for measuring the ability of the production indicator to be within required limits.

4.2   Evolution of the SPI system from a social perspective

During the interview with the IT top manager prior to investigating this particular SPI system, the quality manager (author) was specifically being told to think about the organization and the systems development processes through the metaphor of a machine. The IT manager made some drawings in the air, indicating that he was thinking in terms of a hydraulic machine pumping information through the organization and out to the users and owners (ministry).

The systems approach used for structuring the problem of investigating the SPI was partly based on SSM-like principles like discussing with various people while drawing "rich pictures" in order to figure out how they differed in their understanding of the system. When doing audits of software engineering practice against the software engineering standards, this feedback was useful for understanding the gaps while not preventing gaps from being documented.

This approach, mixing conversations with measurements, became the implementation method that was followed consistently during the three years of the experiment.

First year: Reporting the findings upwards in the system caused emotional stir. People felt they were doing as best as they could, performing and documenting much better than what was required by the standards, and felt humiliated and demotivated by quality audits giving them scores in terms of numbers ("quality index") and so on. They wrote a letter to the director general (head of the larger organization) and complained about the situation. The quality manager never got a copy of the letter, but was told by the IT manager that there were some misunderstandings and that quality audits should continue as planned.

Second year: Based on previous year's unfortunate circumstances, it was important to be gentle yet sufficiently specific in order to help the software unit to improve. However, as new versions of documents were audited, the same errors and lack of compliance with standards remained. Little improvement. The people said they did not have time to improve, just to do what was absolutely necessary. Besides, they felt quality audits focused too much on process and forgot about the product. They said they took pride in producing products of high quality, and methods (means) for achieving such excellent results were of less importance as long as the results were good.

Third year: Trying to respond seriously to what people were saying, the same audits from the previous year were repeated but now expanded in order to include product quality indicators. Using statistical analysis, the quality management people found that the main production indicator for the system was rapidly declining, as could be seen from updates of the annual Cpk capability index (Deming, 1994). When presenting this finding to the systems and software people, they said this had to be the result of socio-geographical dynamics, not a phenomenon they could control. When asked about whether it would be a good idea to improve the prediction algorithm that caused the problems, they said they had no time for dealing with such issues. It was too difficult. They had been told to follow a given formula, and it was not their task to analyse whether this formula was optimal or not.

In 2005, after the study was completed, the people in this particular unit took part in rewriting software engineering standards to be used for further SPI. When the software engineering standards were updated, many of the changes in the methods and standards were of a kind that would give higher score according to the quality audit system but would make the method it self significantly worse. For instance, the process of updating requirement documents was eliminated.

5   DISCUSSION AND CONCLUSION

The development of the SPI system followed the three stages of TSI. Creativity: The quality manager was explicitly told to think about the organization as a machine. Choice and implementation: According to Flood (1993, p. 81), typical systems methodologies fitting with the machine metaphor are the classical management frameworks described by Taylor and Fayol. In order to carry out the technical part of quality audits, this was done according to the professional guidelines of quality engineering, i.e. in a machine-like manner.

However, this rigid design proved useful in making people respond and reflect upon the standards they had defined for their own work. When presenting the results of audits, a "soft systems approach" was used, in order to figure out what people were thinking, how one could solve the situation together, asking people what they would do if they were responsible for doing quality audits etc.

Unlike Flood's attempts to ask critical questions for making people reflect, the method of trying to force people to follow their own standards by first "measuring the facts" and then doing SSM-like discussion, worked well for creating debate. Particularly the way audits and quality reports were widely distributed made the QMS into a "conflict machine".

5.1   The illusion of excellence as a mental prison

It is not too difficult to see how the organization was imprisoned in a belief of high quality and continuous improvement, while the measurement of practice against standard indicated low degree of compliance with internal quality standards and continuous spiralling in the wrong direction. Similar to the cases reported by Brunsson et al (2000), the organization had locked itself in a situation where there was no measurable feedback on whether they were doing the right thing or not, only good intensions, hard work, and occasional verbal feedback if production went well.

It did not improve matters that the internal audit had investigated the unit, been impressed by standards, written procedures and system documentation without going into depth when analysing how this was used. The result of this may have been twofold; firstly adding to the beliefs of the organizational unit that they were doing things as expected, and secondly enrolling the internal audit into the same "fake quality" belief system, as it would be easier to accept the happy belief that the unit was doing fine rather than to question the quality of their own audit methods.

Although not specifically mentioned in the case study, as it happened prior to the time when the TSI experiment was carried out, the national audit had done a similar overview audit to what the internal audit later did, also contributing to the general belief that everything was fine. In other words, it would almost come as a surprise if these people were not trapped in an illusion of excellence and internal bliss, like Adorno's interpretation of Odysseus and the lotus eaters (Sherratt, 2000).

5.2   The liberation process

As explained in the story, the "fake quality" was easily revealed through quality audits as what people were saying did not fit the results of the audits. When confronted with the facts, the response was a mixture of surprise, irritation and what they described as "unfair game" of being measured and having the measurements distributed upwards and sideways in the organization. The crash between their self-perception of what they were doing and the measurements caused emotional outbursts and intense debate.

In other words, liberation through quality management was in this case a process of agony and frustration, and it remained a difficult process during all three years of the experiment. While there were no dramatic changes during the period of experimentation, there were signs of improvement in terms of discussion and awareness of quality management issues that seemed to have been more or less totally ignored after the QMS had been documented and made into "shelfware".

Although some of this liberation resulted in attempts to fight the quality department and attempts to change the software engineering standards for producing better score without resulting in higher quality, the main reason for applying critical theory as a foundation for SPI should not be to force people follow standards or force them do what the quality department wants them to do, but it should be to generate debate about standards and make people take responsibility for their own software engineering processes.

The fact that the software engineers got the methodology group to remove the maintenance of the requirements documents from the software engineering methodology (end of section 4.2), despite the fact that the organization was required to keep a ten year record of requirements, was an interesting example of how SPI can be a political game of accepting and distributing responsibility. Although a strategy like this would be helpful for improving the score for the software engineers, the overall impact on the organization would be a step backwards down the maturity ladder if assessments had been done through CMM or similar SPI models (Zahran, 1998).

5.3   Theoretical implications for the TSI model in software process improvement

Although the SPC diagram and statistical reasoning in section 4.1 do not contain sufficient data for making judgements that would convince a properly trained quality engineer, the results are consistent with the interpretative narrative.

The interpretative part of the study provide the key insights on what happened, although a rich case like this contains actors and actions responding and reacting in different ways. By thinking about SPI as knowledge management rather than control, the design idea of using (1) horizontal benchmarking, (2) vertical jump-reporting and (3) improvisation for preventing those in power to destroy the TSI implementation, made the SPI system work successfully as a "conflict machine".

Although three years was a rather short period for a case like this, and the fact that the design was particularly made to fit with the internal power struggles in a hierarchical public sector organization, the design idea (section 2.2) worked well, making a theoretical contribution on how TSI can be applied in the software industry.

The overall interpretation of the case study is that the use of critical thinking as a foundation for SPI was a fruitful idea that should lead to more empirical research.

References

Argyris, C. and Schön, D.A. (1978). Organizational Learning: A Theory of Action Perspective. Addison-Wesley, Reading, Massachusettes.

Beckford, J. (2002). Quality. 2nd Edtion. Routledge, London.

Beckford, J. (2009). Quality. 3nd Edtion. Routledge, London.

Beer, S. (1968). Management Science. Aldus, London.

Beer, S. (1972). Brain of the Firm. Wiley, Chichester.

Bénézech, D., Lambert, G. and Lanoux, B. (2001). Completion of knowledge codification: an illustration through the ISO 9000 standards implementation process. Research Policy, 30, 1395-1407.

Berlinksi, D. (1976). On Systems Analysis: An essay concerning the limitations of some mathematical methods in the social, political and biological sciences, MIT Press, London.

Braverman, H. (1974). Labour and Monopoly Capital: The Degradation of Work in the Twentieth Century, Monthly Review Press, New York.

Brunsson, N. et al. (2000). A World of Standards, Oxford University Press, Oxford.

Checkland, P. (1981). Systems Thinking, Systems Practice. Wiley, Chichester.

Clark, T.J. (1999). Success Through Quality: Support Guide for the Journey to Continuous Improvement, ASQ Quality Press: Milwaukee, Wisconsin.

Crosby, P.B. (1979). Quality is Free, MacGraw-Hill, New York.

Davenport, T. and Prusak, L. (1998). Working Knowledge: How organizations manage what they know. Harvard Business School Press, Boston, Massachusettes.

Deming, E.W. (1986). Out of the Crisis, MIT University Press, Cambridge, Massachusettes.

Deming, E.W. (1994). The New Economics, MIT University Press, Cambridge, Massachusettes.

DiStefano, J.J., Stubberud, A.R. and Williams, I.J. (1990). Schaum's Outline of Feedback and Control Systems. Second Edition. McGraw-Hill, New York.

Flood, R.L. (1993). Beyond TQM. John Wiley & Sons, Chichester.

Flood, R.L. (1994). I think that I should say something about total systems intervention (TSI): About TSI being used. Systems Practice, 7 (5), 565-567.

Flood, R.L. (2006). The Relationship of 'Systems Thinking' to Action Research. In Handbook of Action Research (Reason, P. and Bradbury, H. Ed.), pp. 117-128, SAGE Publications, London.

Flood, R.L. and Jackson, M.C (1991). Creative Problem Solving: Total Systems Intervention. Wiley, Chichester.

Flood, R.L. and Romm, N.R.A. (1996). Diversity Management: Triple loop learning. Wiley, Chichester.

Green, S.M. (1992). Total systems intervention: Organisational communication in North Yorkshire Police, Systemic Practice, 5 (6), 586-600.

Hevner, A.R., March, S.T., Park, J. and Ram, S. (2004). Design science in information systems research. MIS Quarterly, 28 (1), 75-105.

Hoyle, D. (2006). ISO 9000 Quality Systems Handbook. Butterworth-Heinemann, Amsterdam.

Iivari, J. (2007). A Paradigmatic Analysis of Information Systems as a Design Science. Scandinavian Journal of Information Systems, 19 (2), 39-64.

Jackson, M.C. (2000). Systems Approaches to Management, Kluwer/Plenum, New York.

Juran, J.M. (2003). Juran on Leadership for Quality: An Executive Handbook, Free Press, New York.

Krick, E.V. (1969). An introduction to engineering and engineering design. Second Edtion. Wiley, New York.

Legge, K. (2002). On Knowledge, Business Consultants and the Selling of Total Quality Management. In Critical Consulting: New Perspectives on the Management Advice Industry (Clark, T. and Fincham, R. Ed.), pp. 74-90, Blackwell, Oxford.

Morgan, G. (1980). Paradigms, Metaphors, and Puzzle Solving in Organization Theory, Administrative Science Quarterly, 25 (4), 605-622.

Roberts, H.V. and Sergesketter, B.V. (1993) Quality is Personal: A foundation for total quality management, Free Press, New York.

Rosenhead, J. and Mingers, J. (2001). Rational analysis for a problematic world revisited: Problem structuring methods for complexity, uncertainty and conflict. Second edition. Wiley, Chichester.

Taiwo, J. (2001). Systems approaches to total quality management. Total Quality Management, 12 (7&8), 967-973.

Tsoukas, H. (1993). The road to emancipation is through organizational development: a critical evaluation of Total Systems Intervention, Systemic Practice and Action Research, 6 (1), 53-70.

Sherratt. Y. (2000). Adorno and Horkheimer's Concept of 'Enlightenment'. British Journal for the History of Philosophy, 8 (3), 521-544.

Shewhart, W.A. (1939). Statistical Method from the Viewpoint of Quality Control, Dover, New York.

Simon, H. (1996). Sciences of the Artificial. Third edition. MIT Press, Massachusettes.

Ulrich, W. (1983). Critical heuristics of social planning, Wiley, New York.

Woodall, W.H. (2000). Controversies and Contradictions in Statistical Process Control. Journal of Quality Technology, 32 (4), 341-350.

Zahran, S. (1998). Software Process Improvement: Practical Guidelines for Business Success. Addison-Wesley, Harlow.

IV

Software Process Improvement: What gets measured gets done

Petter Øgland
Department of Informatics, University of Oslo, Norway
petterog@ifi.uio.no

Abstract. A software quality management system (QMS) has been designed in a democratic fashion by programmers and has been approved by management. In order to motivate the programmers in following their own standards, measurement feedback is used for creating social pressure (peer pressure and management pressure). In nine out of ten cases this approach has been successful. Could the failure of the tenth case be an indication of the statement "what gets measured gets done" not being as obviously true as it is sometimes assumed to be in management literature? Trying to investigate this by reflecting on seven years of conversations with programmers and managers, various explanations are presented. Few seem to have any validity. The most likely explanation seems to be that "what gets measured gets done" is a statement about group behaviour. When it comes to individuals or very small groups, special predicaments may make behaviour less predictable. The theoretical insights for QMS design, provided by this case study, is that the "what gets measured gets done" design approach might prove more efficient if one manages to conceptualize lumps of individuals as self-managing teams or groups.

Introduction

The use of measurements in feedback loops plays a fundamental role in software process improvement (Sommerville, 2001). Not only are measurements useful for getting objective knowledge on process characteristics, but the measurement process may have motivational implications by itself as illustrated by the "what gets measured gets done" principle often mentioned in management literature (e.g. Waterman & Peters, 1982).

The purpose of this introduction is to describe the background for a case study where the "what gets measured gets done" principle was used for designing a quality management system (QMS) for COBOL software. The design of the system is treated as part of the background for the study, and thus presented in this introduction, where the motivation for research comes from unexpected results from how the QMS is performing.

Background for case study

Within the IT department of a Scandinavian public sector finance institution the lack of standardized software development practices has caused critical situations when trying to rotate software among programmers or whenever new programmers enter or old programmers leave. A near-fatal incident in 1997, where one of the main programmers responsible for vital parts of a nationally critical software system tragically died and left the remaining programmers with almost incomprehensible code to handle, caused the organization to rethink its strategies of software development. The IT strategy document of 1998 emphasized the need for developing and following internal programming standards that were compliant with international software standards. There were also updates in the IT security policies in 2000. Interviews with programmers and managers 2000-2008, carried out by the author of this paper (who was working as a quality manager from 2000-2005), indicated that all shareholders seemed to agree on the seriousness of the situation and all seemed to agree on the need for developing and implementing common standards (Ogland, 2006).

Designing a quality management system

In trying to solve the practical problem of making programmers align with common standards and make sure that all software, new and old, is gradually made compliant with the standards, a small quality management system (QMS) was designed by focusing on the following ideas:

- *Participatory Design* (the programmers themselves designing both the standard and the management system for making sure the standard is being followed)
- *Double-loop learning* (create a system that not only makes software comply with standards but also helps reflect upon whether the standards should be improved or revised)
- *"What gets measured gets done"* (performance is evaluated by measurements and used for objective feedback)

Consistent with ideas of Participatory Design, a system for guiding and monitoring the process of standardizing the software was developed by the programmers themselves. The system consisted of an internal standard for the development of COBOL software, developed according to the local procedure used for developing standards, a software program for testing business software against a given set of tests (a subset of all the tests implied by the standard), and the management of the system consisting of one of the programmers running the test program and giving the results to the quality coordinator (external to the group) while the quality coordinator did statistical analyses and returned the results to the programmers.

The QMS was designed as a "double-loop learning" system (Argyris & Schön, 1978, pp. 1-6) as illustrated in figure 1. An initial programming standard was designed by the programmers and then used for testing the software. As deviations from standard ("defects") were discovered, "single-loop learning" consisted of eliminating the defects and making software more uniform and hopefully more accessible for all programmers. The outer loop in figure 1 is a design feature to stimulate debate on whether the initial standard is too flexible, too restrictive or whether it could be "improved" in some way or another ("double-loop learning").

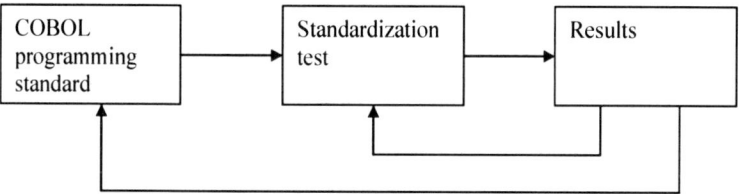

Figure 1. Software quality management system designed as a "double-loop learning" system

Immediately after the system was implemented in 2000, single-loop learning set in as measured in terms of the defect level systematically decreasing in most of the software packages being monitored. A few years later, in 2003, there was an instance of double-loop learning as the programmers decided that the initial version of the standard was too restrictive, resulting in the standard and the test program being redefined (Ogland, 2006).

Another important part of the design for the QMS was stimulating improvement by benchmarking annual defect levels and annual improvement results among the various projects and informing all shareholders of the results, as illustrated in figure 2 with management pressure and peer pressure indicated through dotted lines.

The idea behind this aspect of the QMS design was to try to create tension needed to prevent the dynamics of the system reaching equilibrium of no further improvement rather than a homeostasis of continuous improvement, as suggested by total quality management theory based on reframing Kurt Lewin's force field theory and action research within the framework of complex adaptive systems (Goldstein, 1996; Øgland, 2006; 2007b).

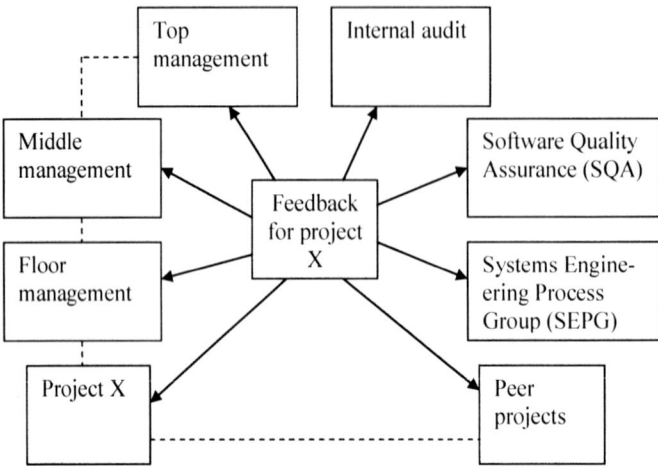

Figure 2. Design for buiding social tension by giving distributed feedback

Observations

While some software projects started the process of standardizing in 1998, as a consequence of the near-fatal incident, the common COBOL software standard was accepted in 2000. There are ten software development projects being run in parallel, each project responsible for standardizing the COBOL software for one particular software system.

The solid curve on the left side diagram in figure 3 shows the results of repeated estimates of "year of zero defects", using linear regression estimates on plots representing the average defect levels for all ten projects. The oscillations in the curve indicate that the estimates are not to be trusted too much. The rapid fall in the curve between 2002 and 2003 is the result of "double-loop learning" (the standard being made less strict, thus producing less "defects" and consequently advancing the expected year of zero defects although the improvement rate is unchanged). The current guess, based on estimates for the last four years, is that all relevant software will be compliant with the given standard around 2011, although the latest point estimate suggests 2014 as year of zero defects.

The diagram on the right hand side of figure 3 shows the latest predictions for year of zero defects for each of the ten projects. While many projects are expected to reach the level of zero defects within a few years, for the tenth project the regression line predicts the year of zero defects lies more than fifty years ahead in time (more than nine standard deviations behind the average zero-defects-year for the other nine projects).

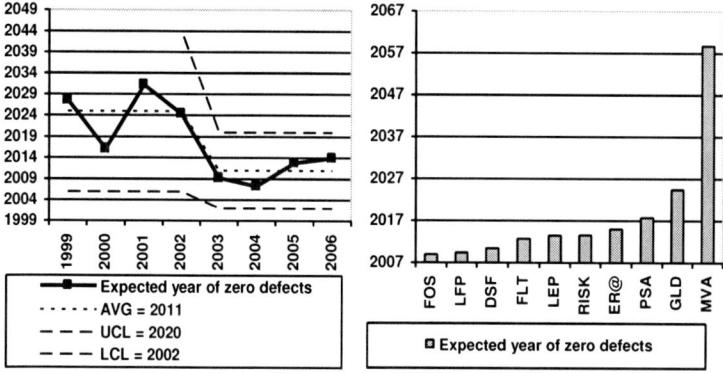

Figure 3. Results of linear regression for predicting the year of zero defects

Evaluating the design in figure 1 and 2 based on the results shown in figure 3, the standardization process is not working as well as one might hope for. Why is the tenth project behaving differently from the others?

Research problem and structure of paper

Considering the ideas informing design of the QMS, such as user participation, flexibility for changing the governing variable, clear feedback in the shape of measurements and metrics and trying to design the management system as a game rather than something opposed upon the workers by management, in one of the ten cases the design is not working as well as the designer (writer of the paper) would have hoped. The research question is stated as:

- Do the observations challenge the assuption of "what gets measured gets done"?

The research question is motivated by the hope that a better understanding of why the tenth project is failing might contribute ideas on how to improve the design of quality management systems, making systems for solving similar problems more efficient and robust.

In the next section, performance measurement systems theory and flow theory will be used to frame the problem within a context that could perhaps provide some ideas for better design of quality management systems. The approach used for gaining insights on the behavior of the tenth project, consists of a series of interviews that have been carried out in combination with looking at output from the QMS in terms of numerical tables and diagrams. A general description of methods and material is presented in the third section while the case study results follow in the fourth section. In the final section the aim is to try to make sense out of the interviews and statistics through a discussion that leads to a conclusion and new design ideas.

Designing software quality management systems

According to Sommerville (2001, p. 536-7), software quality management can be structured into three principal activities:

1. *Quality assurance.* The establishment of a framework of organizational procedures and standards which lead to high-quality software.

2. *Quality planning.* The selection of appropriate procedures and standards from this framework and the adaptation of these for a specific software project.

3. *Quality control.* The definition and enactment of processes which ensure that the project quality procedures and standards are followed by the software development team.

Furthermore, there are two types of standards that may be established as part of the quality assurance process (Sommerville, 2001, p. 539):

1. *Product standards.* These are standards that apply to the software product being developed. They include document standards such as the structure of the requirements document which should be produced, documentation standards such as a standard comment header for an object class definition and coding standards which define how a programming language should be.

2. *Process standards.* These are standards that define the processes which should be followed during software development. They may include definitions of specifications, design and validation processes and a description of the documents which must be generated in the course of these processes.

According to this classification, the standardization method described in the introduction can be described as a product standard although the method in itself may be seen as a process standard.

Concerning some of the problems described in the introduction, Sommerville (2001, p. 540-1) describe these as well-know and gives advice on how to avoid such problems.

> Software engineers sometimes consider standards to be bureaucratic and irrelevant to the technical activity of software development. This is particularly likely when the standards require tedious form-filling and work recording. Although they usually agree about the general need for standards, engineers often find good reasons why standards are not necessarily appropriate to their particular project.
>
> To avoid these problems, quality managers who set the standards need to be adequately resourced and should take the following steps:
>
> 1. Involve software engineers in the development of product standards. They should understand the motivation behind the development of the standard and be committed to these standards. The standards document should not simply state a standard to be followed but should include a rationale of why particular standardization decisions have been made.
>
> 2. Review and modify standards regularly to reflect changing technologies. Once standards are developed they tend to be enshrined in a company standards handbook and there is often a reluctance to change them. A standards handbook is essential but it should evolve with changing circumstances and technology.
>
> 3. Provide software tools to support standards wherever possible. Clerical standards are the cause of many complaints because of the tedious work involved in implementing them. If tool support is available, there is not a great deal of additional effort involved in development to the standards.

Sommerville does not include advice on what to do when these design principles have been used and some of the software engineers still ignore the standards, as was the case mentioned in the introduction.

Offen and Jeffrey (1997) include issues such as "a quality environment has already been established" and "there is senior management/sponsor commitment" in their list of success factor framework in related research on establishing software measurement programs (using the M3P model), but they make no suggestions on how to succeed with the model if these two factors are not present. On the contrary, they report problems with installing a measurement program in a government organization where success factors were not present.

In a comparative study of two organizations IS and ES implementing software metrics programs, Hall and Fenton (1997) draw some conclusions on practitioner attitude:

> One of the most important factors in metrics program success is practitioner attitude: If you fail to generate positive feelings toward the program, you seriously undermine your likelihood of success.
>
> A significant influence on attitude towards metrics was job seniority. In both organizations, managers were much more positive than develops about metrics use, introduction, and

management. Furthermore, the more senior managers were, there more enthusiastic there were about using metrics. At IS, for example, 87 percent of senior managers were positive about metrics compared to 72 percent of middle managers and 45 percent of junior analysts and programmers.

However, we also found that developers were more positive about metrics than conventional wisdom has led us to believe (Tom DeMarco suspected this was the case.) It is generally thought, especially by managers, that developers are unenthusiastic about quality mechanisms like metrics and cannot see their value. Our results actually show that 80 percent of ES developers and 50 percent of IS developers were positive about metrics use.

It has been said that when developers are asked their opinion about software quality mechanisms, they say such things are useful, but when they're asked to participate they find many reasons why their work must be exempt. This could explain the positive attitudes towards metrics what we found in this study. If this is the case – and develops are only positive about metrics in the abstract – then organizations need to work toward realizing this positive potential. In any case, the relationship between positive perceptions and negative action warrants more research.

A difference between the measurement system design described in the introductory section and the designs of the systems described by Hall and Fenton is the fact that the quality standards, measurements and metrics were defined by the software engineers themselves without management interference beyond the fact that the standards were sanctioned by management and the feedback was not only given to the engineers but also given to managers and other process shareholders.

Although some of the research on the design of software measurement systems mentioned above uses ethnographic studies as a research approach, the researchers do not explicitly suggest applying ethnographic studies as an integrated part of the ongoing QMS implementation processes. Sommerville (2001, p. 562) recommends, however, ethnographic studies as a technique for process analysis in order to understand the nature of software development as a human activity on a more general basis, not discussing software measurements in particular but development in general.

What gets measured gets done

There are numerous references to the principle of "what gets measured gets done" in management and quality control literature. The principle is attributed to Mason Haire in the following context (quoted in Lynch & Cross, 1995, p. 159):

> What gets measured gets done. If you are looking for quick ways to change how an organization behaves, change the measurement system.

There are numerous references to this principle in management and quality control literature (e.g. Peters & Waterman, 1982). Based on literature research carried out so far, it has been difficult to find research questioning or contradicting Haire's statement, although some researchers mention the effect of unexpected results of using measurements, e.g. Behn (2003):

> "What gets measured gets done" is, perhaps, the most famous aphorism of performance measurement. If you measure it, people will do it. Unfortunately, what people measure often is not precisely what they want done. And people – responding to the explicit or implicit incentives of the measurement – will do what people are measuring, not what these people actually want done. [...] Thus, although performance measures shape behavior, they may shape behavior in both desirable and undesirable ways.

Although it has been difficult finding research that challenges the verbatim "what gets measured gets done", there has been written extensively on similar phenomena, such as "the Hawthorne effect". The Hawthorne effect refers to the work efficiency studies carried out by the Hawthorne Works outside Chicago 1924-32 and is sometimes described as "a short-term improvement caused by observing worker performance" (Landsberger, 1968). There seems to be some controversy as to whether the data from the experiments actually support the anecdote about workers increasing their productivity because of the presence of the observers or whether the "Hawthorne effect" is management mythology unsupported by empirical evidence (Wikipedia, 2008).

Other effects of similar nature to "what gets measured gets done" and the "Hawthorne effect" include the "Pygmalion effect" and the "placebo effect".

Participatory Design

Among the web sites for the Computer Professionals for Social Responsibility organization there is a web page suggesting that there can be no single definition of Participatory Design (PD) as PD practitioners are so diverse in their perspectives, backgrounds and areas of concern (CPSR, 2008). Nevertheless, the following list of issues is used for giving some guidelines on the sort of thinking that is associated with PD:

- Respect the users of technology, regardless of their status in the workplace, technical know-how, or access to their organization's purse strings. View every participant in a PD project as an expert in what they do, as a stakeholder whose voice needs to be heard.

- Recognize that workers are a prime source of innovation, that design ideas arise in collaboration with participants from diverse backgrounds, and that technology is but one option in addressing emergent problems.

- View a "system" as more than a collection of software encased in hardware boxes. In PD, we see systems as networks of people, practices, and technology embedded in particular organizational contexts.

- Understand the organization and the relevant work on its own terms, in its own settings. This is why PD practitioners prefer to spend time with users in their workplaces rather than "test" them in laboratories.

- Address problems that exist and arise in the workplace, articulated by or in collaboration with the affected parties, rather than attributed from the outside.

- Find concrete ways to improve the working lives of co-participants by, for example, reducing the tedium associated with work tasks; co-designing new opportunities for exercising creativity; increasing worker control over work content, measurement and reporting; and helping workers communicate and organize across hierarchical lines within the organization and with peers elsewhere.

- Be conscious of one's own role in PD processes; try to be a "reflective practitioner."

For the purpose of designing quality management systems it is not obvious that a PD approach may be the best approach. Some quality control experts seem to be of the persuasion that it is the people who do the work who are best capable of describing their processes, but there are others who believe that those doing the work are inside the system and thus not able to see the system properly in the same way as an external specialist would do (e.g. Deming, 1992, p. 54).

Materials and Methods

Insights related to why a certain group of software engineers appears to be behaving inconsistently with the principle "what gets measured gets done" is needed in order to improve the design of the QMS outlined in the introductory section. If one were to give a procedural description P of the management system from the introduction, i.e. a flowchart or a detailed list of steps of what is actually being done in order to monitor and provide feedback to the software engineers standardizing COBOL software, the aim of the research is to come up with a revised procedure P' that would generate better results than P.

From this perspective, the research process can be seen as an integrated part of an engineering process that consists of finding the optimal procedural design $P*$ for this particular quality control problem. The current research does not aim for an optimal design, but conceptually it could be possible to think of iterations of design research that would produce a series of designs that would ultimately converge into an optimal design where improvement is no longer possible; P, P', P'', ..., $P*$.

In traditional engineering literature, science and engineering have sometimes been described as inverse processes. Trying to explain the difference between science and engineering to engineering students, Krick (1969, p. 36-7) explains as follows:

Full appreciation of the role of engineering is difficult if you do not understand the basic distinction between science and engineering. They differ with respect to the basic processes characteristic of each (research versus design), predominant day-to-day concerns, and primary end product (knowledge versus physical contrivances).

Science is a body of knowledge, specifically, man's accumulated understanding of nature. Scientists direct their efforts primarily to improving this understanding. They search for useful explanations, classifications, and means of predicting natural phenomena. In his search for new knowledge the scientist engages in a process called research and in so doing he devotes much of his time to the following activities:

- Hypothesizing explanations of natural phenomena.
- Obtaining data with which to test these theories.
- Conceiving, planning, instrumenting, and executing experiments.
- Analyzing observations and drawing conclusions.
- Attempting to describe natural phenomena in the language of mathematics.
- Attempting to generalize from what has been learned.
- Making known his findings through articles and papers.

The scientist's prime objective is knowledge as an end in itself.

In contrast, the usual end product of the engineer's efforts is a physical device, structure, or process. Let there be no mistake – the gyroscope, the weather satellite, the radio telescope, the electrocardiograph, the nuclear power station, the electronic computer, and the artificial kidney are the fruits of engineering. The engineer develops these contrivances through a create process referred to as design (in contrast to the scientist's central activity – research). Some of the engineer's prime concerns as he executes this process are the economic feasibility, the safeness, the public acceptance, and the manufacturability of his creations. In contrast, the scientist's prime concerns as he performs his function include the validity of his theories, the reproducibility of his experiments, and the adequacy of his methods of observing natural phenomena.

In the case of quality engineering, i.e. the engineering standards and procedures to be included in a quality management system, Krick's references to natural science could be replaced with social science. Juran (1964) suggests that the relationship between management and social research can be seen as identical to the relationship between engineering and natural science.

The design cycle in figure 4 illustrates engineering design and design research as reverse processes.

The major difference between the diagram in figure 4 and the original diagram in Krick's book is that the process named "monitoring the system" has been replaced by "design research"; the tagging of the bottom arrow. What this means in the context of this paper is that not only has the procedure P been monitored in terms of plotting results to graphs and interviewing the people involved, but the procedure P has been identified as a special case of a class of procedures that consist of measuring performance, plotting and sharing the results as joint feedback to the group. Typical examples of such procedures would be the regular evaluations ("sprints") that are carried out as a part of agile software development practices such as Scrum (Schwaber, 2004). The goal is then to question the statement "what gets measured gets done" within this general context of measurement and feedback driven software development, rather than just adding practical knowledge to the practical quality engineering problem in question.

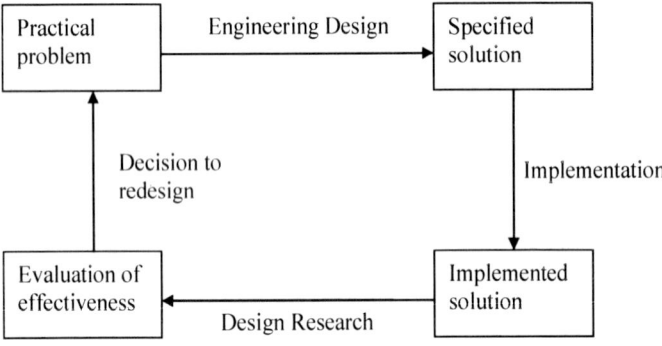

Figure 4. Design Research Cycle (adapted from Krick, 1969, p. 160)

The research design has been inspired by an attempt to interpret aspects of "science of the artificial" (Simon, 1996) in the context of the "research wheel" as described by Rudestam and Newton (1992, pp. 5-8). The process of integrating engineering and research into the same process should be consistent with the research activities defined by March and Smith (1995) as is also the idea of a procedure P' being the output of this kind of research. It is also the belief of the author that the research method explained is in compliance with the seven guidelines for design science as suggested by Hevner et al. (2004).

In previous papers based on earlier stages of the same case study, the action research approach has been used (Ogland, 2006; 2007a; 2007b). However, as pointed out by Cole, Purao, Rossi & Sein (2005), action research and design research have much in common, even to the extent that it may even be possible to see them as special cases of a generalized "action design science". The reason why design research has been chosen rather than action research in this third iteration of the same "action design research" study is the author's impression that action research seems more useful for researching topics in psychology or sociology while trying to create organizational change while design research aims at adding to the knowledge of designing artifacts (e.g. quality management systems) while, similarly, trying to create organizational change. In other words, while the aim of this paper is to add insights on how interventions in a software engineering culture can create organizational change, the intervention has to be of a kind that can be described as a procedure to be added as part of the quality management system of the organization.

Data collection and analysis

Certain parts of the data collection and analysis consist of the data collection and analysis done as a part of the running of the quality management system, as illustrated in figure 3. As the researcher is also the designer of the system, all system documentation, input and output for the system have been ready at hand. Furthermore, it has been possible to collect data on the cost of running the system (in terms of man-hours spent by the engineer/researcher for running and improving the system) and other measurement related to the management of the system.

When it comes to understanding the weaknesses of the design in terms of understanding why the quality control principle of "what gets measured gets done" seem to have been violated to a certain degree for at least one of the projects that interact with the system, it is necessary to conduct interviews with the people involved. Not only the software engineers apparently not behaving as expected are necessary to interview, but also their managers who are the ones who are responsible for standards and procedures being followed. In order to get an even fuller picture of the environment, various other system shareholders have been interviewed, such as software engineers who have been behaving particularly consistent with the expectations of the systems, managers on different levels and people responsible for software engineering process improvement and software quality assurance.

However, as the engineering design of the COBOL standardization quality management system started as a quality engineering project and has only more recently been transformed into a action/design research project, interviews, conversations and observations done up until quite recently have been done either as a part of managing and improving the system and partly at random intervals in an unplanned manner.

Furthermore, while many of the principles from ethnographic studies (e.g. Silverman, 2004) have been followed as an integrated part of the application of international guidelines on how to conduct quality audits (ISO, 2002), neither tape recorders nor notebooks have been used. At certain periods the researcher was also not allowed to interview software engineers (unless accompanied by a manager), something that often resulted in interviews not being conducted, although the QMS has been running continuously for seven years.

As the system has interfaced with ten project groups, normal management procedure for the running of the QMS should have consisted of carrying out seventy (or more) interviews with software engineers plus additional interviews with managers and other shareholders. However, due to restrictions mentioned and sometimes practical difficulties in making meetings with the software engineers, the research so far has consisted of about 40-50 interviews and/or conversations.

The data analysis has consisted of the researcher trying to remember what has been said and discussed and then trying to make sense out of this (Weick, 1995, pp. 1-16) for the purpose of understanding how to improve the efficiency of the quality management system.

Population characteristics

The interpretative part of the study has consisted of interviewing members from ten projects over a period of seven years. The projects were managed by three group leaders, handling a total of about 40 programmers.

Seven of the projects were related to software to be maintained in consistency with annual waterfall-like life cycles (Sommerville, 2001, p. 45-6), while the remaining three projects were related to on-line computer systems that followed principles more in the style of evolutionary development (Sommerville, 2001, p. 46-8).

The distribution between male and female programmers was about 50/50. The age distribution was from about mid thirties to mid sixties, with most of the people being in the age slot between 40 and 50. Each of the ten projects are manned with 2 to 6-7 people.

The tenth project consists of two people, one person responsible for the MVA system (female, age approx. 40) and one person responsible for the ER system (male, age approx. 50). Although the two systems do not interact functionally, source code is stored on the same disk on the mainframe which is the domain that defines the tenth project.

Results

In the first part of figure 5, the progress is compared between the average defect level of the first nine projects and defect level of the tenth project. The second part of the figure compare the progress rate for each of the ten projects as defined by the regression line made up of plotted values from 2004 and onwards. Due to the revision of the software standard in 2002/2003, the gap produced by the revision is a cause of changes in the evaluation system and not due to "dramatic improvements" (as mentioned in the introductory section), thus making period from 2004 and onwards more suitable for predicting future progress than looking at the complete time series.

By visually inspecting the right-hand diagram in figure 5, it is possible that the improvement rate for the solid line was slightly more rapid in the earlier period 1998-2002 than it was in the later period 2003-2006 (although not obvious). The "year of zero defects" results in figure 3 were based on making the best linear fit for the observations 2003-2006 and then calculate where that line would cross the x axis. Perhaps it would be more realistic to believe that the improvements would reach asymptotically towards zero (never reaching the "year of zero defects"), but for the case of trying to understand why the tenth project behaves radically different from the other projects, the linear regression model is mathematically simpler to deal with and provides a good enough approximation for investigating this particular problem.

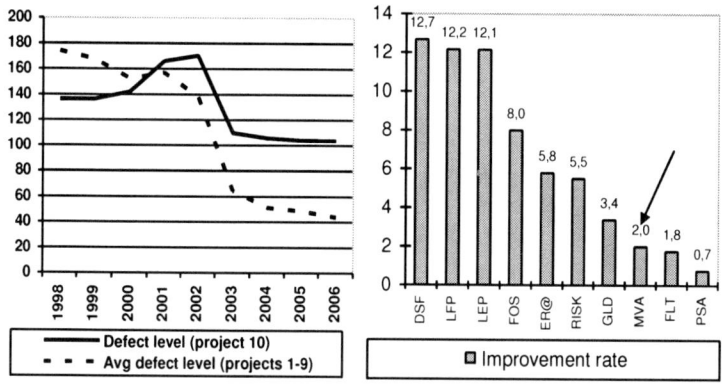

Figure 5. Defect index for the tenth project compared with the average defect index for the remaining nine projects

The individual improvement rates on the right-hand side of figure 5 shows that then tenth project (MVA) is not the project progressing at the slowest rate. In fact, there are two projects making even less annual progress (FLT and PSA). However, when we compare the columns in this figure 5 with the columns in figure 3, the reason why the projects FLT and PSA score better is because the software they represent have already been standardized to a high level and it is no longer necessary to improve at a very rapid rate in order to reach the "year of zero defects" within a timeline that is comparable with most of the other projects.

Discussions with representatives of the tenth project

During the time of the first conversations, in 2000, the project coordinator for the tenth project was sharing office with the project coordinator for one of the more consistently successful projects (FOS). When discussing first year results with the FOS project coordinator it was possible also to give some hints to the other project coordinator. As can be seen in figure 5, there was no progress in the tenth project the first few years, and as the quality manager (writer of this paper) was of the persuasion that positive results should be give positive and explicit feedback while negative results should be handled more diplomatically, the discussion with the coordinator of the tenth project mostly consisted in saying that the defect level of the software was not bad compared to defect levels in other projects (actually the defect level was better than average as can be seen in figure 5).

The coordinator for the tenth project responded to this by asking whether it was necessary to comply with the standard. From the viewpoint of the quality manager this question was surprising as the point of quality management is to make sure that all standards and procedures are being followed unless there should be some well-argued reason for not doing so. The answer the project coordinator was given was that it could perhaps be a good idea to try to do some small improvements, as most of the other projects were already focused on standardizing and were already producing good results.

Annual conversations during the next few years were of a similar kind. The statistics showed little improvement, but conversations were kept on a friendly level, emphasizing that the project was still scoring okay with respect to benchmark results and also discussing the rationale behind the standardization process, namely to make sure that it should be possible for programmer A to take care of software developed by programmer B in an easy manner as they were both following the same programming standard.

When the 2001 results arrived, however, it was necessary to make inquiries into why the results now not only showed lack of improvement but were in fact getting worse. This year it was not possible to conduct an interview with the project coordinator, but discussing the issue with a project member, he said that they had been discussing the issue of trying to take the standardization challenge more seriously. He found the issue of the defect level getting worse both surprising and amusing, but after some reflection he suggested that the reason might have something to do with development of new programs often consisted of making copies of old programs as a starting point, and if those old programs contained lots of defects, these defects would be copied over to the new programs and thus increase the total level of defects.

The next year the defect level increased even more, but after having pointed this out to a higher level manager, the quality manager was told that he would not be allowed to do more interviews with the tenth project.

The role of the software development model

When confronted with lack of progress in project ten as compared with the nine other projects, the head of the software maintenance department suggested that this could perhaps be explained due to the software development model. The tenth project consisted of making "evolutionary" updates (Sommerville, 2001, pp.

46-8) on a "real-time" system (monthly production runs) while many of the other projects dealt with annual production systems. In the case of annual production systems, the maintenance process followed a strict procedure of updates in specification documents, design documents, programming, testing, production and evaluation in compliance with various annual waterfall models (Sommerville, 2001, pp. 45-6). Working within disciplined waterfall framework, it should not be a great surprise that the standardization of software for systems following such a rigid development model would be more quickly standardized than systems without such a rigid model, using a more evolutionary approach.

His conclusion was that we should not interview the people in the tenth project as they were probably doing their best, and being confronted with poor trend data would only make them annoyed and less productive.

However, the tenth project was not the only project following an "evolutionary development" software process model. In figure 6 below the progress results from the tenth project is compared with progress results from the RISK project and the DSF project.

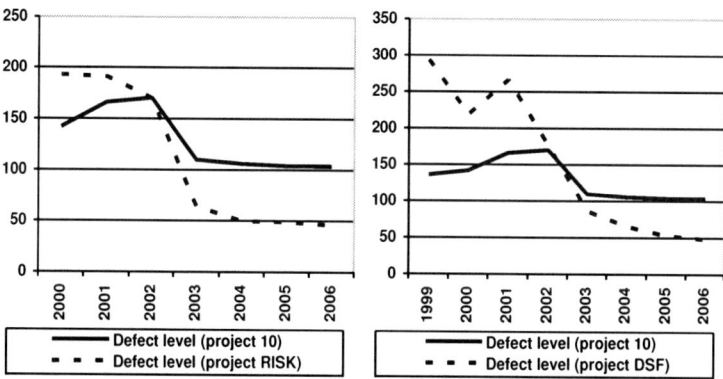

Figure 6. Comparison of progress on the tenth project and two other projects that also maintain software within the framework of an "evoluationary development" software process modell.

The diagram on the left-hand side of figure 6 seems somewhat consistent with the hypothesis that it might be more difficult to create improvement for "evolutionary development" systems where standardization is not part of a well-defined and time-bound waterfall phase for "implementation and unit testing". The diagram on the right-hand side of figure 6, however, shows good results from a project trying to standardize software within the framework of evolutionary development.

In both comparisons, the progress during the last few years (since 2003) is more rapid for the reference projects that in the case of the tenth project, as can be seen from the diagram in figure 6 where the prognosis for when the tenth project will be completed is far beyond the time horizon for the reference projects.

The Pygmalion effect

In the year 2000, the quality manager (writer of this paper) was able to discuss some issues of software quality assurance with a visiting SQA person from a large CMMI-level 5 company in India. This was the time when the COBOL standard had been developed and the first iteration of the quality control was about to commence. The discussion evolved around the idea of internal benchmarking and distribution of results as a way for creating needed and sufficient tension for creating improvements, as illustrated in figure 2 and explained in the introduction of this paper. Personally, he would not try something like that, he said, as he expected benchmarking to create little motivation for improvement for those who got top results and would probably work like negative motivation for those who got bottom results.

Reflecting upon this discussion, perhaps the reason for the poor performance in the tenth project could have something to do with the tenth project repeatedly receiving poor benchmark results, each time contributing to a manifestation of a poor self-image that the programmers were poor performers and there consequently being no reason to improve as the results only verified their own pessimistic beliefs.

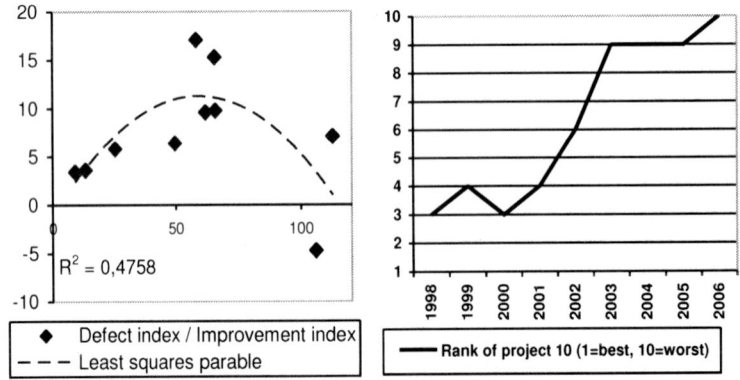

Figure 7. (a) Parabolical relationship between defect indexes and improvement indexes, and (b) history of defect benchmark results (rank) for the tenth project when compared with the others.

Producing a scatter diagram with defect level along the x axis and improvement rates along the y axis, the pattern suggested by the Indian SQA consultant actually seem to be confirmed (right-hand side of diagram in figure 7).

Using a parabolic regression curve to model the quality improvements (from the past to the present year) as a function of the quality level from the past year, the tenth project fits on the far left (low quality, little improvement) while projects on the far right are those of high quality and little improvement. Those who score low and those who score high on the benchmark results show trends of little annual improvement. Those who are ranked in the middle range of the benchmark results show trends of great improvement.

However, the diagram on the right-hand side shows that the tenth project has not always been the worst project. In fact, it started out as one of the best and has gradually fallen down on the ranking table. There is no indication of the motivation for standardization having changed during the seven years the tenth project has been observed, although it has been ranked among the best, the mid-level and the worst. Project performance for the tenth project has been consistently below the performance level of the other projects all the time.

Interview with IT top management

At the time when the tenth project had reached a climax of not only failing to improve but actually getting less and less compliant with the standards over several years, the quality manager (writer of this paper) brought the issue up with the IT director general. The IT director general asked whether the quality managers had any ideas why it was like this, why this particular project was performing totally opposite of the other projects. As the quality manager answered that he did not know, the IT director general took up the issue with his board of managers on the next weekly meeting. Although it is unclear what was said during this meeting and what was communicated down the line of three management levels above the software engineers in the tenth project, after this incident the tenth project has been reporting slow but steady improvements, as can be seen in the time series diagrams in figures 6 and 7.

Due to business reorganization in 2007, the former IT director general was replaced with one of the people who had previously been on his board of senior managers. As a part of the ongoing research on how to improve the QMS design, in February 2008 the new director was asked whether he had any suggestions on what could be the reason why the tenth project was consistently performing at a significantly worse than the other projects. The new IT director general, who previously had worked mostly with external consultant software engineers (for large software development projects) rather than in-house software maintenance engineers, interpreted the situation as typical for difficulty of working with in-house people in a public sector organization.

In private organizations it is possible to remove people not willing to follow the rules of the organization, he said, but in a large public sector organization the employers are protected in ways that makes it close to impossible to handle difficult employees.

Self-assessment: Quality costs

Total quality costs are sometimes defined as prevention costs plus appraisal costs plus failure costs (ASQ, 2008). While the cost of failure, such as the cost of having people trying to make changes into source code they have difficulty understanding, may be difficult to predict, the prevention costs are kept at a minimum by having the software engineers themselves decide which programs to standardize and when to do this (as long as all programs are standardized in the long run). The appraisal costs are the costs of running and improving the quality management system. The running of the system, consisting of collecting numerical data, carrying out the statistical analysis, producing written feedback and conducing interviews, plus writing and annual evaluation report of about 100 pages (25,000 words), amounts to about 70 man-hours (about one man-day for each of the ten projects each year). Improving the system by the use of action research or design research, including the writing of academic papers at a quality that will get them accepted in decent academic outlets, can be costly although exact man-hours haven't been calculated yet.

There have been some minor changes in the system from year to year, trying to improve efficiency and make the process more "scientific" (i.e. compliant with action research and/or design research), but the basic principles of measuring software against a common standard, benchmarking and distributing the results has remained the same all along since the first year the system was run.

Discussion

The study was not designed to compare and contrast a PD approach with a non-PD approach for developing standards and quality management systems. However, the study indicates that it is possible to get quite far by a quantitative engineering approach, producing 90% "automatic improvement" in this particular case. For the final 10%, nevertheless, the mechanical approach does not work (as of yet) and it is necessary to carry out some kind of qualitative studies in order to find out what actually happens in the social world and see whether this might give some insights that could be used for improving upon the design described in the introductory section.

As was mentioned in the theory section, ethnographic studies should be treated not only as an academic research approach but as an integrated part of software engineering when trying to understand the nature of software engineering as a human activity (Sommerville, 2001, p. 562). One of the reasons for the prolonged weak results for the tenth project may have something to do with a lack of initiative in terms of carrying out interpretative research to find out in more detail what the software engineers in question were thinking and feeling rather than simply rely on the behaviorist hypothesis of "what gets measured gets done".

On the other hand, as mentioned in the results part, the quality manager / researcher was at times not allowed to interview these people as some of the managers was of the opinion that it would be better to leave these people alone doing their best than to provoke them by asking them about the quality management system.

This protective attitude among some of the managers is different from the case studies reported by Hall and Fenton (1997). In other studies it seems to be more common that managers are focused on standards, measurements, control and improvement. Following the logic implied by the new IT director general, the reason why there seems to be less focus on control and improvement in public sector organizations may be because the survival of the organization does not depend on customers to the same degree as private organizations, and the fact that strong unions and protective culture makes it difficult to apply the philosophy of "managing by measuring" anyway.

Participatory Design

One success factor often mentioned for implementing software measurement systems is the importance of having management commitment (e.g. Offen and Jeffrey, 1997). When there is little management commitment, as in this case, it may be useful to design a quality management system that exploit those few elements of management commitment there might be or to create an illusion of management commitment and use that illusion in order to try to create sufficient social pressure to make sure that people comply with the system (Øgland, 2007b).

Where PD has sometimes been motivated as a part of political research where the aim has been to create a greater level of democracy in the work place or a better culture for communication, in the COBOL programmer case the aim has been that the programmers themselves should take responsibility for the quality of their work by defining the standards, the procedures and measurement systems themselves rather than having such elements pushed upon them from above.

What gets measured gets done?

In nine of the ten projects, the results were consistent with "what gets measured gets done". This observation is consistent with certain leadership theories, such as the principle that whatever management focuses on tends to get done (Schein, 1985). In this case study, however, the managers did not show much interest in measurements. Rather than getting enthusiastic about the improvement trends, they got worried about non-optimal trends and sometimes tried to argue against measuring or prevent the researcher for doing qualitative studies that might help to understand why the trends were not as good as expected.

In this respect the software measurement design seems to have more in common with agile software development methods such as Scrum where the Scrum coordinator (Scrum Master) is not a traditional project manager in terms of being responsible for progress, but the Scrum Master is a person who, among other things, is responsible for collecting and presenting statistics while it is the team itself that decides what to do (Schwaber, 2004, p. 6-7).

If one should read a "what gets measured gets done" principle into the Scrum framework, an essential part of the Scrum philosophy seems to be the focus on self-managed development teams. Many of the COBOL projects could be defined as self-managed teams in a similar way, as there is no real management pressure and the benchmark statistics are used for turning the process of standardization more into a game-like process. As reported in a previous paper focusing on the programmers who were the leaders in the standardization game, not all the programmers within the group were equally enthusiastic about being measured and benchmarked, but the fact that the group consisted of several people a culture of quality improvement emerged and made the project excel (Ogland, 2006).

In the case of the tenth project, the project consists of a group of one (or two). There are also other projects that consist only of one person, and still perform fairly well, e.g. the RISK project, but a single person project might be more vulnerable. The fact that the tenth project behaves in a different way than the other projects may not be as surprising after all. The implications in Mason Haire's "what gets measured gets done" quote, as stated in the theory section is a statement about organizational change, not of individual change.

In the case of the tenth project, the more recent measurements show a slight improvement, something that appears to be a consequence of top management involvement. The fact that summary statistics were reported to top management over several years did not seem to have much of an impact on the tenth project, but when there was top management action, improvement were quick to follow.

Conclusions and further research

When doing interviews with various actors in order to get various interpretations on why the project is behaving differently, there are three main suggestions:

1) The software life-cycle is different
2) The programmers are badly motivated by repeatedly being ranked as worst in class, thus accepting this image and becoming worst in class
3) The attempt to socially construct peer pressure and management pressure is not successful. The programmers continue to act as if they were living on an isolated island.

It was shown that neither the first nor the second point is valid. In the case of the first point, there are other projects with a similar underlying life-cycle model that create better improvement results. In the case of the second point, the tenth project has not always been worst-in-class. In the beginning the project was performing better than average but as no action was taken, the project gradually fell down the ranking list until it became "worst-in-class".

Although the current IT director general made a rather cynical remark about problems with management of behavior in public sector organizations, the comment seems to carry a certain level of truth. If people decide not to follow internal rules and regulations, it may be that such problems need different management methods than some of the most common methods used in private organizations.

The "what gets measured gets done" principle is extracted from a statement about organizational change. It may be "common knowledge" that the principle works for groups of people (Behn, 2003), but whether it works on individuals is not so clear. At least this study has illustrated the principle being set to use for a period of seven years with poor results in one case.

The theoretical contribution from this research is that quality management systems design based on "what gets measured gets done" should make sure that the topology of the larger socio-technical system does not fragment into isolated islands. It may not be possible for the designer of the quality management system to suggest that programmers are periodically rotated among various groups or that they add practices such as peer review of source code, as there may be organizational reasons why such changes may be difficult to achieve, but it should be within the responsibility of the QMS designer to question whether it may be possible to strengthen the social network of programmers so they may be able to communicate and exchange views on the QMS process as something they share.

If it should happen that the key person in the tenth project should either be moved to another project or this person should be asked to be member of another standardization project in addition to the tenth project, an interesting hypothesis for further research would be to investigate whether the socialization within a new project would carry back inspiration for increasing the improvement rate for the tenth project.

References

Argyris, C. and Schön, D. (1978). *Organizational Learning: A Theory of Action Perspective*, Addison-Wesley Publishing Company: Reading, Massachusettes.

ASQ (2008). Cost of Quality (COQ), http://www.asq.org/learn-about-quality/cost-of-quality/overview/overview.html (accessed on April 8th, 2008)

Behn, R.D. (2003). "Why Measure Performance? Different Purposes Require Different Measures", *Public Administration Review*, vol. 63, no. 5., 586-606.

Cole, R., Purao, S., Rossi M. & Sein, M.K. (2005). "Being proactive: where action research meets design research", *Proceedings of the Twenty-Sixth International Conference on Information Systems*, 325-336.

CPSR (2008). *What is Participatory Design?* http://www.cpsr.org/issues/pd/introInfo, (accessed on March 28th 2008)

Deming, W.E. (1992). *The New Economics for Industry, Government, Education, Second Edition*, The MIT Press: Cambridge, Massachusettes.

Goldstein, J. (1994). *The Unshackled Organization: Facing the Challenge of Unpredictability Through Spontaneous Reorganization*, Productivity Press: Portland, Oregon.

Hall, T. and Fenton, N. (1997). "Implementing Effective Software Metrics Programs", *IEEE Software*, vol. 14, no. 2, 55-64.

Hevner, A., March, S., Park, J., and Ram, S. (2004). "Design Science in Information Systems Research," *MIS Quarterly*, vol. 28, no. 1, 75-105.

Hoyle, D. (2006). *ISO 9000 Quality Management Systems Handbook, Fifth Edition*, Butterworth-Heinemann: London.

Imai, K. (1986). *Kaizen: The Key to Japan's Competitive Success*. McGraw-Hill: New York.

ISO (2002). *Guidelines for qualtiy and or environmental management systems auditing (ISO 19011:2002)*, International Standards Organization: Geneva.

Juran, J.M. (1964). *Managerial Breakthrough*, McGraw-Hill: New York.

Krick, E.V (1969). *An Introduction to Engineering and Engineering Design, Second Edition*, John Wiley & Sons: New York.

Landsberger, H. (1968). *Hawthorne Revisited*, Cornell University: New York.

Lynch, R. and Cross. K. (1995) *Measure Up!: Yardsticks for Continuous Improvement*, Wiley: New York.

March, S.T. & Smith, G.F. (1995). "Design and natural science research on information technology", *Decision Support Systems*, vol. 15, no. 4, 251-266.

Offen, R.J. and Jeffrey, R. (1997). "Establishing Software Measurement Programs", *IEEE Software*, vol. 7, no. 1, 39-54.

Peters, T. & Waterman, R.H. (1982). *In Search of Excellence: Lessons From America's Best-Run Companies*, Harpercollins: New York.

Rudestam, K.E. & Newton, R.R. (1992). *Surviving your Dissertation: A Comprehensive Guide to Content and Process*, Sage Publishing: London.

Schein, E. (1985). *Organizational culture and leadership: A dynamic view*, Jossey-Bass: San Francisco.

Schlickman, J. (2003). *ISO 9000 Quality Management Systems Design*, ASQ Quality Press: New York.

Schwaber, K. (2004). *Agile Project Management with Scrum*, Microsoft Press: Redmond, Washington.

Seddon, J. (2006). *The Vanguard Standards: A systems thinker's guide to interpretation and use of ISO 9000:2000*, http://www.lean-service.com/3-1.asp

Silverman, D. (2004). *Qualitative Research: Theory, Method and Practice, Second Edition*, Sage Publications: London.

Simon, H.A. (1996). *The Sciences of the Artificial, Third Edition*, The MIT Press, Cambridge, Massachusettes.

Sommerville, I. (2001). *Software Engineering, 6th Edition*, Addison-Wesley: Harlow, England.

Vaishnavi, V., & Kuechler, W. (2006). Design Research in Information Systems. Retrieved April 12, 2007, from http://www.isworld.org/Researchdesign/drisISworld.htm

Weick, K.E. (1995). *Sensemaking in Organizations*, Sage Publications: London.

Wikipedia (2008). Hawthorn effect. Retrieved February 3rd 2008, from http://en.wikipedia.org/wiki/Hawthorne_effect

Ogland, P. (2006). "Using internal benchmarking as strategy for cultivation: A case of improving COBOL software maintainability". *29th Information Systems Research in Scandinavia (IRIS 29): "Paradigms Politics Paradoxes"*, 12-15 August, 2006, Helsingør, Denmark.

Ogland, P. (2007a). "Improving Research Methodology as a part of doing Software Process Improvement", *30th Information Systems Research in Scandinavia (IRIS 30): "Models, Methods and Messages"*, 11-14 August, 2007, Tampere, Finland.

Ogland, P. (2007b). "Designing quality management systems with minimal management commitment", *Systemist*, vol. 29, no. 3, 101-112.

Designing quality management systems as complex adaptive systems

Petter Øgland

Department of Informatics, University of Oslo, Norway

Abstract

Complex adaptive systems research adds to the theory of how to design systems that are resilient to change in turbulent environments. This paper reports a case story about using complex adaptive systems theory for designing a quality management system in a politically turbulent organization. The story explains how the quality management system evolved rapidly, exploiting the turbulence of the organization, but collapsed after six years. Through an analysis and discussion of what went wrong, three key issues are identified and explained; (1) topology of quality management systems, (2) controlling the controllers, and (3) projects perspective vs. systems perspective. Implications for a revised design strategy are discussed.

Key words: Quality management, ISO 9000, Complex Adaptive Systems (CAS).

Introduction

In much of the literature on how to design quality management systems there is an implied understanding of stability in terms of focus on the importance of having management commitment, building a quality culture, improving the organizational processes on a project-by-project basis, consistent with Lewin's unfreeze-change-freeze method (French & Bell, 1995; Gold, 1999; Juran 1965; 1993; Beckford, 2002). The quality management expert W.E. Deming often used a "funnel experiment" in his seminars, dropping marble balls through a funnel and record where they hit while trying to aim a given goal and reduce variation, to illustrate how improvement efforts outside the state of statistical control has a tendency for making the situation even worse (Deming, 1986; 1994).

However, the organizational reality of quality management that practitioners have to deal with is often significantly different from ideal assumptions of organizational stability. Organizations may be in constant turmoil due to reorganizations, change of personnel, fluctuations in leadership style due to various "fads" or turbulence as a consequence of unpredictability of market and customers. One stream of development in quality management literature during the past 15 years has been a growing awareness of how to use insights from the natural sciences, biology in particular, for evolving organizational theory that give strategies for adaptation and survival in turbulent situations (e.g. Goldstein, 1994, Dooley, 1995; Wheatley, 1999; Capra, 2002).

As some researchers have pointed out (e.g. Stacy et al, 2000), much of this type of writing, using complexity theory as a basis for understanding organizations, is basically of metaphorical nature, often used for packing old ideas in new language rather than producing new approaches to meet the radically different reality of having to deal with turbulence. The aim of this paper is to describe and analyse an attempt to use aspects of complex adaptive systems (CAS) theory for giving a normative rather than an interpretative theory of QMS design. Through the description and analysis of this case, the aim is to add insights to the research question on how to design quality management systems that are resilient to the shocks generated by turbulence in organizations and in organizational environments.

In the following section there is a description of the CAS framework used, relating the framework to previous use in quality management literature and how it relates to complexity theory and the theory of management and organizations in general. This is followed by a section that describes how the empirical research is set up. The next two sections present results in terms of first telling the story of how the life cycle of a particular quality management design and then a discussion aimed at giving insights for the CAS design approach by interpreting the success and the failure of the design as it was implemented.

Complex adaptive systems as a quality management approach

Various writers discuss complexity theory and complex adaptive systems (CAS) in different ways (e.g. Waldrop, 1992; Johnson, 2002; Gribbin, 2004). The approach used in this paper is based on a framework by Kelly (1994). His framework was one of the first to try to summarize some of the insights from the Santa Fe Institute and other complexity research communities in a way that made an impact on quality management research (Dooley et al, 1995; Dooley, 1996; 1997).

Kelly's main metaphors for explaining what a complex adaptive system is, are flocks of birds, ant colonies, bee hives and how investigation of such biological populations have inspired robotics design (e.g. Brooks & Flynn, 1989; Brooks, 2002) and computer programming (Holland, 1995; 1998). In the final chapter of the book, the ideas for design are summarised as the 'nine laws of God' (Kelly, 1994, pp. 468-472).

- ❑ Distribute being
- ❑ Control from the bottom up
- ❑ Cultivate increasing returns
- ❑ Grow by chunking
- ❑ Maximize the fringes
- ❑ Honour your errors
- ❑ Pursue no optima; have multiple goals
- ❑ Seek persistent disequilibrium
- ❑ Change changes itself

Although there are other lists and other ways of presenting CAS design principles (e.g. Axelrod & Cohen, 2000), this simple list can work as a checklist for evaluating or discussing whether a given QMS design has been developed in compliance with CAS or not. Unlike the more technical framework suggested by Axelrod & Cohen, using a language that is more similar to how the computer programmer might conceptualise CAS, Kelly's nine principles provide a mixture of how a CAS might be designed and how the system is expected to behave. This mixture seems like a good idea when the framework is intended primarily for evaluation rather than design. However, as will be explained in the case study, the intuitive nature of Kelly's framework was also of practical use when designing a purely technical quality management system that does not necessarily contain all the theoretical ideas used by more detailed CAS frameworks (Øgland, 2000).

Is complexity theory a fundamental challenge to systems thinking?

Much of the literature on complexity and organizations describe the non-linear view of the world as a radical break with earlier scientific traditions, and the organizational theory needs to be brought up to date with the current state of natural science as we are no longer living in a world dictated by the science of Descartes and Newton (Wheatley, 1999; Capra, 2002; Stacy et al, 2000).

If complexity science is inconsistent with conventional systems theory, there might be a problem with using CAS as a design principle for quality management systems. However, not all systems experts see the move from general systems theory (GST) to CAS to be a change in ontology and epistemology. Simon (1996, chapter 7) argues that the history of systems theory can be seen as consisting of three main events. Around the beginning of the 20th century, the first wave of systems thinking focused on holism in various forms. With the advent of cybernetics, GST, operational research, and computers in the 1950s, a new wave of systems thinking emerged. The more recent interest in chaos, complexity, fractals, and non-linear equations can be seen as a further extension of the same systems ideas.

In his attempt to show how post-modern thought links with the development in mathematics for the past 150 years, Tasic (2001, p. 156) points out that ill-conditioned mathematical weather models, sometimes referred to as "butterfly effect" models, as a butterfly flapping its wings on one part of the planet may cause severe storms on another part of the planet, are descriptions of the mathematical models and not descriptions of the world itself. In other words, the fact that our mathematical models are unstable or not capable of making predictions beyond a certain level, does not necessarily mean that it is impossible to make such predictions, only that the particular model is not capable of doing it. As Tasic points out, writers from the community of organizational studies trying to use ideas from modern physics and complexity science often seem to confuse the natural scientist's notion of real world phenomenon and the conceptual model of the phenomenon.

As a part of the theoretical foundation referred to in the ISO 9000 standards, there is a list of eight management principles, including "principle 5: Systems approach to management" (Hoyle, 2006, pp. 30-31). From a strictly scientific point of view, there seems to be no reason why one should not be able to use CAS as a design principle rather than, for example, GST or management cybernetics. From the perspective of how Simon is describing the development of systems thinking, it is only a question of using different mathematical framework for describing the quality management dynamics. Adding or subtracting a component to a mathematical equation may have a profound impact on solution strategies, but it will not have any consequences in the area of epistemology.

As Dooley (1997) suggests that the learning aspects inherent in total quality management theory could be used for creating loosely coupled self-managing systems, the argument in this paper is intended to be seen as an effort to show how Dooley's ideas on using CAS as a basis for total quality management (TQM) leads to practical implementations and how such implementations return insights for more refined CAS-based QMS design theory.

Materials and methods

In order to reflect on aspects of CAS theory for designing quality management systems, 15 years of practical experimentation of quality management design will be described and discussed in the following manner:

- ❑ In the period 1992-99, the CAS principles described by Kelly (1994) were used for developing a computer-based quality management system for handling meteorological data. This activity is documented through 295 technical publications, 111 administrative publications, and 31 scientific publications. The writer of this paper was the main designer of the system, so much of the analysis is done as self-reflection. An interview with the manager of the organization and the computer programmer now responsible for the system was conducted in order to understand the impact of the QMS on the current organization and how the QMS has been working from 1999 until present.

- ❑ In the period 2000-2005, the ideas from the CAS-based design of the QMS in the technical organization were used as a framework for designing a QMS in a large public sector organization that handled financial data. In 2005 the QMS collapsed, but since 2006 there has been an attempt to rebuild it through the process of action research (Coghlan & Brannick, 2001). The documentation for this system consisted of 61 administrative publications, 45 technical publications and 17 scientific publications.

- ❑ The main focus of analysis in the case study is on the collapse of the QMS designed for the organization dealing with financial data. As the writer of this paper was the quality manager and main designer of the QMS, the analysis is primarily done in the form of self-reflection, using the documentation from both organizations as reference for making sure that design issues are not forgotten. As the case story will show that it was internal problems in the quality department and the organization of that department within the total organization that were the main cause of collapse, interviews have been conducted with a national board of ISO 9000 experts during the annual national conference of 2006.

- ❑ In order to get additional viewpoints on the collapse, trying to understand some of the issues that surfaced on the ISO 9000 conference, interviews and discussions have also been conducted with a selected group of people from the organization where the QMS was implemented. As the plan is to continue the development of the QMS through the process of aligning with academia and reshaping the QMS design process into a process of action research, the interviews and discussions were balanced between finding out why things went wrong and how to use such insights for further design.

In the first part of the case story, when designing a quality management system for meteorological data, the organization consisted of about 40 people, about two thirds being scientists or engineers. The remaining lot were responsible for punching meteorological data from handwritten reports into the computer database, doing some kind of elementary manual quality control of the data, and interfacing with the public in case of producing computer printouts of standardized weather and climate statistics or giving simple information over the phone. The design of quality management system was more or less a purely technical design, automatically scheduled by computer to move data between various data tables and filter out suspicious observations due to statistical controls. Most of the 31 scientific publications mentioned in this case relate to the development of statistical quality control methods while the technical reports dealt with how these methods were implemented within the system.

In the second part of the story, the organization addressed consisted of about 300 people dealing with design, implementation and running of systems that had to do with the national financial infrastructure. The design of the quality management system in this case was primarily focused on controlling and improving the work processes of these people, often using whatever procedures and standards already in existence in the organization as a starting point. The technical and administrative publications relate to the documentation of the system and the documentation of the performance of the system. The 17 scientific publications are mostly a result of academic papers written about the system in retrospect or papers written as a part of reshaping parts of the project into action research. The first nine publications, however, were papers published in a journal internal to the organization, partly to motivate the organization in questions of quality management but also to report progress and discuss insights.

The ISO 9000 experts were interviewed at the 9th annual QUALIS conference. This is a national conference made up of people who are certified ISO 9000 quality managers or certified ISO 9000 quality auditors who meet to discuss ideas and challenges related to ISO 9000 quality management. The annual attendance is about 25-35 people, with 28 experts attending in the 2006 conference when the interviews were done. The data collection consisted of first sending out a survey to the people on the invitation list, requesting response on six questions that were relevant for the issues discussed in this paper and other more general issues. Based on the response and answers from this query, informal interviews and discussions were carried out as an integrated part of attending the conference.

The final part of the case study, dealing with the issue of trying to understand why the QMS design failed and finding ways to start a more sustainable redesign, consisted of a series of interviews and conversations with various managers within the organization. A long series of informal discussions were done with the person who took over the responsibility as quality manager. Questions and exchange of ideas were done in face-to-face meetings, over the phone and by e-mail. More formal interviews were done with the IT manager, who was the formal owner of the QMS and who had also requested the writer to continue QMS design in the shape of research while another person was given formal responsibility for further improvement of the QMS. As there was a reorganization in 2007, the position of IT manager was given to another person, who is now the person subject to formal interviews. Main ideas from conversations were recorded on paper in the shape of diagrams and handwritten notes.

Results from case study

Designing a computer-based quality management system for handling technical data

Use of complex adaptive systems as a design strategy for developing a computer-based quality management system for dealing with technical data evolved as a consequence of dealing with uncertainty rather than something that was specifically planned at the beginning. On the contrary, the initial strategy for designing and implementing a database system on a new mainframe computer, both rebuilding and improving on the earlier system that was being used on the old computer, followed a conventional systems development method going through stages of requirement specifications, design of new solution, implementation, test and delivery of new system (Moe, 1995).

However, due to the complexity of the original solution, lack of experience among the in-house people who were supposed to develop the system, a few cases of conflicting personal agendas among key personnel, internal politics based on the prestige of the new system, the need to start producing output from the system while it was still in the stage of being specified or designed etc., resulted in the project being more chaotic than anticipated and the initial release of the new system not being able to perform as well as the old system. As soon as the formal project was completed, however, the new system quickly improved through the use of informal prototyping and application-by-application development to satisfy internal needs among climate researchers and external customers.

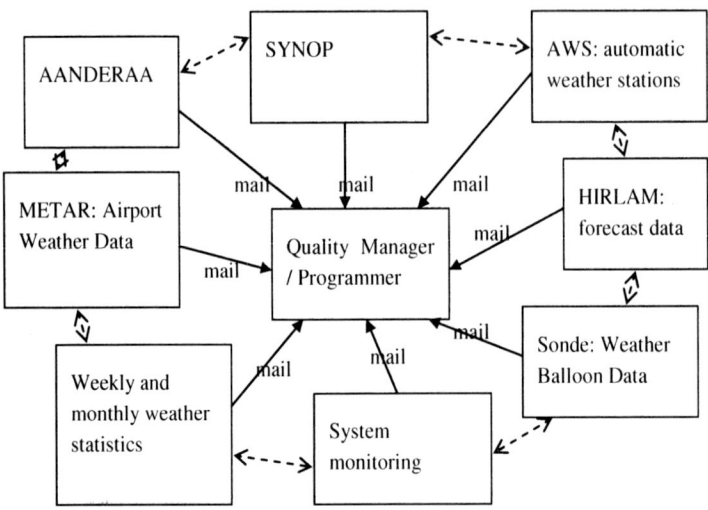

Figure 1 Topology for the technical quality management system

The writer of this paper, being the designer (and implementer) of the quality management aspects of the system, was puzzled by the apparent failure of the highly structured and management-driven development method and the rapid success of the make-up-as-you-go-along approach. During the period of formal development, much time had been spent on project administration and developing documents related to specifications and design, but as implementation was commencing, most of the earlier documentation turned out to lack sufficient detail, based on wrong premises, not correctly mapped, not relevant due to new technological developments etc. Beyond the minimum solution delivered by the project, the actual system was mostly developed afterwards. At this time, complexity theory was starting to become a popular topic. Accidentally discovering a book on complexity theory (Kelly, 1994) resulted in insights not only on why the formal top-down project management method failed to work in a somewhat turbulent context, but it also provided ideas on how to exploit the turbulence for making a resilient QMS design (Øgland, 2000).

The general CAS design principle, inspired by Kelly and his "nine laws", is illustrated in figure 1. The first and most important idea was to "distribute being" in terms of designing the system in the shape of several computer programs that worked independently of each other, but where they were nevertheless loosely linked in terms of how quality control of one type of data used data from another type as reference. The main way they were linked together, however, was how they were programmed to report all error and warning messages into the mailbox of the programmer. Which program to focus on for the day was then decided by the programmer through the use of Pareto analysis and run charts (Øgland, 1999).

The approach worked. The CAS approach focused on evolving the system by starting with simple computer programs that were gradually linked with other programs, and there was no overall design or idea on how the system was evolving, it was simply reshaped each time a new type of data was included or new quality control mechanisms were developed.

Based on interviews conducted in April 2008, none of the original components of the system were any longer in operational use. Although the topology diagram in figure 1 indicates dashed lines between the various components, basically the system was a star topology, meaning that removing the central node would quickly make the whole system collapse, which is also what happened. However, the QMS worked successfully for many years, and a part of the expectations of the CAS design is that of focusing narrowly in time and allowing for changes and adaptations as it develops, and the QMS had now been replaced by a new QMS.

Using the insights from the technical experiment for designing an ISO 9000 system

Having spent seven years developing quality control methods for weather observations seemed like good motivation for developing a quality management system in an equally complex socio-technical system of IT related personnel developing and maintaining computer systems for handling part of the national financial infrastructure. Based on the previous experience of the insufficiency of a management driven waterfall project that would perhaps take another seven years before it started to produce results, the starting point this time was to conceptualize the organization as a garden and then start cultivating whatever practises people were following, encourage what seemed to be working (and was compliant with ISO 9001 requirements) and ignore practices that did not fit into this picture.

In the technical system, the agents within the CAS conceptualization consisted of computer programs having simple strategies that consisted of doing what they were programmed to do, like moving data between different databases, performing statistical quality control, or producing climate statistics for use among climate researchers and the public in general. In the case of the QMS for handling the workforce that were responsible for systems development and systems maintenance, it was not obviously clear from the outset whether the population defined by the CAS should be the people or the processes within the organization. According to one of the management principles in ISO 9000, the aim is to manage the processes, not necessarily the people (Hoyle, 2006, pp. 29-30), although the involvement of people is also listed among the ISO 9000 management principles (ibid, pp. 28-29).

Focusing on the processes and procedures rather than the people when trying to create organizational change seemed to have the advantage of not interfering with what the local experts were doing, but rather evolve the system in terms of giving the power and incentives in order to have them develop standards and measurement systems themselves, so they would be more capable of planning, predicting and improving their own work processes. Furthermore, this approach meant that whatever rules and regulations that were already in place were a part of the current state of the CAS, regardless of whether the current system was muddled, inconsistent, partly out of use, or partly replaced by practice sidestepping the formal procedures. Focusing on the processes and procedures rather than the people seemed highly consistent with the CAS-design of the earlier technical QMS.

Organizational development by focusing on structure

Even though the CAS design focused on the documented part of the quality management system, the aim of the initiative was to get people to take more responsibility for their own work in terms of figuring out how work could be done simpler, more efficient, with a fewer errors, more coordinated with respect to how others in the organization are doing their work and so on. The general idea was consequently to get the people themselves to evaluate the current procedures and then allow them to rewrite the procedures if that would be beneficial for themselves and the organization as a whole.

Defining an active population of processes for investigation consisted of focusing on areas in the organization where there was a general management focus, and/or where it would be easy to include measurements, build feedback routines and generate continuous improvement. From there on, the idea was generally to "go with the flow" in terms of not trying to invent or introduce new ideas, but rather focus on quality control mechanisms already in existence and add measurements to these. This approach would fit with the requirements in chapter 8 of the ISO 9001:2000 standard, and by focusing on the measurements aspects of ISO 9001 it seemed as if the quality management system would develop more or less by itself, not following any particular goals or timelines beyond regular assessments against various relevant quality management standards.

The first successful control routine to emerge from this approach, after seeding several attempts that did not catch on, was a control routine to make sure that software was developed according to common standards (Øgland, 2007). After having established a routine that addressed quality control on the factory floor of computer programming, the next idea was to use the dynamics of "positive feedback" in terms of adding features to this successful mechanism that would make aspects of the quality control system climb up the organization to meet with top management. As top management involvement mainly consisted of providing signatures for critical productions, the approach was to start a series of quality audits that would produce a document, comprising software evaluation and other types of evaluations, which could be presented to top management as part of decision documentation for giving the signature for production. By presenting and formulating the quality controls in a given manner, it was possible to see the process as a part of "management review" of the quality system, as defined in chapter 5 of the ISO 9001:2000 standard.

The next step was to involve the Ministry of Finance and the National Audit as part of the quality management system, without asking or discussing, but simply by looking at what the organization was doing and how exchange of data could be monitored and used as a part of the ever-growing quality management system.

Despite the fact that this quality management system design process was more or less completely "out of control", evolving in an opportunistic rather than planned manner, it was efficient in establishing quality control methods to meet with the international standards. However, it also caused discussion and debate. As the operational mechanism for creating necessary and sufficient organizational tension, for reflecting and rewriting current internal rules and standards, consisted of auditing against such rules and standards, unfortunate trends not fitting with hidden agendas of the organization were sometimes made visible, causing a fair amount of stir. The quality manager (author of this paper) spent much time being the centre of controversy. Nevertheless, bringing issues to the surface usually resulted in various types of actions, often working as a good motivation for making people take responsibility for their own work practices and rewriting procedures and standards to fit better with what they were actually trying to achieve.

The diagram in figure 2 shows the quality management system in a way that makes it comparable with the structure of the technical system from the previous experiment.

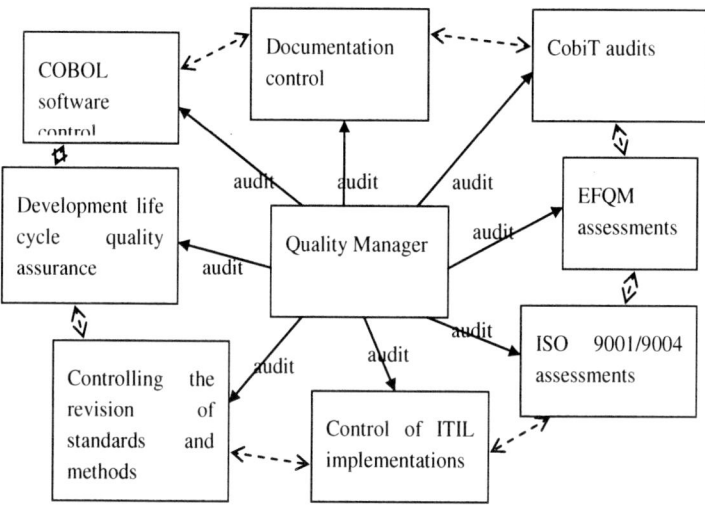

Figure 2 Topology for the socio-technical quality management system

Just as in the previous case, the processes were initially running independently of each other, but by auditing different processes against standards, it became possible to benchmark process performance, and the dotted lines indicate efforts in trying to make the system more connected through communication of benchmark results. Similar to the technical system, however, the topology for the operation of the QMS is the same sort of star topology, meaning that everything more or less depends on the component in the centre of the figure.

In order to avoid a collapse similar to how the technical system collapsed, the quality manager tried various ways of making the system more robust, such as including people with various sorts of competence in the quality department, networking with the internal audit, taking part in a national quality management network for public sector organizations, networking with similar organizations in other Nordic countries, and trying to involve the National Audit in the quality management.

Some of the most important efforts were the attempts to try to influence the rewriting of the current procedures and methods to include measurements and elementary statistical quality control, such as statistical process control (SPC) and Pareto analysis, as a part of the method. By having both the data collection and much of the analysis moved from the central node in figure 2 and have it distributed within the methods applied in the other nodes of the diagram, perhaps even have the methods integrated in the computer-based information infrastructure, would clearly make the QMS less vulnerable. This was, however, difficult to achieve.

The diagram in figure 3 illustrates the history of the QMS so far. The black arrow showing the rapid improvements during the period 2000-2004 is supposed to indicate what was experienced as an exponential growth in terms of how the system evolved from success building on success in starting with simple ideas that worked and got gradually more complex with time.

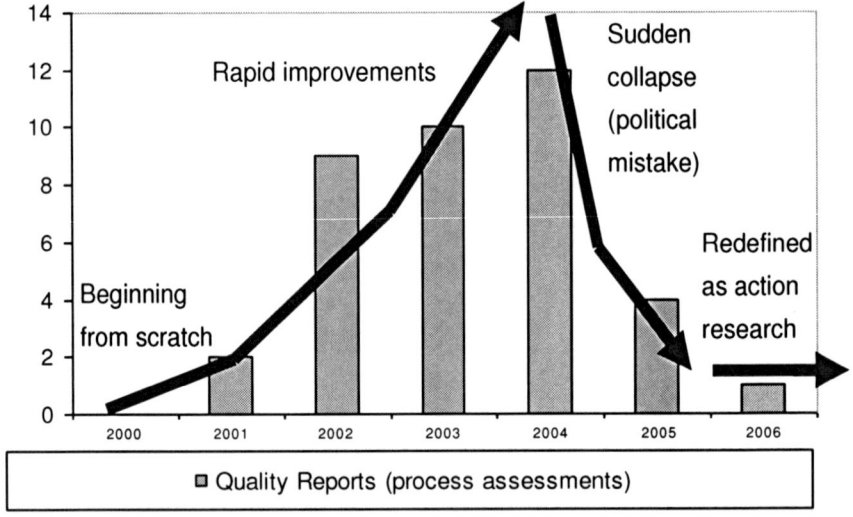

Figure 3 Visual summary of the QMS development

Although the CAS-based QMS design was based on the idea that tensions and conflict was necessary for getting the system made, after five years of successful quality management the quality manager made some political mistakes and was consequently moved into another department. The QMS collapsed, although there is now another attempt to rebuild by aligning with academia and doing quality audits in the shape of action research rather than the more conventional earlier approach.

How the system collapsed

Various attempts were done in order to teach people the principles of ISO 9000, asking managers to define measurements, teaching statistical quality control to staff etc., but with limited success. The only way to get the workers to pay attention to quality control routines was by helping them in doing and analysing measurements, using the principle of "what gets measured gets done" as a deliberate part of the quality system design (Øgland, 2008) and otherwise document and distribute documents on a wide scale to create an illusion of management commitment to quality in order to make the workers focused (Øgland, 2007).

One of the key elements of quality control was the top management signature for starting critical production. Conducting quality audits along the development cycle and hand in the audit results as an appendix to the production signature sheet was good timing for getting management commitment for further process improvement. Rather than having a special meeting for presenting quality challenges and making priorities on how to improve for the next financial year, this part of the ISO 9001 requirements (clause 5.6), could be easily implemented as a part of the annual production year, evaluating the QMS related to the specific production line just before the system got signed off. Not only was this practical from the point of view of getting management signatures, but it was also a good moment for having completed a QMS evaluation as any problems that might occur during production could then be used for systematically improving the way the QMS had been evaluated.

On the other hand, at the moment of production sign-off, many people had worked extra hard to make sure that production would run smoothly, so it was not necessarily the psychologically best moment for giving people feedback on how they had been following various standards and procedures. Perhaps they had even deliberately avoided certain procedures in order to make sure that everything would work out fine. Because of this, it was necessary to be less exploratory and more specific in how audits and investigations were being done, focusing on the most important issues, and presenting the results in a constructive manner.

Inspired by Deming's example of how to break down a bank into organizational units and define objectives to improve in each such unit, including the unit for "productivity and quality analysis" (Deming, 1986, pp. 227-238), it seemed like a good idea to for the quality management unit to carry out self-assessments against ISO 9001 and various other standards that were being used in the organization. The quality manager believed not only would this contribute valuable experience in how to interpret the standards and testing various audits and assessments on the group before going into the field, but also that this approach might make the quality management people starting to talk the same language so that everybody would understand more clearly what the expectations of the job were.

However, the quality management people responded far more violently in being measured and asked to follow standards than anybody else in organization. In fact, when the people who spent all of their working hours on measuring and evaluating others were themselves measured and evaluated against international standards on how to do quality audits, IT audits, quality management etc., this quickly escalated into a situation where the quality manager was removed from his position into a position where he was supposed to do research on quality management while another person (previously second in command in the quality department) should handle the quality management issues.

Why the quality management system collapsed

From the perspective of the quality manager (writer of this paper), the fragile topology illustrated in figure 2 and the ongoing tensions generated by "what gets measured gets done" among workers and visualizing trends that might not fit with the political games carried out by various actors in management, were sufficient reasons for not feeling too secure about the robustness of the QMS design.

However, as the idea of "taking ones own medicine" in terms of applying ISO 9000 on the quality organization as an isolated sub-organization within the larger organization seemed like a good idea at the time, the negative reaction among fellow quality management experts within the organization was highly surprising. In order to get a better understanding of why this didn't work out as expected, one of the first investigations carried out within the new position of being expected to the quality management research, was to attend a national conference of certified ISO 9000 quality experts to figure out whether what had happened within the organization was a special cause due to the people involved or whether it might be part of a larger pattern.

By first doing an e-mail survey, prior to meeting people at the conference, six of the twenty-eight (21%) responded. Five of the respondents were clearly negative, as if the answers to the questions were more or less obvious. One person shaped his argument in pro/contra-reasoning, but still ended up being negative.

1. *If I were a single-person consultancy service specialising in quality management (e.g. giving courses in ISO 9001 or aiding organizations in building ISO 9001 quality management systems, "quality management for hire" etc) should I then adjust my consultancy management system to comply with the ISO 9001:2000 standard? Why - why not?*

2. *If I were a quality manager in a given organization (head of the "quality department"), independent of any requirements that might give for the organization as a whole, should I consider my own department as a single unit and make the management system for this unit compliant with ISO 9001:2000? Why – why not?*

The reason they were against applying ISO 9000 for themselves consisted of responses like (1) too much paper work, (2) too much attention to the system brings attention away from the customer, (3) more important to have all relevant information in the head that having things written down, (4) "twenty-five years of experience tells me that this is a bad idea".

The only person trying to do a balanced review, said that ISO 9001:2000 may force people to follow the routines and standards they have themselves developed, and in the case of being an ISO 9000 consultant, being certified against the ISO 9001:2000 standard this might give good publicity. Concerning the second question, he answered that the Quality Department would become competent in understanding ISO 9001:2000, but he believed focusing too much focus on the standard may lead the Quality Department into becoming isolated from the organization as a whole.

During the conference, various discussions and interviews made it possible to get more elaborate insights on these particular answers and also get responses from others who had not participated in the survey. However, not too many insights resulted from these conversations. People who were clearly trained in convincing others on why ISO 9000 might be useful for systematic performance improvement did not feel convinced that they should apply the same standards on themselves.

Based on a psychological case study of F.W. Taylor, the father of scientific management and thus the grandfather of quality management, one might speculate that people who get involved in quality management are of a particular psychological disposition, that they compensate for certain personal problems by focusing on controlling others (Kakar, 1971), but this conflicts with the fact that there is a body of quality management literature that deals with the principles of organizational quality management by emphasizing the importance of the quality people following standards and quality management principles (e.g. Roberts & Sergesketter, 1993; Deming, 1986).

Although, the investigation indicated that the behaviour of the quality people in the case study was not an isolated case, the behaviour is still inconsistent with standards and best practices used for evaluating quality management. In other words, the CAS-based QMS design should probably have anticipated some of the problems with self-directed measurements, but rather than avoiding the issue, more proper care should perhaps have been given on how to design such self-reflective standards and measurements.

Why did the opinion of the quality people matter?

Although the ISO 9001 standard requires that the quality manager shall report directly to the head of the organization (clause 5.5.2), sometimes top management may choose to meet this requirement by making the report from quality management to top management through a dotted line on the organizational chart while the solid line of responsibility may go through other departments. In this case, there was a dotted line to IT management where all the relevant quality management decisions were taken, although practical administrative issues were handled by having the quality department report to the projects department.

Although the different points of perspective seem more apparent in retrospect, quality management is sometimes seen as a part of operational research (e.g. Deming, 1994), meaning that understanding the organization as a system and identifying feedback loops for repeated measurement and documentation of continual improvement is of imperative importance in QMS design. In order to be evaluated as an efficient project manager, on the other hand, vital parameters may be issues such as being able to deliver projects on time, within cost and with a "good enough" quality. In trying to do a study through the use of soft systems methodology (Checkland, 1981), it seems reasonable to believe that one might easily end up with rich pictures indicating very different understandings of what the system is and how the system works.

This impression was further clarified by the fact that the projects people did not seem very enthusiastic about the CAS-design, feeling more comfortable with a project approach. An ISO 9001:2000 project was established in 2004, following the conventional project management principles of scoping the work, establishing steering groups, reference groups, involvement of external experts etc. Shortly before a large reorganization was carried out in 2007, the ISO 9001:2000 project was put more or less on ice as it turned out that the external consultants were too expensive, they did not properly understand the dynamics of the organization, and top management got too busy with other things than to continue monitoring the quality management project.

Another indication of the QMS failure being of systemic nature rather than caused by individuals, was the story of the new quality manager.

The new person being asked to accept the role of quality manager had been working as a part of the group for a few years and had a very good background from science and engineering. His approach was different. Based on many years of industrial experience, it was clear that he had no intension of doing the same political mistakes. Having a practical and soft-spoken engineering approach, during interviews he nevertheless explained that he had great difficulty in understanding organizational politics, feeling sidestepped in important issues related to the development of the quality management system, and generally feeling disconcerted. In some of the later interviews, he explained that he had more or less given up quality management altogether, rather focusing on project management as this made him feel much more valuable in terms of actually getting work done and being visible to the organization.

Starting from scratch again

While a somewhat stressful situation at the time, being asked to give up operational quality management in order to pursue a career in quality management research was an interesting move when viewed in retrospect. The writer turned organizational researcher in the staff of the IT director, thus moved away from the people who saw the world from a projects perspective and into the world of a person who had a systems perspective of the organization. The challenge now was to reframe the earlier 15 years of quality management engineering into the perspective of research, trying to figure out how to achieve similar QMS design results or perhaps even better QMS design results when describing the design process as a research process (action research process) rather than a conventional quality management process.

In 2007, during a major reorganization, it was decided that the IT department should no longer exist in its current shape. The IT director was asked to become a representative of OECD in Paris, and the project manager became the new IT director. The writer was consequently reorganized to report to the new IT director, but with his new organizational responsibilities, interviews and discussions with the new IT director indicated a new way of thinking that was clearly much more systems-like. As the new IT director now had to live with the responsibilities of his former projects – and not only ship and deliver – his new way of thinking about the organization seemed to fit with the new responsibilities. From the present perspective, this seems like good soil for starting a new quality management systems design, a design based on evolutionary CAS development methods rather than the waterfall project methods that had previously failed.

In recent interviews, the new IT director emphasizes issues such as:

- ❏ The organization needs to reduce costs, even though the latest IT projects have produced costly solutions that eats a fair amount of the annual budgets

- ❏ Too much of the production is manually driven, and should be automated to reduce errors and costs

- ❏ There is need for more improvement of test routines to prevent costly errors in production

- ❏ While the earlier organization was a sequence of silos with little communication between them, the current organization is becoming more like layers of tilted silos with little communication between management levels.

- ❏ Present IT models, such as IS Lite, the Y model and quality management framework such as ITIL have so far been costly and less successful than anticipated

- ❏ The quality management system should to a greater extent be linked with the part of the management system that communicates directly with the Ministry of Finance

❑ The quality management system should be coordinated with the risk management method developed and implemented by the internal audit

❑ There should be a gradual change from reactive quality control to proactive quality assurance

❑ The definition and implementation of Service Level Agreements (SLA) should be an important area of investigation for quality management

❑ There should be a focus on investigating process improvement and quality management efforts that were started prior to reorganization but where there seems to be less focus now

As the research continues and slowly tries to encapsulate the aspects of the quality management system that was previously made through internal consultancy, some of the ideas listed above might serve as starting point for processes to address when starting new loops of process improvement.

Discussion

Although some comments could have been made on how the technical quality management system from the first part of the case story fitted with the CAS theory, the discussion focuses on the life cycle of the socio-technical quality management system illustrated in figure 3. The first part of the discussion consists of addressing each of the "nine laws" of CAS design as defined by Kelly (1994, chapter 24). The second part addresses three key issues related to the QMS design failure, and discusses these issues in terms of implications for revised CAS-based strategies for QMS design.

How did the QMS design fit with the CAS design framework?

Insights reported from the case study, with some additional comments for explaining additional case study details, is used below to show how the QMS design fitted with the CAS design ideas suggested by Kelly through his list of "nine laws".

Distribute being

As was illustrated in both the case of the technical quality management system and the socio-technical quality management system, the system itself consisted of various entities that were loosely or tightly coupled in some way or another. This approach made the system robust in the way that the failure or shut-down of one particular computer program or one particular organizational process did not cause failure or shut-down for the system as a whole.

However, when the total system ultimately failed, the systemic reason for this was that the quality manager was also a part of the system. In fact, he was the central node in a complex adaptive system that was structured as a star topology. Both the technical system and the socio-technical system failed in the same way. Shortly after the key person in the middle of the star topology was removed from the structure, the structure collapsed. If one should compare this with complex adaptive systems in nature, such as flocks of birds or streams of fish, the natural design is generally more robust in the sense that it does not depend on one particular member for its survival.

Although there were various attempts of improving the robustness of the QMS by having the quality department aligning with various other actors, the method of building and improving quality management systems by performing audits is a type of activity that many are reluctant to do, as it is an intellectual challenge which has a tendency for creating negative emotional feedback. It is the sort of activity that probably only "die hard" quality management people would feel emotionally rewarding to do.

On the other hand, if one were to redesign this approach as research (doing audits as a way of collecting research data), while the emotional feedback for improving the organization would still be mostly negative from the organization itself, feedback from the academic community could perhaps compensate for this as the method itself seems to work quite well. Nevertheless, it is not a robust design as it depends to a very large degree on one particular member of the organization.

Control from the bottom up

An aspect that caused serious problems, was the idea to try to make the quality management system self-referential or "autopoietic" through the mechanism of making twofold use of certain quality standards and methods. The ISO 9001:2000 standard was used both for evaluating the organization and for making self-assessments within the group of quality management people. The aim of the ISO 9001:2000 quality standard is to improve management systems, but the explicit aim of improving performance was not much of an issue neither among the quality people within the organization nor among the quality experts interviewed at the QUALIS conference. They responded to ISO 9001:2000 as a tool for regulation, and although they might believe that it could help the organization as a whole to improve, they did not want to apply ISO 9001:2000 on themselves.

Nevertheless, the control mechanism applied within the CAS-design of the QMS was not to interfere in how the standards, procedures and control mechanisms were designed by the people responsible for each of the relevant processes. The role of the quality department was to conduct audits for checking whether such local control system existed and whether they were performing as expected. Control was being carried out from the bottom up, although the quality department could perhaps be seen as a top-down mechanism for checking (controlling) whether the local controls were working.

Cultivate increasing returns

The bar diagram in figure 3, documenting some of the measurable aspects of the QMS life cycle, shows that the first period from the conception of the quality management system design, until it reached a peak and collapsed, was a period characterised by exponential growth. By starting many improvement processes in parallel, leaving some to die while others where nurtured and grown until they reached into other and more high level improvement processes, the system grew in an exponential way. The development method was a typical example of "success building upon success". What were not fully explained in the case study though were the limits to growth in terms of the quality department having limited resources for doing audits. Even though the audit processes themselves got more standardized and more efficient, there would clearly have been a point where it would be difficult to start more auditing (without hiring more people) and then the system would have reached some kind of stasis. On the other hand, this type of speculation does not necessarily contradict the principle of "cultivate increasing returns", as there are limits to growth in most ecological systems.

Grow by chunking

Kelly (1994, p. 469) explains what he means by growth by chunking:

"The only way to make a complex system that works is to begin with a simple system that works. Attempts to instantly install highly complex organization – such as intelligence or a market economy – without growing it, inevitably leads to failure."

The approach used within the organization consisted of working with process improvement at various levels. Some processes were chosen because they were "low hanging fruit" in terms of easy for producing results in terms of continuous process improvement, while other processes were chosen because they involved interaction with top management at critical moments such as signing off production of tax cards or pre-completed self-declarations. All such process improvement projects started at a very simple level, simply counting the number of defects when comparing software documentation with software documentation standards or comparing the actual software with the software standards. As the process improvement processes were aligned with the annual business cycles, with each year the processes were slightly changed, and gradually more and more processes interacted with each other and started evolving a sort of quality management ecology of standards, procedures, measurements, statistical results and action plans.

Maximize the fringes

As illustrated in the case, the design method did not focus on putting the organization in turning everybody into believing the same sort of thing. The general idea was just to support people with measurements and statistics on what they were doing, often making conflicts of interest more visible and thus heating up organizational temperature. The general idea was not primarily to make people more happy, but to make them reflect more on what they were doing, and ultimately make them more conscious of the quality of their own work and how that quality of work affected others in the organization.

Honour your errors

As the aim of quality management systems is to create process improvement, there is always a need to do assessments to figure out the current level as a baseline for measuring further improvement. This principle does consequently not necessarily have anything to do with the fact that CAS was used as a design principle, but rather a consequence of the nature of quality management. It could be pointed out, however, that although the ISO 9001 standard require an organization to provide evidence of improvement (e.g. clause 8.5), such "evidence" is always object to interpretations and what counts as improvement or not may be an issue of debate or negotiation between process owners and process auditors. Nevertheless, in this particular case, all processes were improving in measurable ways as a consequence of the QMS methodology.

Pursue no optima; have multiple goals

While both the organizations in the case story would probably be able of state their ultimate goals as keeping relevant departments of the ministry happy, making sure there are no problems found as a consequence of national audit or that the general public are sufficiently satisfied with the services that the organizations deliver, the QMS itself was designed in a way that consisted of running a large number of audit projects at the same time. Even though one might argue that the aim of the QMS was to optimize the quality costs of the organizations, i.e. making sure that the costs of appraisals, corrections and preventions were kept at an optimal level, the system itself had no way of figuring out how to do this. Although there were cost limits to how many quality audits (appraisals) could be done, based on how many people were employed in the quality department, the cost of corrections could at best be estimated based on risk analysis, and there were no formal methods of measuring the cost of the people in the organization developing and improving structures and methods (preventive action) as this was either integrated with normal work or done without measuring the costs.

Seek persistent disequilibrium

Similar to Kurt Lewin's T-group studies (Gold, 1999), the CAS method for QMS design was a way of stimulating debate and controversy rather than searching for a state of equilibrium where all organizational members were happy. Unlike Lewin, however, the process did not go through stages of un-freeze-change-freeze but simply tried to create continuous tension by giving feedback on all processes in order to make it easier for the people to do small improvements rather than to leave things as they were. Having the organization maintain disequilibrium was a part of the QMS design.

Change changes itself

The final of Kelly's laws seems more to be an observation of how complex adaptive systems work rather than a design rule. If one were to interpret the statement as a design rule, the key idea would perhaps be to make sure that it is possible for the organization to change itself. The way this was done within the organization was by having the workers themselves design the standards to be followed and then use audits and measurements of performance against these standards as a way of probing whether the standards were acceptable or needed further improvement. In several cases, standards were redesigned as an immediate consequence of the standards being put to use and results being distributed to various process stakeholders. Sometimes such changes resulted in the standards being improved (from the viewpoint of the quality department) while at other times it resulted in the standards being made more flexible. Anyway the standards were being changed, illustrating how change in processes caused change in the standards the processes were based upon, and thus fitting with the idea of "change changes itself".

How did the CAS design framework explain the problems with the QMS design?

In the case story there are three issues that are particularly relevant to the collapse of the QMS. Firstly, there is the issue of the QMS star topology, having the robustness of the system depending on one particular component. Secondly, there is the issue of people working with audits and quality management being sensitive to being audited and measured themselves. Finally, there is the issue of understanding work in terms of projects or systems.

Quality management systems topology

Kelly (1994, chapter 2) uses ant colonies and bee hives as examples of complex adaptive systems. Removing one ant or one bee does not necessarily have a consequence on the colony or the hive as a system. However, one might wonder what happens if one were to remove the queen ant or the queen bee. Although the colony or hive might survive for a while, complex adaptive systems in nature also seem to contain special components that if they do not behave as leaders of the system at least they have an important role in how the system is coordinated.

On the other hand, while the quality control department had to actively control (audit) that the distributed control mechanisms in the organization were functioning, the role of the queen bee or queen ant appears to be a more passive part of the system (ibid, p. 5). Perhaps it might be possible to compare this with the sociology of science in the way that there are often a few researchers whose work are referred to much more than anything else within the community. Although such writers may be considered central nodes in the network, removing such nodes perhaps causing complete fields of research to collapse, they themselves may not have an active part in the management of the network beyond being beacons for navigation and coordination for the other researchers in the community.

A challenge for further improvement of the QMS design strategy is consequently to investigate ways of making the quality manager and the quality department more passive (implicitly managing rather than explicitly managing) and invisible while at the same time sustaining and increasing in momentum as the central node of the network. As mentioned in the case study, there was an effort on trying to embed quality control and monitoring into the automated information infrastructure of the organization. While this was not particularly successful in the case study, it nevertheless seems like a natural goal of a CAS-based QMS design strategy.

Controlling the controllers

Although it was not perfectly clear whether the particular quality management staff in the case study where behaving contrary to expected behaviour of quality personnel, or whether they might be part of a typical pattern, as the interview with the ISO 9000 experts seemed to indicate, the issue of "controlling the controllers" should be addressed as a part of the CAS-based QMS design. It does not seem to follow directly from the CAS approach itself. What the quality manager (writer of this paper) tried to do in order to improve the performance of the quality department was to try to make the quality coordinators themselves suggest how they wanted their work to be measured, in order to focus on process improvement, but all attempts, whether they were based on individual suggestions, international standards on how quality management should be done, or if it was simply to measure individual performance in relation to what the group as a whole were trying to achieve, all such efforts were met with hostility. Reflecting on various reasons for quality management people not wanting to be measured by their own standards, three explanations come to mind.

- The reluctance of being measured could be an issue of "knowing too much about the profession", as is sometimes argued in the case of "doctors being the worst patients" (Lam, 1990).

- Another possibility might be that many people involved in quality management are deliberately searching for staff positions where they can be seen as doing something vague but important, giving them personal flexibility in how they spend their day without risk of being evaluated in terms of productivity (Maier, 2004).

- A third possibility might be that they know they are not behaving according to the standards of the profession (deliberately or not), and do not see anything gained by having this documented (Marquez, 2001).

In this particular case study, however, the reason the people behaved the way they did still remains a mystery open to further investigations.

Projects and systems

An obvious answer to the conflict in organizational perspectives from the point of view of the projects people and the quality people could be that one should follow the requirements of the ISO 9001 standard and quality management literature (e.g. Deming, 1986; Juran, 1993; Beckford, 2002), namely that the quality organization should be reporting directly to the board of directors, as the organization would like the perspective of the quality management people to reflect the perspective of the top management. In practice, however, the people responsible for quality management may not be in a situation where they can influence the position of the quality department on the organizational chart, and may thus try to make the best out of situation. The case study tells a story of how networking and designing quality management processes into vital steps of business processes helped drive through improvement in areas that were outside of the scope of responsibility of the projects department. Nevertheless, not aligning quality management with the specific interests of the projects department also made the quality department less important for the projects department and ultimately expendable. While the first quality manager focused on top management interests regardless of the projects department, the second quality manager focused on the internal interests of the projects department regardless of top management. Neither approach was sustainable in the long run.

In retrospect, there are three alternative strategies that seem interesting and relevant.

- Trying to balance work between spending time on quality assurance inside a particular project, while also spending time improving the total organization.

- Define and manage some kind of TQM or ISO 9000 project that is formally dressed up as a project, but in reality follows the CAS-principles of cultivating a quality management system.

- Abandon the quality department and inhabit some other kind of department where one can do the same kind of work, although describing it as organizational development or security system development or whatever might fit the people in that department.

What happened in the case study was something very similar to the third alternative, redefining the QMS design as an action research process, and so far this looks like a very good strategy indeed.

References

Axelrod, R. & Cohen, M.D. (2000) Harnessing Complexity: Organizational Implications of a Scientific Frontier, Basic Books, New York.

Beckford, J. (2002) Quality: A Critical Introduction. Second edition, Routledge, UK.

Brooks, R. & Flynn, A. (1989) 'Fast, cheap, and out of control: a robot invasion of the solar system', Journal of The British Interplanetary Society, Vol 42 pp. 418-485.

Brooks. R. (2002) Flesh and machines: how robots will change us, Pantheon Books, New York.

Capra, F. (2002) The Hidden Connections: Integrating the biological, cognitive and social dimensions of life into a science of sustainability, Doubleday, New York.

Checkland, P. (1981) Systems Thinking Systems Practice, Wiley, Chichester.

Coghlan, D. and Brannick, T. (2001). Doing Action Research in Your Own Organization, SAGE Publications, London.

Deming, E.W. (1986) Out of the Crisis, MIT Press, USA.

Deming, E.W. (1994) The New Economics, Second Edition, MIT Press, USA.

Dooley, K., Johnson, T. and Bush, D. (1995) 'TQM, chaos, and complexity' Human Systems Management, Vol 14 No 4 pp 1-16.

Dooley, K. (1996) 'A Nominal Definition of Complex Adaptive Systems,' The Chaos Network, Vol 8 No 1 pp. 2-3.

Dooley, K. (1997) 'A complex adaptive system model of organizational change', Nonlinear dynamics, psychology and life sciences, Vol 1 No 1 pp. 69-97.

French, W.L. and Bell, C.H. (1995) Organizational Development: Behavioural Science Interventions for Organizational Improvement, 5th Edition, Prentice Hall, New York.

Gold, M. (ed.) (1999) The Complete Social Scientist: A Kurt Lewin Reader, APA Books, Washington.

Goldstein, J. (1994) The Unshackled Organization: Facing the challenge of upredictability through spontaneous reorganization, Productivity Press, Portland.

Gribbin, J. (2004) Deep Simplicity: Chaos, complexity and the emergence of life, Penguin, London.

Holland, J.H. (1995) Hidden Order: How adaptation builds complexity, Addison-Wesley, New York.

Holland, J.H. (1998) Emergence: From chaos to order, Oxford University Press, Oxford.

Hoyle, D. (2006) ISO 9000 Quality Systems Handbook, Fifth Edition, Butterworth-Heinemann, London.

Johnson, S. (2002) Emergence: The connected lives of ants, brains, cities and software, Schribner, New York.

Juran, J.M. (1965) Managerial Breakthrough: A New Concept of the Manager's Job, McGraw-Hill Educational, New York.

Juran, J.M. (1993) Juran on Quality by Design, Free Press, New York.

Kakar, S. (1971) Frederick Taylor: A study in personality and innovation, MIT Press, Massachusettes.

Kelly, K. (1994) Out of Control: The New Biology of Machines, Social Systems and the Economic World, Addison-Wesley, New York.

Lam, C. (1990) 'Doctor, how about you own health?', The Hong Kong Practitioner, Vol 12 No 12 pp 1191-1192.

Maier, C. (2004) Bonjour Paresse: De l'art et de la nécessité d'en faire le moin possible en entreprise, Editions Gallimard, Paris.

Marquez, L. (2001) 'Helping Healthcare Providers Perform According to Standards', Operations Research Issue Paper, Vol 2 No 3, USAID, USA.

Moe, M. (1995) KLIBAS – The DNMI Climatological Database System, DNMI Report no. 22/95 KLIMA, Oslo.

Øgland, P. (1999) Quality Control of Meteorological Observations from the DNMI – Airport Weather Stations: The ALF/METAR Routine, DNMI Report no. 26/99, KLIMA, Oslo.

Ogland, P. (2000) 'Quality Assurance of Data Flow and Systems Management at DNMI' in: M. Moe (ed.), Eumetnet ECSN Project: Climate Databases. Proceedings from the Oslo workshop 11.-12. October 1999, DNMI Report no. 05/00 KLIMA, Oslo, pp 56-62.

Ogland, P. (2007) 'Designing quality management systems with minimal management commitment', Systemist, Vol 29 No 3 pp 101-112.

Ogland, P. (2008) 'Software Process Improvement: What gets measured gets done', 31st Information Systems Research in Scandinavia (IRIS 31): "Challenging the Future: Context, Participation and Services", 9-12 August 2008, Åre, Sweden.

Roberts, H.V. & Sergesketter, B.F. (1993) Quality is Personal: A Foundation for Total Quality Management, Free Press, New York.

Simon, H. (1996) The Sciences of the Artificial, Third Edition, The MIT Press, Cambridge, Massachusettes.

Stacey, R.D., Griffin, D. & Shaw, P. (2000) Complexity and Management: Fad or radical challenge to systems thinking?, Routledge, London.

Tasic, V. (2001) Mathematics and the Roots of Postmodern Thought, Oxford University Press, Oxford.

Waldrop, M.M. (1992) Complexity: The emerging science at the edge of order and chaos, Touchstone, New York.

Wheatley, M. (1999) Leadership and the New Science: Discovering order in a chaotic world, Berrett-Koehler Publishers, New York.

VI

Designing quality management systems with minimal management commitment

Øgland, Petter

Department of Informatics, University of Oslo, Norway

Abstract

In literature on quality management design it is "common knowledge" that quality management will not work without management commitment. But, not always is it possible to achieve management commitment, so what to do then? Based on a longitudinal study of quality management design in a software development organisation, a systems thinking approach is presented and discussed. The main idea is that management commitment is observed through the eyes of the people being managed, and may thus be created as an illusion to compensate for a lack of the real thing. The case study shows how this can be done in a way easy to replicate.

Introduction

Beckford (2002: 311) concludes his discussion of quality management from a systems perspective by saying that "management commitment is the single most critical issue in the pursuit of quality. Without it, the programme will fail – as so many do".

However, in a busy software development environment, there may be limits to how much management can dedicate itself to setting quality objectives, making quality plans, reading defect reports and doing quality management systems reviews. The real problem of many software development organisations may thus be related to the problem of *how to design quality management systems with minimal management commitment.*

In this paper, a study of COBOL computer programmers is used as an example in order to illustrate design challenges and design ideas for a software quality management system (QMS) with minimal management commitment. The theory presented in section two refers to programmer psychology, programming standards and QMS design. In section three follows a description of the research methodology, which in this case has been chosen as design research. Results are presented in section four, and in section five follows a discussion of what has been learned through the failures and problems with the current QMS design.

Theory

The theory chapter does not aim to give a complete description of the fields discussed, but try to emphasise aspects of domain knowledge and QMS knowledge that is expected to be to of significant importance for good QMS design in an environment consisting of COBOL programmers.

Psychology of COBOL programmers

Strauss (in: Davis & Hersh, 1986: 179-186) discusses the psychology of computer programmers by starting with the comment that computer programmers are people who would much rather communicate with machines than people. He suggests that the psychology of the computer programmer may be somewhat similar to the psychology of the formula one race car driver, in terms of having a total dependence on the surrounding technology and thus expressing oneself through technology. Furthermore, he suggests that computer programming is basically something that has to be experienced from within, as it from the outside may look both forbidding and dull.

Weinberg (1971) provides a more positive picture of programmers in terms of social skills and interests, but to a certain degree the message is the same. Computer programming is associated with the ability to sustain long attention spans and the ability to concentrate. Although Csikszentmihalyi (1992) does not focus exclusively on computer programmers when researching how flow and happiness is achieved through an "autotelic" personality, his theories on how flow is achieved through relaxed balance between skills and challenges makes computer programmers an interesting example, as they frequently seem to be in states of flow for long periods of time. The activity of writing computer code is an activity that requires both discipline and creativity, and could perhaps be used as a prime example of how to achieve intellectual flow.

Programming standards and participatory design

The COBOL programming language appeared in 1959 and is one of the oldest programming languages still in use. The programming standard was designed by a committee. Is has later been redesigned as ANSI standards as COBOL-68, COBOL-74, COBOL-85 and COBOL 2002 (Ghezzi & Jazayeri, 1997).

COBOL 85 was not compatible with earlier versions. Furthermore, older versions of COBOL lacked local variables, and could not support structured programming. Joseph Brophy, of Travelers Insurance, spearheaded an effort to inform users of COBOL of the heavy reprogramming costs of implementing the new standard. As a result, the ANSI COBOL Committee received more than 3,200 letters from the public, mostly negative, requiring the committee to make changes (Wikipedia, 2007).

Standards may stir up controversy. Not particularly focused on design of internal programming standards, the Scandinavian countries in the 1960s and 1970s developed an approach to design called "participatory design" as an attempt to actively involve end-users in the design process to ensure the product designed met their needs and would be usable (Bjerknes, Ehn and Kyng, 1987).

Using academia as a part of organisational design

The Scandinavian studies of participatory design experiments were facilitated as collaborative research between industry and academia. One way of trying to achieve the effect of combining action and research is through the method of "action research" (Reason and Bradbury, 2006).

One of the more recent applications of action research in the Scandinavian community has been in the area of researching health information systems in the developing world. One of the major theoretical insights gained from these studies has been that one can use the international network of scientists as a platform for building a network of information systems in developing countries. Information systems researchers function as an "information infrastructure" for practical development of health information systems to build upon this infrastructure, just like computer systems are being built upon the information infrastructure of the Internet (Braa, Monteiro and Sahay, 2004).

Design of quality management systems

The international standard ISO 9001:2000 provides a set of requirements that define the internationally agreed upon concept of a quality management system. The standard is generic, and may be applied to all sorts of organisations or parts of organisations, regardless of size, sector and line of business. The requirements are grouped into a structure (ISO 9001 model) illustrated in figure 1.

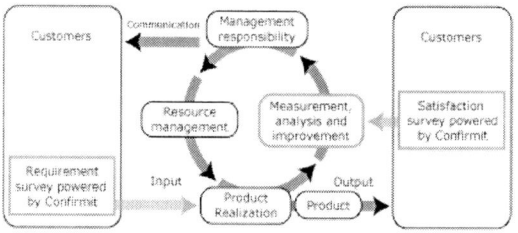

Figure 1 ISO 9001 model (http://www.confirmit.com/solutions/subject/iso_9000/print.asp)

Along with ISO 9001 there are a number of other international guidelines and standards that give requirements and expectations for design in more specific areas, such as the guidelines ISO 90003 for interpreting the ISO 9001 requirements in a software development organisation, or standards ISO 12207 for managing the software development lifecycle.

As the ISO 9001 standard is a list of requirements for producing a certifiable quality management system, it does not give advice on how to design the QMS in order to fit with both the organisation and the requirements of the standard. As pointed out by Seddon (2000), providing a good QMS design that fits with the ISO 9001 requirements is not a trivial task, illustrating his point by giving examples of cases where bad QMS design has resulted in poor quality or causing the situation to become even worse than it was before the QMS was implemented. A design approach that is more likely to succeed, he suggests, is to apply the systems thinking approach that he finds in the writings of Deming (1986; 1992).

Methodology

Design research

Simon (1996) argues that the research approach used for investigating the natural world is not the best approach for investigating the artificial world, and he defines design research as a scientific method that is different both from the positivist methods used in natural science and also different from the phenomenological methods used for understanding purpose and meaning.

The illustration in figure 2 is inspired by the guidelines provided by the Association of Information Systems (AIS, 2007) for using design research to study information systems. The inner loop turning clock-wise illustrates a typical systems developing method consisting of four steps. First the problem is formulated and a design process is used for providing a solution in the shape of a model. The model is then implemented as a system, and the system is run and monitored in order to perform an evaluation. The evaluation is used for identifying opportunities for improvement, and the cycle starts again.

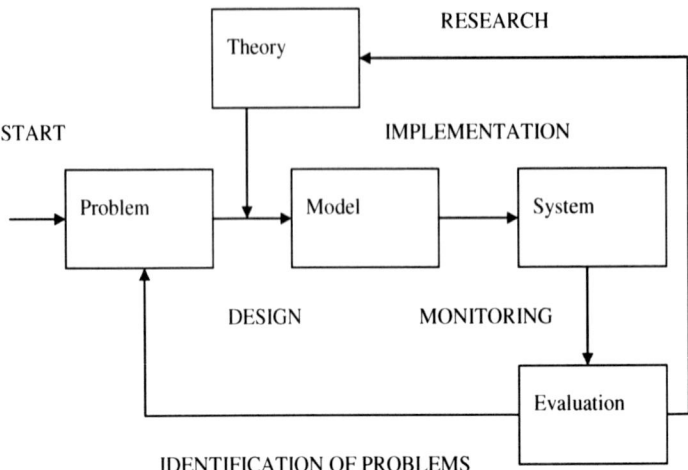

Figure 2 System design and design research

Design research is represented by the process that runs from the evaluation of a system, focusing on the problems and challenges of the system in action, in order to contribute to the theory that was used in the design. This simplified description of design research corresponds with how design and research are sometimes viewed as inverse processes (e.g. Krick, 1965).

The socio-technical quality management system

The ISO 9001:2000 standard contains requirements both with respect to humans and artefacts, meaning that the quality management system cannot only be understood as the quality manual, procedures and other documents, but the QMS must be seen as the total socio-technical system consisting of the humans and non-humans that collaborate in managing the organisation with respect to quality.

In this study, the writer of this paper has been working as a management consultant within the IT function of a large Scandinavian public sector organisation during the period from 2000 to 2007. The aim of this particular case study is to investigate the design of a subsystem of the total QMS that deals specifically with making COBOL programmers following programming standards.

The aim of the QM subsystem is to make the COBOL software more easily maintainable. In 1997 one of the COBOL programmers died, and others had to step in to maintain and improve critical software. As there was no standardised way of programming, the situation got critical, and it became obvious to everybody that there was an intense need to make sure that all COBOL software was standardised and restructured to fit with modern principles of structured programming. In the strategic plan for the IT department, published in 1998, it was stated that all COBOL software should be compliant with internal standards based on the COBOL 85 standard and good programming practice.

The QM subsystem consists of three groups of programmers, comprising 40 COBOL programmers and three managers. These managers report to the software maintenance manager. The software maintenance manager reports to the head of the IT department. During the first five years of this study, the management consultant reported to the innovation manager, and the innovation manager reported to the head of the IT department. For the past two years, the management consultant has reported directly to the head of the IT department. The COBOL software consisted of about 1.4 million lines of code, distributed among 10 software projects.

Results

In order to design the details of the QMS in figure 1, the diagram in figure 3 illustrates relationships and flows in the part of the QMS called "product realization".

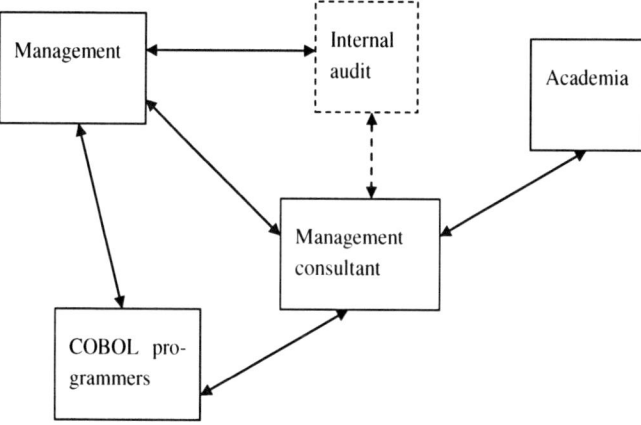

Figure 3 COBOL standardisation management system ("product realisation" in QMS)

In this design the term "management consultant" is used as the term for describing an owner of the QMS, meaning that this is a person who can destroy the system (Checkland, 1981).

Interaction between consultant and programmers

The interface between the consultant and the programmers consists of the consultant producing a note summarising the situation for the particular group of programmers, including statistical trends illustrating how the group is progressing towards the goal of making the software compliant with the standard ("zero defects"), a statistically estimated guess on how long it will take until they have completed the task (if continuing at current speed), and benchmarking results of the group against fellow groups.

The note is presented to a representative of the group of programmers during an improvised interview. The consultant is thus observing the reactions of the programmer when confronted with the statistics, and they are able to discuss the situation.

If the representative of the programming group is not available, the statistics are delivered by post, and the consultant will not be able to observe reactions. In such cases, the consultant sometimes talks to the manager instead, especially if the statistical trends seem to go in the wrong direction.

Interaction between consultant and management

Given the initial problem of lack of management commitment, one of the core design ideas was to minimize the interaction between consultant and management. In order to utilise the principles of "what managers focus on tends to get done" (Schein, 1992), it seemed worth a try just to send a copy of the evaluation results to management so that the programmers understood that managers where being informed.

By the end of each annual cycle, a full report was constructed. As the aim of the report has gradually been to develop theory that would improve the relationship with academia, the report was difficult to understand both for programmers and managers, but according to the "what gets focused gets done" hypothesis, the important issue was to make visible that quality control and academic research was getting done rather than what was the details of the academic work. The practical aspects, i.e. whether the trends showed improvement or not, were explained through executive summaries.

Interaction between consultant and internal audit

As the purpose of the internal audit is to make sure that the internal control is working properly, the annual reports from the standardisation project were also distributed to the internal audit. Just like in the case of management, the design idea behind this interface had more to do with getting the programmers to see that the internal audit were being informed than with what the internal audit were actually doing with the information they were being given. Actually, as the internal audit was a small group of people with a large internal control system to monitor, the consultant never got any feedback on the COBOL project, and never bothered to discuss this particular project with the internal audit.

Although not illustrated on figure 3, there was a continuous effort to enlarge the system by including various actors such as the National Audit, the National Quality Management Organisation and a "best practice" network of similar organisations from neighbouring countries. The idea remained the same; to give the programmers an illusion of management commitment by becoming the centre of a system that was growing all the time, over seven years. However, just like the case of the internal audit, none of these new components of the system showed any interest whatsoever in what was going on, and had no interest in performing mutual benchmarks, exchanging "best practices" or doing any sort of interaction.

Interaction between consultant and academia

Due to challenges in the organisation due to programmers not being to happy with being monitored and management not being too happy with being given statistics that indicate the processes are not running as smoothly as one would like, there is a looming chance that management will terminate the system and the consultant being unable to perform process improvement.

The reason for including academia in the QMS design is thus to use the "cultural capital" of academia as a source of power make making the QMS survive despite producing statistics that may challenge the organisation. The general idea is to use the QMS for improving the organisation rather than having the organisation terminate the QMS.

So far, three academic conference papers have been produced. One paper got accepted at a Scandinavian workshop conference on information systems research. The other paper got rejected at a European information systems conference, but was modified and got accepted for a Scandinavian workshop conference. The current paper was accepted for a systems society conference. The research questions and research approach has been slightly changed based on the feedback received through each conference feedback.

Discussion

As the hypothesis for the paper is that the current QMS design is a successful design, the purpose of this discussion is to try to explain why the design appears successful and to challenge the hypothesis by focusing on some of the weaker aspects of the design.

Overview of significant findings

Designing an environment for the COBOL programmers

When there are weak ties with management, the design idea suggests this to be compensated by stronger ties with the programmers, or at least a method for providing the programmers with an experience that would be somewhat similar to having strong management commitment.

The idea informing this particular QMS design was Csikszentmihalyi's studies of "flow" and happiness (Csikszentmihalyi, 1992). By presenting the programmers with trend curves and Pareto diagrams illustrating how they were performing against the standard and against each other, this was supposed to help the programmers find the right balance between challenge and mastery, and thus use these statistics as a way of achieving flow. Consistent with Csikszentmihalyi's theories, there were no incentives associated with the numerical feedback beyond the fact that the programmers knew that the information was also presented to management, internal audit and, more recently, also used as input for academic research. According to flow theory, the state of relaxed happiness is most easily achieved by the autotelic personality, i.e. the state of doing work for the pleasure of doing it.

From a systemic perspective, the focus of the design was to create an environment that would make the programmers work as an adaptive and evolving system, and there was consequently no need to investigate too deeply what the programmers where thinking. Preferably, in order to achieve flow, they should not be thinking too self-consciously about the standards and measurements, but just raise their personal standards to gradually match with the challenges provided by the QMS.

Applying participatory design for developing programming standards

In order to prevent unnecessary resistance and complaints from the programmers about being alienated by the internal programming standards, having the standards forced upon them, or making questions concerning the competence of the standards, one of the QMS design ideas was to have the programmers themselves design the internal programming standard, but nevertheless make sure that it was formulated in terms of explicit demands ("shalls"), so that it would be easy to produce measurement software that could be used for checking COBOL software for non-compliance with the standard. In collaboration with the programmers, various parts of literature on programming practice was used, such as Dijkstra (1968), the introductory chapter in Aho, Hopcroft and Ullman (1983) and various pieces of advice found on the internet.

Both the standard and the measurement system derived from the standard were discussed and developed among the programmers, and was signed by management, thus showing a minimal management commitment.

Whether the involvement of the programmers through a participatory design of having them design their own standards was necessary or not for achieving a good QMS design is difficult to say. Despite having defined the standards themselves, they were not particularly happy with being forced to follow a standard, although each and every one seem to be quite happy with their fellow programmers being forced to follow it.

Differences as compared to traditional QMS design

Although the Toyota quality management system seems to have been based on a similar systems thinking type of design (Fujimoto, 1999), during the literature research done as a preparation for this study, no traditional QMS design literature was found to support the idea of designing quality management systems with minimal management commitment. On the contrary, the advise found in all the literature studied, including Tricker (2005), Schlickman (2002), Deming (1986), Crosby (1979), Juran (2006), and the ISO 9000 guidelines, were supportive of the comments made by Beckford in the introduction of this paper. However, looking at the discussion forum of the American Society for Quality (ASQ, 2007) there is a thread related to complexity theory in quality management. It is possible that there may be some similarities between the design approach presented in this paper and how complex adaptive systems (CAS) may be used as a theory for QMS design (e.g. Dooley et al, 1995).

The importance of aligning with academia

As illustrated in the story of the internal audit and other units, people tend to be interested in collaboration only when they are being forced to collaborate or there are clear indications of "what's in it for me". The internal audit and the national audit were interested in auditing according to their own audit plans, and had little use or interest in being fed with additional information. People working with quality management systems in other organisations were focused on their own problems, and had little interest in cooperation or learning by benchmarking. Also, from the perspective of management, such informal international quality management networks were of little use as they could not be used for any political purpose unless the relationships were made tighter through formalisations, and if it should turn out that the benchmarks turned out less favourable for the organisation, this would only produce yet another threat for the destruction of the QMS.

Using academia as a component in the QMS design, however, proved to be a much more useful idea, provided one could find the right academic niche, such as scientists researching general systems theory, management systems theory or information systems theory. Establishing a contact between the management consultant working with the day to day practical problems of QMS design and information systems scientists developing theories on management information systems design, and testing such theories through a network of international information systems studies, proved to be a success.

Unless the previous relationships, that were established in order to create an illusion of management commitment, the relationship with academia was a different type of relationship as it was a two-way relationship for creating a research-action process that would be of mutual interest. Besides, establishing contacts with academia was something that gave prestige to management, and thus reducing the risk of the QMS being destroyed.

Consideration of the findings in light of exiting research studies

It is "common knowledge" in quality management literature in general and software process improvement management literature in particular that quality management systems are difficult to design, difficult to implement, and seldom have a life span longer than two years Furthermore, in order to achieve success, there are several factor that need to be present, such as management commitment, measurements connected to economic parameters and other issues that seem important but may be difficult to achieve.

In the study documented through this paper, none of the usual "must have" conditions are present, and yet the QMS has lasted for over seven years and is still viable. What seems to be radically different in this particular study, as compared to others studies, is the emphasis on treating the organisation as a system. Rather than starting by a detailed clock-work design of each component of the system and making sure that everything is perfectly optimal, the driving idea has been to view the QMS as an organic entity and try to produce and environment for the system that may work as a learning environment, appealing to the sportsmanship, pride, pleasure of doing good work, etc of the programmers by providing them with numerical feedback.

Implications for current theory

Looking at the issue of designing quality management systems from a soft systems perspective rather than a hard systems perspective, makes it possible to challenge the assumption of management commitment. What this particular case study illustrates is that lack of management commitment can be compensated by trying to establish and illusion of management commitment. What matters is not what the situation looks like for somebody observing the system from the outside, but what the situation looks like from the perspective of the COBOL programmers. If it is possible to convince the COBOL programmers that there is a strong management commitment, meaning that following programming standards and producing high quality maintainable software is something that is considered to be of great importance, then it doesn't really matter what management may think.

Although such ideas are not specifically discussed by Seddon (2000), the ideas seem to fit well with his soft-systems interpretation of Deming's later writing (Deming, 1992).

Careful examination of findings that fail to support the hypothesis

Checkland (1981: 318) uses the term "system owner" for the person or persons who might be capable of destroying the system. In the case of the quality management system discussed here, the main owners seem to be the head of the IT department, the management consultant and the COBOL programmer who is delivering statistics to the management consultant. As this particular programmer is about to retire, something have to be done if the QMS is not to be destroyed, and it clearly reveals that depending too much on key personnel for running is a bad design feature in the long run, although it was perhaps an essential feature of the early design, in order to build on the few key people who had the knowledge and motivation for making the system work.

Whether the management consultant is capable of destroying the system or not is not of great concern for the management consultant per se, but it ties him up with this particular quality management project, demanding resources and making him less flexible in order to investigate similar projects. Of course, from the perspective of the organisation, it may not be all that useful to have projects depending too much on singular people.

The greatest threat to the system, however, is top management. The design of the QMS is based on the assumption that "no news is good news" whenever management is concerned. If the statistical trends do not show improvement, it may be easier for management to shut down the system and play ignorant than actually do something about it. Thus the problem of the management consultant is to convince management that everything is fine and working smoothly while, on the other hand, convincing that programmers that they need to shape up and focus on keeping with the programming standards and generally improving whatever they are doing. On the other hand, if the programmers are stressed too much, they may complain to management, thus making management shutting down the quality management system anyway.

Limitations of the study that might affect the validity or generalisation of the results

It is difficult to generalise from a single case study. There are various factors that might be questioned, such as the study being carried out among software programmers in a Scandinavian public sector organisation. Software programmers may respond differently to standards, measurements and quality management systems than other professions. Scandinavian culture may be different to other cultures. Public sector may be different to private sector. Nevertheless, the study provides a method and a repeatable example of what has been successful in one organisation. As the results appears to be contrary to common knowledge among academics and practitioners in management consulting, the study should at least be a possible reference point for doing more studies of a similar kind.

Recommendations for further research

Although the ISO 9001 requirement standard is used as a part of the theory in this study, the QMS design in section four was not fully compliant with ISO 9001:2000. In developing a design theory for quality management systems with minimal management commitment, it would be interesting to investigate to which extent such a theory could be generalised for designing quality management systems compliant with the international minimum requirements for quality management systems, i.e. ISO 9001. In this context, it is particularly interesting that there are clauses in ISO 9001:2000 setting requirements to management commitment, something that would make the "management without managers" approach (Koch and Godden, 1996) interesting to study.

Implications for professional practice or applied settings

As this paper documents the personal experience of an internal quality management consultant in a public sector IT organisation, the story of the QMS design has been a story of personal transformation from a traditional analytical quality management approach to a systems thinking quality management approach. The experience has not been an experience of finding anything wrong with the

ISO 9000 standards or experts in industrial engineering, but rather an experience in terms of ideas from typical "hard systems thinkers" proving even more insightful when combined with a "soft systems approach".

Although the ideas in this study are influenced by how various systems models may be used for augmenting the quality management strategies, as suggested by Beckford (2002), the results from the study are more optimistic than Beckford, suggesting that even with minimal management support, the quality manager (management consultant) need not despair. Insights from systems thinking may stimulate good results.

References

Aho, A.V., Hopcroft, J.E. and Ullman, J. (1983) Data structures and algorithms, Addison-Wesley, USA.

AIS (2007) Association for Information Systems, Design Research in Information Systems, http://www.isworld.org/Researchdesign/drisISworld.htm

ASQ (2007) American Society for Quality, Discussion Boards, Complexity Theory in Quality, http://www.asq.org/discussionBoards/forum.jspa?forumID=50

Beckford, J. (2002) Quality: A Critical Introduction. Second edition, Routledge, UK.

Bjerknes, G., Ehn, P., & Kyng, M. (Eds.), Computers and Democracy - A Scandinavian Challenge, Aldershot, UK.

Braa, J., Monteiro, E. and Sahay, S. (2004) 'Networks of Action' MIS Quarterly, Vol 28 pp 1-26.

Checkland, P. (1981) Systems Thinking, Systems Practice, Wiley, UK.

Crosby, P.B. (1979) Quality is Free, Signet, USA.

Csikszentmihalyi, M. (1992) Flow: The Psychology of Happiness, Rider, USA.

Deming, E.W. (1986) Out of the Crisis, MIT Press, USA.

Deming, E.W. (1992) The New Economics, MIT Press, USA.

Dijkstra, E.W. (1968) 'Go To Statement Considered Harmful' Communications of the ACM, Vol 11 No 3 pp 147-48.

Davis, J.D. and Hersh, R. (1986). Descartes' Dream: The World According to Mathematics, HBJ, New York.

Dooley, K., Johnson, T. and Bush, D. (1995) 'TQM, chaos, and complexity' Human Systems Management, Vol 14 No 4 pp 1-16.

Flood, R.L. (1993) Beyond TQM, John Wiley and Sons, UK.

Fujimoto, T. (1999) The Evolution of a Manufactoring System at Toyota, Oxford University Press, USA.

Ghezzi, C. and Jazayeri, M. (1997) Programming Language Concepts, Wiley, USA.

Juran, J.M. (2006) Juran on Quality by Design: The New Steps for Planning Quality into Goods and Services, Free Press, USA.

Koch, R. and Godden, I. (1996) Managing without Management: A Post-Management Manifesto for Business Simplicity, Nicholas Brealy Publishing, UK.

Krick, E.V. (1965) An Introduction to Engineering and Engineering Design, Wiley, USA.

Reason, P. and Bradbury, H. (2006) Handbook of Action Research: Concise Paperback Edition, Sage, UK.

Schein, E. (1992) Organisational Culture and Leadership, Pfeiffer Wiley, USA.

Schlickman, J. (2003) ISO 9001:2000 Quality Management System Design, Artech House Publishers, USA.

Seddon, J. (2000) The Case Against ISO 9000: How to Create Real Quality in your Organisation, Oak Tree Press, UK.

Simon, H. (1996) The Sciences of the Artificial, MIT Press, USA.

Tricker, R. (2005) ISO 9001:2000 for Small Businesses, Butterworth-Heinemann, UK.

Weinberg, G. (1971) The Psychology of Computer Programming, Dorset House, USA.

Wikipedia (2007) COBOL, http://en.wikipedia.org/wiki/Cobol

THE ADJUDICATION COMMITTEE'S EVALUATION OF THE CANDIDATE'S DISSERTATION

(Is to be submitted to the Department 5 weeks prior to the planned disputation, the evaluation must reach the Faculty no later than 4 week before the planned defence)

The adjudication committee has had the following members:

Professor Jan Ljungberg, Department of Applied Information Technology IT-University, Göteborg University

Professor Anita Mirijamdotter, Informatics Department, Linnaeus University,

Professor Ole Hanseth, Institutt for informatikk, Universitetet i Oslo

Petter Øgland has written the dissertation with the title:

" Mechanism design for total quality management: Using the bootstrap algorithm for changing the control game"

Evaluation of the candidate's dissertation, each of the following aspects must be answered:

The dissertations field of research:

The field of research is Total Quality Management (TQM) and Quality Management Systems (QMS) in relation to information systems development and information infrastructures.

The content and objective of the dissertation (short description, work of great merit and other important details on the theoretical and/or experimental side should be mentioned):

The dissertation includes 6 individual papers and a kappa which summaries the contributions of the papers and synthesises the findings to reflect the overall objective. The candidate addresses Total Quality Management (TQM) as a methodology for improving software development processes. He points at difficulties to implement TQM and suggests building on a design theory, the Bootstrap Algoritm (BA), to overcome theses difficulties. The research then sets out to explore the stability and robustness of the BA approach including its impact for successful TQM implementation and proposes a set of hypothesis, which is then operationalized into research questions. The lenses used for investigating the appropriateness of the BA algorithm for successful TQM implementation are game theories and systems theory.

The objective is to contribute to successful TQM implementation in complex environments (both technical and social complexity).

The candidate's original contribution and independence in research:

The candidate applies a set of theories on the problem of TQM implementation, like the bootstrap algorithm theory (as applied on designing information infrastructures), game theory (especially the monopoly model) and systems theories to address implementation in social and technical complex environments. His studies are characterised by reflective practice (reflections on practice and reflections in practice), which he illustrates through the methodology of Canonical Action Research. The principles of this research methodology are most appropriate to the candidate's action oriented approach. His empirical research is reported in three cycles which span for almost 20 years. Each cycle represents gradual advancement of findings of the applicability of the chosen theoretical lenses.

The dissertation represents clearly a large amount of work and delivers good insights on the problems to successfully implement a quality management system, and how to possibly overcome them.

The contributions are, in particular

- application of the bootstrap algorithm for the design of TQM implementations

- application of game theories for exploring TQM implementation

- longitudinal research on TQM implementation

The scientific standard of the dissertation (strength and weaknesses):

The dissertation is a well-written thesis with mature and deep theoretical discussions. The reference list is impressive, and it is obvious that the author is familiar with the theories he is discussing. A core set of theories (systems theory, the monopoly model and the bootstrap algorithm) are intelligently used on TQM implementation issues occurring in an action research project spanning over almost 20 years.

Some weaknesses:

TQM is an organizational change/development method. There is very little discussion in the thesis about organizational change and no relation to the change discourse. Still quite much reference to general change literature is used to set the stage for TQM. Positioning the thesis in a more generic change discourse could have led to a more general discussion of the results of the thesis.

The merits of TQM are basically taken for granted; no critical discussion of TQM is taking place.

The relation and differentiation between TQM and Quality Management Systems (QMS) are omitted.

Altogether, this leads to a slightly unclear positioning.

Although, an in many ways impressive theoretical discussion, the down side is that the thesis become somewhat eclectic. It is not totally convincing that all the theories that are presented are really needed, and how they sometimes hang together. Some cuts from Occam's razor would have been beneficial to the thesis.

The candidate's perspective on the research area and his/her ability to view own research in a greater context:

The candidate has been exploring the issue of TQM implementation through many years of practice. He relates this experience to applicable action research methodology to make sense of his process and to explicate the findings. He also creatively includes theories and models taken from other domains to enable viewing the research from novel perspectives.

The candidate relates his approach to the prevailing scientific discourse on epistemological traditions. He prefers to illustrate how he relates to different epistemologies depending on his research phase rather than position himself. This is not common from a scientific perspective. However, from the viewpoint of practice this is understandable.

The technical quality of the dissertation (outline, depiction, general impression, level within an international setting):

The dissertation kappa is mostly very pedagogically and well written and refers to the content and contributions of the individual papers in several places. It is well balanced in terms of the content of individual chapters.

However, the Introduction is a bit lengthy. Here the basic theories (TQM and Bootstrap Algorithm, BA) are briefly presented, including relating game models to TQM and a systems model to TQM and BA. The chapter also includes identified knowledge gaps in BA research when related to TQM, which are then formulated as hypothesis to be addressed in the dissertation. This means that this first chapter builds up a complex argumentation for the approach of this research and includes a variety of perspectives including combining these in a creative manner. So it is not altogether clear what the research is about and aims to achieve until other chapters have been studied.

Other comments (any dissents in the committee should be mentioned here):

The report shall conclude whether the dissertation is worthy of being defended:

☒ The dissertation is worthy of defense without changes

☐ The dissertation is worthy of defense, but the dissertation or the scientific work has minor shortcomings that should be corrected before the defense. The candidate should normally be able to do this within two months. No re-examination is necessary.

☐ The dissertation is possibly worthy of defense, but the dissertation or the scientific work has major shortcomings that should be corrected before it can be defended. The candidate should normally be able to do this within six months. The dissertation should be re-examined by the original adjudication committee before final approval for defense.

☐ The dissertation or the scientific work falls short of the standards required for a PhD, and it is found not worthy of defense.

PLACE: Gothenburg **DATE:** 2013-10-24

SIGNATURES:

Jan Ljungberg	**Anita Mirijamdotter**	**Ole Hanseth**
Opponent 1	Opponent 2	Administrator

March 5th, 2006

Department of Informatics
University of Oslo
P.O. Box 1080, Blindern, 0316 Oslo (Norway)

The role of the quality manager in large public sector organizations: Project proposal

1. Background

Information systems development (ISD) involves risk, and failures remain common despite advances in development tools and technologies. While the Norwegian Tax Authorities (NTAX) have generally received positive publicity with respect to their efforts on improving public services, there is a high level of complexity in running software development projects and maintaining software solutions. There is a high level of interaction between departments within NTAX and a low tolerance for error. The organization is constantly being monitored by the Department of Finance (FIN) and the Auditors General (AG).

As strategy for preventing problems, NTAX use various quality assurance methods, such as developing and improving technical schemes and management methods, certifying personnel to international standards, and participating in networks for sharing best practices.

The current quality assurance approach is developed as a set of policies, strategies and standards, defined as a part of the information security management system (NTAX, 1996), and to be used as a part of the general NTAX management system. The Quality Management System (QMS) was operationally implemented five years later by appointing a Quality Manager for coordinating the Quality Function (Quality Management Organization) (NTAX, 2001).

There are many challenges in managing the Quality Function, and from the point of view of NTAX, it is important to understand how to organize and utilize quality management in a manner that both generates efficient quality improvement and fits with corporate culture (NTAX, 1997; DNV, 2005).

2. Quality management in complex bureaucratic organizations

A recent external investigation of the IT function of NTAX concluded that NTAX could be interpreted as a Machine Bureaucracy developing in the direction of an Administrative Adhocracy (Mintzberg, 1983; Statskonsult, 2002). When standardized and repetitive routines of the tax administration are taken over by computers, the computer department automatically grows in power, regardless of how power may have been defined according to the organizational charts.

From a quality management point of view, this is interesting in two aspects. Firstly, the power relationships defined on the organizational charts may not be the best way to understand the operational QMS. Secondly, the IT strategy and the methods of further computerizing the Machine Bureaucracy could have a major strategic importance for how the QMS is maintained and improved.

As quality management normally works within the paradigm of viewing the organization as a cybernetic system to be optimized (Morgan, 1997: chapter 3), the Administrative Adhocracy produces a challenge in terms of a paradigm of complexity, flow and growth (ibid: chapter 8). Some writers (e.g. Kelly, 1994: 196) have pointed out that the Japanese quality management

P.1

practices (for the IT function) follow this new paradigm (see also: Liker, 2004; Womack & Jones, 2003).

One of the core ideas in complexity theory as applied to management problems, is to let go of central planning and control, but rather distribute the system into weakly tied units and let this loosely connected system steer itself bottom-up (e.g. Kelly, 1994: 468-469).

However, in order to let loose on the overall control, more control much be put into each separate unit. Kelly (ibid: 469) describes this as the "Fourth Law of God", stating that "the only way to make a complex system work is to begin with a simple system that works; [...an ecology] is created from assembling it incrementally from simple modules that can operate independently."

If we regard the QMS as a Complex Adaptive System (CAS) (Battram, 1996), the Fourth Law could be interpreted as controlling and improving the complete QMS by making sure each weakly tied unit follows a *strictly deterministic logic* like, say, a computer program. According to the CAS theory, this would constitute a robust strategy for making the organization "automatically" grow, long-term, in the direction of "organizational excellence" (Oakland, 2001).

Without explicitly referring to the theory of CAS, it is my impression that similar ideas are prevalent in the information systems research environment at UiO. It has, for instance, been suggested (Hanseth, 2005) that insights from current research on broadband deployment and development of communication standards (research that reveal CAS-like structures and strategies), should be used for implementing information systems in health-care organizations.

At the moment there seems to be much interest in applying complexity theory into the area of organization and management research (Stacey et al, 2000; Urry, 2003), including the problems of quality management (Dooley et al, 1995). The idea of seeing the quality manager as an actor (component) within a CAS seems to be implicit in some of this research (e.g. Dooley, 2002), but investigations of the role of the quality manager as a leverage node of the system (and what the programmable logic of this node might be) appears to be unexplored territory.

3. Research Objective

The object of the research is to investigate the problem of quality management within the dynamics of an organization transforming itself from a Machine Bureaucracy to an Administrative Adhocracy, narrowing in on the role of the quality manager as a node of the QMS viewed as a CAS.

There are three main questions I would like to address:

- Is it possible to describe a simple logic of quality management as if the quality manager and the rest of the quality management personnel were robots?
- How does one create "robotic" quality coordinators as actors in a CAS?
- What is the impact of this approach?

I plan to investigate these questions by researching literature, interviewing quality management personnel, finding out what they do and why. To which extent the quality managers can document significant trends of organizational improvement (7 years or more), as a result of the quality management approach, will be of particular interest.

Framework for literature research and interviews will be drawn from clause 5.5.2 in ISO 9001:2000 and various aspects of CMM / ISO 15504, ISO 12207, ISO 19011, CobiT, TickIT, ITIL, internal goals and regulations of the organization and what else might help define the role of the quality manager.

4. Research Methods

The method will focus on building a general QMS model based on the CAS point of view. The model should be sufficiently abstract to fit various organizations, but also sufficiently detailed to be used for predicting performance (on a simple level) of a concrete Quality Function, such as the NTAX Quality Function, and also other organizations if possible.

For building such a model, literature on organizations, management and complexity need to be done, emphasizing the dynamics of an organization from a Machine Bureaucracy to an Administrative Adhocracy.

Data collection will focus on interviewing and assessing the quality manager and key personnel within his circle of influence. The assessments will be structured according to various quality management standards, and will be based on available documentation. Interviews will be done partly to validate the assessments and partly as interpretive investigations in order to understand how the world-view of the quality manager is compliant with the conditions of the CAS model. If there seems to be a reasonable level of consistency, then the method will focus on how to use CAS as a language for discussing management issues.

A typical way of doing assessments of the quality manager could be to ask the questions in ISO 9004 (ISO, 2000c: Appendix A) and categorize the results according to the ISO 9004 maturity scale from 1 to 5. The parts of the CMM / ISO 15504 and CobiT assessments standards that relate to quality management could be used in a consistent manner.

In general the research will follow the conventions of Management Research (Easterby-Smith et al, 2002; Collis & Hussey, 2003), including aspects of Action Research when needed, although further details have to be discussed with each of the quality managers that are to be used as research subjects in the investigation.

5. Research Design

The larger part of the empirical work will have to concentrate on the quality management organization of NTAX, but in order to have reference data, similar types of interviews and assessments should also be done for other organizations, e.g. NTAX subcontractors, DNV and USIT.

Prof. Jens Kaasbøll of UiO has accepted the role of primary supervisor on behalf of UiO. Dr. Lars Bratthall of Det Norske Veritas (DNV Research) has accepted the role of secondary supervisor on behalf of DNV.

If it will become necessary to look for further case studies (independent organizations) for comparative analysis or testing ideas in other environments, Dr. Bratthall has suggested DNV may be able to provide samples on a case to case basis.

At the moment, UiO is carrying out research related to the development of information systems in healthcare, both nationally and in third-world countries. It seems reasonable to expect that there should be much to benefit from a co-ordination between the research proposed in this document and organizational and management research already being carried out.

6. Expected outputs

The general output questions formulated as part of the research objective (questions a, b, and c in section 3 above) are expected to be answered by creating the following outputs:

(a) One or more models, describing how various quality managers are understanding their organizations; analysis and discussions of these models in respect to how they appear useful within the framework of TQM and complexity theory.

(b) Descriptions of various types of patterns of behavior for the quality manager (i.e. what the quality manager actually does, regardless of what the mental models identified under point a might indicate); analysis and discussion of this behavior related to the aim of quality management in complex organizations and some general guidelines on what might be an optimal approach given the type of organization under consideration.

(c) Development of an hypothesis or some ideas in respect of how the CAS approach can compensate for management commitment, change of leadership, internal politics and other issues that are critical for more standard approaches to quality management.

Although the focus of the research is on the role of the quality manager, the way to evaluate the work of the quality manager is through the quality, productivity and flexibility of the organization in whole. It is expected that the output of the research will contribute in saying something about how the performance of the quality manager contributes to the performance of the organization in whole.

The results are expected to be published in journals dealing with quality management, organizational change and information systems (information infrastructure), such as *Quality Management Journal, Journal for Quality and Participation, Information and Organization, Organization Science, Organization* and *The Scandinavian Journal of Information Systems*.

7. Other benefits

The research process is expected to benefit internal quality monitoring and control in the organizations investigated as we try to integrate the research with what is the current quality control focus of each particular organization.

In the case of NTAX the most interesting improvement areas are expected to be those already being monitor by FIN and AG.

8. Budget

The research is fully financed by the Norwegian Tax Authorities.

Researcher's Contact

The researcher concerned (Petter Øgland) is presently situated within the Norwegian Tax Administration. His contact address is: Directorate of Taxes, IT Department, P.O. Box 6300 Etterstad, 0603 OSLO; phone no.: +47 22 07 74 17; e-mail: petter.ogland@skatteetaten.no.

References

Easterby-Smith, M., Thorpe, R. and Lowe, A. (2002) *Management Research: An Introduction.* 2nd Edition. Sage Publications: London.

Battram, A. (1996) *Navigating Complexity: The Essential Guide to Complexity Theory in Business and Management,* The Industrial Society: London.

Collis, J. and Hussey, R. (2003) *Business Research: A practical guide for undergraduate and postgraduate students,* 2nd Edition, Palgrave Macmillan: New York.

DNV (2005) *Kvalitetsarbeid i IT-funksjonen, Vurdering av systemet for kvalitetsstyring i IT-funksjonen i Skattedirektoratet,* Rapport unntatt offentlighet, 03.10.2005, Det Norske Veritas: Høvik.

Dooley, K. (2002) "Organizatonal Complexity," *International Encyclopedia of Business and Management,* M. Warner (ed.), Thompson Learning: London, p. 5013-5022.

Dooley, K., T. Johnson, and D. Bush (1995) "TQM, chaos, and complexity", *Human Systems Management,* 14(4): 1-16.

Hanseth, O. (2005) "Globally Scaleable Information Structures" presentation at *PhD Days Workshop in Information systems, 30 Sept – 1 Oct 2005,* Department of Informatics, University of Oslo: Oslo.

ISO (2000a) *Quality management systems – Fundamentals and vocabulary (ISO 9000:2000),* International Standards Organization: Geneve.

ISO (2000b) *Quality management systems – Requirements (ISO 9001:2000),* International Standards Organization: Geneve.

ISO (2000c) *Quality management systems – Guidelines for performance improvements (ISO 9004:2000),* International Standards Organization: Geneve.

Kelly, K. (1994) *Out Of Control: The New Biology of Machines, Social Systems and the Economics World,* Addison-Wesley: New York.

Liker, J. (2004) *The Toyota Way,* Addison-Wesley: New York.

Morgan, G. (1997) *Images of Organization,* SAGE Publishing: London.

Mintzberg, H. (1983) *Structure in Fives: Designing Effective Organizations,* Prentice-Hall: Upper Saddle River, New Jersey.

NTAX (1997) *Strategi, politikk og standarder for IT-sikkerhet i Skatteetaten,* Version 2.1, SKD no. 6/96, Directorate of Taxes: Oslo.

NTAX (1998) Strategisk plan for bruk av IT i Skatteetaten, Version 1.3, SKD no. 62/96, Directorate of Taxes: Oslo.

NTAX (2001) *Stillingsbeskrivelse – Kvalitetssjef (underdirektør),* Notat 21.03.01, Directorate of Taxes, IT department: Oslo.

Oakland, J.S. (2001) *Total Organizational Excellence: Achieving World-Class Performance,* Butterworth-Heinemann: Oxford.

Statskonsult (2002) *Organisering av IT-funksjonen i Skatteetaten,* Statskonsult: Oslo.

Urry, J. (2003) *Global Complexity,* Polity: Cambridge.

Womack, J.P. and Jones, D.T. (2003) *Lean Thinking: Banish Waste and Create Wealth in Your Corporation*, 2nd Edition, Free Press Business.

Lightning Source UK Ltd.
Milton Keynes UK
UKOW05n2225241114

242125UK00002B/23/P